Learn Three.js
Third Edition

Programming 3D animations and visualizations for the web
with HTML5 and WebGL

Jos Dirksen

BIRMINGHAM - MUMBAI

Learn Three.js
Third Edition

Commissioning Editor: Amarabha Banerjee
Acquisition Editor: Reshma Raman
Content Development Editor: Arun Nadar
Technical Editor: Surabhi Kulkarni
Copy Editor: Safis Editing
Project Coordinator: Sheejal Shah
Proofreader: Safis Editing
Indexer: Mariammal Chettiyar
Graphics: Jason Monteiro
Production Coordinator: Deepika Naik

First published: October 2013

Second edition: March 2015

Third edition: August 2018

Production reference: 1310818

Published by Packt Publishing Ltd.
Livery Place
35 Livery Street
Birmingham
B3 2PB, UK.

ISBN 978-1-78883-328-8

www.packtpub.com

`mapt.io`

Mapt is an online digital library that gives you full access to over 5,000 books and videos, as well as industry leading tools to help you plan your personal development and advance your career. For more information, please visit our website.

Why subscribe?

- Spend less time learning and more time coding with practical eBooks and Videos from over 4,000 industry professionals

- Improve your learning with Skill Plans built especially for you

- Get a free eBook or video every month

- Mapt is fully searchable

- Copy and paste, print, and bookmark content

PacktPub.com

Did you know that Packt offers eBook versions of every book published, with PDF and ePub files available? You can upgrade to the eBook version at `www.PacktPub.com` and as a print book customer, you are entitled to a discount on the eBook copy. Get in touch with us at `service@packtpub.com` for more details.

At `www.PacktPub.com`, you can also read a collection of free technical articles, sign up for a range of free newsletters, and receive exclusive discounts and offers on Packt books and eBooks.

Contributors

About the author

Jos Dirksen has worked as a software developer and architect for more than a decade. He has a lot of experience in a large range of technologies, ranging from backend technologies, such as Java and Scala, to frontend development using HTML5, CSS, and JavaScript. Besides working with these technologies, Jos also regularly speaks at conferences and likes to write about new and interesting technologies on his blog. He also likes to experiment with new technologies and see how they can best be used to create beautiful data visualizations.

He is currently working as a freelance full-stack engineer on various Scala and JavaScript project.

Previously, Jos has worked in many different roles in the private and public sectors, ranging from private companies such as ING, ASML, Malmberg, and Philips to organizations in the public sector, such as the Department of Defense.

About the reviewer

Francesco Strazzullo is a frontend engineer and trainer for extrategy. He loves to share what he learns in his job by writing on his blog or presenting a new talk at a conference or a local JavaScript user group. During his free time, he likes to relax by playing with his PlayStation or cooking.

Packt is searching for authors like you

If you're interested in becoming an author for Packt, please visit authors.packtpub.com and apply today. We have worked with thousands of developers and tech professionals, just like you, to help them share their insight with the global tech community. You can make a general application, apply for a specific hot topic that we are recruiting an author for, or submit your own idea.

Table of Contents

Preface   1

Chapter 1: Creating Your First 3D Scene with Three.js   7
  Requirements for using Three.js   11
  Getting the source code   13
    Using Git to clone the repository   13
    Downloading and extracting the archive   14
    Testing the examples   15
      Python-based web servers should work on most Unix/macOS systems   15
      Npm-based web server if you've worked with Node.js   16
      Portable version Mongoose for macOS and/or Windows   16
      Running from the filesystem by disabling security exceptions in Firefox and
      Chrome   17
  Creating the HTML skeleton   19
  Rendering and viewing a 3D object   21
  Adding materials, lights, and shadows   26
  Expanding your first scene with animations   29
    Introducing requestAnimationFrame   30
    Animating the cube   32
    Bouncing the ball   33
  Using dat.GUI to make experimenting easier   35
  Automatically resize the output when the browser size changes   38
  Summary   39

Chapter 2: The Basic Components that Make Up a Three.js Application   41
  Creating a scene   42
    The basic functionality of a scene   42
    Adding fog to the scene   50
    Using the overrideMaterial property   51
  Geometries and meshes   53
    The properties and functions of a geometry   54
    Functions and attributes for meshes   61
  Different cameras for different uses   68
    Orthographic camera versus perspective camera   69
    Looking at specific points   74
  Summary   77

Chapter 3: Working with Light Sources in Three.js   79
  The different kinds of lighting provided by Three.js   80
  Basic lights   81
    THREE.AmbientLight   81

Using the THREE.Color object | 85
THREE.SpotLight | 89
THREE.PointLight | 97
THREE.DirectionalLight | 103
Special lights | 106
THREE.HemisphereLight | 106
THREE.AreaLight | 108
Lens flare | 110
Summary | 115

Chapter 4: Working with Three.js Materials | 117
Understanding common material properties | 118
Basic properties | 119
Blending properties | 121
Advanced properties | 122
Starting with a simple mesh | 123
THREE.MeshBasicMaterial | 124
THREE.MeshDepthMaterial | 128
Combining materials | 130
THREE.MeshNormalMaterial | 133
Multiple materials for a single mesh | 137
Advanced materials | 139
THREE.MeshLambertMaterial | 140
THREE.MeshPhongMaterial | 142
THREE.MeshStandardMaterial | 144
THREE.MeshPhysicalMaterial | 146
Creating your own shaders with THREE.ShaderMaterial | 147
Materials you can use for a line geometry | 155
THREE.LineBasicMaterial | 155
THREE.LineDashedMaterial | 158
Summary | 159

Chapter 5: Learning to Work with Geometries | 161
The basic geometries provided by Three.js | 163
2D geometries | 163
THREE.PlaneGeometry | 164
THREE.CircleGeometry | 166
THREE.RingGeometry | 169
THREE.ShapeGeometry | 171
3D geometries | 177
THREE.BoxGeometry | 177
THREE.SphereGeometry | 178
THREE.CylinderGeometry | 181
THREE.ConeGeometry | 184
THREE.TorusGeometry | 186
THREE.TorusKnotGeometry | 188
THREE.PolyhedronGeometry | 190

THREE.IcosahedronGeometry   193
THREE.TetrahedronGeometry   194
THREE.OctahedronGeometry   195
THREE.DodecahedronGeometry   196

Summary   197

Chapter 6: Advanced Geometries and Binary Operations   199
THREE.ConvexGeometry   200
THREE.LatheGeometry   202
Creating a geometry by extruding   204
  THREE.ExtrudeGeometry   204
  THREE.TubeGeometry   206
  Extruding from SVG   208
THREE.ParametricGeometry   211
Creating 3D text   215
  Rendering text   215
  Adding custom fonts   218
Using binary operations to combine meshes   220
  The subtract function   222
  The intersect function   227
  The union function   229
Summary   230

Chapter 7: Points and Sprites   231
Understanding points   232
THREE.Points and THREE.PointsMaterial   236
  Styling particles with the HTML5 canvas   239
    Using HTML5 canvas with THREE.CanvasRenderer 239
    Using HTML5 canvas with WebGLRenderer   242
  Using textures to style particles   245
Working with sprite maps   254
Creating THREE.Points from an advanced geometry   259
Summary   261

Chapter 8: Creating and Loading Advanced Meshes and Geometries 263
Geometry grouping and merging   263
  Grouping objects together   264
  Merging multiple meshes into a single mesh   267
Loading geometries from external resources   270
  Saving and loading in Three.js JSON format   271
  Saving and loading THREE.Mesh   271
  Saving and loading a scene   274
  Working with Blender   279
    Installing the Three.js exporter in Blender 280
    Loading and exporting a model from Blender 282
Importing from 3D file formats   285
  The OBJ and MTL formats   285

Loading a COLLADA model 290
Loading models from other supported formats 292
Show proteins from PDB 298
Creating a particle system from a PLY model 303
Summary 304
Chapter 9: Animations and Moving the Camera 307
Basic animations 307
Simple animations 308
Selecting objects 310
Animating with Tween.js 313
Working with the camera 317
TrackballControls 319
FlyControls 321
FirstPersonControls 323
OrbitControl 325
Morphing and skeletal animation 327
Animation with morph targets 329
Animation with a mixer and morph targets 329
Using multiple THREE.AnimationClip objects 337
Animation using bones and skinning 340
Creating animations using external models 344
Creating a bones animation using Blender 346
Loading an animation from a COLLADA model 350
Animation loaded from a Quake model 353
Using the gltfLoader 355
Visualize motions captured models using the fbxLoader 356
Loading legacy DirectX models through the xLoader 359
Visualizing a skeleton with the BVHLoader 360
Reusing models from the SEA3D project 362
Summary 364
Chapter 10: Loading and Working with Textures 365
Using textures in materials 365
Loading a texture and applying it to a mesh 366
Using a bump map to create wrinkles 375
Achieving more detailed bumps and wrinkles with a normal map 377
Using a displacement map to alter the position of vertices 379
Adding subtle shadows with an ambient occlusion map 380
Creating fake shadows using a lightmap 383
Metalness and roughness maps 385
Alpha map 387
Emissive map 389
Specular map 391
Creating fake reflections using an environment map 393
Advanced usage of textures 401

Custom UV mapping   401
Repeat wrapping   406
Rendering to a canvas and using it as a texture   408
Using the canvas as a texture   409
Using the canvas as a bump map   411
Using the output from a video as a texture   413
Summary   414

Chapter 11: Render Postprocessing   415
Setting up Three.js for postprocessing   416
Creating THREE.EffectComposer   417
Configuring THREE.EffectComposer for postprocessing   418
Updating the render loop   418
Postprocessing passes   420
Simple postprocessing passes   422
Using THREE.FilmPass to create a TV-like effect   423
Adding a bloom effect to the scene with THREE.BloomPass   424
Output the scene as a set of dots   426
Showing the output of multiple renderers on the same screen   427
Additional simple passes   428
Advanced EffectComposer flows using masks   429
Advanced pass - Bokeh   434
Advance pass - ambient occlusion   438
Using THREE.ShaderPass for custom effects   439
Simple shaders   442
Blurring shaders   448
Creating custom postprocessing shaders   452
Custom grayscale shader   452
Creating a custom bit shader   456
Summary   459

Chapter 12: Adding Physics and Sounds to Your Scene   461
Creating a basic Three.js scene with physics   462
Physi.js material properties   469
Physi.js supported shapes   472
Using constraints to limit the movement of objects   478
Using PointConstraint to limit movement between two points   479
Hinge constraints   482
Limiting movement to a single axis with SliderConstraint   486
Creating a ball-and-socket-joint-like constraint with ConeTwistConstraint   488
Creating detailed control with DOFConstraint   490
Add sound sources to your scene   494
Summary   498

Other Books You May Enjoy   499

Index   503

Preface

Over the last couple of years, browsers have gotten more powerful and are capable of delivering complex applications and graphics. Most of this, though, is standard 2D graphics. All modern browsers have adopted WebGL, which allows you to not just create 2D applications and graphics in the browser, but also create beautiful and high-performance 3D applications using the capabilities of the GPU.

Programming WebGL directly, however, is very complex. You need to know the inner details of WebGL and learn a complex shader language to get the most out of WebGL. Three.js provides a very easy-to-use JavaScript API around the features of WebGL, so you can create beautiful 3D graphics without having to learn the details of WebGL.

Three.js provides a large number of features and APIs you can use to create 3D scenes directly in your browser. In this book, you'll learn all the different APIs Three.js has to offer through lots of interactive examples and code samples.

Who this book is for

This book is great for everyone who already knows JavaScript and wants to start with creating 3D graphics that run in any browser. You don't need know anything about advanced math or WebGL; all that is needed is a general knowledge of JavaScript and HTML. The required materials and examples can be freely downloaded and all tools used in this book are open source. So, if you've ever wanted to learn how to create beautiful, interactive 3D graphics that run in any modern browser, this is the book for you.

What this book covers

Chapter 1, *Creating Your First 3D Scene with Three.js*, covers the basic steps you need to take to get started with Three.js. You'll immediately create your first Three.js scene, and at the end of this chapter you'll be able to create and animate your first 3D scene directly in your browser.

Chapter 2, *The Basic Components That Make Up a Three.js Application*, explains the basic components that you need to understand when working with Three.js. You'll learn about lights, meshes, geometries, materials, and cameras. In this chapter, you also get an overview of the different lights Three.js provides and the cameras you can use in your scene.

Chapter 3, *Working with Light Sources in Three.js*, dives deeper into the different lights you can use in your scene. It shows examples and explains how to use a SpotLight, a DirectionLight, an AmbientLight, a PointLight, a HemisphereLight, and an AreaLight. Additionally, it also shows how to apply a lens flare effect on your light source.

Chapter 4, *Working with Three.js Materials*, talks about the materials available in Three.js that you can use on your meshes. It shows all the properties you can set to configure the materials for your specific use and provides interactive examples to experiment with the materials that are available in Three.js.

Chapter 5, *Learning to Work with Geometries*, is the first of two chapters that explore all the geometries that are provided by Three.js. In this chapter, you'll learn how to create and configure geometries in Three.js and you can experiment, using the provided interactive examples, with geometries such as Plane, Circle, Shape, Cube, Sphere, Cylinder, Torus, TorusKnot, and PolyHedron.

Chapter 6, *Advanced Geometries and Binary Operations*, continues where the previous chapter left off. It shows you how to configure and use the more advanced geometries that are provided by Three.js, such as Convex and Lathe. In this chapter, you'll also learn how to extrude 3D geometries from 2D shapes and how you can create new geometries by combining geometries using binary operations.

Chapter 7, *Points and Sprites*, explains how to use the sprites and points from Three.js. You'll learn how to create a point cloud from scratch, and from existing geometries. In this chapter, you'll also learn how you can modify the way the individual points look through the use of sprites and materials.

Chapter 8, *Creating and Loading Advanced Meshes and Geometries*, shows you how to import meshes and geometries from external sources. You'll learn how to use Three.js' internal JSON format to save geometries and scenes. This chapter also explains how to load models from formats such as OBJ, DAE, STL, CTM, PLY, and many more.

Chapter 9, *Animations and Moving the Camera*, explores the various types of animations you can use to make your scene come to life. You'll learn how to use the Tween.js library together with Three.js, and you'll learn how to work with animation models based on morhps and skeletons.

Chapter 10, *Loading and Working with Textures*, expands on Chapter 4, *Working with Three.js Materials*, where materials were introduced. In this chapter, we dive into the details of textures. This chapter introduces the various types of textures that are available and how you can control how a texture is applied to your mesh. Additionally, in this chapter you are shown how you can directly use the output from HTML5 video and canvas elements as input for your textures.

`Chapter 11`, *Render Postprocessing*, explores how you can use Three.js to apply postprocessing effects to your rendered scene. With postprocessing you can apply effects such as blur, tiltshift, and sepia to your rendered scene. Besides this, you'll also learn how to create your own postprocessing effect and create a custom vertex and fragment shader.

`Chapter 12`, *Adding Physics and Sounds to Your Scene*, explains how you can add physics to your Three.js scene. With physics you can detect collisions between objects, make them respond to gravity, and apply friction. This chapter shows how to do this with the Physijs JavaScript library. Additionally, this chapter also shows how you can add positional audio to a Three.js scene.

To get the most out of this book

To get the most out of this book, you need to know a little bit of JavaScript and follow the instructions in the first chapter to set up a local web server and get the samples for this book.

Download the example code files

You can download the example code files for this book from your account at `www.packtpub.com`. If you purchased this book elsewhere, you can visit `www.packtpub.com/support` and register to have the files emailed directly to you.

You can download the code files by following these steps:

1. Log in or register at `www.packtpub.com`.
2. Select the **SUPPORT** tab.
3. Click on **Code Downloads & Errata**.
4. Enter the name of the book in the **Search** box and follow the onscreen instructions.

Once the file is downloaded, please make sure that you unzip or extract the folder using the latest version of:

- WinRAR/7-Zip for Windows
- Zipeg/iZip/UnRarX for Mac
- 7-Zip/PeaZip for Linux

The code bundle for the book is also hosted on GitHub at `https://github.com/PacktPublishing/Learn-Three.js-Third-Edition`. In case there's an update to the code, it will be updated on the existing GitHub repository.

We also have other code bundles from our rich catalog of books and videos available at https://github.com/PacktPublishing/. Check them out!

Download the color images

We also provide a PDF file that has color images of the screenshots/diagrams used in this book. You can download it here: https://www.packtpub.com/sites/default/files/downloads/LearnThreeDotjsThirdEdition_ColorImages.pdf.

Conventions used

There are a number of text conventions used throughout this book.

CodeInText: Indicates code words in text, database table names, folder names, filenames, file extensions, pathnames, dummy URLs, user input, and Twitter handles. Here is an example: "The learning-threejs-third directory will now contain all the examples that are used throughout this book."

A block of code is set as follows:

```
<!DOCTYPE html>
<html>

<head>
    <title>Example 01.01 - Basic skeleton</title>
    <meta charset="UTF-8" />
    <script type="text/javascript" charset="UTF-8"
src="../../libs/three/three.js"></script>
    <script type="text/javascript" charset="UTF-8"
src="../../libs/three/controls/TrackballControls.js"></script>
    <script type="text/javascript" src="./js/01-01.js"></script>
    <link rel="stylesheet" href="../../css/default.css">
</head>
```

When we wish to draw your attention to a particular part of a code block, the relevant lines or items are set in bold:

```
var scene = new THREE.Scene();
var camera = new THREE.PerspectiveCamera(45, window.innerWidth /
window.innerHeight, 0.1, 1000);
var renderer = new THREE.WebGLRenderer();
renderer.setClearColor(new THREE.Color(0x000000));
renderer.setSize(window.innerWidth, window.innerHeight);
```

Any command-line input or output is written as follows:

```
chrome.exe --disable-web-security
```

Bold: Indicates a new term, an important word, or words that you see onscreen. For example, words in menus or dialog boxes appear in the text like this. Here is an example: "When you hit the **addCube** button, a new object is created."

Warnings or important notes appear like this.

Tips and tricks appear like this.

Get in touch

Feedback from our readers is always welcome.

General feedback: Email feedback@packtpub.com and mention the book title in the subject of your message. If you have questions about any aspect of this book, please email us at questions@packtpub.com.

Errata: Although we have taken every care to ensure the accuracy of our content, mistakes do happen. If you have found a mistake in this book, we would be grateful if you would report this to us. Please visit www.packtpub.com/submit-errata, selecting your book, clicking on the Errata Submission Form link, and entering the details.

Piracy: If you come across any illegal copies of our works in any form on the Internet, we would be grateful if you would provide us with the location address or website name. Please contact us at copyright@packtpub.com with a link to the material.

If you are interested in becoming an author: If there is a topic that you have expertise in and you are interested in either writing or contributing to a book, please visit authors.packtpub.com.

Reviews

Please leave a review. Once you have read and used this book, why not leave a review on the site that you purchased it from? Potential readers can then see and use your unbiased opinion to make purchase decisions, we at Packt can understand what you think about our products, and our authors can see your feedback on their book. Thank you!

For more information about Packt, please visit packtpub.com.

Creating Your First 3D Scene with Three.js 1

Over recent years, modern browsers have acquired powerful features that can be accessed directly from JavaScript. You can easily add video and audio with the HTML5 tags and create interactive components through the use of the HTML5 canvas. Together with HTML5, modern browsers also support WebGL. With WebGL, you can directly make use of the processing resources of your graphics card and create high-performance 2D and 3D computer graphics. Programming WebGL directly from JavaScript to create and animate 3D scenes is a very complex, verbose and error-prone process. Three.js is a library that makes this a lot easier. The following list shows some of the things that are very easy to do with Three.js:

- Creating simple and complex 3D geometries
- Creating **Virtual Reality (VR)** and **Augmented Reality (AR)** scenes
- Animating and moving objects through a 3D scene
- Applying textures and materials to your objects
- Making use of different light sources to illuminate the scene
- Loading objects from 3D-modeling software
- Adding advanced postprocessing effects to your 3D scene
- Working with your own custom shaders
- Creating point clouds

With a couple of lines of JavaScript, you can create anything, from simple 3D models to photorealistic real-time scenes, as shown in the following screenshot (see it yourself by opening `http://www.vill.ee/eye/` in your browser):

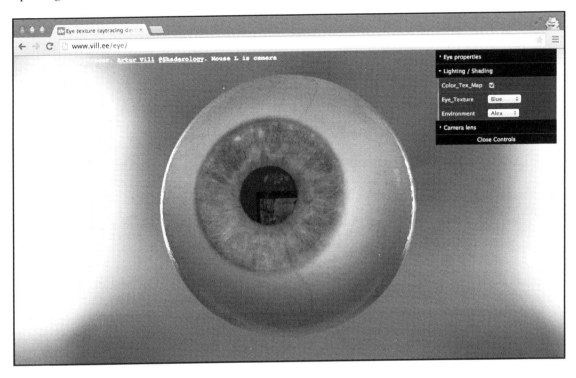

In this chapter, we'll directly dive into Three.js and create a couple of examples that show you how Three.js works, and which you can use to play around with. We won't dive into all the technical details yet; that's something you'll learn in the following chapters. In this chapter, we'll cover the following points:

- The tools required to work with Three.js
- Downloading the source code and examples used in this book
- Creating your first Three.js scene
- Improving the first scene with materials, lights, and animations
- Introducing a couple of helper libraries for statistics and controlling the scene

We'll start this book with a short introduction to Three.js and then quickly move on to the first examples and code samples. Before we get started, let's quickly look at the most important browsers out there and their support for WebGL. All modern browsers on desktop, as well as on mobile, currently support WebGL. The only browser where you have to take care of is the mobile Opera Mini browser. This browser has the option to render pages through the Opera servers, which often prevents JavaScript from working. Since version 8, however, the default mode of Opera Mini is to use the iOS Safari engine, which does support JavaScript and WebGL. You can still configure this browser, though, to use *mini mode*, which will render pages through the Opera servers and won't support WebGL in that case.

Basically, Three.js runs on any modern browser with the exception of older versions of IE. So, if you want to use an older version of IE, you've got to take an additional step. For IE 10 and older, there is the IEWebGL plugin, which you can get from `https://github.com/iewebgl/iewebgl`. This plugin is installed inside IE 10 and older versions and enables WebGL support for those browsers.

So, with WebGL, you can create interactive 3D visualizations that run very well on desktops as well as on mobile devices.

In this book, we'll focus mostly on the WebGL-based renderer provided by Three.js. There is, however, also a CSS 3D-based renderer, which provides an easy API to create CSS 3D-based 3D scenes. A big advantage of using a CSS 3D-based approach is that this standard is supported on all mobile and desktop browsers and allows you to render HTML elements in a 3D space. We'll show how to use the CSS 3D browser in `Chapter 7`, Points and Sprites.

In this chapter, you'll directly create your first 3D scene and will be able to run this in any of the browsers mentioned previously. We won't introduce too many complex Three.js features yet, but, at the end of this chapter, you'll have created the Three.js scene you can see in the following screenshot:

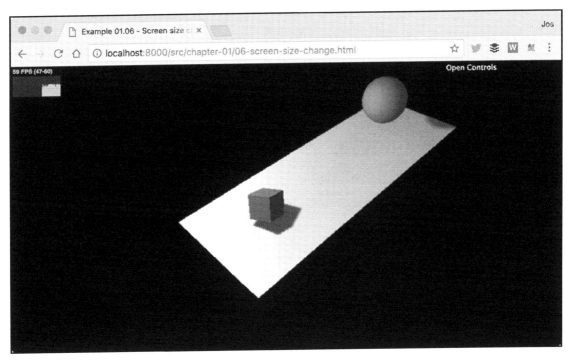

59 FPS (47-60)

For this first scene, you'll learn about the basics of Three.js and also create your first animation. Before you start your work on this example, in the next couple of sections, we'll first look at the tools you need to easily work with Three.js and how you can download the examples shown in this book.

Requirements for using Three.js

Three.js is a JavaScript library, so all you need to create Three.js WebGL applications is a text editor and one of the supported browsers to render the results. I would like to recommend the following JavaScript editors, which I've used extensively over the last couple of years on various projects:

- **Visual Studio Code**: This free editor from Microsoft runs on all major platforms and provides great syntax highlighting and smart completion based on types, function definitions, and imported libraries. It provides a very clean interface and is great for working on JavaScript projects. It can be downloaded from here: https://code.visualstudio.com/.
- **WebStorm**: This editor from the JetBrains guys has great support for editing JavaScript. It supports code completion, automatic deployment, and JavaScript debugging directly from the editor. Besides this, WebStorm has excellent GitHub (and other version control systems) support. You can download a trial edition from http://www.jetbrains.com/webstorm/.
- **Notepad++**: Notepad++ is a general-purpose editor that supports code highlighting for a wide range of programming languages. It can easily layout and format JavaScript. Note that Notepad++ is only for Windows. You can download Notepad++ from http://notepad-plus-plus.org/.
- **Sublime Text Editor**: Sublime is a great editor that offers very good support for editing JavaScript. Besides this, it provides many very helpful selections (such as multiple-line select) and edit options, which, once you get used to them, provide a really good JavaScript-editing environment. Sublime can also be tested for free and can be downloaded from http://www.sublimetext.com/.

Even if you don't use any of these editors, there are a lot of editors available, open source and commercial, that you can use to edit JavaScript and create your Three.js projects, since all you need is the ability to edit text. An interesting project you might want to look at is http://c9.io. This is a cloud-based JavaScript editor that can be connected to a GitHub account. This way, you can directly access all the source code and examples from this book and experiment with them.

Besides these text-based editors that you can use to edit and experiment with the sources from this book, Three.js currently also provides an online editor itself.

With this editor, which you can find at http://threejs.org/editor/, you can create Three.js scenes using a graphical approach.

I mentioned that most modern web browsers support WebGL and can be used to run Three.js examples. I usually run my code in Chrome. The reason is that most often, Chrome has the best support and performance for WebGL and it has a really great JavaScript debugger. With this debugger, which is shown in the following screenshot, you can quickly pinpoint problems, for instance, using breakpoints and console output. This is exemplified in the following screenshot. Throughout this book, I'll give you pointers on debugger usage and other debugging tips and tricks:

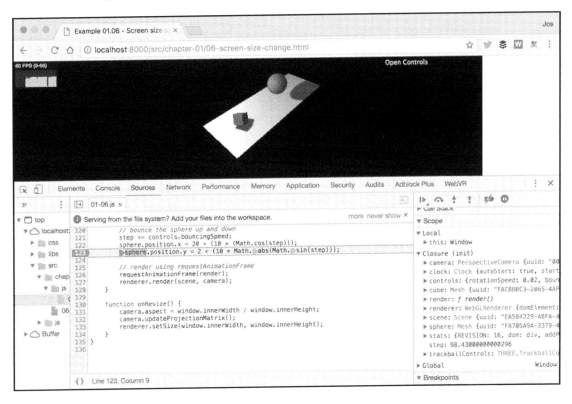

60 FPS (0-60)

That's enough by way of an introduction for now; let's get the source code and start with the first scene.

Getting the source code

All the code for this book can be accessed from GitHub (`https://github.com/`). GitHub is an online Git-based repository that you can use to store, access, and version source code. There are a couple of ways that you can get the sources for yourself:

- Clone the Git repository
- Download and extract the archive

In the following two paragraphs, we'll explore these options in a bit more detail.

Using Git to clone the repository

Git is an open source distributed version control system that I used to create and version all the examples in this book. For this, I used GitHub, a free, online Git repository. You can browse this repository from this link: `https://github.com/josdirksen/learning-threejs-third`.

To get all the examples, you can clone this repository using the `git` command-line tool. To do this, you first need to download a Git client for your operating system. For most modern operating systems, a client can be downloaded from `http://git-scm.com`. After installing Git, you can use this to get a *clone* of this book's repository. Open a command prompt and go to the directory where you want to download the sources. In that directory, run the following command:

```
git clone https://github.com/josdirksen/learning-threejs-third
```

This will start downloading all the examples, as shown in the following screenshot:

The `learning-threejs-third` directory will now contain all the examples that are used throughout this book.

Downloading and extracting the archive

If you don't want to use Git to download the sources directly from GitHub, you can also download an archive. Open `https://github.com/josdirksen/learning-threejs-third` in a browser and click on the **Clone or download** button on the right-hand side. This will give you the option to download all the sources in a single ZIP file:

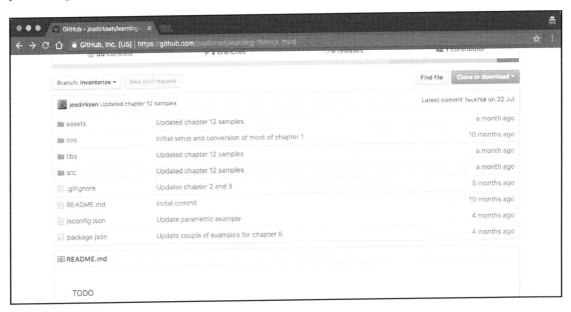

Extract this to a directory of your choice, and you'll have all the examples available.

Downloading the example code: You can also download the example code files from your account at `http://www.packtpub.com` for all the Packt Publishing books you have purchased. If you purchased this book elsewhere, you can visit `http://www.packtpub.com/support` and register to have the files emailed directly to you.

Testing the examples

Now that you've downloaded or cloned the source code, let's do a quick check to see whether everything is working and make you familiar with the directory structure. The code and examples are organized per chapter. There are two different ways of viewing examples. You can either open the extracted or cloned folder in a browser directly and look at and run a specific example, or you can install a local web server. This first approach will work for most of the basic examples, but when we start loading external resources, such as models or texture images, just opening the HTML file isn't enough. In this case, we need a local web server to make sure the external resources are loaded correctly. In the following section, we explain a couple of different ways you can set up a simple local web server for testing. If you can't set up a local web server but use Chrome or Firefox, we also provide an explanation on how to disable certain security features so that you can even test without a local web server.

Setting up a local web server is very easy depending on what you've already got installed. In here, we list a couple of examples on how to do this. There are many different ways of doing this, depending on what you've already got installed on your system.

Python-based web servers should work on most Unix/macOS systems

Most Unix/Linux/macOS systems already have Python installed. On those systems, you can very easily start a local web server:

```
> python -m SimpleHTTPServer
Serving HTTP on 0.0.0.0 port 8000 ...
```

Do this in the directory where you checked out / downloaded the source code.

Npm-based web server if you've worked with Node.js

If you've already done some work with Node.js, there is good chance you've got npm installed. With npm, you have two simple options to set up a quick local web server for testing. The first option uses the `http-server` module, as follows:

```
> npm install -g http-server
> http-server
Starting up http-server, serving ./ on port: 8080
Hit CTRL-C to stop the server
```

Alternatively, you can also use the `simple-http-server` option, as follows:

```
> npm install -g simple-http-server
> nserver
simple-http-server Now Serving: /Users/jos/git/Physijs at
http://localhost:8000/
```

A disadvantage of this second approach, however, is that it doesn't automatically show directory listings when browsing the sources, whereas the first approach does.

Portable version Mongoose for macOS and/or Windows

If you haven't got Python or npm installed, there is a simple, portable web server, named Mongoose, that you can use. First, download the binaries for your specific platform from `https://code.google.com/p/mongoose/downloads/list`. If you are using Windows, copy it to the directory containing the examples and double-click on the executable to start a web browser serving the directory it is started in.

For other operating systems, you must also copy the executable to the target directory, but instead of double-clicking on the executable, you have to launch it from the command line:

In both cases, a local web server will be started on port `8080`. The following screenshot shows the output when you open a browser to a locally running Mongoose server:

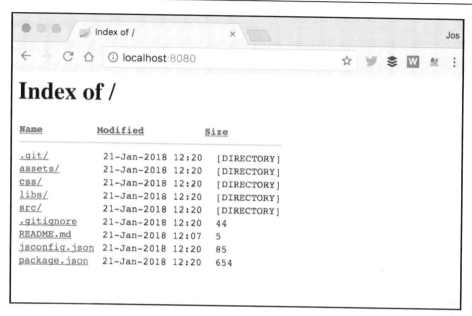

All the examples are in the `src` folder. By just clicking on a chapter in this folder, we can show and access all the examples for that specific chapter. If we discuss an example in this book, we'll refer to the specific name and folder so that you can directly test and play around with the code.

Running from the filesystem by disabling security exceptions in Firefox and Chrome

If you use Chrome to run the examples, there is a way to disable some security settings so that you can use Chrome to view the examples without requiring a web server. Note that you shouldn't do this on a browser you use on the internet since it can leave you open to all kinds of malicious code. To do this, you have to start Chrome in the following way:

- For Windows, you call the following:

```
chrome.exe --disable-web-security
```

- On Linux, do the following:

```
google-chrome --disable-web-security
```

- And on macOS, you disable the settings by starting Chrome like this:

```
open -a "Google Chrome" --args --disable-web-security
```

When you start Chrome this way, you can access all the examples directly from the local filesystem.

For Firefox users, we need to take a couple of different steps. Open Firefox and, in the URL bar, type `about:config`. This is what you'll see:

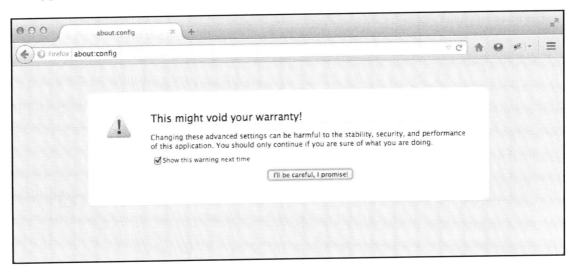

Warning window

On this screen, click on the **I'll be careful, I promise!** button. This will show you all the available properties you can use to fine-tune Firefox. In the search box on this screen, type in `security.fileuri.strict_origin_policy` and change its value to `false`, just as we did in the following screenshot:

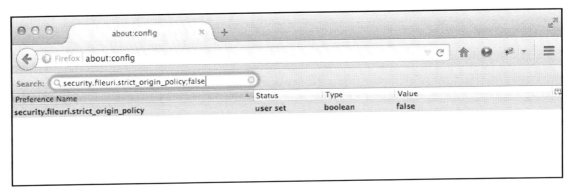

At this point, you can also use Firefox to directly run the examples provided in this book. Now that you've either got a web server installed, or disabled the necessary security settings, it is time to start creating our first Three.js scene.

Creating the HTML skeleton

The first thing we need to do is create an empty skeleton page that we can use as the base for all our examples, as follows:

```html
<!DOCTYPE html>
<html>

<head>
    <title>Example 01.01 - Basic skeleton</title>
    <meta charset="UTF-8" />
    <script type="text/javascript" charset="UTF-8"
src="../../libs/three/three.js"></script>
    <script type="text/javascript" charset="UTF-8"
src="../../libs/three/controls/TrackballControls.js"></script>
    <script type="text/javascript" src="./js/01-01.js"></script>
    <link rel="stylesheet" href="../../css/default.css">
</head>

<body>
    <!-- Div which will hold the Output -->
    <div id="webgl-output"></div>

    <!-- Javascript code that runs our Three.js examples -->
    <script type="text/javascript">
        (function () {
            // contains the code for the example
            init();
        })();
    </script>
</body>

</html>
```

As you can see from this listing, the skeleton is a very simple HTML page, with only a couple of elements. In the <head> element, we load the external JavaScript libraries that we'll use for the examples. For all the examples, we'll at least need to load the Three.js library, three.js. And we also load a controller, TrackballControls.js, which allows you to use your mouse to rotate and pan around the scenes. The last JavaScript file we load in the <head> section is the file that contains the example code. For this first example, it is called 01-01.js. Finally, in the <head> element, we load a CSS file, which contains some simple styles (for example, the styles in the default.css file remove any scrollbars when we create a full-page Three.js scene). In the <body> element of this page, you can see a single <div> element. When we write our Three.js code, we'll point to the output of the Three.js renderer to that element. At the bottom of this page, you can see a bit of JavaScript. In this function, which is called when the page is loaded, we call init(). The init() function is defined in the 01-01.js file and will set up the Three.js scene. For this example, the init() function in the 01-01.js file is very simple and just prints out the Version of Three.js we're using:

```
function init() {
    console.log("Using Three.js version: " + THREE.REVISION);
}
```

If we open this file in our browser and look at the console output, you should see something like this:

In the `<head>` element we included the sources for Three.js. Three.js comes in two Versions:

- `three.min.js`: This is the library you'd normally use when deploying Three.js sites on the internet. This is a mini version of Three.js, created using UglifyJS, which is a quarter of the size of the normal Three.js library. All the examples and code used in this book are based on Three.js r95, which was released in July 2018.
- `three.js`: This is the normal Three.js library. We use this library in our examples since it makes debugging much easier when you can read and understand the Three.js source code.

In the next section, you'll learn how to add the first couple of 3D objects and render them to the `<div>` element we defined in our HTML skeleton.

Rendering and viewing a 3D object

In this step, you'll create your first scene and add a couple of objects and a `camera`. Our first example will contain the following objects:

Object	Description
Plane	This is a two-dimensional rectangle that serves as our ground area. In the second screenshot of this chapter, this is rendered as the gray rectangle in the middle of the scene.
Cube	This is a three-dimensional cube, which we'll render in red.
Sphere	This is a three-dimensional sphere, which we'll render in blue.
Camera	The `camera` determines what you'll see in the output.
Axes	These are the x, y, and z axes. This is a helpful debugging tool to see where the objects are rendered in 3D space. The x axis is colored red, the y axis is colored green, and the z axis is colored blue.

I'll first show you how this looks in code (the source with comments can be found in `chapter-01/js/01-02.js`), and then I'll explain what's happening:

```
function init() {
    var scene = new THREE.Scene();
    var camera = new THREE.PerspectiveCamera(45, window.innerWidth /
window.innerHeight, 0.1, 1000);
    var renderer = new THREE.WebGLRenderer();
    renderer.setClearColor(new THREE.Color(0x000000));
    renderer.setSize(window.innerWidth, window.innerHeight);
```

```
    var axes = new THREE.AxesHelper(20);
    scene.add(axes);

    var planeGeometry = new THREE.PlaneGeometry(60, 20);
    var planeMaterial = new THREE.MeshBasicMaterial({
        color: 0xAAAAAA
    });

    var plane = new THREE.Mesh(planeGeometry, planeMaterial);
    plane.rotation.x = -0.5 * Math.PI;
    plane.position.set(15, 0, 0);
    scene.add(plane);

    // create a cube
    var cubeGeometry = new THREE.BoxGeometry(4, 4, 4);
    var cubeMaterial = new THREE.MeshBasicMaterial({
        color: 0xFF0000,
        wireframe: true
    });
    var cube = new THREE.Mesh(cubeGeometry, cubeMaterial);
    cube.position.set(-4, 3, 0);
    scene.add(cube);

    // create a sphere
    var sphereGeometry = new THREE.SphereGeometry(4, 20, 20);
    var sphereMaterial = new THREE.MeshBasicMaterial({
        color: 0x7777FF,
        wireframe: true
    });
    var sphere = new THREE.Mesh(sphereGeometry, sphereMaterial);
    sphere.position.set(20, 4, 2);
    scene.add(sphere);

    // position and point the camera to the center of the scene
    camera.position.set(-30, 40, 30);
    camera.lookAt(scene.position);

    // add the output of the renderer to the html element
    document.getElementById("webgl-
output").appendChild(renderer.domElement);

    // render the scene
    renderer.render(scene, camera);
}
```

If we open this example in the browser, we see something that resembles what we're aiming at (see the screenshot at the beginning of this chapter), but it is still a long way off, as follows:

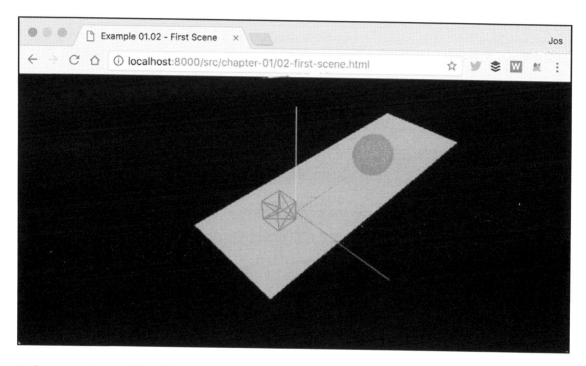

Before we start making this more beautiful, I'll first walk you through the code one step at a time so that you understand what the code does:

```
var scene = new THREE.Scene();
var camera = new THREE.PerspectiveCamera(45, window.innerWidth /
window.innerHeight, 0.1, 1000);
var renderer = new THREE.WebGLRenderer();
renderer.setClearColor(new THREE.Color(0x000000));
renderer.setSize(window.innerWidth, window.innerHeight);
```

At the top of the example, we create a `scene`, a `camera`, and a `renderer`. The `scene` object is a container that is used to store and keep track of all the objects we want to render and all the lights we want to use. Without a `THREE.Scene` object, Three.js isn't able to render anything. More information on the `THREE.Scene` object can be found in `Chapter 2`, *The Basic Components that Make Up a Three.js Application*. The sphere and the cube we want to render will be added to the scene later on in the example.

In this first fragment, we also create a camera object. The camera object defines what we'll see when we render a scene. In Chapter 2, *The Basic Components That Make Up a Three.js Application*, you learn more about the arguments you can pass into the camera object. Next, we define renderer. The renderer object is responsible for calculating what the scene object will look like in the browser based on what the camera is looking at. We create a WebGLRenderer that uses your graphics card to render the scene in this example.

 If you look through the source code and the documentation of Three.js (which you can find at http://threejs.org/), you'll notice that there are different renderers available besides the WebGL-based one. There is a canvas-based renderer, a CSS-based renderer, and even an SVG-based one. Even though they work and can render simple scenes, I wouldn't recommend using them. They're not actively developed anymore, very CPU-intensive, and lack features such as good material support and shadows.

We set the background color of renderer to black (new THREE.Color(0X000000)) with the setClearColor function and tell renderer how large the scene needs to be rendered using the setSize function. By passing in the window.innerWidth and window.innerHeight, we use all the screen space available.

So far, we've got a basic empty scene, a renderer, and a camera. There is, however, nothing yet to render. The following code adds the lines showing the axis and the plane:

```
var axes = new THREE.AxesHelper(20);
scene.add(axes);

var planeGeometry = new THREE.PlaneGeometry(60, 20);
var planeMaterial = new THREE.MeshBasicMaterial({
    color: 0xAAAAAA
});
var plane = new THREE.Mesh(planeGeometry, planeMaterial);
plane.rotation.x = -0.5 * Math.PI;
plane.position.set(15, 0, 0);
scene.add(plane);
```

As you can see, we create an `axes` object (the passed-in value determines the size of the lines representing the *x*, *y*, and *z* axes) and use the `scene.add` function to add these axes to our scene. Next, we create the plane. This is done in two steps. First, we define what the plane looks like using the new `THREE.PlaneGeometry(60,20)` code. In this case, it has a width of `60` and a height of `20`. We also need to tell Three.js what this plane looks like (for example, its color and its transparency). In Three.js, we do this by creating a material object. For this first example, we'll create a basic material (`THREE.MeshBasicMaterial`) with the color `0xAAAAAA`. Next, we combine these two into a `Mesh` object and assign that to the `plane` variable. Before we add `plane` to the scene, we need to put it in the correct position; we do this by first rotating it 90 degrees around the *x* axis, and next, set its position in the scene using the position property. If you're already interested in the details of this, look at the `06-mesh-properties.html` example from the code folder of `Chapter 2`, *The Basic Components That Make Up a Three.js Application*, which shows and explains rotation and positioning. All we then need to do is add `plane` to `scene`, just like we did with `axes`.

The `cube` and `sphere` objects are added in the same manner, but with the `wireframe` property set to `true`, which tells Three.js to show us a wireframe and not a solid object. Now, let's move on to the final part of this example:

```
camera.position.set(-30, 40, 30);
camera.lookAt(scene.position);

document.getElementById("webgl-output").appendChild(renderer.domElement);
renderer.render(scene, camera);
```

At this point, all the elements we want to render are added to the scene at the correct positions. We've already mentioned that the `camera` defines what will be rendered. In this piece of code, we position the `camera` using the `set` function to hover above our scene (we can also use `position.x`, `position.y`, and `position.z` to set the individual parts of the camera's position). To make sure the `camera` is looking at our objects, we use the `lookAt` function to point it at the center of our scene, which is located at position (0, 0, 0) by default. All that is left to do is append the output from the `renderer` to the `<div>` element of our HTML skeleton. We use standard JavaScript to select the correct output element and append it to our `div` element with the `appendChild` function. Finally, we tell `renderer` to render `scene` using the `camera` object provided.

In the next couple of sections, we'll make this scene more interesting by adding lights, shadows, more materials, and even animations.

Adding materials, lights, and shadows

Adding new materials and lights in Three.js is very simple and is implemented in pretty much the same way as we explained in the previous section. We start by adding a light source to the scene (for the complete source, look at `js/03-03.js`), as follows:

```
var spotLight = new THREE.SpotLight(0xFFFFFF);
spotLight.position.set(-40, 40, -15);
spotLight.castShadow = true;
spotLight.shadow.mapSize = new THREE.Vector2(1024, 1024);
spotLight.shadow.camera.far = 130;
spotLight.shadow.camera.near = 40;
```

`THREE.SpotLight` illuminates our scene from its position (`spotLight.position.set(-40, 60, -10)`). We tell it that we want it to cast a shadow by setting the `castShadow` property to `true`. In the code, you can see that we also set some additional properties on the light: `shadow.mapSize`, `shadow.camera.far`, and `shadow.camera.near`. Without going into too much detail, these properties define how sharp and detailed our rendered shadow will appear. We'll explain these properties in more detail in Chapter 3, *Working with the Different Light Sources Available in Three.js*. If we render the scene this time, however, you won't see any difference from the previous one. The reason is that different materials respond differently to light. The basic material we used in the previous example (`THREE.MeshBasicMaterial`) doesn't do anything with the light sources in the scene. They just render the object in the specified color. So, we have to change the materials for `plane`, `sphere`, and `cube` to the following:

```
var planeGeometry = new THREE.PlaneGeometry(60,20);
var planeMaterial = new THREE.MeshLambertMaterial({color:
    0xffffff});
var plane = new THREE.Mesh(planeGeometry, planeMaterial);
...
var cubeGeometry = new THREE.BoxGeometry(4,4,4);
var cubeMaterial = new THREE.MeshLambertMaterial({color:
    0xff0000});
var cube = new THREE.Mesh(cubeGeometry, cubeMaterial);
...
var sphereGeometry = new THREE.SphereGeometry(4,20,20);
var sphereMaterial = new THREE.MeshLambertMaterial({color:
    0x7777ff});
var sphere = new THREE.Mesh(sphereGeometry, sphereMaterial);
```

In this piece of code, we changed the materials for our objects to `MeshLambertMaterial`. This material, `MeshPhysicalMaterial` and `MeshStandardMaterial` (and the deprecated `MeshPhongMaterial`) are the materials Three.js provides that take light sources into account when rendered.

The result, shown in the following screenshot, however, still isn't what we're looking for:

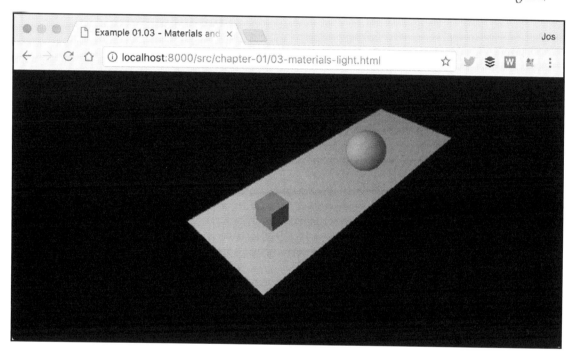

We're getting there, and the cube and sphere are looking a lot better. What is still missing, though, are the shadows. Rendering shadows takes a lot of computing power and, for that reason, shadows are disabled by default in Three.js. Enabling them, though, is very easy. For shadows, we have to change the source in a couple of places, as follows:

```
renderer.setClearColor(new THREE.Color(0x000000));
renderer.setSize(window.innerWidth, window.innerHeight);
renderer.shadowMap.Enabled = true;
```

The first change we need to make is to tell `renderer` that we want shadows. You do this by setting the `shadowMap.Enabled` property to `true`. If you look at the result from this change, you won't notice anything different yet. That is because we need to explicitly define which objects cast shadows and which objects receive shadows. In our example, we want the sphere and the cube to cast shadows on the ground plane. You do this by setting the corresponding properties on those objects:

```
plane.receiveShadow = true;
...
cube.castShadow = true;
...
sphere.castShadow = true;
```

Now, there is just one more thing to do to get the shadows. We need to define which light sources in our scene will cast shadows. Not all the lights can cast shadows, and you'll learn more about that in Chapter 3, *Working with the Different Light Sources Available in Three.js*, but THREE.SpotLight, which we used in this example. We only need to set the correct property, as shown in the following line of code, and the shadows will finally be rendered:

```
spotLight.castShadow = true;
```

And, with this, we get a scene complete with shadows from our light source, as follows:

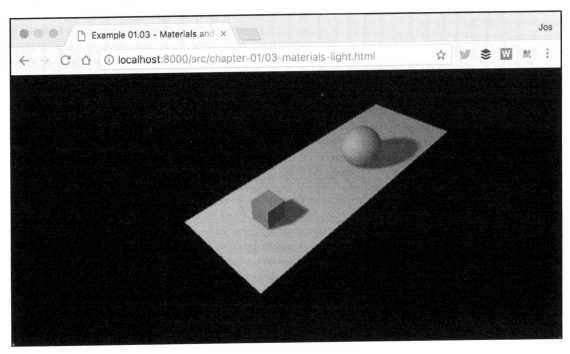

If you look at the code in 01-03.js, you can see that we also create a scene with different objects. You can use this for yourself by removing the comments for the createXXX functions. Once you do that, and remove the objects we added previously, you can see how shadows work with a slightly more complex scene. How the result from that scene appears can be seen in the following screenshot.

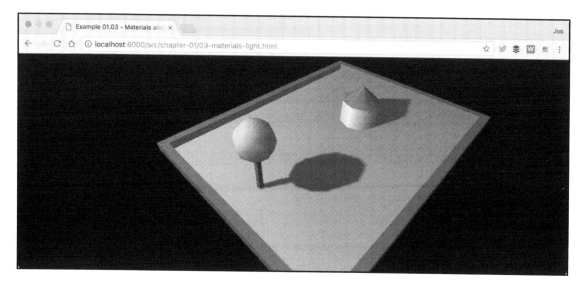

The last feature that we'll add to this first scene is some simple animation. In Chapter 9, *Animations and Moving the Camera*, you'll learn more advanced animation options.

Expanding your first scene with animations

If we want to animate the scene, the first thing that we need to do is find some way to re-render the scene at a specific interval. Before HTML5 and the related JavaScript APIs came along, the way to do this was using the setInterval(function, interval) function. With setInterval, we could specify a function that, for instance, would be called every 100 milliseconds. The problem with this function is that it doesn't take into account what is happening in the browser. If you were browsing another tab, this function would still be fired every couple of milliseconds. Besides that, setInterval isn't synchronized with the redrawing of the screen. This can lead to higher CPU usage, flickering, and generally poor performance.

Introducing requestAnimationFrame

Modern browsers luckily have a solution for that with the `requestAnimationFrame` function. With `requestAnimationFrame`, you can specify a function that is called at an interval. You, however, don't define this interval. This interval is defined by the browser. You do any drawing you need to do in the supplied function, and the browser will make sure it is painted as smoothly and efficiently as possible. Using this is really simple (the complete source can be found in the `04-04.js` file); you just create a function that handles the rendering:

```
function renderScene() {
  requestAnimationFrame(renderScene);
  renderer.render(scene, camera);
}
```

In this `renderScene` function, we call `requestAnimationFrame` again, to keep the animation going. The only thing we need to change in the code is that instead of calling `renderer.render` after we've created the complete scene, we call the `renderScene` function once to initiate the animation:

```
...
document.getElementById("webgl-output")
  .appendChild(renderer.domElement);
renderScene();
```

If you run this, you won't see any changes yet compared to the previous example because we haven't animated anything yet. Before we add the animation, though, we introduce a small helper library that gives us information about the frame rate the animation is running at. This library, from the same author as Three.js, renders a small graph that shows us information about the rate at which the scene is rendered.

To add these statistics, we first need to include the library in the `<head>` element of the HTML, as follows:

```
<script type="text/javascript" src="../../libs/util/Stats.js"></script>
```

The only thing left to do is initialize the statistics and add them to the page:

```
function initStats(type) {

    var panelType = (typeof type !== 'undefined' && type) && (!isNaN(type))
? parseInt(type) : 0;
    var stats = new Stats();

    stats.showPanel(panelType); // 0: fps, 1: ms, 2: mb, 3+: custom
    document.body.appendChild(stats.dom);
```

```
      return stats;
  }
```

This function initializes the statistics and, based on the passed in `type` variable renders the frames per second, the time it took to render the frame, or the amount of allocated memory. At the beginning of our `init()` function, we'll call this function, and we've got `stats` enabled, as follows:

```
function init(){

  var stats = initStats();
  ...
}
```

> Since this is something we want to add to each example, we don't add the `initStats` function to the sources of our examples, but this function, together with other useful helper functions, are added to the `util.js` file.

This file is included in the header of the HTML pages as follows:

```
<script type="text/javascript" src="../js/util.js"></script>
```

The only thing left to do now is to tell the `stats` object when we're in a new rendering cycle. We do this by adding a call to the `stats.update` function in our `renderScene` function, as follows:

```
function renderScene() {
  stats.update();
  ...
  requestAnimationFrame(renderScene);
  renderer.render(scene, camera);
}
```

If you run the code with these additions, you'll see the statistics in the upper left-hand corner, as shown in the following screenshot:

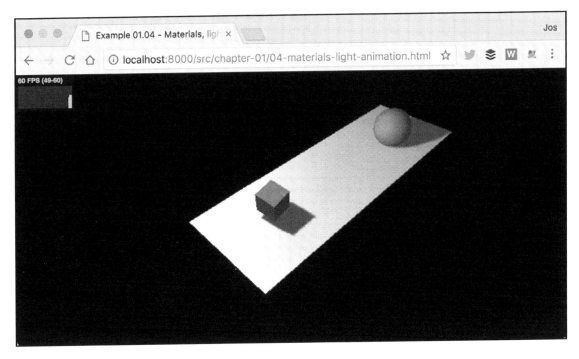

60 FPS (49-60)

Animating the cube

With `requestAnimationFrame` and the statistics configured, we've got a place to put our animation code. In this section, we'll expand the `renderScene` function with code that will rotate our red cube around all of its axes. Let's start by showing you the code:

```
function renderScene() {
  ...
  cube.rotation.x += 0.02;
  cube.rotation.y += 0.02;
  cube.rotation.z += 0.02;
  ...
  requestAnimationFrame(renderScene);
  renderer.render(scene, camera);
}
```

That looks simple, right? What we do is that we increase the `rotation` property of each of the axes by `0.02` every time the `renderScene` function is called, which shows up as a cube smoothly rotating around all of its axes. Bouncing the blue ball isn't much harder.

Bouncing the ball

To bounce the ball, we once again add a couple of lines of code to our `renderScene` function, as follows:

```
var step=0;
function renderScene() {
  ...
  step+=0.04;
  sphere.position.x = 20 + 10*(Math.cos(step));
  sphere.position.y = 2 + 10*Math.abs(Math.sin(step));
  ...
  requestAnimationFrame(renderScene);
  renderer.render(scene, camera);
}
```

With the cube, we changed the `rotation` property; for the sphere, we're going to change its `position` property in the scene. We want the sphere to bounce from one point in the scene to another with a nice, smooth curve. This is shown in the following diagram:

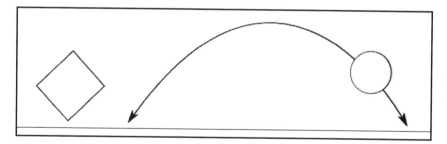

For this, we need to change its position on the *x* axis and its position on the *y* axis. The `Math.cos` and `Math.sin` functions help us create a smooth trajectory using the `step` variable. I won't go into the details of how this works here. For now, all you need to know is that `step+=0.04` defines the speed of the bouncing sphere. In `Chapter 8`, *Creating and Loading Advanced Meshes and Geometries*, we'll look in much more detail at how these functions can be used for animation, and we'll explain everything. Here's how the ball looks in the middle of a bounce:

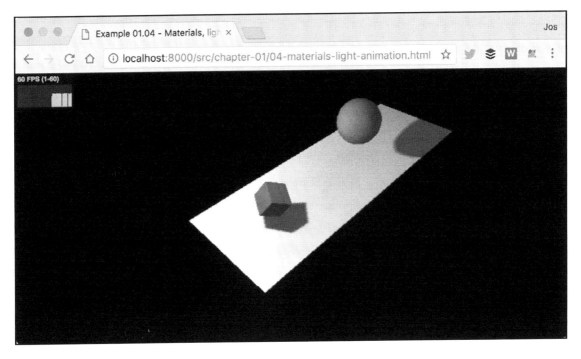

60 FPS (1-60)

Before wrapping up this chapter, we must add one more element to our basic scene. When working with 3D scenes, animations, colors, and properties like that, it often requires a bit of experimenting to get the correct color or speed. It would be very easy if you could just have a simple GUI that allows you to change these kinds of properties on the fly. Luckily, there is!

Using dat.GUI to make experimenting easier

A couple of employees from Google created a library called dat.GUI (you can find the documentation online at http://code.google.com/p/dat-gui/), which allows you to very easily create a simple user interface component that can change variables in your code. In the last part of this chapter, we'll use dat.GUI to add a user interface to our example that allows us to do the following:

- Control the speed of the bouncing ball
- Control the rotation of the cube

Just like we had to do for the statistics, we first add this library to the <head> element of our HTML page, as follows:

```
<script type="text/javascript" src="../../libs/util/dat.gui.js"></script>
```

The next thing we need to configure is a JavaScript object that will hold the properties we want to change using dat.GUI. In the main part of our JavaScript code, we add the following JavaScript object, as follows:

```
var controls = new function() {
  this.rotationSpeed = 0.02;
  this.bouncingSpeed = 0.03;
}
```

In this JavaScript object, we define two properties: this.rotationSpeed and this.bouncingSpeed, and their default values. Next, we pass this object into a new dat.GUI object and define the range for these two properties, as follows:

```
var gui = new dat.GUI();
gui.add(controls, 'rotationSpeed', 0, 0.5);
gui.add(controls, 'bouncingSpeed', 0, 0.5);
```

The rotationSpeed and bouncingSpeed properties are both set to a range of 0 to 0.5. All we need to do now is make sure that in our renderScene loop, we reference these two properties directly so that when we make changes through the dat.GUI user interface, it immediately affects the rotation and speed of bounce of our objects, as follows:

```
function renderScene() {
  ...
  cube.rotation.x += controls.rotationSpeed;
  cube.rotation.y += controls.rotationSpeed;
  cube.rotation.z += controls.rotationSpeed;
  step += controls.bouncingSpeed;
  sphere.position.x = 20 +(10 * (Math.cos(step)));
```

```
        sphere.position.y = 2 +(10 * Math.abs(Math.sin(step)));
        ...
    }
```

Now, when you run this example (`05-control-gui.html`), you'll see a simple user interface that you can use to control the bouncing and rotation speeds. A screenshot of the bouncing ball and the rotating cube is shown here:

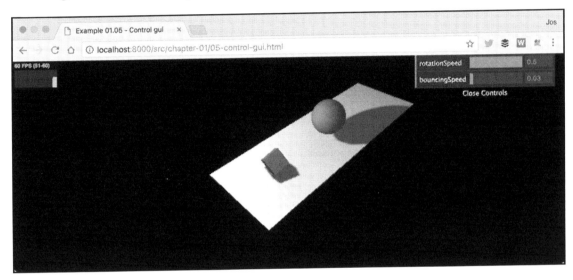

60 FPS (51-60)

Remember that in the HTML skeleton we showed at the beginning of this chapter, we include the `TrackballControls.js` JavaScript file. With this file, we can control the `camera` used in the scene, as we'll explain in more detail in `Chapter 9`, *Animations and Moving the Camera*. For now, we'll just enable this control by adding a couple lines of JavaScript. The first thing we need to do is initialize the trackball controls. Since these controls respond to **Document Object Model (DOM)** element events, we need to make sure we add the following lines after this call:

```
document.getElementById("webgl-output").appendChild(renderer.domElement);
// add the two lines below
var trackballControls = initTrackballControls(camera, renderer);
var clock = new THREE.Clock();
```

The `initTrackballControls` function is defined in `utils.js`, which we mentioned earlier. In later chapters, we'll go into more detail regarding how this works. Now, we also need to update the `render` function as follows:

```
function render() {
    trackballControls.update(clock.getDelta());
    ...
}
```

At this point, we're done. If you open the `05-control-gui.html` example again, you can move your mouse and left-click to rotate the `camera`. If you press S when moving your mouse, you can zoom in and out, and, if you press D, you can pan around the scene. This, for instance, allows you to view the scene from a different side:

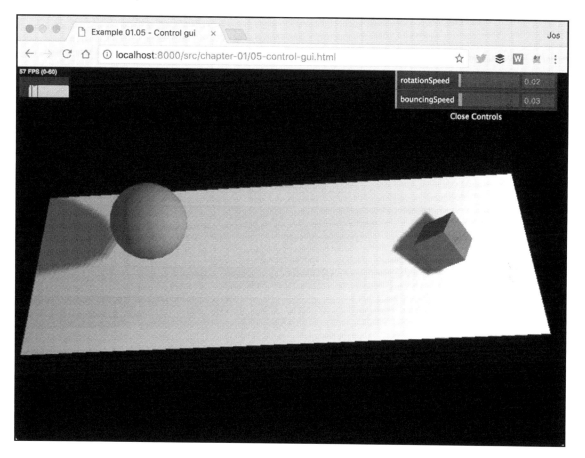

57 FPS (0-60)

All the examples from now on will use these controls by default, so you can easily look at different parts of the rendered scene.

If you've looked at the examples in your browser, you might have noticed that when you change the size of your browser, the scene doesn't automatically scale. In the next section, we'll add this as a final feature for this chapter.

Automatically resize the output when the browser size changes

Changing the `camera` when the browser is resized can be done pretty simply. The first thing we need to do is register an event listener as follows:

```
window.addEventListener('resize', onResize, false);
```

Now, whenever the browser window is resized, the `onResize` function, which we'll specify next, is called. In this `onResize` function, we need to update the `camera` and `renderer`, as follows:

```
function onResize() {
  camera.aspect = window.innerWidth / window.innerHeight;
  camera.updateProjectionMatrix();
  renderer.setSize(window.innerWidth, window.innerHeight);
}
```

For the `camera`, we need to update the `aspect` property, which holds the aspect ratio of the screen, and for the `renderer`, we need to change its size. The final step is to move the variable definitions for `camera`, `renderer`, and `scene` outside of the `init()` function so that we can access them from different functions (such as the `onResize` function), as follows:

```
var camera;
var scene;
var renderer;

function init() {
  ...
  scene = new THREE.Scene();
  camera = new THREE.PerspectiveCamera(45, window.innerWidth /
    window.innerHeight, 0.1, 1000);
  renderer = new THREE.WebGLRenderer();
  ...
}
```

Summary

That's it for the first chapter. In this chapter, we showed you how to set up your development environment, how to get the code, and how to get started with the examples provided with this book. You further learned that to render a scene with Three.js, you first have to create a THREE.Scene object, add a camera, a light, and the objects that you want to render. We also showed you how you can expand this basic scene by adding shadows and animations. Lastly, we added a couple of helper libraries. We used dat.GUI, which allows you to quickly create control user interfaces, and we added stats.js, which provided feedback on the frame rate and other metrics at which your scene is rendered.

In the next chapter, we'll expand on the example we created here. You'll learn more about the most important building blocks that you can use in Three.js.

2
The Basic Components that Make Up a Three.js Application

In the previous chapter, you learned the basics of Three.js. We looked at a couple of examples, and you created your first complete Three.js application. In this chapter, we'll dive a bit deeper into Three.js and explain the basic components that make up a Three.js application. In this chapter, you'll explore the following topics:

- The main components that you can use to create a Three.js application
- What you can do with the `THREE.Scene` object
- How geometries and meshes are related
- The difference between the orthographic and perspective `cameras`

We'll start by looking at how you can create a scene and add objects.

Creating a scene

In the previous `Chapter 1`, *Creating Your First 3D Scene with Three.js*, you created `THREE.Scene`, so you already know the basics of Three.js. We saw that for a scene to show anything, we need four types of component:

Component	Description
Camera	This determines what is rendered on the screen.
Lights	These have an effect on how materials are shown and are used when creating shadow effects (discussed in detail in `Chapter 3`, *Working with the Different Light Sources Available in Three.js*).
Objects	These are the main objects that are rendered from the perspective of the `camera`, they include cubes, spheres, and point clouds.
Renderer	Uses the `camera` and the information from the scene to draw the output on the screen.

`THREE.Scene` serves as the container for the lights and the objects. `THREE.Scene` itself doesn't have that many options and functions.

`THREE.Scene` is a structure that is sometimes also called a scene graph. A scene graph is a structure that can hold all the necessary information of a graphical scene. In Three.js, this means that `THREE.Scene` contains all the objects, lights, and other objects necessary for rendering. It is interesting to note that a scene graph, as the name implies, isn't just an array of objects; a scene graph consists of a set of nodes in a tree structure. Each object you can add to the scene in Three.js, and even `THREE.Scene` itself, extends from a base object named `THREE.Object3D`. A `THREE.Object3D` object can also have its own children, which you can use to create a tree of objects that Three.js will interpret and render.

The basic functionality of a scene

The best way to explore the functionality of a scene is by looking at an example. In the source code for this chapter, you can find the `01-basic-scene.html` example. We'll use this example to explain the various functions and options a scene has. When we open this example in the browser, the output will look similar to what's shown in the next screenshot (and remember that you can use the mouse in combination with the `a`, `s`, and `d` keys to move, zoom, and pan around the rendered scene):

60 FPS (1-60)

This looks like the examples we saw in Chapter 1, *Creating Your First 3D Scene with Three.js*. Even though the scene looks pretty empty, it already contains a couple of objects. Looking at the source for this example (02-02.js), we can see that we used the scene.add(object) function from the THREE.Scene object to add THREE.Mesh (the ground plane you see), THREE.SpotLight, and THREE.AmbientLight. The THREE.Camera object is added automatically by Three.js when you render the scene, so you don't need to add it to the scene itself. Take a look at the following source code for this scene:

```
var scene = new THREE.Scene();
var camera = new THREE.PerspectiveCamera(45, window.innerWidth
  / window.innerHeight, 0.1, 100);
scene.add(camera);
...
var planeGeometry = new THREE.PlaneGeometry(60,40,1,1);
var planeMaterial = new THREE.MeshLambertMaterial({color: 0xffffff});
var plane = new THREE.Mesh(planeGeometry,planeMaterial);
...
scene.add(plane);
var ambientLight = new THREE.AmbientLight(0x3c3c3c);
scene.add(ambientLight);
```

```
...
var spotLight = new THREE.SpotLight(0xffffff, 1.2, 150, 120);
spotLight.position.set(-40, 60, -10);
spotLight.castShadow = true;
scene.add(spotLight);
```

Before we look deeper into the THREE.Scene object, we'll first explain what you can do in the demo, and after that, look at the code. Open the 01-basic-scene.html example in your browser and look at the Controls in the upper-right corner, which you can see in the following screenshot:

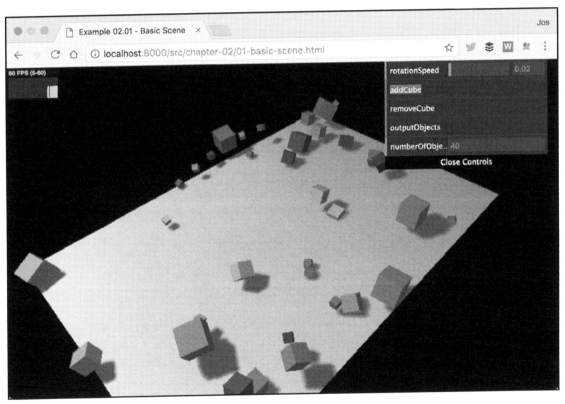

60 FPS (5-60)

With these controls, you can add a cube to the scene, remove the cube that was last added to the scene, and show all the current objects that the scene contains in the console of your browser. The last entry in the Controls section shows the current number of objects in the scene. What you'll probably notice when you start up the scene is that there are already four objects in the scene. These are the ground plane, the ambient light, and the spotlight we mentioned earlier. We'll look at each of the functions in the Controls section and start with the easiest one, addCube, as follows:

```
this.addCube = function() {

    var cubeSize = Math.ceil((Math.random() * 3));
    var cubeGeometry = new THREE.BoxGeometry(cubeSize, cubeSize, cubeSize);
    var cubeMaterial = new THREE.MeshLambertMaterial({color: Math.random() *
0xffffff });

    var cube = new THREE.Mesh(cubeGeometry, cubeMaterial);
    cube.castShadow = true;
    cube.name = "cube-" + scene.children.length;
    cube.position.x= -30 + Math.round(Math.random() * planeGeometry.width));
    cube.position.y= Math.round((Math.random() * 5));
    cube.position.z= -20 + Math.round((Math.random() *
planeGeometry.height));

    scene.add(cube);
    this.numberOfObjects = scene.children.length;
};
```

This piece of code should be pretty easy to read by now. Not many new concepts are introduced here. When you hit the **addCube** button, a new THREE.BoxGeometry object is created whose width, height, and depth are set to a random value between 1 and 3. Besides a random size, the cube also gets a random color, and a random position.

A new element that we introduce here is that we also give the cube a name using its name attribute. Its name is set to cube-, appended with the number of objects currently in the scene (scene.children.length). A name is very useful for debugging purposes but can also be used to directly access an object from your scene. If you use the THREE.Scene.getObjectByName(name) function, you can directly retrieve a specific object and, for instance, change its location without having to make the JavaScript object a global variable. You might wonder what the last line does. The numberOfObjects variable is used by our control GUI to list the number of objects in the scene. So, whenever we add or remove an object, we set this variable to the updated count.

The next function we can call from the control GUI is removeCube. As the name implies, clicking on the **removeCube** button removes the last added cube from the scene. In code, it looks like this:

```
this.removeCube = function() {
  var allChildren = scene.children;
  var lastObject = allChildren[allChildren.length-1];
  if (lastObject instanceof THREE.Mesh) {
    scene.remove(lastObject);
    this.numberOfObjects = scene.children.length;
  }
}
```

To add an object to the scene, we use the add function. To remove an object from the scene, we use, not very surprisingly, the remove function. Since Three.js stores its children as a list (new ones are added at the end), we can use the children property, which contains an array of all the objects in the scene, from the THREE.Scene object to get the last object that was added. We also need to check whether that object is a THREE.Mesh object to avoid removing the lights. After we've removed the object, we once again update the GUI property, numberOfObjects, that holds the number of objects in the scene.

The final button on our GUI is labeled **outputObjects**. You probably already clicked on this and nothing seemed to happen. This button prints out all the objects that are currently in our scene to the web browser console, as shown in the following screenshot:

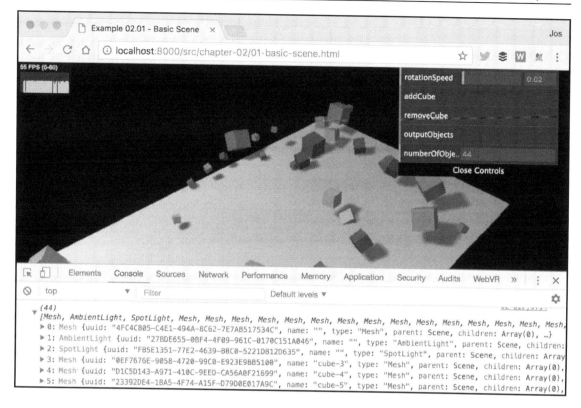

55 FPS (0-60)

The code to output information to the **Console** log makes use of the built-in `console` object:

```
this.outputObjects = function() {
  console.log(scene.children);
}
```

This is great for debugging purposes, and especially when you name your objects, it's very useful for finding issues and problems with a specific object in your scene. For instance, the properties of `cube-17` look like this (if you already know the name, you could use `console.log(scene.getObjectByName("cube-17")` to output only that single object):

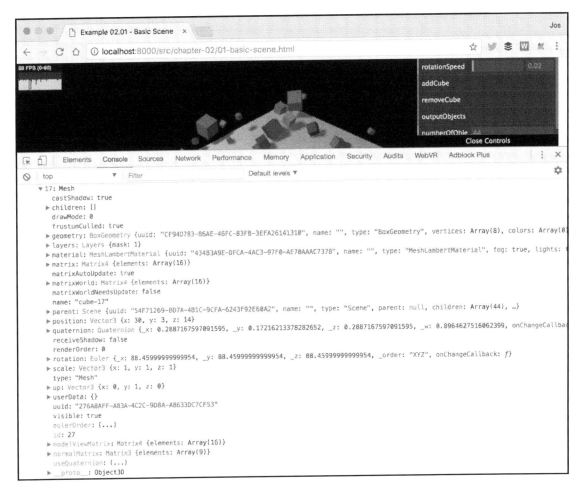

58 FPS (1-80)

So far, we've seen the following scene-related functionality:

- `THREE.Scene.Add`: This adds an object to the scene
- `THREE.Scene.Remove`: This removes an object from the scene

- THREE.Scene.children: This gets a list of all the children in the scene
- THREE.Scene.getObjectByName: This gets a specific object, by name, from the scene

These are the most important scene-related functions, and most often, you won't use any more than these. There are, however, a couple of helper functions that could come in handy, as is shown in the following code fragment.

As you saw in Chapter 1, *Creating Your First 3D Scene with Three.js*, we used a render loop to render the scene. Let's look at that loop for this example:

```
function render() {
  stats.update();
  scene.traverse(function(++6+obj) {
    if (obj instanceof THREE.Mesh && obj != plane ) {
      obj.rotation.x+=controls.rotationSpeed;
      obj.rotation.y+=controls.rotationSpeed;
      obj.rotation.z+=controls.rotationSpeed;
    }
  });

  requestAnimationFrame(render);
  renderer.render(scene, camera);
}
```

Here, we see the THREE.Scene.traverse() function being used. We can pass a function to the traverse() function that will be called for each child of the scene. If a child itself has children, remember that a THREE.Scene object can contain a tree of objects. The traverse() function will also be called for all the children of that object. You traverse through the complete scene graph.

We use the render() function to update the rotation for each of the cubes (note that we explicitly ignore the ground plane). We could also have done this by iterating ourselves over the children property array using a for loop or with forEach since we've only added objects to THREE.Scene and haven't created a nested structure.

Before we dive into the details of THREE.Mesh and THREE.Geometry, I'd like to show you two interesting properties that you can set on the THREE.Scene object: fog and overrideMaterial.

Adding fog to the scene

The fog property lets you add a fog effect to the complete scene; the farther an object is from the camera, the more it will be hidden from sight, as shown in the following screenshot:

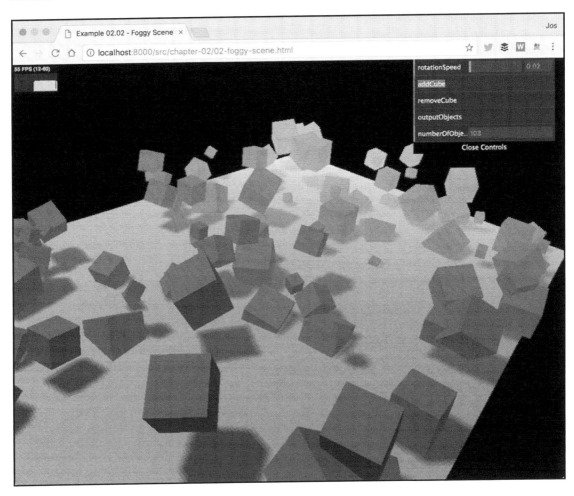

55 FPS (12-60)

To best see the effect of the added fog, use the mouse to zoom in and out, and you'll see the cubes being affected by the fog. Enabling fog is really easy in Three.js. Just add the following line of code after you've defined your scene:

```
scene.fog = new THREE.Fog( 0xffffff, 0.015, 100 );
```

Here, we define a white fog (0xffffff). The preceding two properties can be used to tune how the mist appears. The 0.015 value sets the near property, and the 100 value sets the far property. With these properties, you can determine where the mist starts and how fast it gets denser. With the THREE.Fog object, the fog increases linearly. There is also a different way to set the mist for the scene; for this, use the following definition:

```
scene.fog = new THREE.FogExp2( 0xffffff, 0.01 );
```

This time, we don't specify near and far, but just the color (0xffffff) and the mist's density (0.01). It's best to experiment a bit with these properties to get the effect you want.

 With THREE.FogExp2, the fog's intensity doesn't increase linearly but grows exponentially with the distance.

Using the overrideMaterial property

The last property we'll discuss for the scene is overrideMaterial. When you use this property, all the objects in the scene will use the material that is set to the overrideMaterial property and ignore the material that is set on the object itself. This is useful when you've got a large set of objects in the scene that all share the same material and material properties. This will improve performance since Three.js only has to manage this single material. In practice, though, you won't often need to use this property.

Use it like this:

```
scene.overrideMaterial = new THREE.MeshLambertMaterial({color: 0xffffff});
```

Upon using the `overrideMaterial` property, as shown in the preceding code, the scene will be rendered like this:

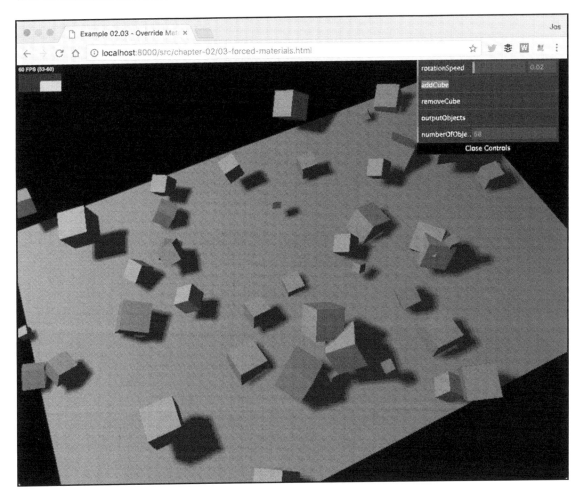

60 FPS (53-60)

In the preceding figure, you can see that all the cubes are rendered using the same material and the same color. In this example, we used a `THREE.MeshLambertMaterial` object as the material. With this material type, we can create non-shiny-looking objects that respond to the lights that are present in the scene. In Chapter 4, *Working with Three.js Materials*, you'll learn more about `THREE.MeshLambertMaterial`.

In this section, we looked at the first of the core concepts of Three.js: `THREE.Scene`. The most important thing to remember about the scene is that it is basically a container for all the objects and lights you want to use when rendering. The following table summarizes the most important functions and attributes of the `THREE.Scene` object:

Function/Property	Description
add(object)	This is used to add an object to the scene. You can also use this function, as we'll see later on, to create groups of objects.
children	This returns a list of all the objects that have been added to the scene, including the camera and lights.
getObjectByName(name, recursive)	When you create an object, you can give it a distinct name. The scene object has a function that you can use to directly return an object with a specific name. If you set the recursive argument to true, Three.js will also search through the complete tree of objects to find the object with the specified name.
remove(object)	If you have a reference to an object in the scene, you can also remove it from the scene using this function.
traverse(function)	The children property returns a list of all the children in the scene. With the traverse function, we can also access these children. With traverse, all the children are passed into the supplied function one by one.
fog	This property allows you to set the fog for the scene. The fog will render a haze that hides faraway objects.
overrideMaterial	With this property, you can force all the objects in the scene to use the same material.

In the next section, we'll take a closer look at the objects that you can add to the scene.

Geometries and meshes

In each of the examples so far, you've seen geometries and meshes being used. For instance, to add a sphere to the scene, we did the following:

```
var sphereGeometry = new THREE.SphereGeometry(4,20,20);
var sphereMaterial = new THREE.MeshBasicMaterial({color: 0x7777ff});
var sphere = new THREE.Mesh(sphereGeometry,sphereMaterial);
```

We define the geometry (`THREE.SphereGeometry`), the shape of an object, and its material (`THREE.MeshBasicMaterial`), and we combined these two in a mesh (`THREE.Mesh`) that can be added to a scene. In this section, we'll take a closer look at geometries and meshes. We'll start with the geometry.

The properties and functions of a geometry

Three.js comes with a large set of geometries out of the box that you can use in your 3D scene. Just add a material, create a mesh, and you're pretty much done. The following screenshot, from example `04-geometries`, shows a couple of the standard geometries available in Three.js:

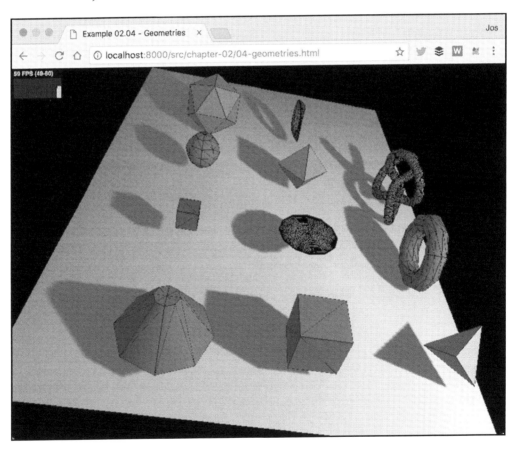

59 FPS (49-60)

In Chapter 5, *Learning to Work with Geometries*, and Chapter 6, *Advanced Geometries and Binary Operations*, we'll explore all the basic and advanced geometries that Three.js has to offer. For now, we'll look in greater detail at what a geometry actually is.

A geometry in Three.js, and in most other 3D libraries, is basically a collection of points in a 3D space, also called **vertices** (where a single point is called a vertex), and a number of faces connecting those points together. Take, for example, a cube:

- A cube has eight corners. Each of these corners can be defined as an x, y, and z coordinate. So each cube has eight points in a 3D space.
- A cube has six sides, with a vertex at each corner. In Three.js, a face always consists of three vertices that make a triangle. So, in the case of a cube, each side consists of two triangles to make the complete side.

When you use one of the geometries provided by Three.js, you don't have to define all the vertices and faces yourself. For a cube, you only need to define the width, height, and depth. Three.js uses that information and creates a geometry with eight vertices at the correct position and the correct number of faces (12 in the case of a cube, 2 triangles per side). Even though you'd normally use the geometries provided by Three.js or generate them automatically, you can still create geometries completely by hand using vertices and faces. This is shown in the following lines of code:

```
var vertices = [
  new THREE.Vector3(1,3,1),
  new THREE.Vector3(1,3,-1),
  new THREE.Vector3(1,-1,1),
  new THREE.Vector3(1,-1,-1),
  new THREE.Vector3(-1,3,-1),
  new THREE.Vector3(-1,3,1),
  new THREE.Vector3(-1,-1,-1),
  new THREE.Vector3(-1,-1,1)
];

var faces = [
  new THREE.Face3(0,2,1),
  new THREE.Face3(2,3,1),
  new THREE.Face3(4,6,5),
  new THREE.Face3(6,7,5),
  new THREE.Face3(4,5,1),
  new THREE.Face3(5,0,1),
  new THREE.Face3(7,6,2),
  new THREE.Face3(6,3,2),
```

```
    new THREE.Face3(5,7,0),
    new THREE.Face3(7,2,0),
    new THREE.Face3(1,3,4),
    new THREE.Face3(3,6,4),
];

var geom = new THREE.Geometry();
geom.vertices = vertices;
geom.faces = faces;
geom.computeFaceNormals();
```

This code shows how to create a simple cube. We define the points that make up this cube in the `vertices` array. These points are connected to create triangular faces, based on their array index, and are stored in the `faces` array. For instance, `new THREE.Face3(0,2,1)` creates a triangular face using the 0, 2, and 1 points from the `vertices` array. Note that you have to take care of the sequence of the vertices used to create `THREE.Face`. The order in which they are defined determines whether Three.js thinks it is a front-facing face (a face facing the `camera`) or a back-facing face. If you create the faces, you should use a clockwise sequence for front-facing faces and a counter-clockwise sequence if you want to create a back-facing face.

In this example, we used a number of `THREE.Face3` elements to define the six sides of the cube, with two triangles for each face. In previous versions of Three.js, you could also use a quad instead of a triangle. A quad uses four vertices instead of three to define the face. Whether using quads or triangles is better is a heated debate raging in the 3D-modeling world. Basically though, using quads is often preferred during modeling since they can be more easily enhanced and smoothed than triangles. For rendering and game engines though, working with triangles is often easier since every shape can be rendered very efficiently using triangles.

Using these vertices and faces, we can now create a new instance of `THREE.Geometry` and assign the vertices to the `vertices` attribute and the faces to the `faces` attribute. The last step is to call `computeFaceNormals()` on the geometry we created. When we call this function, Three.js determines the *normal* vector for each of the faces. This is the information Three.js uses to determine how to color the faces based on the various lights in the scene.

With this geometry, we can now create a mesh, just like we saw earlier. We've created an example that you can use to play around with the position of the vertices, and which also shows the individual faces. In example `05-custom-geometry`, you can change the position of all the vertices of a cube and see how the faces react. This is shown in the following screenshot (should the control GUI be in the way, you can hide it by pressing *H*):

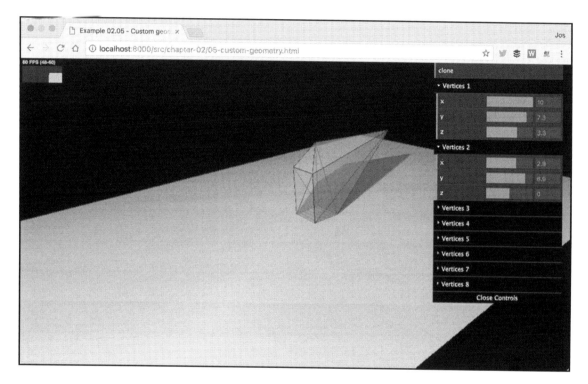

60 FPS (48-60)

This example, which uses the same setup as all our other examples, has a `render` loop. Whenever you change one of the properties in the drop-down control box, the cube is rendered based on the changed position of one of the vertices. This isn't something that works out of the box. For performance reasons, Three.js assumes that the geometry of a mesh won't change during its lifetime. For most geometries and use cases, this is a very valid assumption. To get our example to work, however, we need to make sure the following is added to the code in the `render` loop:

```
mesh.children.forEach(function(e) {
    e.geometry.vertices = vertices;
    e.geometry.verticesNeedUpdate = true;
```

```
    e.geometry.computeFaceNormals();
});
```

In the first line, we point the vertices of the mesh you see onscreen to an array of updated vertices. We don't need to reconfigure the faces since they are still connected to the same points they were before. After we've set the updated vertices, we need to tell the geometry that the vertices need to be updated. We do this by setting the `verticesNeedUpdate` property of the geometry to `true`. Finally, we do a recalculation of the faces to update the complete model using the `computeFaceNormals` function.

The last geometry functionality we'll look at is the `clone()` function. We mentioned that the geometry defines the form and shape of an object, and combined with a material, we create an object that can be added to the scene to be rendered by Three.js. With the `clone()` function, as the name implies, we can make a copy of the geometry and, for instance, use it to create a different mesh with a different material. In the same example, `05-custom-geometry`, you can see a **clone** button at the top of the control GUI, as in the following screenshot:

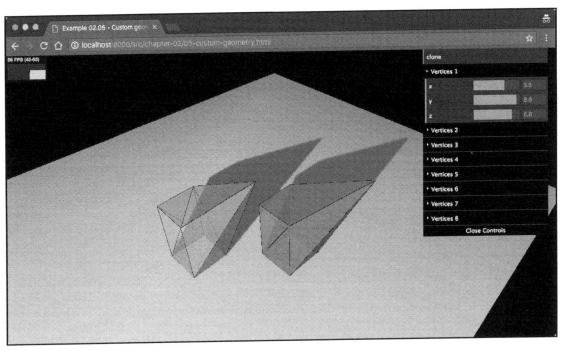

If you click on this button, a clone (a copy) will be made of the geometry as it currently is, a new object is created with a different material, and it is added to the scene. The code for this is rather simple but is made a bit more complex because of the materials I used. Let's take a step back and look at how the green material for the cube was created, as shown in the following code:

```
var materials = [
    new THREE.MeshLambertMaterial({opacity: 0.6, color: 0x44ff44,
transparent: true}),
    new THREE.MeshBasicMaterial({color: 0x000000, wireframe: true})
];
```

As you can see, I didn't use a single material, I used an array of two materials. The reason is that besides showing a transparent green cube, I also wanted to show you the wireframe since that shows up very clearly where the vertices and faces are located. Three.js, of course, supports using multiple materials when creating a mesh. You can use the `SceneUtils.createMultiMaterialObject` function for this, as shown in the following code:

```
var mesh = THREE.SceneUtils.createMultiMaterialObject( geom, materials);
```

In this function, Three.js doesn't just create one `THREE.Mesh` object, it creates one for each material you specified and puts these meshes in a group (a `THREE.Object3D` object). This group can be used in the same manner as you've used the `scene` object. You can add meshes, get objects by name, and so on. For instance, to make sure all the children of the group cast shadows, do the following:

```
mesh.children.forEach(function(e) { e.castShadow = true });
```

Now, let's get back to the `clone()` function we were discussing:

```
this.clone = function() {
  var clonedGeom = mesh.children[0].geometry.clone();
  var materials = [
    new THREE.MeshLambertMaterial( { opacity:0.6, color: 0xff44ff,
transparent:true } ),
    new THREE.MeshBasicMaterial( { color: 0x000000, wireframe: true } )
  ];
```

```
    var mesh2 = THREE.SceneUtils.createMultiMaterialObject(clonedGeom,
materials);
    mesh2.children.forEach(function(e) {e.castShadow=true});
    mesh2.translateX(5);
    mesh2.translateZ(5);
    mesh2.name="clone";
    scene.remove(scene.getObjectByName("clone"));
    scene.add(mesh2);
}
```

This piece of JavaScript is called when the **clone** button is clicked on. Here, we clone the geometry of the first child of our cube. Remember, the mesh variable contains two children; it contains two `Three.Mesh` objects, one for each material we specified. Based on this cloned geometry, we create a new mesh, aptly named `mesh2`. We move this new mesh using translate functions (more on this in Chapter 5, *Learning to Work with Geometries*), remove the previous clone (if present), and add the clone to the scene.

In the previous section, we used `createMultiMaterialObject` from the `THREE.SceneUtils` object to add a wireframe to the geometry we created. Three.js also provides an alternative way of adding a wireframe using `THREE.WireframeGeometry`. Assuming you have a geometry called `geom`, you can create a wireframe geometry from that: `var wireframe = new THREE.WireframeGeometry(geom);`. Next, you can draw the lines of this geometry, using the `Three.LineSegments` object, by first creating a `var line = new THREE.LineSegments(wireframe)` object, and then add it to the scene: `scene.add(line)`. Since this helper internally is just a `THREE.Line` object, you can style how the wireframe appears. For instance, to set the width of the wireframe lines, use `line.material.linewidth = 2;`.

That's enough on geometries for now.

Functions and attributes for meshes

We've already learned that to create a mesh, we need a geometry and one or more materials. Once we have a mesh, we add it to the scene and it's rendered. There are a couple of properties you can use to change where and how this mesh appears on the scene. In this first example, we'll look at the following set of properties and functions:

Function/Property	Description
position	This determines the position of this object relative to the position of its parent. Most often, the parent of an object is a THREE.Scene object or a THREE.Object3D object.
rotation	With this property, you can set the rotation of an object around any of its axes. Three.js also provides specific functions for rotations around an axis: rotateX(), rotateY(), and rotateZ().
scale	This property allows you to scale the object around its x, y, and z axes.
translateX(amount)	This property moves the object a specified amount along the x axis.
translateY(amount)	This property moves the object a specified amount along the y axis.
translateZ(amount)	This property moves the object a specified amount over the z axis. For the translate functions, you could also use the translateOnAxis(axis, distance) function, which allows you to translate the mesh a distance along a specific axis.
visible	If you set this property to false, THREE.Mesh won't be rendered by Three.js.

As always, we have an example ready for you that will allow you to play around with these properties. If you open `06-mesh-properties.html` in your browser, you get a drop-down menu where you can alter all these properties and directly see the result, as shown in the following screenshot:

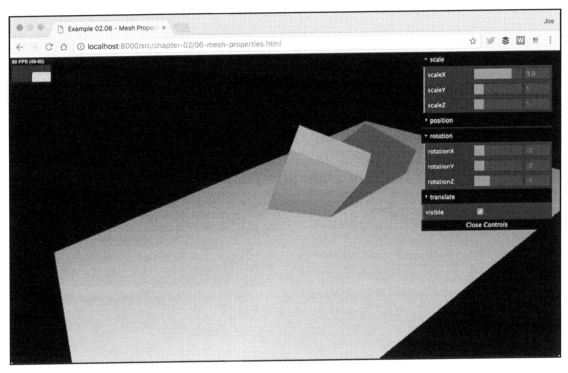

60 FPS (49-60)

Let me walk you through them; I'll start with the position property. We've already seen this property a couple of times, so let's quickly address it. With this property, you set the *x*, *y*, and *z* coordinates of the object. This position is relative to its parent object, which is normally the scene you add the object to, but could also be a THREE.Object3D object or another THREE.Mesh object. We'll get back to this in Chapter 5, *Learning to Work with Geometries*, when we look at grouping objects. We can set an object's position property in three different ways. We can set each coordinate directly:

```
cube.position.x = 10;
cube.position.y = 3;
cube.position.z = 1;
```

However, we can also set all of them at once, as follows:

```
cube.position.set(10,3,1);
```

There is also a third option. The `position` property is `THREE.Vector3` object. That means we can also do the following to set this object:

```
cube.postion = new THREE.Vector3(10,3,1)
```

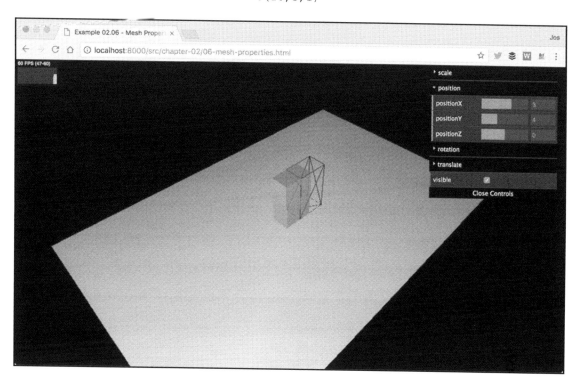

60 FPS (40-60)

However, if we now move the group around, the offset will remain the same. In Chapter 5, *Learning to Work with Geometries*, we'll look deeper into parent-child relations and how grouping affects transformation, such as scaling, rotation, and translation.

OK, next on the list is the rotation property. You've already seen this property being used a couple of times here and in the previous Chapter 1, *Creating Your First 3D Scene with Three.js*. With this property, you set the rotation of the object around one of its axes. You can set this value in the same manner as we did the position. A complete rotation, as you might remember from math class, is *2 x π*. You can configure this in Three.js in a couple of different ways:

```
cube.rotation.x = 0.5*Math.PI;
cube.rotation.set(0.5*Math.PI, 0, 0);
cube.rotation = new THREE.Vector3(0.5*Math.PI,0,0);
```

If you want to use degrees (from 0 to 360) instead, we'll have to convert those to radians. This can be easily done like so:

```
Var degrees = 45;
Var inRadians = degrees * (Math.PI / 180);
```

You can play around with this property using the 06-mesh-properties.html example.

The next property on our list is one we haven't talked about: `scale`. The name pretty much sums up what you can do with this property. You can scale the object along a specific axis. If you set the scale to values lesser than one, the object will shrink, as shown in the following screenshot:

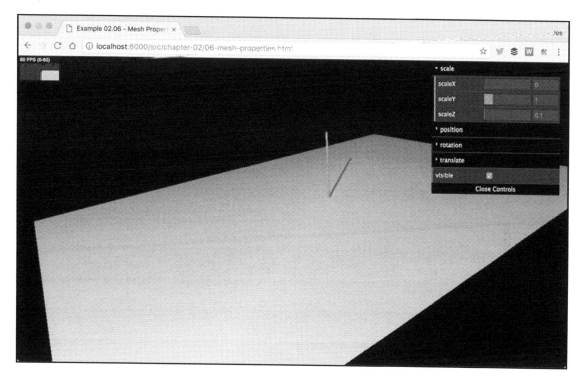

60 FPS (0-60)

When you use values greater than one, the object will become larger, as shown in the following screenshot:

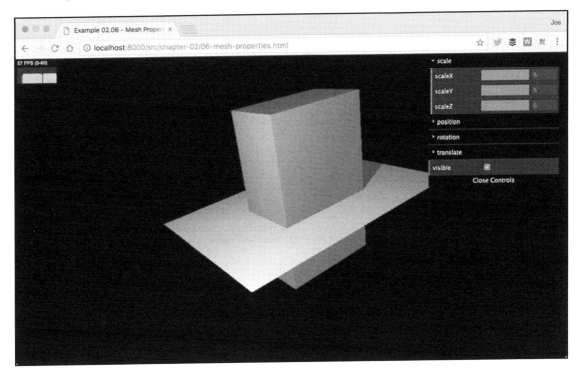

57 FPS (0-60)

The next part of the mesh that we'll look at is the translate functionality. With translate, you can also change the position of an object, but instead of defining the absolute position where you want the object to be, you define where the object should move to, relative to its current position. For instance, we have a sphere that is added to a scene, and its position has been set to (1, 2, 3). Next, we translate the object along its x axis: translateX(4). Its position will now be (5, 2, 3). If we want to restore the object to its original position, we do this: translateX(-4). In the 06-mesh-properties.html example, there is a menu tab called **translate**. From there, you can experiment with this functionality. Just set the translate values for x, y, and z and hit the **translate** button. You'll see the object being moved to a new position based on these three values.

The last property you can use from the menu in the top-right corner is the visible property. If you click on the **visible** menu item, you'll see that the cube becomes invisible:

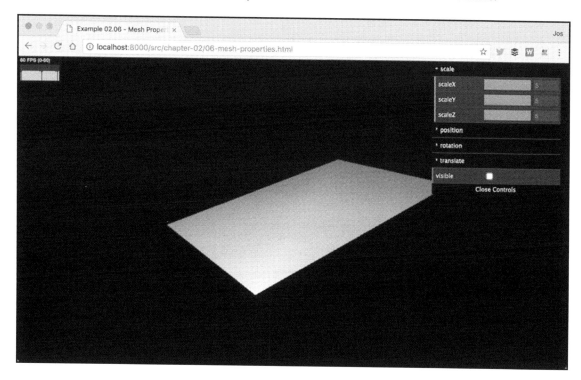

60 FPS (0-60)

When you click on it, the cube becomes visible again. For more information on meshes, geometries, and what you can do with these objects, check out Chapter 5, *Learning to Work with Geometries*, and Chapter 7, *Points and Sprites*.

Different cameras for different uses

There are two different `camera` types in Three.js: the orthographic `camera` and the perspective `camera`. In `Chapter 3`, *Working with the Different Light Sources Available in Three.js*, we'll take a much more detailed look at how to work with these `cameras`, so in this chapter, we'll stick to the basics. Note that Three.js also provides a couple of very specific `cameras` for creating scenes that can be viewed using 3D glasses or VR gear. We won't go into detail for those `cameras` in this book, since they work exactly the same as the `cameras` explained in this chapter.

> If you're looking for simple VR cameras, you can use `THREE.StereoCamera` to create 3D scenes that are rendered side to side (standard stereo effect), use a parallel barrier (as 3DS provides), or provide an anaglyph effect where the different views are rendered in different colors.
> Alternatively, Three.js has some experimental support for the WebVR standard, which is supported by a number of browsers (for more info, see `https://webvr.info/developers/`). To use this, not that much needs to change. You just set `renderer.vr.enabled = true;` and Three.js will handle the rest. The Three.js website has a couple of examples where this property and some other features of Three.js support for WebVR are demonstrated: `https://threejs.org/examples/`.

For now, we focus on the standard perspective and orthographic `cameras`. The best way to explain the differences between these `cameras` is by looking at a couple of examples.

Orthographic camera versus perspective camera

In the examples for this chapter, you can find a demo called `07-both-cameras.html`.
When you open this example, you'll see something like the following:

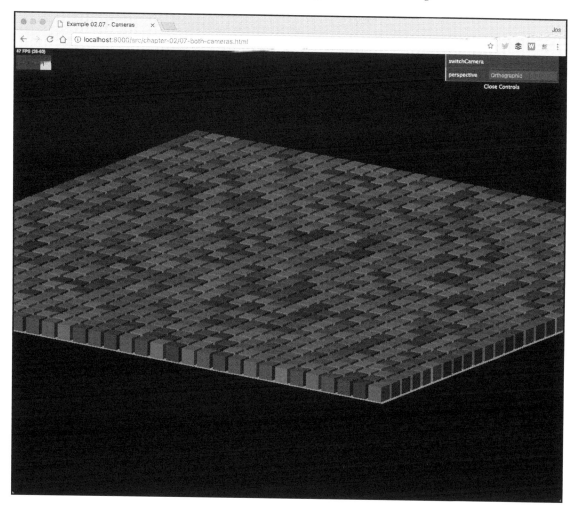

47 FPS (26-60)

This is called a perspective view and is the most natural view. As you can see from this figure, the farther away the cubes are from the camera, the smaller they are rendered. If we change the camera to the other type supported by Three.js, the orthographic camera, you'll see the following view of the same scene:

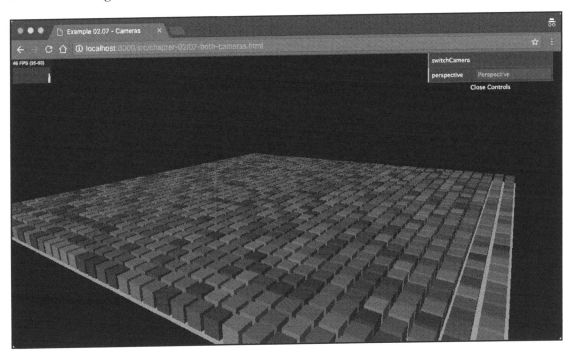

With the orthographic `camera`, all the cubes are rendered the same size; the distance between an object and the `camera` doesn't matter. This is often used in 2D games, such as *SimCity 4* and old versions of *Civilization*:

In our examples, we'll use the perspective `camera` the most since it best resembles the real world. Switching `cameras` is easy. The following piece of code is called whenever you hit the switch `camera` button on the `07-both-cameras` example:

```
this.switchCamera = function() {
  if (camera instanceof THREE.PerspectiveCamera) {
    camera = new THREE.OrthographicCamera(
        window.innerWidth / - 16,
        window.innerWidth / 16,
        window.innerHeight / 16,
        window.innerHeight / - 16,
        -200, 500 );
    camera.position.x = 120;
    camera.position.y = 60;
    camera.position.z = 180;
    camera.lookAt(scene.position);
    this.perspective = "Orthographic";
  } else {
    camera = new THREE.PerspectiveCamera(45, window.innerWidth /
window.innerHeight, 0.1, 1000);

    camera.position.x = 120;
    camera.position.y = 60;
    camera.position.z = 180;
```

```
            camera.lookAt(scene.position);
            this.perspective = "Perspective";
        }
    };
```

In this code fragment, you can see that there is a difference in the way we create the `camera`. Let's look at `THREE.PerspectiveCamera` first. This `camera` takes the following arguments:

Argument	Description
fov	**Field Of View (FOV)** is the part of the scene that can be seen from the position of the `camera`. Humans, for instance, have an almost 180-degree FOV, while some birds might even have a complete 360-degree FOV. But since a normal computer screen doesn't completely fill our vision, a smaller value is often chosen. Generally, for games, a FOV between 60 and 90 degrees is chosen. *Good default:* 50
aspect	This is the aspect ratio between the horizontal and vertical sizes of the area where we're rendering the output. In our case, since we use the entire window, we just use that ratio. The aspect ratio determines the difference between the horizontal FOV and the vertical FOV. *Good default:* `window.innerWidth / window.innerHeight`
near	The `near` property defines from how close to the `camera` Three.js should render the scene. Normally, we set this to a very small value to directly render everything from the position of the `camera`. *Good default:* 0.1
far	The `far` property defines how far the `camera` can see from the position of the `camera`. If we set this too low, a part of our scene might not be rendered, and if we set it too high, in some cases, it might affect the rendering performance. *Good default:* 1000
zoom	The `zoom` property allows you to zoom in and out of the scene. When you use a number lower than 1, you zoom out of the scene, and if you use a number higher than 1, you zoom in. Note that if you specify a negative value, the scene will be rendered upside down. *Good default value:* 1

The following diagram gives a good overview of how these properties work together to determine what you see:

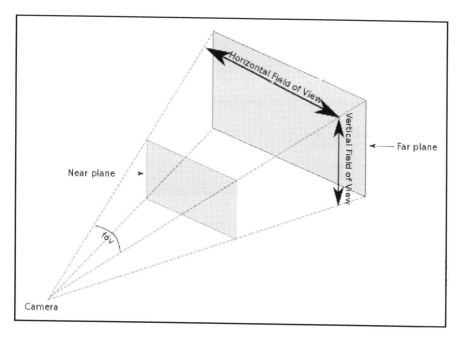

The fov property of the camera determines the horizontal FOV. Based on the aspect property, the vertical FOV is determined. The near property is used to determine the position of the near plane, and the far property determines the position of the far plane. The area between the near plane and the far plane will be rendered.

To configure the orthographic camera, we need to use other properties. The orthographic projection isn't interested in which aspect ratio to use or with what FOV we look at the scene since all the objects are rendered at the same size. When you define an orthographic camera, you define the cuboid area that needs to be rendered. The properties for the orthographic camera reflect this, as follows:

Argument	Description
left	This is described in the Three.js documentation as *Camera frustum left plane*. You should see this as the left-hand border of what will be rendered. If you set this value to -100, you won't see any objects that are farther to the left-hand side.
right	The right property works in a way similar to the left property, but this time, to the other side of the screen. Anything farther to the right won't be rendered.
top	This is the top position to be rendered.

bottom	This is the bottom position to be rendered.
near	From this point, based on the position of the camera, the scene will be rendered.
far	To this point, based on the position of the camera, the scene will be rendered.
zoom	This allows you to zoom in and out of the scene. When you use a number lower than 1, you'll zoom out of the scene; if you use a number higher than 1, you'll zoom in. Note that if you specify a negative value, the scene will be rendered upside down. The default value is 1.

All these properties can be summarized in the following diagram:

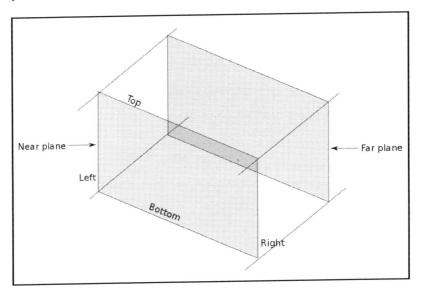

Looking at specific points

So far, you've seen how to create a camera and what the various arguments mean. In Chapter 1, *Creating Your First 3D Scene with Three.js*, you also saw that you need to position your camera somewhere in the scene, and that the view from that camera is rendered. Normally, the camera is pointed to the center of the scene: position (0,0,0). We can, however, easily change what the camera is looking at, as follows:

```
camera.lookAt(new THREE.Vector3(x,y,z));
```

I've added an example where the `camera` moves, and the point it is looking at is marked with a red dot, as follows:

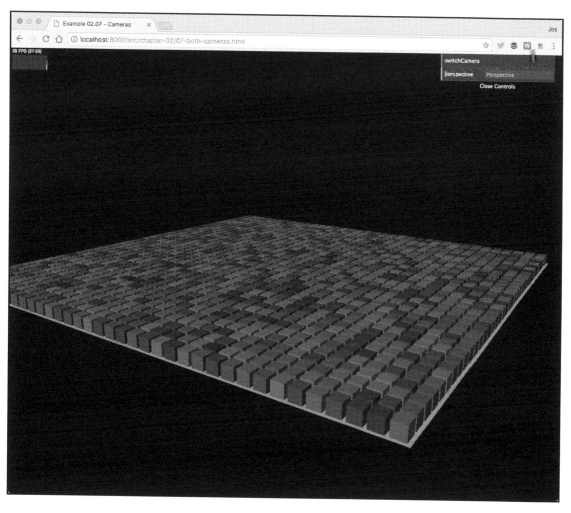

47 FPS (26-60)

If you open the `08-cameras-lookat` example, you'll see the scene moving from left to right. The scene isn't really moving. The `camera` is looking at different points (see the red dot in the center), which gives the effect that the scene is moving from left to right. In this example, you can also switch `camera` types. If you switch to the orthographic `camera`, you see that changing the point the `camera` looks at has pretty much the same effect as with `THREE.PerspectiveCamera`. The interesting part to notice, though, is that with `THREE.OrthographicCamera`, you can clearly see that the sizes of all the cubes stay the same regardless of where the `camera` is looking, and the distance of a cube to the position of the `camera`:

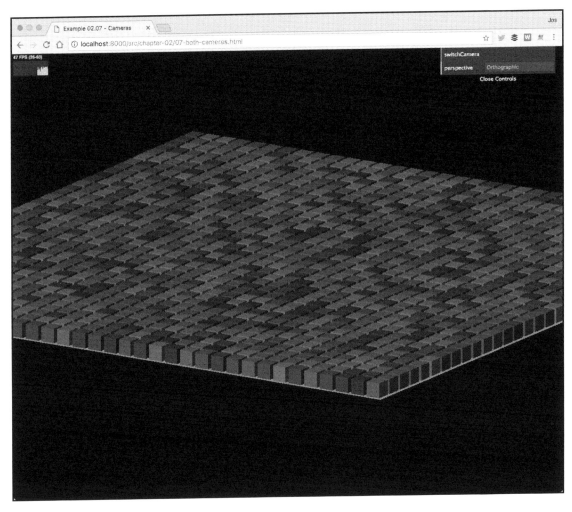

47 FPS (26-60)

When you use the `lookAt` function, you point the `camera` at a specific position. You can also use this to make the `camera` follow an object around the scene. Since every `THREE.Mesh` object has a position that is a `THREE.Vector3` object, you can use the `lookAt` function to point to a specific mesh in the scene. All you need to do is this: `camera.lookAt(mesh.position)`. If you call this in the render loop, you'll make the `camera` follow an object as it moves through the scene.

Summary

We discussed a lot in this second introductory chapter. We showed the functions and properties of `THREE.Scene` and explained how you can use these properties to configure your main scene. We also showed you how to create geometries. You can either create them from scratch using a `THREE.Geometry` object or use any of the built-in geometries Three.js provides. Finally, we showed you how to configure the two main `camera`s Three.js provides. `THREE.PerspectiveCamera` renders a scene using a real-world perspective, and `THREE.OrthographicCamera` provides the fake 3D effect often seen in games. We've also covered how geometries work in Three.js and you can now easily create your own geometries from the standard geometries provided by Three.js or by crafting them by hand.

In the next chapters, we'll look at the various light sources that are available in Three.js. You'll learn how the various light sources behave, how to create and configure them, and how they affect different materials.

Working with Light Sources in Three.js 3

In Chapter 1, *Creating Your First 3D Scene with Three.js*, you learned about the basics of Three.js, and in Chapter 2, *The Basic Components that Make Up a Three.js Application*, we looked a bit deeper at the most important parts of the scene: the geometries, meshes, and cameras. You might have noticed that we skipped exploring the details of lights in that chapter even though they make up an important part of every Three.js scene. Without lights, we won't see anything rendered (unless you use basic or wireframe materials). Since Three.js contains a large number of lights, each of which has a specific use, we'll use this chapter to explain the various details of the lights and prepare you for the upcoming chapters on material usage.

 WebGL itself doesn't have inherent support for lighting. Without Three.js, you would have to write specific WebGL shader programs to simulate these kinds of lights. A good introduction on simulating lighting in WebGL from scratch can be found at https://developer.mozilla.org/en-US/docs/Web/WebGL/Lighting_in _WebGL.

In this chapter, you'll learn about the following subjects:

- The light sources that are available in Three.js
- When a specific light source should be used
- How you can tune and configure the behavior of all these light sources
- As a bonus, we'll also quickly look at how you can create lens flares

As with all the chapters, we have a lot of examples that you can use to experiment with the lights' behavior. The examples shown in this chapter can be found in the chapter-03 folder of the supplied sources.

The different kinds of lighting provided by Three.js

There are a number of different lights available in Three.js that all have specific behavior and usages. In this chapter, we'll discuss the following set of lights:

Name	Description
THREE.AmbientLight	This is a basic light, the color of which is added to the current color of the objects in the scene.
THREE.PointLight	This is a single point in space from which light spreads in all directions. This light can't be used to create shadows.
THREE.SpotLight	This light source has a cone-like effect like that of a desk lamp, a spot in the ceiling, or a torch. This light can cast shadows.
THREE.DirectionalLight	This is also called infinite light. The light rays from this light can be seen as parallel, like, for instance, the light from the sun. This light can also be used to create shadows.
THREE.HemisphereLight	This is a special light and can be used to create more natural-looking outdoors lighting by simulating a reflective surface and a faintly illuminating sky. This light also doesn't provide any shadow-related functionality.
THREE.AreaLight	With this light source, instead of a single point in space, you can specify an area from which light emanates. THREE.AreaLight doesn't cast any shadows.
THREE.LensFlare	This is not a light source, but with THREE.LensFlare, you can add a lens flare effect to the lights in your scene.

This chapter is divided into two main parts. First, we'll look at the basic lights: THREE.AmbientLight, THREE.PointLight, THREE.SpotLight, and THREE.DirectionalLight. All these lights extend the base THREE.Light object, which provides shared functionality. The lights mentioned here are simple lights that require a little setting up and can be used to recreate most of the required lighting scenarios. In the second part, we will look at a couple of special-purpose lights and effects: THREE.HemisphereLight, THREE.AreaLight, and THREE.LensFlare. You'll probably only need these lights in very specific cases.

Basic lights

We'll start with the most basic of the lights: THREE.AmbientLight.

THREE.AmbientLight

When you create THREE.AmbientLight, the color is applied globally. There isn't a specific direction this light comes from, and THREE.AmbientLight doesn't contribute to any shadows. You would normally not use THREE.AmbientLight as the single source of light in a scene since it colors all the objects in the same color, regardless of shape. You use it together with other lighting sources, such as THREE.SpotLight or THREE.DirectionalLight, to soften the shadows or add some additional color to the scene. The easiest way to understand this is by looking at the 01-ambient-light.html example in the chapter-03 folder. With this example, you get a simple user interface that can be used to modify THREE.AmbientLight that is available in this scene. Note that in this scene, we also have THREE.SpotLight, which adds additional lighting and provides shadows.

In the following screenshot, you can see that we used a scene from Chapter 1, *Creating Your First 3D Scene with Three.js*, and made the color and intensity of THREE.AmbientLight configurable. In this example, you can also turn off the spotlight to see what the effect of THREE.AmbientLight is on its own:

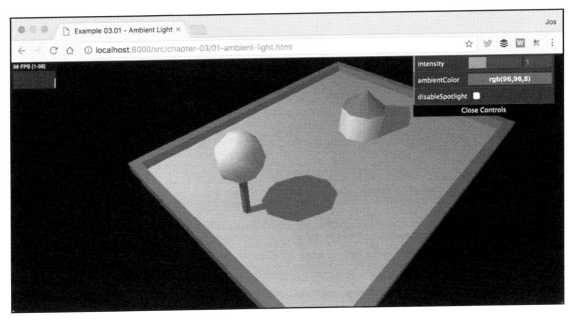

56 FPS (1-56)

The standard color we set in the code for this scene is #606008. This is a hexadecimal representation of a color. The first two values specify the red part of the color, the next two values specify the green part, and the last two values specify the blue part. In the UI for this example, the decimal values are shown.

In this example, we use a very dimmed color that we mainly use to smoothen the hard shadows our meshes cast to the ground plane. You can change the color to a more prominent yellow/orange color (`rgb(190, 190, 41)`) with the menu in the top-right corner, and then the objects will have a sun-like glow over them. This is shown in the following screenshot:

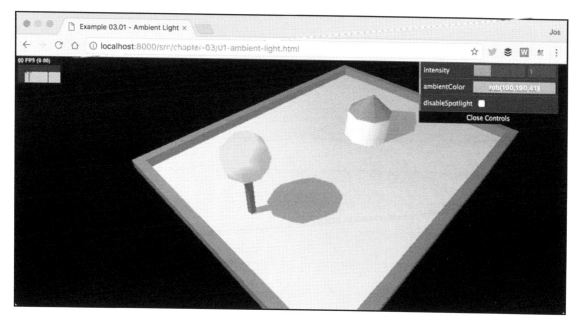

60 FPS (0-60)

As the screenshot image shows, the yellow/orange color is applied to all the objects and casts a glow over the complete scene. What you should remember when working with this light is that you should be very conservative with the color you specify. If the color you specify is too bright, you'll quickly get a completely oversaturated image. Besides the color, we can also set the intensity of the light. This determines how much THREE.AmbientLight affects the colors in the scene. If we turn it down, only a little of the color is applied to the objects in the scene. If we turn it up, our scene becomes really bright:

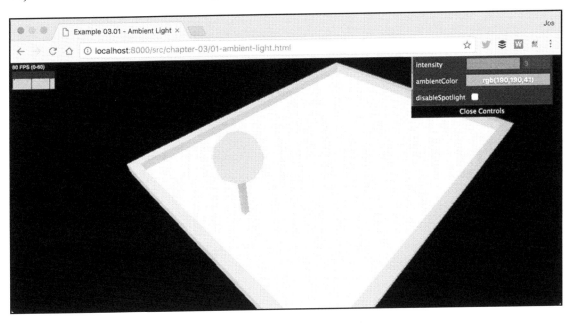

60 FPS (0-60)

Now that we've seen what it does, let's look at how you can create and use THREE.AmbientLight. The next couple of lines of code show you how to create THREE.AmbientLight and also show how to connect this to the GUI Controls menu, which we already saw in the previous chapters:

```
var ambientLight = new THREE.AmbientLight("#606008");
scene.add(ambientLight);

...

var controls = new function () {
  this.intensity = ambientLight.intensity;
  this.ambientColor = ambientLight.color.getStyle();
  this.disableSpotlight = false;
};
```

```
var gui = new dat.GUI();
gui.add(controls, 'intensity', 0, 3, 0.1).onChange(function (e) {
  ambientLight.color = new THREE.Color(controls.ambientColor);
  ambientLight.intensity = controls.intensity;
});
gui.addColor(controls, 'ambientColor').onChange(function (e) {
  ambientLight.color = new THREE.Color(controls.ambientColor);
  ambientLight.intensity = controls.intensity;
});
gui.add(controls, 'disableSpotlight').onChange(function (e) {
  spotLight.visible = !e;
});
```

Creating `THREE.AmbientLight` is very simple and only takes a couple of steps. `THREE.AmbientLight` doesn't have a position and is applied globally, so we only need to specify the color (in hex), `new THREE.AmbientLight("#606008")`, and add this light to the scene, `scene.add(ambientLight)`. Optionally, we can also provide an additional value in this constructor for the `intensity` of this light. Since we didn't specify it here, it uses a default `intensity` of 1. In the example, we bind the `color` and the `intensity` of `THREE.AmbientLight` to the Controls menu. To do this, you can use the same kind of configuration we used in the previous two chapters. The only change is that instead of using the `gui.add(...)` function, we use the `gui.addColor(...)` function to control the color. This creates an option in the Controls menu, with which we can directly change the color of the passed-in variable. In the code, you can see that we use the `onChange` feature of `dat.GUI: gui.addColor(...).onChange(function(e){...})`. With this function, we tell `dat.GUI` to call the passed-in function each time the color changes. In this specific case, we set the `color` of `THREE.AmbientLight` to a new value. In a similar way, we make sure that changes in the `intensity` control are also applied to the ambient light used in the scene.

Using the THREE.Color object

Before we move on to the next light, we're going to look closer at the `THREE.Color` object. In Three.js, when you need to provide a color (for example, for materials, lights, and so on.) you can pass in a `THREE.Color` object, or Three.js will create one from a passed-in string value, as we've seen for `THREE.AmbientLight`. Three.js is very flexible when parsing the input for the `THREE.Color` constructor. You can create a `THREE.Color` object in the following ways:

- **Empty constructor**: `new THREE.Color()` will create a white color object.
- **Hex value**: `new THREE.Color(0xababab)` will parse the passed-in hex value and create a color from that. This is the preferred way of creating colors.

- **Hex string**: `new THREE.Color("#ababab")` will create a color based on the passed-in CSS color string.
- **RGB string**: `new THREE.Color("rgb(255, 0, 0)")` or `new THREE.Color("rgb(100%, 0%, 0%)")` .
- **Color name**: You can use named colors as well—`new THREE.Color( 'skyblue' )`.
- **HSL string**: If you like working in the HSL domain, instead of the RGB domain, you can pass in the HSL values—`new THREE.Color("hsl(0, 100%, 50%)")`.

- **Separate RGB values**: And you can specify the individual RGB components on a scale from 0 to 1—`new THREE.Color( 1, 0, 0 )`.

If you want to change the color after construction, you'll have to create a new `THREE.Color` object or modify the internal properties of the current `THREE.Color` object. The `THREE.Color` object comes with the following functions to set and get information about the current object:

Name	Description
`set(value)`	Set the value of this color to the supplied hex value. This hex value may be a string, a number, or an existing `THREE.Color` instance.
`setHex(value)`	Set the value of this color to the supplied numeric hex value.
`setRGB(r,g,b)`	Set the value of this color based on the supplied RGB values. The values range from 0 to 1.
`setHSL(h,s,l)`	Set the value of this color on the supplied HSL values. The values range from 0 to 1. A good explanation of how HSL works for configuring colors can be found at http://en.wikibooks.org/wiki/Color_Models:_RGB,_HSV,_HSL.
`setStyle(style)`	Set the value of this color based on the CSS way of specifying colors. For instance, you could use `"rgb(255,0,0)"`, `"#ff0000"`, `"#f00"`, or even `"red"`.
`copy(color)`	Copy the color values from the `THREE.Color` instance provided to this color.
`copyGammaToLinear(color)`	Set the color of this object based on the `THREE.Color` instance supplied. The color is first converted from the gamma color space to the linear color space. The gamma color space also uses RGB values, but uses an exponential scale instead of a linear one.
`copyLinearToGamma(color)`	Set the color of this object based on the `THREE.Color` instance supplied. The color is first converted from the linear color space to the gamma color space.

`convertGammaToLinear()`	This converts the current color from the gamma color space to the linear color space.
`convertLinearToGamma()`	This converts the current color from the linear color space to the gamma color space.
`getHex()`	Return the value from this color object as a number: 435241.
`getHexString()`	Return the value from this color object as a hex string: "0c0c0c".
`getStyle()`	Return the value from this color object as a CSS-based value: "rgb(112,0,0)".
`getHSL(optionalTarget)`	Return the value from this color object as a HSL value. If you provide the `optionalTarget` object, Three.js will set the h, s, and l properties on that object.
`offsetHSL(h, s, l)`	Add the h, s, and l values provided to the h, s, and l values of the current color.
`add(color)`	This adds the r, g, and b values of the color supplied to the current color.
`addColors(color1, color2)`	Add `color1` and `color2`, and set the value of the current color to the result.
`addScalar(s)`	Add a value to the RGB components of the current color. Bear in mind that the internal values use a range from 0 to 1.
`multiply(color)`	Multiply the current RGB values with the RGB values from `THREE.Color`.
`multiplyScalar(s)`	This multiplies the current RGB values with the value supplied. Bear in mind that the internal values use a range from 0 to 1.
`lerp(color, alpha)`	This finds the color that is between the color of this object and the color supplied. The alpha property defines how far between the current color and the supplied color you want the result to be.
`equals(color)`	This returns `true` if the RGB values of the `THREE.Color` instance supplied match the values of the current color.
`fromArray(array)`	This has the same functionality as `setRGB`, but now the RGB values can be provided as an array of numbers.
`toArray`	This returns an array with three elements, [r, g, b].
`clone()`	This creates an exact copy of this color.

In the preceding table, you can see that there are many ways in which you can change the current color. A lot of these functions are used internally by Three.js, but they also provide a good way to easily change the color of lights and materials, without having to create and assign new THREE.Color objects.

Before we move on to the discussion on THREE.PointLight, THREE.SpotLight, and THREE.DirectionalLight, let's first highlight their main difference, that is, how they emit light. The following diagram shows how these three light sources emit light:

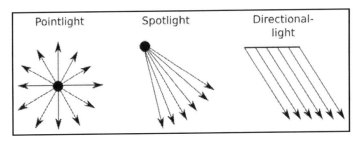

You can see the following from this diagram:

- THREE.PointLight emits light from a specific point in all directions.
- THREE.SpotLight emits light from a specific point in a cone-like shape.
- THREE.DirectionalLight doesn't emit light from a single point, but emits light rays from a 2D plane, where the rays are parallel to each other.

We'll look at these light sources in more detail in the next few sections; let's start with THREE.SpotLight.

THREE.SpotLight

THREE.SpotLight is one of the lights you'll use most often (especially if you want to use shadows). THREE.SpotLight is a light source that has a cone-like effect. You can compare this with a flashlight or a lantern. This light has a direction and an angle at which it produces light. The following screenshot shows what using THREE.SpotLight looks like (02-spot-light.html):

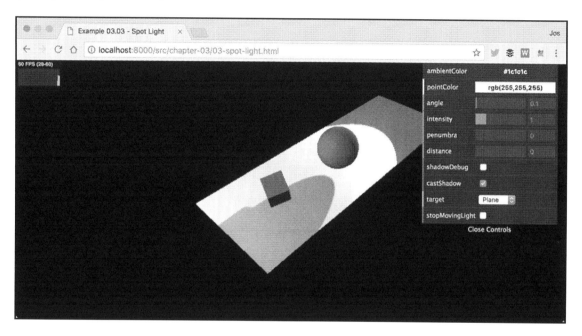

60 FPS (28-60)

The following table lists all the properties that you can use to fine-tune `THREE.SpotLight`. First, we'll look at the properties specific to the light behavior; after that, we'll look at the properties that allow you to control how the shadows are rendered:

Property	Description
angle	This determines how wide the beam emerging from this light is. This is measured in radians and defaults to `Math.PI/3`.
castShadow	If set to `true`, this light will create shadows. See the following table on how to configure the shadows.
color	This is the color of the light.
decay	This is the amount the intensity diminishes the farther away from the light source it gets. A `decay` of 2 leads to more realistic light, and the default value is 1. This property only has effect when the `physicallyCorrectLights` property is set on the `WebGLRenderer`.
distance	When this property is set to a non 0 value, the light intensity will decrease linearly from the set intensity at the light's position to 0 at this distance.
intensity	This is the intensity the light shines with. This defaults to 1.
penumbra	The percentage at the edge of the spotlight's coin, which is smoothed (blurred) to 0. Takes a value between 0 and 1, and the default is 0.
position	This is the position of the light in `THREE.Scene`.
power	The light's power when being rendered in physical correct mode (enable this by setting the `physicallyCorrectLights` property set on the `WebGLRenderer`). This is measured in lumens and the default value is `4*Math.PI`.
target	With `THREE.SpotLight`, the direction it is pointed in is important. With the `target` property, you can point `THREE.SpotLight` to look at a specific object or position in the scene. Note that this property requires a `THREE.Object3D` object (such as `THREE.Mesh`). This is in contrast to the cameras we saw in Chapter 2, *Basic Components That Make Up a Three.Js Application*, that use `THREE.Vector3` in their `lookAt` function.
visible	If this is set to `true` (the default), this light is turned on, and if this is set to `false`, the light is turned off.

When you enable the shadow for THREE.SpotLight, you can control how that shadow is rendered. You can control this through the shadow property of a THREE.SpotLight:

Property	Description
shadow.bias	The shadow bias moves the cast shadow away or toward the object casting the shadow. You can use this to solve some strange effects when you work with very thin objects (a good example can be found at: http://www.3dbuzz.com/training/view/unity-fundamentals/lights/8-shadows-bias). If you see strange shadow effects, small values (for example, 0.01) for this property can often resolve the issue. The default value for this property is 0.
shadow.camera.far	This determines what distance from the light shadows should be created. The default value is 5000. Note that you can also set all the other properties provided for THREE.PerspectiveCamera, which we showed in Chapter 2, *Basic Components That Make Up a Three.js Scene*.
shadow.camera.fov	This determines how large the field of view used to create shadows is (see the *Different cameras for different uses* section in Chapter 2, *Basic Components That Make Up a Three.js Scene*). The default value is 50.
shadow.camera.near	This determines what distance from the light shadows should be created. The default value is 50.
shadow.mapSize.width and shadow.mapSize.height	This determines how many pixels are used to create the shadow. Increase this when the shadow has jagged edges or doesn't look smooth. This can't be changed after the scene is rendered. The default value for both is 512.
shadow.radius	When this value is set to values higher than 1, the edge of the shadows will be blurred. This won't have any effect if the shadowMap.type of the THREE.WebGlRenderer is set to THREE.BasicShadowMap.

Creating THREE.SpotLight is very easy. Just specify the color, set the properties you want, and add it to the scene, as follows:

```
var spotLight = new THREE.SpotLight("#ffffff");
spotLight.position.set(-40, 60, -10);
spotLight.castShadow = true;
spotLight.shadow.camera.near = 1;
spotLight.shadow.camera.far = 100;
spotLight.target = plane;
spotLight.distance = 0;
spotLight.angle = 0.4;
spotLight.shadow.camera.fov = 120;
```

You can see that we create an instance of THREE.SpotLight and set the various properties to configure the light. We also explicitly set the castShadow property to true because we want shadows. We also need to point THREE.SpotLight somewhere, which we do with the target property. In this case, we point it at the plane object. When you run the example (02-spot-light.html), you'll see a scene like the following screenshot:

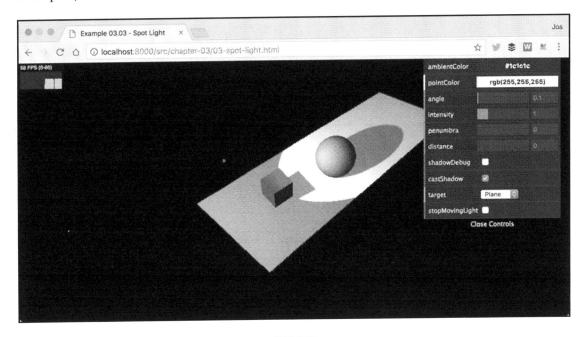

58 FPS (0-60)

In this example, you can set a number of properties specific to `THREE.SpotLight`. One of them is the `target` property. If we set this property to the blue sphere, the light will focus at the center of the sphere even if the sphere moves around the scene. When we created the light, we aimed it at the ground plane, and in our example, we can also aim it at the other two objects. But what if you don't want to aim the light at a specific object, but rather at an arbitrary point in space? You can do that by creating a `THREE.Object3D()` object like this:

```
var target = new THREE.Object3D();
target.position = new THREE.Vector3(5, 0, 0);
```

Then, set the target property of `THREE.SpotLight`:

```
spotlight.target = target
```

In the table at the beginning of this section, we showed a couple of properties that can be used to control how the light emanates from `THREE.SpotLight`. The `distance` and `angle` properties define the shape of the cone of light. The `angle` property defines the width of the cone, and with the `distance` property, we set the length of the cone. The following diagram explains how these two values together define the area that will receive light from `THREE.SpotLight`:

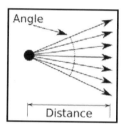

Usually, you won't really need to set these values since they come with reasonable defaults, but you can use these properties, for instance, to create a THREE.SpotLight that has a very narrow beam or quickly decreases in light intensity. The last property you can use to change the way THREE.SpotLight produces light is the penumbra property. With this property, you set from where the intensity of the light decreases at the edge of the light cone. In the following screenshot, you can see the result of the penumbra property in action. We have a very bright light (high intensity) that rapidly decreases in intensity as it moves at the edge of the cone:

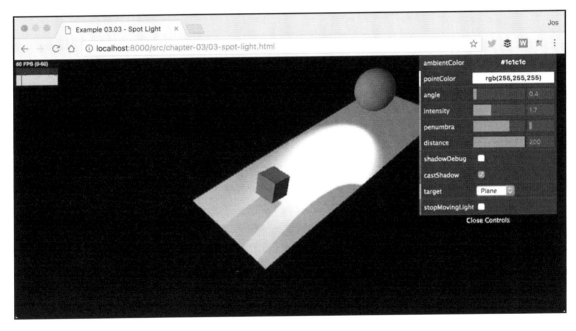

60 FPS (0-60)

Before moving on to the next light, we'll quickly look at the shadow-related properties available to THREE.SpotLight. You've already learned that we can get shadows by setting the castShadow property of THREE.SpotLight to true (and, of course, making sure that we set the castShadow property for objects that should cast shadows, and that we set the receiveShadow property, for objects that should show a shadow, on the THREE.Mesh objects in our scene). Three.js also allows you very fine-grained control on how the shadow is rendered. This is done by a couple of properties we explained in the table at the beginning of the section. With shadow.camera.near, shadow.camera.far, and shadow.camera.fov, you can control how and where this light casts a shadow. This works in the same way as the perspective camera's field of view we explained in Chapter 2, *Basic Components That Make Up a Three.Js Application*. The easiest way to see this in action is by adding THREE.CameraHelper; you can do this by checking the menu's shadowDebug checkbox. This shows, as you can see in the following screenshot, the area that is used to determine the shadows for this light:

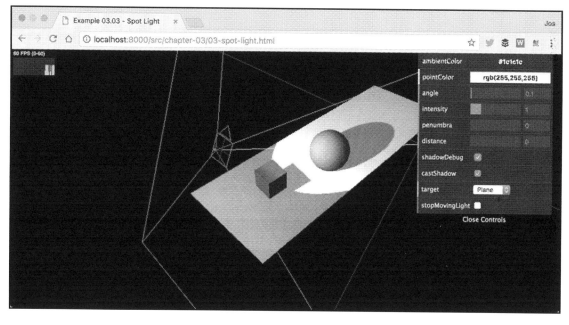

60 FPS (0-60)

When debugging issues with shadows, adding THREE.CameraHelper is really useful. To do this, just add the following lines:

```
var debugCamera = new THREE.CameraHelper(spotLight.shadow.camera);
scene.add(debugCamera)
```

If you want to debug `THREE.SpotLight` itself, Three.js also provides `THREE.SpotLightHelper`, which shows the shape of the `THREE.SpotLight`. To add this helper, you can use the following piece of code:

```
var helper = new THREE.SpotLightHelper(spotLight);
scene.add(helper);

function render() {
  ...
  helper.update();
  ...
}
```

The result is that we can very easily track the shape and direction of our light:

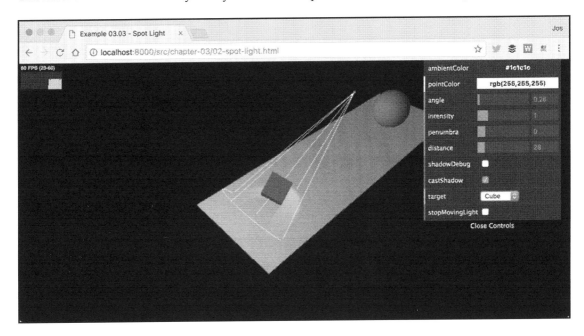

60 FPS (23-60)

I'll end this section with a couple of pointers, just in case you run into issues with shadows:

- If the shadow looks blocky, you can either increase the `shadow.mapSize.width` and `shadow.mapSize.Height` properties and make sure the area that is used to calculate the shadow tightly wraps your object. You can use the `shadow.camera.near`, `shadow.camera.far`, and `shadow.camera.fov` properties to configure this area.
- Remember that you not only have to tell the light to cast shadows, but also have to tell each geometry whether it will receive and/or cast shadows by setting the `castShadow` and `receiveShadow` properties.

- If you use thin objects in your scene, you might see strange artifacts when you render shadows. You can use the `shadow.bias` property to slightly offset the shadows, which will often fix these kinds of issues.
- If you want to have softer shadows, you can set a different `shadowMapType` value on `THREE.WebGLRenderer`. By default, this property is set to `THREE.PCFShadowMap`; if you set this property to `PCFSoftShadowMap`, you get softer shadows.

THREE.PointLight

`THREE.PointLight` in Three.js is a light source that shines light in all directions emanating from a single point. A good example of a point light is a signal flare fired in the night sky. Just as with all the lights, we have a specific example you can use to play around with `THREE.PointLight`. If you look at `03-point-light.html` in the `chapter-03` folder, you can find an example where a `THREE.PointLight` light is moving around a simple Three.js scene.

The following screenshot shows an example of this:

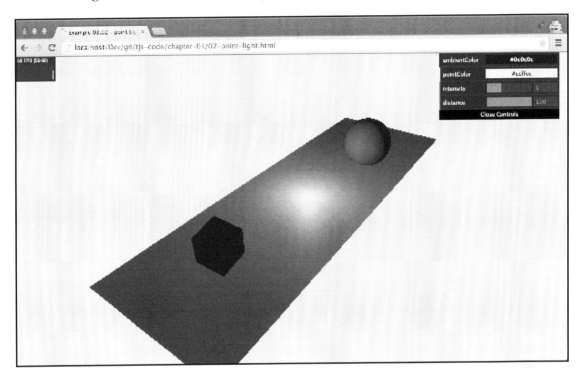

In this example, THREE.PointLight moves around the scene we already saw in Chapter 1, *Create Your First 3D Scene with Three.js*. To make it more clear where THREE.PointLight is, we move a small orange sphere along the same path. As this light moves around, you'll see the scene being illuminated by this light on different sides.

If you've worked with older versions of Three.js, you might have noticed that, earlier, THREE.PointLight wasn't able to cast shadows. With the latest versions of Three.js, THREE.PointLight is now also able to cast shadows, just like THREE.SpotLight and THREE.DirectionalLight.

THREE.PointLight shares a number of properties with THREE.SpotLight, which you can use to configure how this light behaves:

Property	Description
color	This is the color of the light.
distance	This is the distance for which the light shines. The default value is 0, which means that the light's intensity doesn't decrease based on distance.
intensity	This is the intensity the light shines with. This defaults to 1.
position	This is the position of the light in THREE.Scene.
visible	If this property is set to true (the default), this light is turned on, and if set it to false, the light is turned off.
decay	This is the amount the intensity diminishes the farther away from the light source it gets. A decay of 2 leads to more realistic light, and the default value is 1. This property only has effect when the physicallyCorrectLights property is set on the WebGLRenderer.
power	This is the light's power when being rendered in physically correct mode (enable this by setting the physicallyCorrectLights property set on the WebGLRenderer). This is measured in lumens and the default value is 4*Math.PI. And is also directly related to the intensity property (power = intensity * 4π).

Besides these properties, the THREE.PointLight's shadow can be configured in the same way as the shadow for THREE.SpotLight. In the next couple of examples and screenshots, we'll show how these properties work for THREE.PointLight. First, let's look at how you can create THREE.PointLight:

```
var pointColor = "#ccffcc";
var pointLight = new THREE.PointLight(pointColor);
pointLight.distance = 100;
scene.add(pointLight);
```

We create a light with a specific `color` property (here, we use a string value; we could also have used a number or `THREE.Color`), set its `position` property, set the `distance` property, and add it to the scene. In the examples for `THREE.SpotLight`, we showed `intensity` and `distance`. You can use these as well for `THREE.PointLight`, as you can see in the following screenshot:

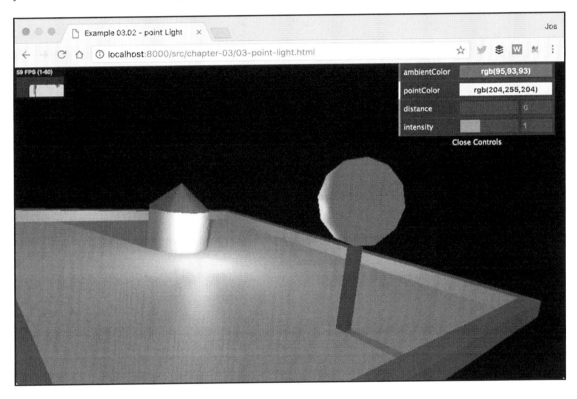

59 FPS (1-60)

You can't set the `power` and `decay` properties in this example; these properties are really useful if you want to simulate real-world scenarios. A good example of this can be found on the Three.js website: `https://threejs.org/examples/#webgl_lights_physical`.

We've seen that with the `intensity` property, you can set how bright a light shines, just like we saw for `THREE.SpotLight`. When using it with `THREE.PointLight`, the result looks like this:

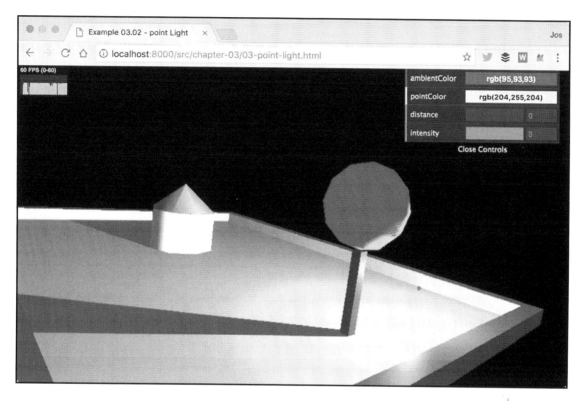

60 FPS (0-60)

The `distance` property of `PointLight` also behaves the same as for `THREE.SpotLight`. For instance, if we have a high `intensity` but a small `distance`, the result looks like this:

60 FPS (0-60)

The `distance` property of `SpotLight` determines how far the light travels from the source before its intensity property is 0. You can set this property like this: `pointLight.distance = 14`. In the preceding screenshot, the light's brightness slowly decreases to 0 at a distance of 14. That's why, in the example, you can still see a brightly lit area, but the light won't reach far. The default value for the `distance` property is 0, which means that the light won't decay over a distance.

THREE.PointLight also uses a camera to determine where to draw the shadows, so you can use THREE.CameraHelper to show what part is covered by that camera, and provides a helper, THREE.PointLightHelper, to show where THREE.PointLight shines its light. With both enabled, you get the following very useful debug information:

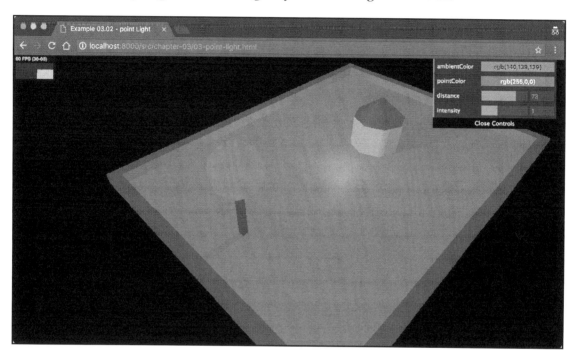

THREE.DirectionalLight

The last of the basic lights we will look at is THREE.DirectionalLight. This type of light can be considered as a light that is very far away. All the light rays it sends out are parallel to each other. A good example of this is the sun. The sun is so far away that the light rays we receive on earth are (almost) parallel to each other. The main difference between THREE.DirectionalLight and THREE.SpotLight (which we saw in the previous section) is that this light won't diminish the farther it gets from the target of THREE.DirectionalLight as it does with THREE.SpotLight (you can fine-tune this with the distance and exponent parameters). The complete area that is lit by THREE.DirectionalLight receives the same intensity of light.

To see this in action, look at the `04-directional-light` example, which is shown here:

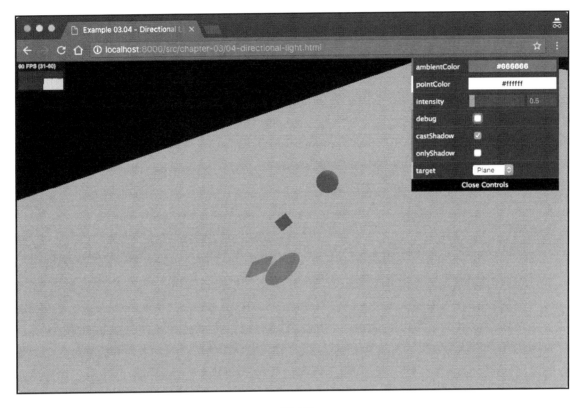

60 FPS (2-60)

As you can see in the preceding screenshot, there isn't a cone of light that is applied to the scene. Everything receives the same amount of light. Only the direction, the color, and the intensity of the light is used to calculate the colors and shadows.

Just as with `THREE.SpotLight`, there are a couple of properties you can set on this light. You can set the `intensity` of the light and the way it casts shadows. `THREE.DirectionalLight` has a lot of properties that are the same as those of `THREE.SpotLight`: `position`, `target`, `intensity`, `castShadow`, `shadow.camera.near`, `shadow.camera.far`, `shadow.mapSize.width`, `shadow.mapSize.width`, and `shadowBias`. For information on those properties, you can look at the preceding section on `THREE.SpotLight`.

If you look back at the `THREE.SpotLight` examples, you can see that we had to define the cone of light where shadows were applied. Since for `THREE.DirectionalLight`, all the rays are parallel to each other, we don't have a cone of light; instead, we have a cuboid area, as you can see in the following screenshot (if you want to see this for yourself, move the camera further away from the scene and check the `debug` checkbox):

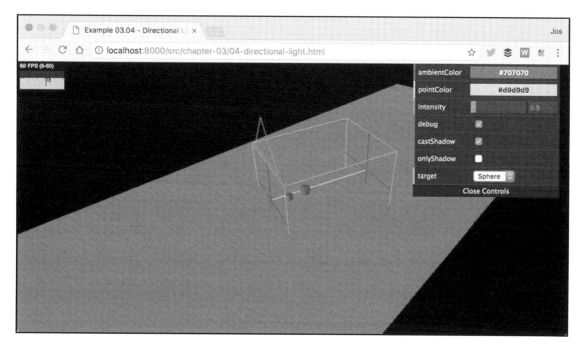

60 FPS (6-60)

Everything that falls within this cube can cast and receive shadows from the light. Just as for `THREE.SpotLight`, the tighter you define this area around the objects, the better your shadows will look. Define this cube using the following properties:

```
directionalLight.castShadow = true;
directionalLight.shadow.camera.near = 2;
directionalLight.shadow.camera.far = 80;
directionalLight.shadow.camera.left = -30;
directionalLight.shadow.camera.right = 30;
directionalLight.shadow.camera.top = 30;
directionalLight.shadow.camera.bottom = -30;
```

You can compare this with the way we configured the orthographic camera in the section on cameras in `Chapter 2`, *Basic Components That Make Up a Three.js Scene*.

Special lights

In this section on special lights, we'll discuss two additional lights provided by Three.js. First, we'll discuss THREE.HemisphereLight, which helps in creating more natural lighting for outdoor scenes; then we'll look at THREE.AreaLight, which emits lights from a large area instead of a single point; and finally, we'll show you how you can add a lens flare effect to your scene.

THREE.HemisphereLight

The first special light we're going to look at is THREE.HemisphereLight. With THREE.HemisphereLight, we can create more natural-looking outdoor lighting. Without this light, we could simulate the outdoors by creating THREE.DirectionalLight, which emulates the sun, and maybe add an additional THREE.AmbientLight to provide some general color to the scene. This, however, won't look really natural. When you're outdoors, not all the light comes directly from above: much is diffused by the atmosphere and reflected by the ground and other objects. THREE.HemisphereLight in Three.js is created for this scenario. This is an easy way to get more natural-looking outdoor lighting. To see an example, look at 05-hemisphere-light.html:

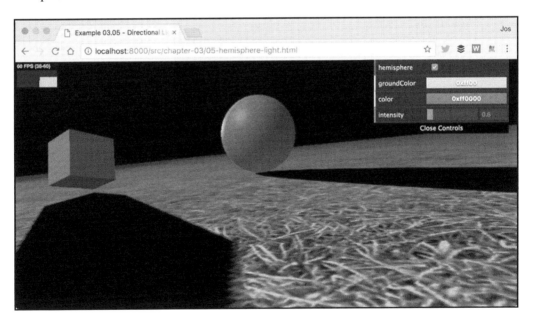

60 FPS (38-60)

This is the first example that loads additional resources and can't run directly from your local filesystem. So if you haven't done so, look at Chapter 1, *Creating Your First 3D Scene with Three.js*, to find out how to set up a local web server or disable the security settings in your browser to make loading external resources work.

If you look closely at the blue sphere, you can see that the ground color of the hemisphere is shown at the bottom of the sphere, and the sky color (set through the color property) is visible at the top of the sphere. In this example, you can turn THREE.HemisphereLight on and off and set these colors and their intensity. Creating a hemisphere light is just as easy as creating any of the other lights:

```
var hemiLight = new THREE.HemisphereLight(0x0000ff, 0x00ff00, 0.6);
hemiLight.position.set(0, 500, 0);
scene.add(hemiLight);
```

You just specify the color that is received from the sky, the color received from the ground, and the intensity of these lights. If you want to change these values later on, you can access them through the following properties:

Property	Description
groundColor	This is the color that is emitted from the ground.
color	This is the color that is emitted from the sky.
intensity	This is the intensity with which the light shines.

THREE.AreaLight

The last real light source we'll look at is `THREE.AreaLight`. With `THREE.AreaLight`, we can define a rectangular area that emits light. In older versions of Three.js, the area light wasn't included, and you had to take a number of additional steps to get it working. In the latest versions of Three.js, however, using `THREE.AreaLight` is very straightforward. Before we look at the details, let's first look at the result we're aiming for (`06-area-light.html` opens this example); the following screenshot shows the result we want to see:

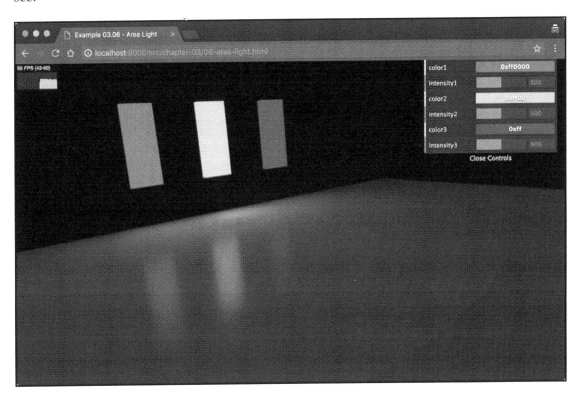

50 FPS (42-60)

What you see in this screenshot is that we've defined three `THREE.AreaLight` objects, each with their own color. You can see how these lights affect the whole area. When we want to use a `THREE.AreaLight`, we have to add one additional import in our HTML file:

```
<head>
  <script type="text/javascript" src="../libs/three.js"></script>
  <script type="text/javascript" src="../libs/stats.js"></script>
  <script type="text/javascript" src="../libs/dat.gui.js"></script>
  <script type="text/javascript"
src="../../libs/three/lights/RectAreaLightUniformsLib.js"></script>
</head>
```

With this additional JavaScript file included, we can start adding `Three.AreaLight` objects. We do this in pretty much the same way as all the other lights:

```
var areaLight1 = new THREE.RectAreaLight(0xff0000, 500, 4, 10);
areaLight1.position.set(-10, 10, -35);
scene.add(areaLight1);
```

In this example, we create a new `THREE.AreaLight`. This light has a color value of `0xff0000`, an intensity value of `500`, and a `width` and `height` of 4 and 10. Just like the other lights, we can use the `position` attribute to set its location in the scene. When you create `THREE.AreaLight`, it will be created as a vertical plane. In our example, we created three `THREE.AreaLight` objects, each with a different color. If you try this yourself for the first time, you might wonder why you don't see anything where you positioned your light. This is because you can't see the light source itself, only the light it emits, which you only see when it touches an object. If you want to recreate what we've shown in the example, you can add a `THREE.PlaneGeometry` or `THREE.BoxGeometry` at the same position (`areaLight1.position`) to simulate the area emitting light, as follows:

```
var planeGeometry1 = new THREE.BoxGeometry(4, 10, 0);
var planeGeometry1Mat = new THREE.MeshBasicMaterial({
  color: 0xff0000
});
var plane1 = new THREE.Mesh(planeGeometry1, planeGeometry1Mat);
plane1.position.copy(areaLight1.position);
scene.add(plane1);
```

You can create really beautiful effects with THREE.AreaLight, but you'll probably have to experiment a bit to get the desired effect. If you pull down the control panel from the top-right corner, you've got some controls you can play around with to set the color and intensity of the three lights from this scene and immediately see the effect, as follows:

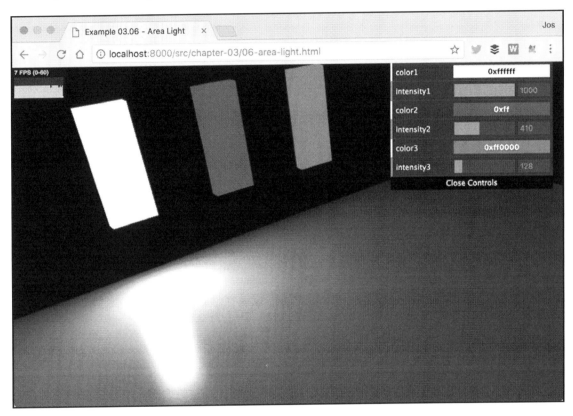

7 FPS (0-60)

Lens flare

The last subject we'll explore in this chapter is lens flares. You are probably already familiar with lens flares. For instance, they appear when you take a photograph directly into the sun or another bright light source. In most cases, you want to avoid this, but for games and 3D-generated images, it provides a nice effect that makes scenes look a bit more realistic.

Three.js also has support for lens flares and makes it very easy to add them to your scene. In this last section, we're going to add a lens flare to a scene and create the output as you can see in the following screenshot; you can see this for yourself by opening `07-lensflares.html`:

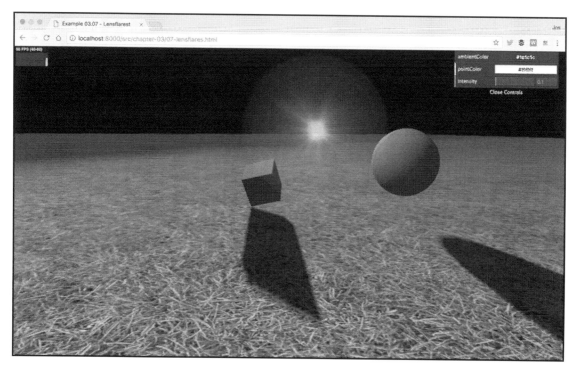

60 FPS (33-60)

We can create a lens flare by instantiating the `THREE.LensFlare` object. The first thing we need to do is create this object. `THREE.LensFlare` takes the following arguments:

```
flare = new THREE.LensFlare(texture, size, distance, blending, color,
opacity);
```

These arguments are explained in the following table:

Argument	Description
texture	A texture is an image that determines the shape of the flare.
size	We can specify how large the flare should be. This is the size in pixels. If you specify −1, the size of the texture itself is used.
distance	This is the distance from the light source (0) to the camera (1). Use this to position the lens flare in the right position.
blending	We can specify multiple textures for the flares. The blending mode determines how these are blended together. The default to use with LensFlare is THREE.AdditiveBlending. There's more on blending in Chapter 4, *Working with Three.js Materials*.
color	This is the color of the flare.
opacity	Defines how transparent the flare is. 0 is completely transparent and 1 is solid.

Let's look at the code used to create this object (see 07-lensflares.html):

```
var textureFlare0 = THREE.ImageUtils.loadTexture
    ("../assets/textures/lensflare/lensflare0.png");

var flareColor = new THREE.Color(0xffaacc);
var lensFlare = new THREE.LensFlare(textureFlare0, 350, 0.0,
    THREE.AdditiveBlending, flareColor);

lensFlare.position.copy(spotLight.position);
scene.add(lensFlare);
```

We first load a texture. For this example, I've used the lens flare texture provided by the Three.js examples, as follows:

If you compare this screenshot with the screenshot at the beginning of this section, you can see that it defines what the lens flare looks like. Next, we define the color of the lens flare using `new THREE.Color( 0xffaacc );`, which gives the lens flare a red glow. With these two objects, we can create the `THREE.LensFlare` object. For this example, we've set the size of the flare to `350` and the distance to `0.0` (directly at the light source).

After we've created the `LensFlare` object, we position it at the location of our light and add it to the scene, which can be seen in the following screenshot:

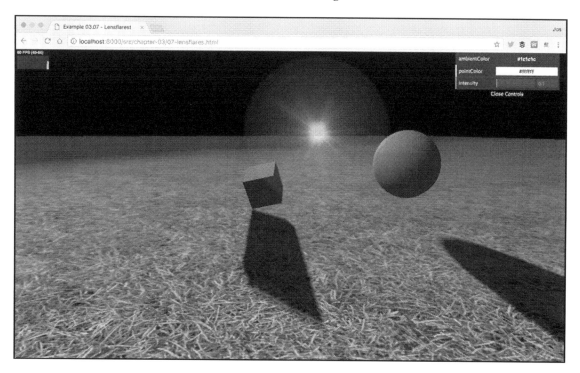

60 FPS (40-60)

It already looks nice, but if you compare this with the screenshot from the beginning of this chapter, you'll notice that we're missing the small round artifacts in the middle of the page. We create these in pretty much the same way as we did the main flare, as follows:

```
var textureFlare3 = THREE.ImageUtils.loadTexture
    ("../assets/textures/lensflare/lensflare3.png");

lensFlare.add(textureFlare3, 60, 0.6, THREE.AdditiveBlending);
lensFlare.add(textureFlare3, 70, 0.7, THREE.AdditiveBlending);
lensFlare.add(textureFlare3, 120, 0.9, THREE.AdditiveBlending);
lensFlare.add(textureFlare3, 70, 1.0, THREE.AdditiveBlending);
```

This time, though, we don't create a new THREE.LensFlare, but use the add function provided by the LensFlare we just created. In this method, we need to specify the texture, size, distance, and blending mode, and that's it.

The add function can take two additional parameters. You can also set the color and the opacity properties of the new flare to add. The texture we use for these new flares is a very light circle; you can see the images used for these flares by looking in the assets/textures/flares/ directory.

If you look at the scene again, you'll see these artifacts appearing at the positions you've specified with the distance argument.

Summary

In this chapter, we covered a lot of information about the different kinds of lights that are available in Three.js. In this chapter, you learned that configuring lights, colors, and shadows is not an exact science. To get the correct result, you should experiment with the different settings and use a `dat.GUI` control to fine-tune your configuration. The different lights behave in different ways and, as we'll see in Chapter 4, *Working with Three.js Materials*, materials respond differently to lights as well. A `THREE.AmbientLight` color is added to each and every color in the scene and is often used to smooth hard colors and shadows. `THREE.PointLight` emits light in all directions and can cast shadows. `THREE.SpotLight` is a light that resembles a flashlight. It has a conical shape, can be configured to fade over distance, and is able to cast shadows. We also looked at `THREE.DirectionalLight`. This light can be compared with a faraway light, such as the sun, whose light rays travel parallel to each other and the intensity of which doesn't decrease the farther away it gets from the configured target, and can also cast shadows. Besides the standard lights, we also looked at a couple of more specialized lights. For a more natural outdoor effect, you can use `THREE.HemisphereLight`, which takes into account ground and sky reflections. `THREE.AreaLight` doesn't shine from a single point, but emits light from a large area. Finally, we showed you how to add a photographic lens flare with the `THREE.LenseFlare` object.

In the chapters so far, we have already introduced a couple of different materials, and in this chapter, you saw that not all materials respond in the same manner to the available lights. In Chapter 4, *Working with Three.js Materials*, we'll give an overview of the materials that are available in Three.js.

Working with Three.js Materials

4

In Chapter 3, *Working with Light Sources in Three.js*, we talked a bit about materials. You learned that a material, together with `THREE.Geometry` forms `THREE.Mesh`. The material is like the skin of the object that defines what the outside of a geometry looks like. For example, a skin defines whether a geometry is metallic-looking, transparent, or shown as a wireframe. The resulting `THREE.Mesh` object can then be added to the scene to be rendered by Three.js. Until now, we haven't really looked at materials in much detail. In this chapter, we'll dive into all the materials Three.js has to offer, and you'll learn how you can use these materials to create good-looking 3D objects. The materials we'll explore in this chapter are shown in the following table:

Name	Description
`MeshBasicMaterial`	This is a basic material that you can use to give your geometries a simple color or show the wireframe of your geometries. This material isn't influenced by lights.
`MeshDepthMaterial`	This is a material that uses the distance from the camera to determine how to color your mesh.
`MeshNormalMaterial`	This is a simple material that bases the color of a face on its normal vector.
`MeshLambertMaterial`	This is a material that takes lighting into account and is used to create dull, non-shiny-looking objects.
`MeshPhongMaterial`	This is a material that also takes lighting into account and can be used to create shiny objects.
`MeshStandardMaterial`	This is a material that uses physical-based rendering to render the object. With physical-based rendering, a physically correct model is used to determine how light interacts with a surface. This allows you to create more accurate and realistic-looking objects.
`MeshPhysicalMaterial`	An extension of `MeshStandardMaterial` that allows more control over the reflection.

MeshToonMaterial	This is an extension of MeshPhongMaterial that tries to make objects look hand-drawn.
ShadowMaterial	This is a specific material that can receive shadows, but the rest is rendered transparent.
ShaderMaterial	This material allows you to specify your own shader programs to directly control how vertices are positioned and pixels are colored.
LineBasicMaterial	This is a material that can be used on the THREE.Line geometry to create colored lines.
LineDashMaterial	This is the same as LineBasicMaterial, but this material also allows you to create a dashed effect.

If you look through the source code of Three.js, you might run into THREE.RawShaderMaterial. This is a specialized material that can only be used together with THREE.BufferedGeometry. This geometry is a specialized form that is optimized for static geometries (for instance, vertices and faces don't change). We won't explore this material in this chapter, but we will use it in *Chapter 11*, *Render Postprocessing*, when we talk about creating custom shaders. In the sources, you can also find THREE.SpriteMaterial and THREE.PointsMaterial. These are materials you use when styling individual points. We won't discuss those in this chapter, but we'll explore them in *Chapter 7*, *Points and Sprites*.

Materials have a number of common properties, so before we look at the first material, THREE.MeshBasicMaterial, we'll look at the properties shared by all the materials.

Understanding common material properties

You can quickly see for yourself which properties are shared between all the materials. Three.js provides a material base class, THREE.Material, that lists all the common properties. We've divided these common material properties into the following three categories:

- **Basic properties**: These are the properties you'll use most often. With these properties, you can, for instance, control the opacity of the object, whether it is visible, and how it is referenced (by ID or custom name).
- **Blending properties**: Every object has a set of blending properties. These properties define how the color of each point of the material is combined with the color behind it.

- **Advanced properties**: There are a number of advanced properties that control how the low-level WebGL context renders objects. In most cases, you won't need to deal with these properties.

Note that, in this chapter, we skip any properties related to textures and maps. Most materials allow you to use images as textures (for instance, a wood-like or stone-like texture). In `Chapter 10`, *Loading and Working with Textures*, we will dive into the various texture and mapping options that are available. Some materials also have specific properties related to animation (for example, `skinning`, `morpNormals`, and `morphTargets`); we'll also skip those properties. These will be addressed in `Chapter 9`, *Animations and Moving the Camera*. The `clipIntersection`, `clippingPlanes`, and `clipShadows` properties will be addressed in `Chapter 6`, *Advanced Geometries and Binary Operations*.

We start with the first set from the list: the basic properties.

Basic properties

The basic properties of the `THREE.Material` object are listed in the following table (you can see these properties in action in the section on `THREE.BasicMeshMaterial`):

Property	Description
id	This is used to identify a material and is assigned when you create a material. This starts at 0 for the first material and is increased by 1 for each additional material that is created.
uuid	This is a uniquely generated ID and is used internally.
name	You can assign a name to a material with this property. This can be used for debugging purposes.
opacity	This defines how transparent an object is. Use this together with the `transparent` property. The range of this property is from 0 to 1.
transparent	If this is set to `true`, Three.js will render this object with the set opacity. If this is set to `false`, the object won't be transparent, just more lightly colored. This property should also be set to `true` if you use a texture that uses an alpha (transparency) channel.
overdraw	When you use `THREE.CanvasRenderer`, it is possible you will see small gaps between the triangles. By setting this property, you can prevent this. A good value is 0.5, and the default is 0.

visible	This defines whether this material is visible. If you set this to `false`, you won't see the object in the scene.
side	With this property, you can define to which side of the geometry a material is applied. The default is `THREE.Frontside`, which applies the material to the front (outside) of an object. You can also set this to `THREE.BackSide`, which applies it to the back (inside), or `THREE.DoubleSide`, which applies it to both sides.
needsUpdate	When Three.js creates a material, it converts it to a set of WebGL instructions. When you want the changes you made in the material to also result in an update to the WebGL instructions, you can set this property to `true`.
colorWrite	If set to `false`, the color of this material won't be shown (in effect, you'll create invisible objects, which occlude objects behind them).
flatShading	Determines whether this material is rendered using flat shading. With flat shading, the individual triangles which make up an object are rendered separately, and aren't combined into a smooth surface.
lights	This is Boolean value that determines whether this material is affected by lights. The default value is `true`.
premultipliedAlpha	Changes the way the transparency of an object is rendered. Defaults to `false`.
dithering	Applies a dithering effect to the rendering material. This can be used to avoid banding. The default is `false`.
shadowSide	Just like the `side` property but, this time, determines which side of the faces casts the shadows. The default is `null`. If `null`, this is determined based on the `side` property like this: • `THREE.Frontside`: Back side • `THREE.Backside`: Front side • `THREE.DoubleSide`: Both sides
vertexColors	You can define individual colors to be applied to each vertex with this property. The default value is `THREE.NoColors`. If you set this value to `THREE.VertexColors`, the colors set in a `THREE.Face3` `vertexColors` array are used to color the individual vertices; if set to `THREE.FaceColors`, the `color` property of each face is used to color that face. This property doesn't work on `CanvasRenderer` but does work on `WebGLRenderer`. Look at the `LineBasicMaterial` example, where we use this property to color the various parts of a line.

	This property determines whether this material is affected by global fog settings. This is not shown in action, but if this is set to `false`, the global fog we saw in `Chapter 2`, *Basic Components That Make Up a Three.js Scene* doesn't affect how this object is rendered.
`fog`	

For each material, you can also set a number of blending properties.

Blending properties

Materials have a couple of generic blending-related properties. Blending determines how the colors we render interact with the colors that are behind them. We'll touch upon this subject a little bit when we talk about combining materials. The `blending` properties are listed in the following table:

Name	Description
`blending`	This determines how the material on this object blends with the background. The normal mode is `THREE.NormalBlending`, which only shows the top layer.
`blendSrc`	Besides using the standard blending modes, you can also create custom blend modes by setting `blendsrc`, `blenddst`, and `blendequation`. This property defines how this object (the source) is blended into the background (the destination). The default `THREE.SrcAlphaFactor` setting uses the alpha (transparency) channel for blending.
`blendSrcAlpha`	This is the transparency of `blendSrc`. The default is `null`.
`blendDst`	This property defines how the background (the destination) is used in blending and defaults to `THREE.OneMinusSrcAlphaFactor`, which means this property too uses the alpha channel of the source for blending but uses 1 (the alpha channel of the source) as the value.
`blendDstAlpha`	This is the transparency of `blendDst`. The default is `null`.
`blendEquation`	This defines how the `blendsrc` and `blenddst` values are used. The default is to add them (`AddEquation`). With these three properties, you can create your own custom blend modes.

The last set of properties is mostly used internally and controls the specifics of how WebGL is used to render the scene.

Advanced properties

We won't go into the details of these properties. These are related to how WebGL works internally. If you do want to know more about these properties, the OpenGL specification is a good starting point. You can find this specification at `http://www.khronos.org/registry/gles/specs/2.0/es_full_spec_2.0.25.pdf`. The following table provides a brief description of these advanced properties:

Name	Description
depthTest	This is an advanced WebGL property. With this property, you can enable or disable the `GL_DEPTH_TEST` parameter. This parameter controls whether the *depth* of a pixel is used to determine a new pixel's value. Normally, you wouldn't need to change this. More information can be found in the OpenGL specifications we mentioned earlier.
depthWrite	This is another internal property. This property can be used to determine whether this material affects the WebGL depth buffer. If you use an object for a 2D overlay (for example, a hub), you should set this property to `false`. Usually, though, you shouldn't need to change this property.
depthFunc	The function to use to compare a pixel's depth. This corresponds to the `glDepthFunc` from the WebGL specifications.
polygonOffset, polygonOffsetFactor, and polygonOffsetUnits	With these properties, you can control the `POLYGON_OFFSET_FILL` WebGL feature. These are normally not needed. For an explanation of what they do in detail, you can look at the OpenGL specifications.
alphatest	This value can be set to a specific value (0 to 1). Whenever a pixel has an alpha value smaller than this value, it won't be drawn. You can use this property to remove some transparency-related artifacts.
precision	Set the precision for this material to one of the following WebGL values: `highp`, `mediump`, or `lowp`.

Now, let's look at all the available materials so that you can see the effect these properties have on the rendered output.

Starting with a simple mesh

In this section, we'll look at a few simple materials: MeshBasicMaterial, MeshDepthMaterial, and MeshNormalMaterial. We start with MeshBasicMaterial.

Before we look into the properties of these materials, here's a quick note on how you can pass in properties to configure the materials. There are two options:

- You can pass in the arguments in the constructor as a parameters object, like this:

```
var material = new THREE.MeshBasicMaterial(
{
  color: 0xff0000, name: 'material-1', opacity: 0.5,
    transparency: true, ...
});
```

- Alternatively, you can also create an instance and set the properties individually, like this:

```
var material = new THREE.MeshBasicMaterial();
material.color = new THREE.Color(0xff0000);
material.name = 'material-1';
material.opacity = 0.5;
material.transparency = true;
```

Usually, the best way is to use the constructor if we know all the properties' values while creating the material. The arguments used in both of these styles use the same format. The only exception to this rule is the color property. In the first style, we can just pass in the hex value, and Three.js will create a THREE.Color object itself. In the second style, we have to explicitly create a THREE.Color object. In this book, we'll use both of these styles.

THREE.MeshBasicMaterial

`MeshBasicMaterial` is a very simple material that doesn't take into account the lights that are available in the scene. Meshes with this material will be rendered as simple, flat polygons, and you also have the option to show the geometry's wireframe. Besides the common properties we saw in the earlier section on this material, we can set the following properties (once again, we ignore the properties which are used for textures, since we'll discuss those in the chapter on textures):

Name	Description
`color`	This property allows you to set the color of the material.
`wireframe`	This allows you to render the material as a wireframe. This is great for debugging purposes.
`wireframeLineWidth`	If you enable the wireframe, this property defines the width of the wires from the wireframe.
`wireframeLinecap`	This property defines how the ends of lines look in wireframe mode. The possible values are `butt`, `round`, and `square`. The default value is `round`. In practice, the results from changing this property are very difficult to see. This property isn't supported on `WebGLRenderer`.
`wireframeLinejoin`	This defines how the line joints are visualized. The possible values are `round`, `bevel`, and `miter`. The default value is `round`. If you look very closely, you can see this in the example using low `opacity` and a very large `wireframeLinewidth` value. This property isn't supported on `WebGLRenderer`.

In the previous chapters, we saw how to create materials and assign them to objects. For `THREE.MeshBasicMaterial`, we do it like this:

```
var meshMaterial = new THREE.MeshBasicMaterial({color: 0x7777ff});
```

This creates a new `THREE.MeshBasicMaterial` and initializes the `color` property to `0x7777ff` (which is purple).

We've added an example that you can use to play around with the
THREE.MeshBasicMaterial properties and the basic properties we discussed in the
previous section, *Basic Properties*. If you open up the 01-basic-mesh-material.html
example in the chapter-04 folder, you'll see a rotating cube like the one shown in the
following screenshot:

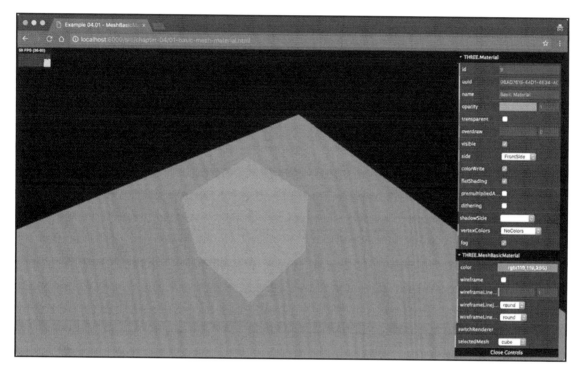

50 FPS (36-60)

This is a very simple object. With the menu in the upper-right corner, you can play around with the properties and select different meshes (and you can also change the renderer). For instance, a gopher with **wireframe** is rendered like this:

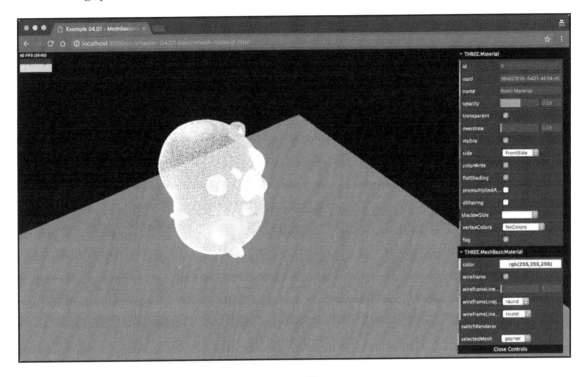

60 FPS (36-60)

You can also select `THREE.CanvasRenderer` to play around with the
`THREE.MeshBasicMaterial` properties like this:

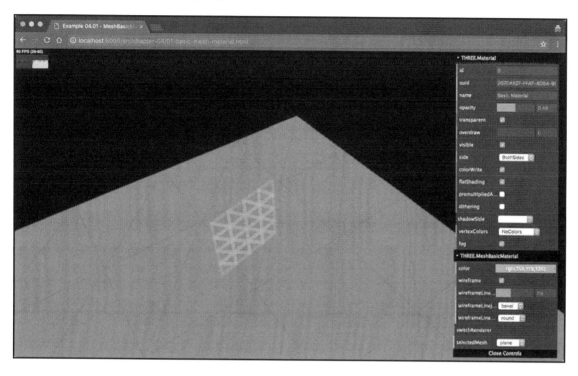

60 FPS (26-60)

One of the properties you can set in this example is the `side` property. With this property,
you define to which side of `THREE.Geometry` the material is applied. You can test how this
property works when you select the plane mesh. Since, normally, a material is only applied
to the front side of a material, the rotating plane will be invisible half the time (when it
shows its back to you). If you set the `side` property to `double`, the plane will be visible the
whole time, since the material is applied to both sides of the geometry. Note, though, that
the renderer will need to do more work when the `side` property is set to `double`, so this
could have an impact on the performance of your scene.

THREE.MeshDepthMaterial

The next material on the list is `THREE.MeshDepthMaterial`. With this material, the way an object looks isn't defined by lights or by a specific material property; it is defined by the distance from the object to the camera. You can combine this with other materials to easily create fading effects. The only relevant properties this material has are the following two that control whether you want to show a wireframe:

Name	Description
`wireframe`	This determines whether or not to show the wireframe.
`wireframeLineWidth`	This determines the width of the wireframe (this will only work with the `THREE.CanvasRenderer`).

To demonstrate this, we modified the cubes example from `Chapter 2`, *Basic Components That Make Up a Three.js Scene* (`02-depth-material` from the `chapter-04` folder). Remember that you have to click on the **addCube** button to populate the scene. The following screenshot shows the modified example:

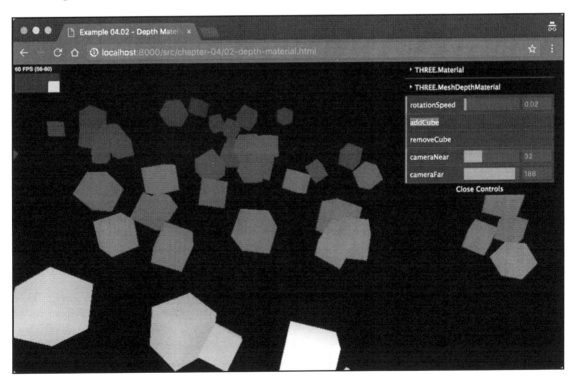

60 FPS (56-60)

This shows the cubes rendered, with the color based on the distance to the camera. Even though the material doesn't have many additional properties to control how an object is rendered, we can still control how fast the object's color fades out. In this example, we exposed the near and far properties of the camera. As you probably remember from Chapter 2, *Basic Components That Make Up a Three.js Scene*, with these two properties, we set the visible area for the camera. Any objects that are nearer to the camera than the near property aren't shown, and any objects further away than the far property also fall outside the camera's visible area.

The distance between the near and far properties of the camera defines the brightness and the rate at which objects fade out. If the distance is very large, objects will only fade out a little as they move away from the camera. If the distance is small, the fade-out will be much more notable (as you can see in the following screenshot):

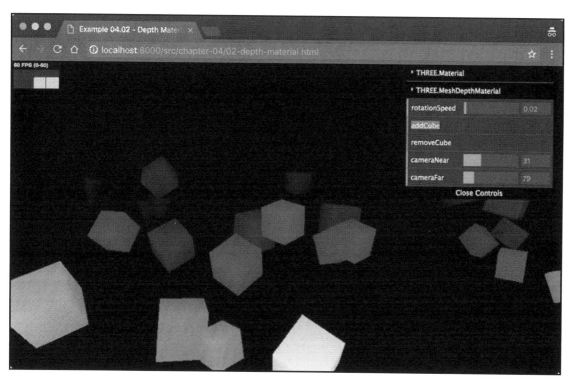

60 FPS (0-60)

Here, the cubes are rendered with a small distance between the near and far properties of the camera. Creating THREE.MeshDepthMaterial is very easy and the object doesn't require any arguments. For this example, we've used the scene.overrideMaterial property to make sure all the objects in the scene use this material without having to explicitly specify it for each THREE.Mesh object:

```
var scene = new THREE.Scene();
scene.overrideMaterial = new THREE.MeshDepthMaterial();
```

The next part of this chapter isn't really about a specific material, but shows a way in which you can combine multiple materials.

Combining materials

If you look back at the properties of THREE.MeshDepthMaterial, you can see that there isn't an option to set the color of the cubes. Everything was decided for you by the default properties of the material. Three.js, however, has the option to combine materials to create new effects (this is also where blending comes into play). The following code shows how we can combine materials:

```
var cubeMaterial = new THREE.MeshDepthMaterial();
var colorMaterial = new THREE.MeshBasicMaterial({color: 0x00ff00,
    transparent: true, blending: THREE.MultiplyBlending})
var cube = new THREE.SceneUtils.createMultiMaterialObject
    (cubeGeometry, [colorMaterial, cubeMaterial]);
cube.children[1].scale.set(0.99, 0.99, 0.99);
```

We get the following green-colored cubes that use the brightness from
THREE.MeshDepthMaterial and the color from THREE.MeshBasicMaterial (open 03-
combined-material.html for this example). The following screenshot
shows the example:

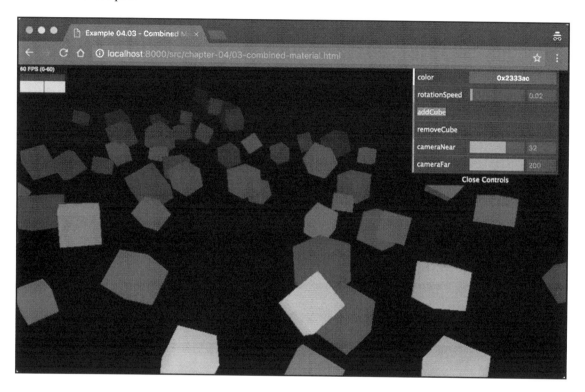

60 FPS (0-60)

Let's look at the steps you need to take to get this specific result. First, we need to create our two materials. For THREE.MeshDepthMaterial, we don't do anything special; for THREE.MeshBasicMaterial, however, we set transparent to true and define a blending mode. If we don't set the transparent property to true, we'll just have solid, green objects since Three.js can't blend the different materials. With transparent set to true, Three.js will check the blending property to see how the green THREE.MeshBasicMaterial object should interact with the background. The background, in this case, is the cube rendered with THREE.MeshDepthMaterial.

For this example, we used THREE.MultiplyBlending. This blend mode multiplies the foreground color with the background color and gives you the desired effect. The last line in this code fragment is also an important one. What happens when we create a mesh with the THREE.SceneUtils.createMultiMaterialObject() function is that the geometry gets copied and two exactly the same meshes are returned in a group. If we render these without the last line, you can often see a flickering effect. This can happen sometimes when objects are rendered one on top of the other and one of them is transparent. By scaling down the mesh created with THREE.MeshDepthMaterial, we can avoid this. To do so, use the following code:

```
cube.children[1].scale.set(0.99, 0.99, 0.99);
```

The next material is also one where we won't have any influence on the colors used in rendering.

THREE.MeshNormalMaterial

The easiest way to understand how this material is rendered is by first looking at an example. Open up the `04-mesh-normal-material.html` example from the `chapter-04` folder. If you select the sphere as the mesh, you'll see something like this (if you set `flatShading` to `true`):

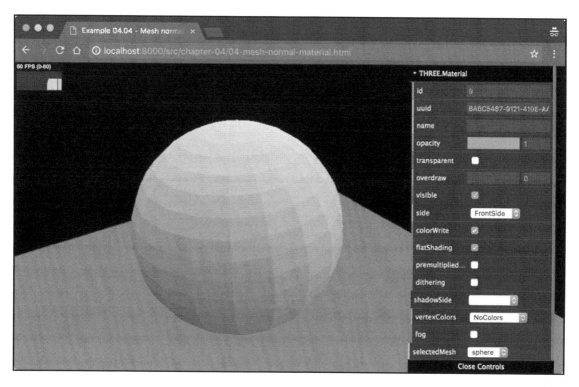

60 FPS (0-60)

As you can see, each face of the mesh is rendered in a slightly different color, and even though the sphere rotates, the colors stay pretty much at the same place. This happens because the color of each face is based on the *normal* pointing out from the face. This normal is the vector perpendicular to the face. The normal vector is used in many different parts of Three.js. It is used to determine light reflections, helps with mapping textures to 3D models, and gives information on how to light, shade, and color pixels on the surface. Luckily, though, Three.js handles the computation of these vectors and uses them internally, so you don't have to calculate or deal with them yourselves. The following screenshot visualizes all the normal vectors of `THREE.SphereGeometry`:

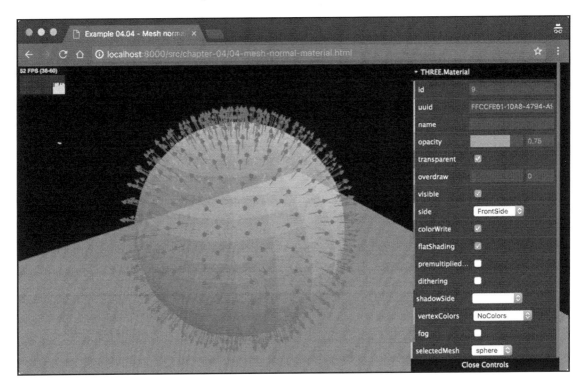

52 FPS (38-60)

The direction this normal points in determines the color a face gets when you use
THREE.MeshNormalMaterial. Since all normals for the faces of a sphere point in a
different direction, we get the colorful sphere you can see in the examples. As a quick side
note, to add these normal arrows, you can use THREE.ArrowHelper like this:

```
for (var f = 0, fl = sphere.geometry.faces.length; f < fl; f++) {
    var face = sphere.geometry.faces[ f ];
    var centroid = new THREE.Vector3(0, 0, 0);
    centroid.add(sphere.geometry.vertices[face.a]);
    centroid.add(sphere.geometry.vertices[face.b]);
    centroid.add(sphere.geometry.vertices[face.c]);
    centroid.divideScalar(3);

    var arrow = new THREE.ArrowHelper(face.normal, centroid, 2,
        0x3333FF, 0.5, 0.5);
    sphere.add(arrow);
}
```

In this code snippet, we iterate through all the faces of THREE.SphereGeometry. For each
of these THREE.Face3 objects, we calculate the center (the centroid) by adding the vertices
that make up this face and dividing the result by 3. We use this centroid, together with
the normal vector of the face, to draw an arrow. THREE.ArrowHelper takes the following
arguments: direction, origin, length, color, headLength, and headWidth.

There are a couple of other properties that you can set on THREE.MeshNormalMaterial:

Name	Description
wireframe	This determines whether or not to show the wireframe.
wireframeLinewidth	This determines the width of the wireframe.

We've already seen `wireframe` and `wireframeLinewidth` in previous examples, so we'll skip those. But let's take this example as an opportunity to look at the `shading` property. With the `shading` property, we can tell Three.js how to render our objects. If you use `THREE.FlatShading`, each face will be rendered as is (as you can see in the previous couple of screenshots), or you can use `THREE.SmoothShading`, which smooth out the faces of our object. For instance, if we render the sphere using `THREE.SmoothShading`, the result looks like this:

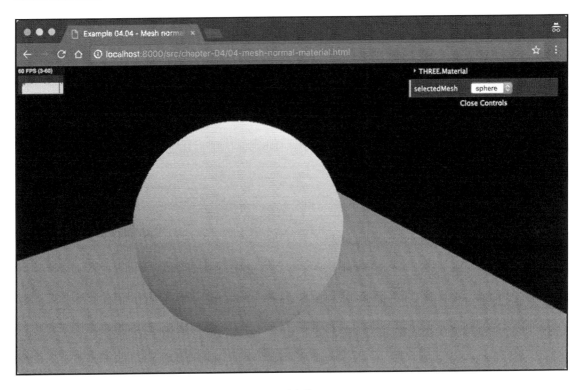

60 FPS (3-60)

We're done with the simple materials, but let's look at one additional subject before moving on. In the next section, we'll look at how you can use different materials for specific faces of a geometry.

Multiple materials for a single mesh

When creating THREE.Mesh, so far we've used a single material. It is also possible to define a specific material for each of the faces of a geometry. For instance, if you have a cube, which has 12 faces (remember, Three.js works with triangles), you can assign a different material (for example, with a different color) to each side of the cube. Doing this is really straightforward, as you can see from the following piece of code:

```
var matArray = [];
matArray.push(new THREE.MeshBasicMaterial( { color: 0x009e60 }));
matArray.push(new THREE.MeshBasicMaterial( { color: 0x0051ba }));
matArray.push(new THREE.MeshBasicMaterial( { color: 0xffd500 }));
matArray.push(new THREE.MeshBasicMaterial( { color: 0xff5800 }));
matArray.push(new THREE.MeshBasicMaterial( { color: 0xC41E3A }));
matArray.push(new THREE.MeshBasicMaterial( { color: 0xffffff }));

var cubeGeom = new THREE.BoxGeometry(3,3,3);
var cube = new THREE.Mesh(cubeGeom, matArray);
```

We first create an array, named matArray, to hold all the materials, and use that array to create THREE.Mesh. What you might notice is that we only create 6 materials, even though we've got 12 faces. To understand how this works, we have to look at how Three.js assigns a material to a face. For this, Three.js uses the materialIndex property of the faces which make up the object. If we look at the materialIndex property of the faces of a THREE.CubeGeometry, we see the following (you can do this from the debugger console of the browser):

```
> cubeGeom.faces.forEach((p,i) => console.log("face " + i + " : "
+p.materialIndex))
face 0 : 0
face 1 : 0
face 2 : 1
face 3 : 1
face 4 : 2
face 5 : 2
face 6 : 3
face 7 : 3
face 8 : 4
face 9 : 4
face 10 : 5
face 11 : 5
```

As you can see, Three.js already groups the sides of a cube together. So instead of having to provide 12 different materials, we only have to provide 6, 1 for each side of the cube. Let's dive a bit deeper into the code and see what you need to do to recreate the following example: a simple 3D Rubik's cube. You can find this example in `05-mesh-face-material.html`. The following screenshot shows this example:

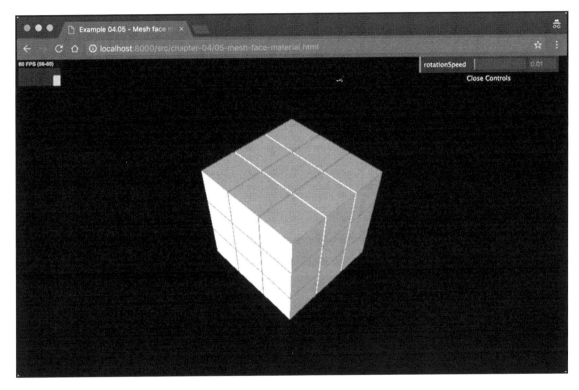

60 FPS (56-60)

This Rubik's cube consists of a number of smaller cubes: three cubes along the x axis, three along the y axis, and three along the z axis. Here's how this is done:

```
var group = new THREE.Mesh();
// add all the Rubik cube elements
var mats = [];
mats.push(new THREE.MeshBasicMaterial({ color: 0x009e60 }));
mats.push(new THREE.MeshBasicMaterial({ color: 0x0051ba }));
mats.push(new THREE.MeshBasicMaterial({ color: 0xffd500 }));
mats.push(new THREE.MeshBasicMaterial({ color: 0xff5800 }));
mats.push(new THREE.MeshBasicMaterial({ color: 0xC41E3A }));
mats.push(new THREE.MeshBasicMaterial({ color: 0xffffff }));
```

```
for (var x = 0; x < 3; x++) {
  for (var y = 0; y < 3; y++) {
    for (var z = 0; z < 3; z++) {
      var cubeGeom = new THREE.BoxGeometry(2.9, 2.9, 2.9);
      var cube = new THREE.Mesh(cubeGeom, mats);
      cube.position.set(x * 3 - 3, y * 3 -3, z * 3 - 3);

      group.add(cube);
    }
  }
}
```

In this piece of code, we first create `THREE.Mesh`, which will hold all the individual cubes (`group`); next, we create the materials for each face and push them to the `mats` array. Then, we create three loops to make sure we create the right number of cubes. In this loop, we create each of the individual cubes, assign the materials, position them, and add them to the group. What you should remember is that the position of the cubes is relative to the position of this group. If we move or rotate the group, all the cubes will move and rotate with it. For more information on how to work with groups, look at `Chapter 8`, *Creating and Loading Advanced Meshes and Geometries*.

If you've opened the example in your browser, you can see that the complete Rubik's cube rotates, and not the individual cubes. This happens because we use the following in our rendering loop:

```
group.rotation.y = step += controls.rotationSpeed;
group.rotation.z = step -= controls.rotationSpeed;
group.rotation.x = step += controls.rotationSpeed;
```

This causes the complete group to rotate around its center `(0, 0, 0)`. When we positioned the individual cubes, we made sure they were positioned around this center point. That's why you see the `- 3` offset in the `cube.position.set(x * 3 - 3, y * 3 - 3, z * 3 - 3);` line of the preceding code.

Advanced materials

In this section, we'll look at the more advanced materials Three.js has to offer. We'll first look at `THREE.MeshPhongMaterial` and `THREE.MeshLambertMaterial`. These two materials react to light sources and can be used to create shiny and dull-looking materials, respectively. In this section, we'll also look at one of the most versatile, but most difficult to use, materials: `THREE.ShaderMaterial`. With `THREE.ShaderMaterial`, you can create your own shader programs that define how the material and object should be shown.

THREE.MeshLambertMaterial

This material can be used to create dull-looking, non-shiny surfaces. This is a very easy-to-use material that responds to the lighting sources in the scene. This material can be configured with a number of properties with the basic properties we've already seen before, so we won't go into the details of those properties, but will focus on the ones specific to this material. That just leaves us with the following two properties:

Name	Description
color	This is the color of the material.
emissive	This is the color this material emits. It doesn't really act as a light source, but this is a solid color that is unaffected by another lighting. This defaults to black. You can use this to create objects that looks like they glow.

This material is created just like all the other ones. Here's how it's done:

```
var meshMaterial = new THREE.MeshLambertMaterial({color: 0x7777ff});
```

For an example of this material, look at `06-mesh-lambert-material.html`. The following screenshot shows this example:

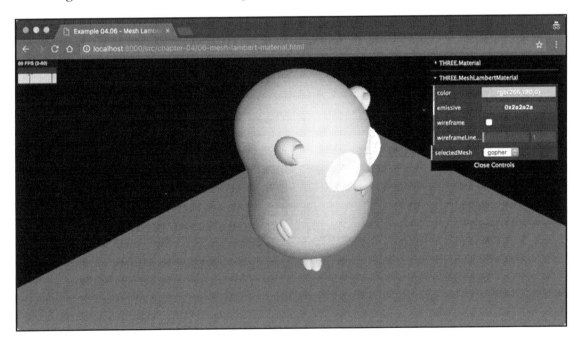

This screenshot shows a gopher, with an orange `color`, and a very light `emissive` glow. One of the interesting features of `THREE.LambertMaterial` is that it also supports the wireframe properties, so you can render a wireframe, that responds to the lights in the scene:

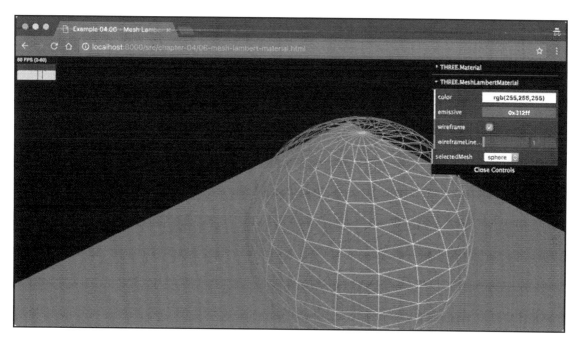

60 FPS (2-60)

As you can see in the preceding screenshots, the material looks rather dull. With `THREE.MeshPhongMaterial`, we can make shiny objects.

THREE.MeshPhongMaterial

With THREE.MeshPhongMaterial, we can create a material that is shiny. The properties you can use for that are pretty much the same as for a non-shiny THREE.MeshLambertMaterial object. In older versions, this was the only material which you could use to make shiny, plastic or metal-like objects. With newer versions of Three.js, if you want more control, you can also use THREE.MeshStandardMaterial and THREE.MeshPhysicalMaterial. We'll discuss both of these materials after we look at THREE.MeshPhongMaterial.

We'll once again skip the basic properties and focus on the properties specific for this material. These properties for this material are shown in the following table:

Name	Description
color	This is the *ambient* color of the material. This works together with the ambient light we saw in the previous chapter. This color is multiplied with the color provided by the ambient light. This defaults to white.
emissive	This is the color this material emits. It doesn't really act as a light source, but this is a solid color that is unaffected by another lighting. This defaults to black.
specular	This property defines how shiny the material is and with what color it shines. If this is set to the same color as the color property, you get a more metallic-looking material. If this is set to gray, it results in a more plastic-looking material.
shininess	This property defines how shiny the specular highlight is. The default value for the shininess is 30. The higher this value is, the shinier the object is.

Initializing a THREE.MeshPhongMaterial material is done in the same way as we've already seen for all the other materials and is shown in the following line of code:

```
var meshMaterial = new THREE.MeshPhongMaterial({color: 0x7777ff});
```

To give you the best comparison, we've created the same example for this material as we did for `THREE.MeshLambertMaterial`. You can use the control GUI to play around with this material. For instance, the following settings create a plastic-looking material. You can find this example in `07-mesh-phong-material.html`:

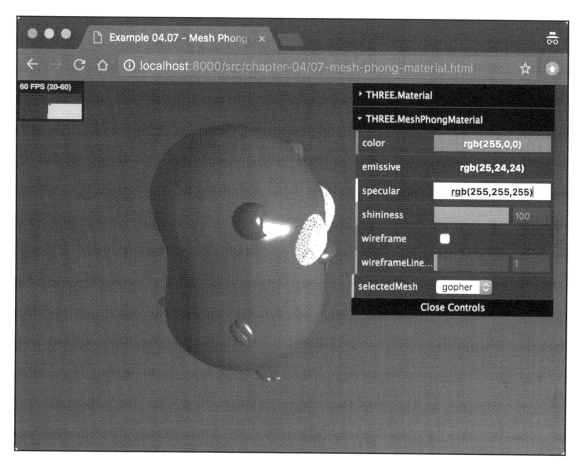

60 FPS (20-60)

This screenshot shows how you can use THREE.MeshPhongMaterial to create plastic-looking objects. Three.js provides an extension to THREE.MeshPhongMaterial to create cartoon-like renderings: THREE.MeshToonMaterial. The properties of THREE.MeshToonMaterial are the same as for THREE.MeshPhongMaterial, Three.js only renders it differently:

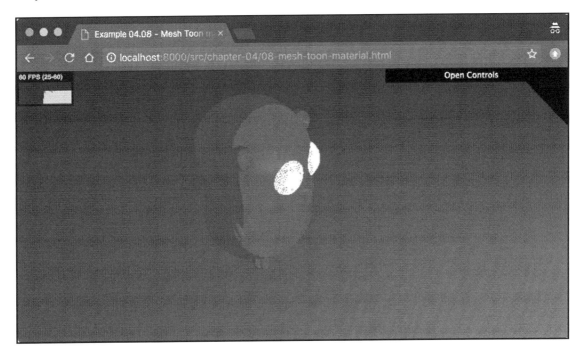

60 FPS (25-60)

We've already mentioned that Three.js provides two additional materials you can use to create realistic-looking materials: THREE.PhysicalMaterial and THREE.StandardMaterial. We'll look at both these materials next.

THREE.MeshStandardMaterial

THREE.MeshStandardMaterial is a material that takes a physics approach to determine how to react to the lighting in the scene. It is a great material for shiny and metal-like materials, and provides a number of properties you can use to configure this material:

Name	Description
metalness	This property determines how much like metal this material is. Non-metallic materials should use a value of 0, metallic materials should use a value close to 1, and the default is 0.5.
roughness	You can also set how rough the material is. This determines how the light that hits this material is diffused. The default is 0.5, a value of 0 is a mirror-like reflection, and a value of 1 diffuses all the light.

Besides these properties, you can also use the color and emissive properties, as well as the properties from THREE.Material, to alter this material. As you can see in the following screenshot, we can use this to simulate a kind of brushed metal look by playing around with the metalness and roughness parameters:

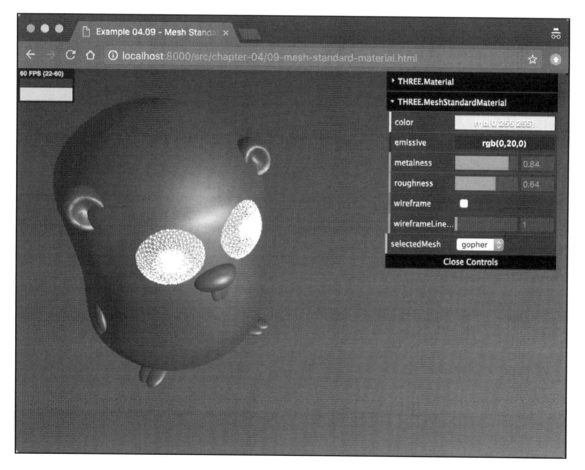

THREE.MeshPhysicalMaterial

A material very close to `THREE.MeshStandardMaterial` is `THREE.MeshPhysicalMaterial`. With this material, you have more control over the reflectivity of the material. This material provides, besides the properties we've already seen for `THREE.MeshPhysicalMaterial`, the following properties to control what the material looks like:

Name	Description
clearCoat	A value indicating a coating layer on top of the material. The higher this value is, the more coating is applied, and the more effective the `clearCoatRoughness` parameter is. This value ranges from 0 to 1 with a default of 0.
clearCoatRoughness	The roughness used for the coating of the material. The rougher it is, the more light is diffused. This is used together with the `clearCoat` property. This value ranges from 0 to 1 with a default of 0.
reflectivity	You can use this property to set the reflectivity of non-metallic materials. So if the `metalness` property is 1 (or near 1), you won't see any effect. The default is 0.5, the minimum is 0, and the maximum is 1.

As we've seen for other materials, it is quite hard to reason about the values you should use for your specific requirements. It's often the best choice to add a simple UI (as we do in the examples) and play around with the values to get to a combination that best reflects your needs. You can see this example in action by looking at the `10-mesh-physical-material.html` example:

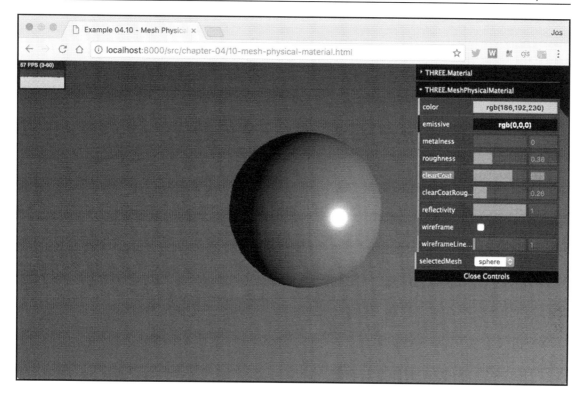

The last of the advanced materials we'll explore is THREE.ShaderMaterial.

Creating your own shaders with THREE.ShaderMaterial

THREE.ShaderMaterial is one of the most versatile and complex materials available in Three.js. With this material, you can pass in your own custom shaders that are directly run in the WebGL context. A shader converts Three.js JavaScript meshes to pixels on screen. With these custom shaders, you can define exactly how your object should be rendered and how to override or alter the defaults from Three.js. In this section, we won't go into the details yet of how to write custom shaders. For more information on that, see Chapter 11, *Render Postprocessing*. For now, we'll just look at a very basic example that shows how you can configure this material.

THREE.ShaderMaterial has a number of properties you can set that we've already seen. With THREE.ShaderMaterial, Three.js passes in all the information regarding these properties, but you still have to process the information in your own shader programs. The following are the properties of THREE.Material that are passed into the shader, and that you can interpret for yourself:

Name	Description
wireframe	This renders the material as a wireframe. This is great for debugging purposes.
Wireframelinewidth	If you enable the wireframe, this property defines the width of the wires from the wireframe.
linewidth	This defines the width of the line to be drawn.
Shading	This defines how shading is applied. The possible values are THREE.SmoothShading and THREE.FlatShading. This property isn't enabled in the example for this material. For example, look at the section on MeshNormalMaterial.
vertexColors	You can define individual colors to be applied to each vertex with this property. This property doesn't work on CanvasRenderer but does work on WebGLRenderer. Look at the LineBasicMaterial example, where we use this property to color the various parts of a line.
fog	This determines whether this material is affected by global fog settings. This is not shown in action. If this is set to false, the global fog we saw in Chapter 2, *Basic Components That Make Up a Three.js Scene*, doesn't affect how this object is rendered.

Besides these properties that are passed into the shader, THREE.ShaderMaterial also provides a number of specific properties you can use to pass in additional information into your custom shader (they might seem a bit obscure at the moment; for more details, see Chapter 11, *Render Postprocessing*), which are as follows:

Name	Description
fragmentShader	This shader defines the color of each pixel that is passed in. Here, you need to pass in the string value of your fragment shader program.
vertextShader	This shader allows you to change the position of each vertex that is passed in. Here, you need to pass in the string value of your vertex shader program.
uniforms	This allows you to send information to your shader. The same information is sent to each vertex and fragment.
defines	Converts to #define code fragments. With these fragments, you can set some additional global variables in the shader programs.
attributes	These can change between each vertex and fragment. They are usually used to pass positional and normal-related data. If you want to use this, you need to provide information for all the vertices of the geometry.
lights	This determines whether light data should be passed into the shaders. This defaults to false.

Before we look at an example, we'll give a quick explanation about the most important parts of ShaderMaterial. To work with this material, we have to pass in two different shaders:

- vertexShader: This is run on each vertex of the geometry. You can use this shader to transform the geometry by moving the position of the vertices around.
- fragmentShader: This is run on each fragment of the geometry. In vertexShader, we return the color that should be shown for this specific fragment.

For all the materials we've discussed until now in this chapter, Three.js provides fragmentShader and vertexShader, so you don't have to worry about them.

For this section, we'll look at a simple example that uses a very simple vertexShader program that changes the *x*, *y*, and *z* coordinates of the vertices of a cube and a fragmentShader program that uses shaders from http://glslsandbox.com/ to create an animating material.

Up next, you can see the complete code for `vertexShader` that we'll use. Note that writing shaders isn't done in JavaScript. You write shaders in a C-like language called **GLSL** (WebGL supports OpenGL ES Shading Language 1.0 — for more information on GLSL, see `https://www.khronos.org/webgl/`), as follows:

```
<script id="vertex-shader" type="x-shader/x-vertex">
  uniform float time;

  void main()
  {
    vec3 posChanged = position;
    posChanged.x = posChanged.x*(abs(sin(time*1.0)));
    posChanged.y = posChanged.y*(abs(cos(time*1.0)));
    posChanged.z = posChanged.z*(abs(sin(time*1.0)));

    gl_Position = projectionMatrix * modelViewMatrix *
        vec4(posChanged,1.0);
  }
</script>
```

We won't go into too much detail here and just focus on the most important parts of this code. To communicate with the shaders from JavaScript, we use something called uniforms. In this example, we use the `uniform float time;` statement to pass in an external value. Based on this value, we change the *x*, *y*, and *z* coordinates of the passed-in vertex (which is passed in as the position variable):

```
vec3 posChanged = position;
posChanged.x = posChanged.x*(abs(sin(time*1.0)));
posChanged.y = posChanged.y*(abs(cos(time*1.0)));
posChanged.z = posChanged.z*(abs(sin(time*1.0)));
```

The `posChanged` vector now contains the new coordinate for this vertex based on the passed-in time variable. The last step we need to perform is pass this new position back to Three.js, which is always done like this:

```
gl_Position = projectionMatrix * modelViewMatrix *
    vec4(posChanged,1.0);
```

The `gl_Position` variable is a special variable that is used to return the final position. Next, we need to create `shaderMaterial` and pass in `vertexShader`. For this, we've created a simple helper function, which we use like this: `var meshMaterial1 = createMaterial("vertex-shader","fragment-shader-1");` in the following code:

```
function createMaterial(vertexShader, fragmentShader) {
  var vertShader = document.getElementById
      (vertexShader).innerHTML;  var fragShader = document.getElementById
```

```
    (fragmentShader).innerHTML;

  var attributes = {};
  var uniforms = {
    time: {type: 'f', value: 0.2},
    scale: {type: 'f', value: 0.2},
    alpha: {type: 'f', value: 0.6},
    resolution: { type: "v2", value: new THREE.Vector2() }
  };

  uniforms.resolution.value.x = window.innerWidth;
  uniforms.resolution.value.y = window.innerHeight;

  var meshMaterial = new THREE.ShaderMaterial({
    uniforms: uniforms,
    attributes: attributes,
    vertexShader: vertShader,
    fragmentShader: fragShader,
    transparent: true

  });
  return meshMaterial;
}
```

The arguments point to the ID of the `script` element in the HTML page. Here, you can also see that we set up a `uniforms` variable. This variable is used to pass information from our renderer into our shader. Our complete render loop for this example is shown in the following code snippet:

```
function render() {
  stats.update();

  cube.rotation.y = step += 0.01;
  cube.rotation.x = step;
  cube.rotation.z = step;

  cube.material.materials.forEach(function (e) {
    e.uniforms.time.value += 0.01;
  });

  // render using requestAnimationFrame
  requestAnimationFrame(render);
  renderer.render(scene, camera);
}
```

You can see that we increase the time variable by `0.01` each time the `render` loop is run. This information is passed into `vertexShader` and used to calculate the new position of the vertices of our cube. Now open up the `08-shader-material.html` example, and you'll see that the cube shrinks and grows around its axis. The following screenshot gives a still image of this example:

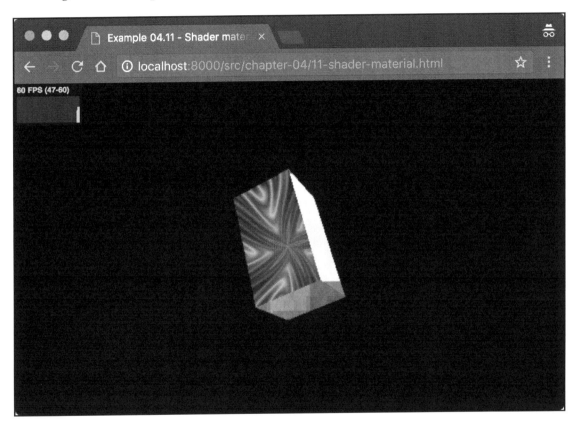

60 FPS (46-60)

In this example, you can see that each of the cube's faces has an animating pattern. The fragment shader that is assigned to each face of the cube creates these patterns. As you might have guessed, we've used `THREE.MeshFaceMaterial` (and the `createMaterial` function we explained earlier) for this:

```
var cubeGeometry = new THREE.CubeGeometry(20, 20, 20);

var meshMaterial1 = createMaterial("vertex-shader", "fragment-
    shader-1");var meshMaterial2 = createMaterial("vertex-shader",
```

```
"fragment-
    shader-2");var meshMaterial3 = createMaterial("vertex-shader",
"fragment-
    shader-3");var meshMaterial4 = createMaterial("vertex-shader",
"fragment-
    shader-4");var meshMaterial5 = createMaterial("vertex-shader",
"fragment-
    shader-5");var meshMaterial6 = createMaterial("vertex-shader",
"fragment-
    shader-6");var material = new THREE.MeshFaceMaterial([meshMaterial1,
    meshMaterial2, meshMaterial3, meshMaterial4, meshMaterial5,
    meshMaterial6]);

var cube = new THREE.Mesh(cubeGeometry, material);
```

The only part we haven't explained yet is `fragmentShader`. For this example, all the `fragmentShader` objects were copied from `http://glslsandbox.com/`. This site provides an experimental playground where you can write and share `fragmentShader` objects. I won't go into the details here, but `fragment-shader-6` used in this example looks like this:

```
<script id="fragment-shader-6" type="x-shader/x-fragment">
    #ifdef GL_ES
    precision mediump float;
    #endif

    uniform float time;
    uniform vec2 resolution;


    void main( void )
    {

      vec2 uPos = ( gl_FragCoord.xy / resolution.xy );

      uPos.x -= 1.0;
      uPos.y -= 0.5;

      vec3 color = vec3(0.0);
      float vertColor = 2.0;
      for( float i = 0.0;  i < 15.0;  ++i ) {
        float t = time * (0.9);

        uPos.y += sin( uPos.x*i + t+i/2.0 ) * 0.1;
        float fTemp = abs(1.0 / uPos.y / 100.0);
        vertColor += fTemp;
        color += vec3( fTemp*(10.0-i)/10.0,  fTemp*i/10.0,
```

```
        pow(fTemp,1.5)*1.5 );
    }

    vec4 color_final = vec4(color, 1.0);
    gl_FragColor = color_final;
  }
</script>
```

The color that finally gets passed back to Three.js is the one set with `gl_FragColor = color_final`. A good way to get a bit more of a feeling for `fragmentShader` is to explore what's available at `http://glslsandbox.com/` and use the code for your own objects. Before we move to the next set of materials, here is one more example of what is possible with a custom `vertexShader` program (`https://www.shadertoy.com/view/MdX3zr`):

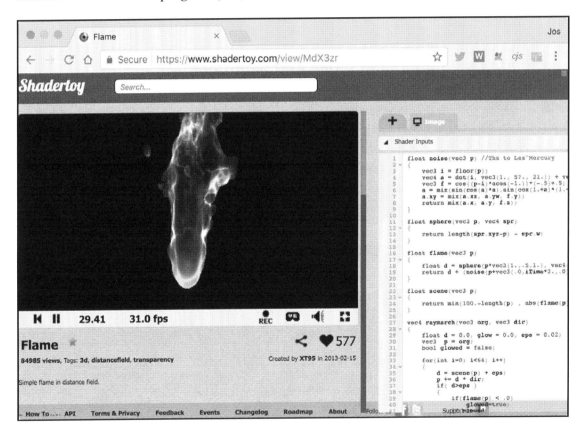

Much more on the subject of fragment and vertex shaders can be found in `Chapter 11`, *Render Postprocessing*.

Materials you can use for a line geometry

The last couple of materials we're going to look at can only be used on one specific mesh: THREE.Line. As the name implies, this is just a single line that only consists of vertices and doesn't contain any faces. Three.js provides two different materials you can use on a THREE.Line geometry, which are as follows:

- THREE.LineBasicMaterial: The basic material for a line allows you to set the colors, linewidth, linecap, and linejoin properties.
- THREE.LineDashedMaterial: This has the same properties as THREE.LineBasicMaterial but allows you to create a *dashed line* effect by specifying dash and spacing sizes

We'll start with the basic variant, and after that look at the dashed variant.

THREE.LineBasicMaterial

The materials available for the THREE.Line geometry are very simple. It inherits all of the properties from THREE.Material, but the following table shows the properties that are most important for this material:

Name	Description
color	This determines the color of the line. If you specify vertexColors, this property is ignored.
linewidth	This determines the width of the line.
linecap	This property defines how the ends of lines look in the wireframe mode. The possible values are butt, round, and square. The default is round. In practice, the results from changing this property are very difficult to see. This property isn't supported on WebGLRenderer.
linejoin	Defines how the line joints are visualized. The possible values are round, bevel, and miter. The default value is round. If you look very closely, you can see this in the example using low opacity and a very large wireframeLinewidth. This property isn't supported on WebGLRenderer.
vertexColors	You can supply a specific color for each vertex by setting this property to the THREE.VertexColors value.

Before we look at an example of LineBasicMaterial, let's first have a quick look at how we can create a THREE.Line mesh from a set of vertices and combine that with LineMaterial to create the mesh, as shown in the following code:

```
var points = gosper(4, 60);
var lines = new THREE.Geometry();
var colors = [];
var i = 0;
points.forEach(function (e) {
  lines.vertices.push(new THREE.Vector3(e.x, e.z, e.y));
  colors[ i ] = new THREE.Color(0xffffff);
  colors[ i ].setHSL(e.x / 100 + 0.5, (  e.y * 20 ) / 300, 0.8);
  i++;
});

lines.colors = colors;
var material = new THREE.LineBasicMaterial({
  opacity: 1.0,
  linewidth: 1,
  vertexColors: THREE.VertexColors });

var line = new THREE.Line(lines, material);
```

The first part of this code fragment, var points = gosper(4, 60);, is used as an example to get a set of *x* and *y* coordinates. This function returns a Gosper curve (for more information, check out http://en.wikipedia.org/wiki/Gosper_curve), which is a simple algorithm that fills a 2D space. What we do next is we create a THREE.Geometry instance, and for each coordinate, we create a new vertex, which we push into the lines property of this instance. For each coordinate, we also calculate a color value that we use to set the colors property.

 In this example, we've set the color using the setHSL() method. Instead of providing values for red, green, and blue, with HSL, we provide the hue, saturation, and lightness. Using HSL is much more intuitive than RGB, and it is much easier to create sets of matching colors. A very good explanation of HSL can be found in the CSS specification: http://www.w3.org/TR/2003/CR-css3-color-20030514/#hsl-color.

Now that we have our geometry, we can create `THREE.LineBasicMaterial` and use this together with the geometry to create a `THREE.Line` mesh. You can see the result in the `12-line-material.html` example. The following screenshot shows this example:

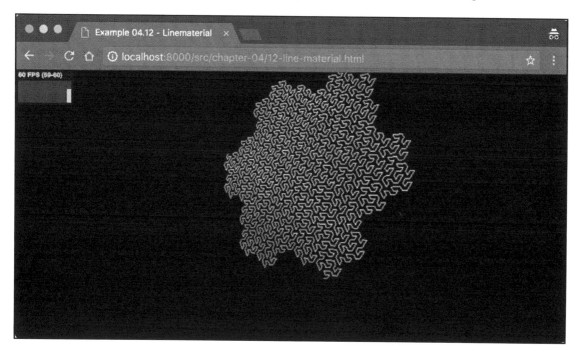

60 FPS (59-60)

This is a line geometry created with `LineBasicMaterial` and using `vertexColors`. The next and last material we'll discuss in this chapter is only slightly different from `THREE.LineBasicMaterial`. With `THREE.LineDashedMaterial`, not only can we color lines, but we can also add a space to the line.

THREE.LineDashedMaterial

This material has the same properties as THREE.LineBasicMaterial and two additional ones you can use to define the dash width and the width of the gaps between the dashes, which are as follows:

Name	Description
scale	This scales dashSize and gapSize. If the scale is smaller than 1, dashSize, and gapSize increase, and if the scale is larger than 1, dashSize, and gapSize decrease.
dashSize	This is the size of the dash.
gapSize	This is the size of the gap.

This material works almost exactly like THREE.LineBasicMaterial. Here's how it works:

```
var material = new THREE.LineDashedMaterial({ vertexColors: true,
    color: 0xffffff, dashSize: 10, gapSize: 1, scale: 0.1 });

var line = new THREE.Line(lines, material);
  line.computeLineDistances();
```

The only difference is that you have to call computeLineDistances() (which is used to determine the distance between the vertices that make up a line). If you don't do this, the gaps won't be shown correctly. An example of this material can be found in 13-line-material-dashed.html and looks like the following screenshot:

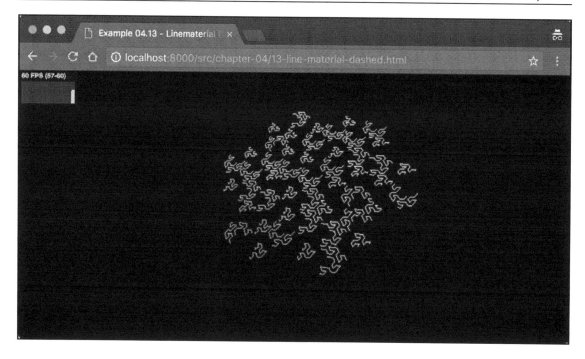

60 FPS (57-60)

Summary

Three.js gives you a lot of materials you can use to skin your geometries. The materials range from the very simple (`THREE.MeshBasicMaterial`) to the complex (`THREE.ShaderMaterial`), where you can provide your own `vertexShader` and `fragmentShader` programs. Materials share a lot of basic properties. If you know how to use a single material, you'll probably also know how to use the other materials. Note that not all materials respond to the lights in your scene. If you want a material that takes lighting into effect, you can usually just use the `THREE.MeshStandardMaterial`. If you need more control, you can also look at `THREE.MeshPhysicalMaterial`, `THREE.MeshPhongMaterial`, or `THREE.MeshLamberMaterial`. Determining the effect of certain material properties just from code is very hard. Often, a good idea is to use a `dat.GUI` approach to experiment with these properties.

Also, remember that most of the properties of a material can be modified at runtime. Some, though (for example, `side`), can't be modified at runtime. If you change such a value, you need to set the `needsUpdate` property to `true`. For a complete overview of what can and cannot be changed at runtime, see the following page:
`https://github.com/mrdoob/three.js/wiki/Updates.`

In this and the previous chapters, we talked about geometries. We used these in our examples and explored a couple of them. In the next chapter, you'll learn everything about geometries and how you can work with them.

5
Learning to Work with Geometries

In the previous chapters, you learned a lot about how to work with Three.js. Now you know how to create a basic scene, add lighting, and configure the material for your meshes. In Chapter 2, *Basic Components That Make Up a Three.js Scene*, we touched upon, but didn't really go into the details of, the available geometries that Three.js provides and that you can use to create your 3D objects. In this and Chapter 6, *Advanced Geometries and Binary Operations*, we'll walk you through all the geometries (except THREE.Line, which we discussed in Chapter 4, *Working with Three.js Materials*) Three.js provides out of the box.

In this chapter, we'll look at the following geometries:

- THREE.CircleGeometry
- THREE.RingGeometry
- THREE.PlaneGeometry
- THREE.ShapeGeometry
- THREE.BoxGeometry
- THREE.SphereGeometry
- THREE.CylinderGeometry
- THREE.ConeGeometry
- THREE.TorusGeometry
- THREE.TorusKnotGeometry
- THREE.PolyhedronGeometry
- THREE.IcosahedronGeometry
- THREE.OctahedronGeometry
- THREE.TetraHedronGeometry
- THREE.DodecahedronGeometry

Before we look into the geometries provided by Three.js, we'll first look a bit deeper into the two main options Three.js provides for representing geometries: a `THREE.BufferGeometry` and a `THREE.Geometry`. In the older Versions of Three.js, all the geometry shapes were based on `THREE.Geometry`. Later, `THREE.BufferGeometry` was introduced, which generally provides better performance, since it can easily get its data to the GPU, but is less easy to use.

With a `THREE.Geometry`, the shape of an object is defined by the following properties:

Property	Description
vertices	The vertices array defines the position of each individual vertex of the model. Vertices are the points that make up a model.
faces	When combining three vertices together, you get a face. This array contains all the faces of the model.

As you can see, `THREE.Geometry` is very easy to reason about. You can directly add points to the model and use them to create new faces or change existing ones. When we look at `THREE.BufferGeometry`, we don't have the `vertices` and `faces` properties, but just have the `attributes` property and optionally the `index` property. These properties are used like this:

Property	Description
attributes	The `attributes` properties are used to store information that can be directly passed to the GPU. For instance, for defining a shape, you define a `Float32Array`, where every three values define the position of a vertex. Each three vertices are then interpreted as a face. This can be defined on a `THREE.BufferGeometry` like this: `geometry.addAttribute( 'position', new THREE.BufferAttribute( arrayOfVertices, 3 ) );`
index	By default, faces don't need to be explicitly defined (each three consecutive positions are interpreted as a single face), but using the `index` property, we can define faces in the same way as we did for a normal `THREE.Geometry`.

For the examples in this chapter, you don't need to think about the differences between these two different types of geometries. If you want to use a `THREE.Geometry`, you can use the geometries shown at the beginning of this chapter. If you want to use the `THREE.BufferGeometry` variant, you just add the word Buffer to the name of the geometry, for example, `THREE.PlaneGeometry` becomes `THREE.PlaneBufferGeometry`. Everything else stays the same. So, let's look at all the basic geometries that Three.js has to offer.

Sometimes, you might need to convert between a `THREE.Geometry`-based shape and a `THREE.BufferGeometry`-based shape. For instance, some of the loaders provided by Three.js load a model into a `THREE.BufferGeometry`. If you want to change some part of the loaded model, it is often easier to convert it into a `THREE.Geometry` and work with the `vertices` and `faces` properties instead of working with the big `attributes` array from a `THREE.BufferGeometry`. To do this, the `THREE.Geometry` provides the `fromBufferGeometry` function, which takes a `THREE.BufferGeometry` and uses that to set the properties of the `THREE.Geometry`. Vice versa, the `THREE.BufferGeometry` has the `fromGeometry` function to set the `attributes` property based on the information from a `THREE.Geometry`. For example, to convert from a `THREE.BufferGeometry` to a `THREE.Geometry`, you can use the following code:

```
var normalGeometry = new THREE.Geometry();
normalGeometry.fromBufferGeometry(bufferGeometry);
```

And vice versa, from a normal `THREE.Geomtry` to a `THREE.BufferGeometry`:

```
var bufferGeometry = new THREE.BufferGeometry();
bufferGeometry.fromGeometry(normalGeometry);
```

The basic geometries provided by Three.js

In Three.js, we have a couple of geometries that result in a 2D mesh and a larger number of geometries that create a 3D mesh. In this section, we'll first look at the 2D geometries: `THREE.CircleGeometry`, `THREE.RingGeometry`, `THREE.PlaneGeometry`, and `THREE.ShapeGeometry`. After that, we'll explore all the basic 3D geometries that are available.

2D geometries

2D objects look like flat objects and, as the name implies, only have two dimensions. The first 2D geometry on the list is `THREE.PlaneGeometry`.

THREE.PlaneGeometry

A `PlaneGeometry` object can be used to create a very simple 2D rectangle. For an example of this geometry, look at the `01-basic-2d-geometries-plane.html` example in the sources for this chapter. A rectangle that was created using `PlaneGeometry` is shown in the following screenshot:

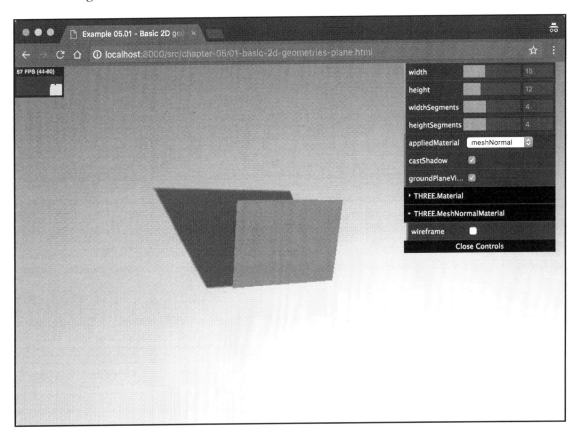

57 FPS (44-60)

In this examples for this chapter, we've added a control GUI that you can use to control the properties of the geometry (in this case, the `width`, `height`, `widthSegments`, and `heightSegments`), and also change the material (and its properties), disable shadows, and hide the ground plane. For instance, if you want to see the individual faces of this shape, you can easily show that by disabling the ground plane, and enabling the `wireframe` property of the selected material:

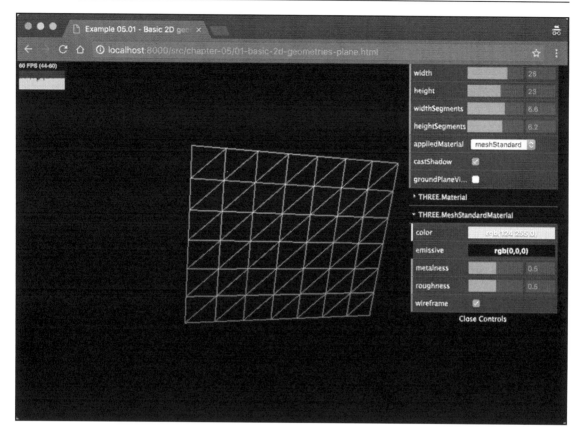

Creating a `THREE.PlaneGeometry` is very simple, and is done as follows:

```
new THREE.PlaneGeometry(width, height, widthSegments, heightSegments);
```

In this example for THREE.PlaneGeometry, you can change these properties and directly see the effect it has on the resulting 3D object. An explanation of these properties is shown in the following table:

Property	Mandatory	Description
width	Yes	This is the width of the rectangle.
height	Yes	This is the height of the rectangle.
widthSegments	No	This is the number of segments the width should be divided into. This defaults to 1.
heightSegments	No	This is the number of segments the height should be divided into. This defaults to 1.

As you can see, this is not a very complex geometry. You just specify the size, and you're done. If you want to create more faces (for example, when you want to create a checkered pattern), you can use the widthSegments and heightSegments properties to divide the geometry into smaller faces.

If you want to access the properties of a geometry after it has been created, you can't just say plane.width. To access the properties of a geometry, you have to use the parameters property of the object. So, to get the width property of the plane object we created in this section, you'd have to use plane.parameters.width.

THREE.CircleGeometry

You can probably already guess what THREE.CircleGeometry creates. With this geometry, you can create a very simple 2D circle (or part of a circle). First, let's look at the example for this geometry, 02-basic-2d-geometries-circle.html. In the following screenshot, you can find an example where we created a THREE.CircleGeometry with a thetaLength value that is smaller than 2 * PI:

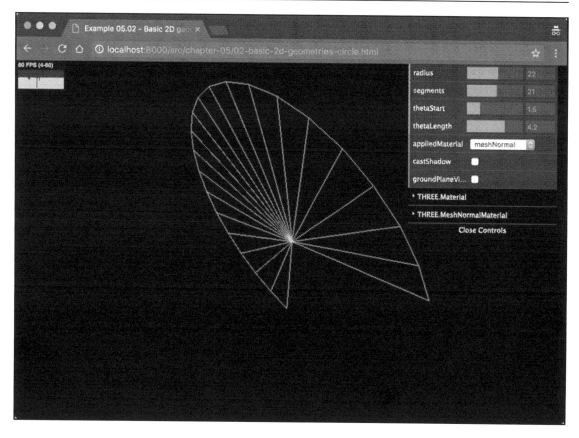

60 FPS (4-60)

 TIP $2 * PI$ represents a complete circle in radians. If you'd rather work with degrees than radians, converting between them is very easy.

The following two functions can help you to convert between radians and degrees, as follows:

```
function deg2rad(degrees) {
  return degrees * Math.PI / 180;
}

function rad2deg(radians) {
  return radians * 180 / Math.PI;
}
```

In this example, you can see and control a mesh that's been created by using `THREE.CircleGeometry`. When you create `THREE.CircleGeometry`, you can specify a few properties that define what the circle looks like, as follows:

Property	Mandatory	Description
radius	No	The radius of a circle defines its size. The radius is the distance from the center of the circle to its side. The default value is 50.
segments	No	This property defines the number of faces that are used to create the circle. The minimum number is 3, and if not specified, this number defaults to 8. A higher value means a smoother circle.
thetaStart	No	This property defines the position from which to start drawing the circle. This value can range from 0 to 2 * PI, and the default value is 0.
thetaLength	No	This property defines to what extent the circle is completed. This defaults to 2 * PI (a full circle) when not specified. For instance, if you specify 0.5 * PI for this value, you'll get a quarter circle. Use this property together with the thetaStart property to define the shape of the circle.

You can create a full circle using the following snippet of code:

```
new THREE.CircleGeometry(3, 12);
```

If you wanted to create half a circle from this geometry, you'd use something like this:

```
new THREE.CircleGeometry(3, 12, 0, Math.PI);
```

This creates a circle with a radius of 3 that is split into 12 segments. The circle starts at a default of 0, and is only drawn halfway since we specify the `thetaLength` as `Math.PI`, which is half a circle.

Before moving on to the next geometry, here's a quick note on the orientation that Three.js uses when creating these 2D shapes (`THREE.PlaneGeometry`, `THREE.CircleGeometry`, `THREE.RingGeometry`, and `THREE.ShapeGeometry`): Three.js creates these objects *standing up*, so they are aligned along the *x-y* plane. This is very logical since they are 2D shapes. However, often, especially with `THREE.PlaneGeometry`, you want to have the mesh lying down on the ground (the *x-z* plane), on some sort of ground area on which you can position the rest of your objects. The easiest way to create a 2D object that is horizontally orientated instead of vertically is by rotating the mesh a quarter rotation backwards (-PI/2) around its *x* axis, as follows:

```
mesh.rotation.x =- Math.PI/2;
```

That's all for `THREE.CircleGeometry`. The next geometry, `THREE.RingGeometry`, looks a lot like `THREE.CircleGeometry`.

THREE.RingGeometry

With `THREE.RingGeometry`, you can create a 2D object that not only closely resembles `THREE.CircleGeometry`, but also allows you to define a hole in the center (see `03-basic-3d-geometries-ring.html`):

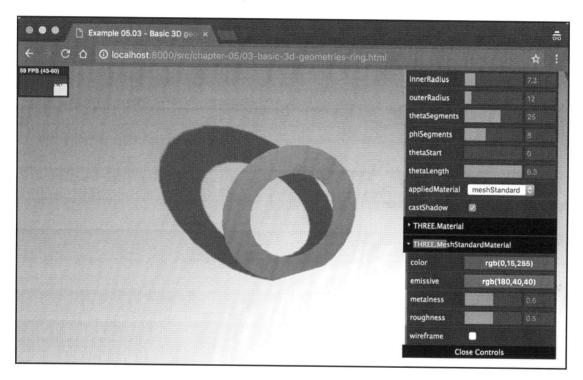

59 FPS (43-60)

`THREE.RingGeometry` doesn't have any required properties (see the following table for the default values), so to create this geometry, you only have to specify the following:

```
Var ring = new THREE.RingGeometry();
```

You can further customize the appearance of the ring geometry by passing the following arguments into the constructor:

Property	Mandatory	Description
innerRadius	No	The inner radius of a circle defines the size of the center hole. If this property is set to 0, no hole will be shown. The default value is 0.
outerRadius	No	The outer radius of a circle defines its size. The radius is the distance from the center of the circle to its side. The default value is 50.
thetaSegments	No	This is the number of diagonal segments that will be used to create the circle. A higher value means a smoother ring. The default value is 8.
phiSegments	No	This is the number of segments required to be used along the length of the ring. The default value is 8. This doesn't really affect the smoothness of the circle but increases the number of faces.
thetaStart	No	This defines the position from which to start drawing the circle. This value can range from 0 to 2 * PI, and the default value is 0.
thetaLength	No	This defines the extent to which the circle is completed. This defaults to 2 * PI (a full circle) when not specified. For instance, if you specify 0.5 * PI for this value, you'll get a quarter circle. Use this property together with the thetaStart property to define the shape of the circle.

The following screenshot shows a wireframe that nicely visualizes the use of `thetaSegments` and `phiSegments`:

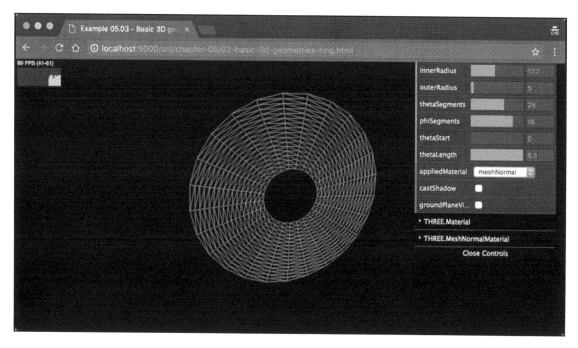

60 FPS (41-61)

In the next section, we'll look at the last of the 2D shapes: THREE.ShapeGeometry.

THREE.ShapeGeometry

THREE.PlaneGeometry and THREE.CircleGeometry have limited ways of customizing their appearance. If you want to create custom 2D shapes, you can use THREE.ShapeGeometry. With THREE.ShapeGeometry, you have a couple of functions you can call to create your own shapes. You can compare this functionality with the `<path` element functionality that is also available to the HTML canvas element and SVG. Let's start with an example, and after that, we'll show you how you can use the various functions to draw your own shape. The `04-basic-2d-geometries-shape.html` example can be found in the sources of this chapter.

The following screenshot shows this example:

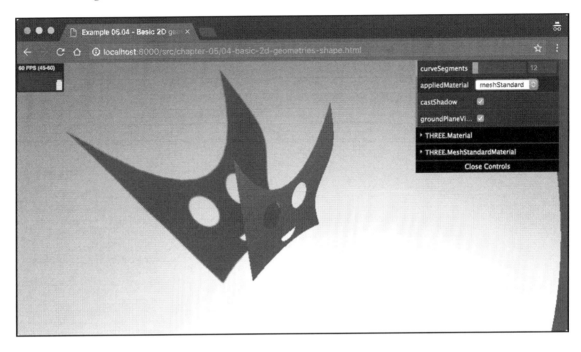

60 FPS (45-60)

In this example, you can see a custom-created 2D shape. Before going into the description of the properties, first, let's look at the code that is used to create this shape. Before we create THREE.ShapeGeometry, we first have to create THREE.Shape. You can trace these steps by looking at the previous screenshot, where we start in the bottom-right corner. Here's how we created THREE.Shape:

```
function drawShape() {
  // create a basic shape
  var shape = new THREE.Shape();

  // startpoint
  shape.moveTo(10, 10);

  // straight line upwards
  shape.lineTo(10, 40);

  // the top of the figure, curve to the right
  shape.bezierCurveTo(15, 25, 25, 25, 30, 40);

  // spline back down
```

```
shape.splineThru(
    [new THREE.Vector2(32, 30),
        new THREE.Vector2(28, 20),
        new THREE.Vector2(30, 10),
    ])

// curve at the bottom
shape.quadraticCurveTo(20, 15, 10, 10);

// add 'eye' hole one
var hole1 = new THREE.Path();
hole1.absellipse(16, 24, 2, 3, 0, Math.PI * 2, true);
shape.holes.push(hole1);

// add 'eye hole 2'
var hole2 = new THREE.Path();
hole2.absellipse(23, 24, 2, 3, 0, Math.PI * 2, true);
shape.holes.push(hole2);

// add 'mouth'
var hole3 = new THREE.Path();
hole3.absarc(20, 16, 2, 0, Math.PI, true);
shape.holes.push(hole3);

// return the shape
return shape;
}
```

In this piece of code, you can see that we created the outline of this shape using lines, curves, and splines. After that, we punched a number of holes in this shape by using the `holes` property of THREE.Shape. In this section, though, we're talking about THREE.ShapeGeometry and not THREE.Shape. To create a geometry from THREE.Shape, we need to pass in THREE.Shape (returned, in our case, from the `drawShape()` function) as the argument to THREE.ShapeGeometry, as follows:

```
new THREE.ShapeGeometry(drawShape());
```

The result from this function is a geometry that can be used to create a mesh. There is also an alternative way of creating THREE.ShapeGeometry when you already have a shape. You can call `shape.makeGeometry(options)`, which will return an instance of THREE.ShapeGeometry (for an explanation of these options, see the following table).

First, let's look at the parameters you can pass into `THREE.ShapeGeometry`:

Property	Mandatory	Description
shapes	Yes	These are one or more `THREE.Shape` objects that are used to create `THREE.Geometry`. You can either pass in a single `THREE.Shape` object or an array of `THREE.Shape` objects.
options	No	You can also pass in some `options` that are applied to all the shapes passed in with the `shapes` argument. An explanation of these options is given here: • `curveSegments`: This property determines how smooth the curves created from the shape are. The default value is 12. • `material`: This is the `materialIndex` property that is used for the faces that are created for the specified shapes. When you use `THREE.MeshFaceMaterial` together with this geometry, the `materialIndex` property determines which of the materials passed in is used for the faces of the shapes passed in. • `UVGenerator`: When you use a texture with your material, the UV mapping determines what part of a texture is used for a specific face. With the `UVGenerator` property, you can pass in your own object, which will create the UV settings for the faces that are created for the shapes passed in. More information on UV settings can be found in Chapter 10, *Loading and Working with Textures*. If none are specified, `THREE.ExtrudeGeometry.WorldUVGenerator` is used.

The most important part of THREE.ShapeGeometry is THREE.Shape, which you use to create the shape, so let's look at the list of drawing functions you can use to create THREE.Shape.

These are actually functions of the THREE.Path object, from which THREE.Shape extends:

Name	Description
moveTo(x,y)	Move the drawing position to the x and y coordinates that are specified.
lineTo(x,y)	Draw a line from the current position (for example, set by the moveTo function) to the x and y coordinates that have been provided.
quadraticCurveTo(aCPx, aCPy, x, y)	There are two different ways of specifying curves. You can use the quadraticCurveTo function, or you can use the bezierCurveTo function (see the following table row). The difference between these two functions is how you specify the curvature of the curve. The following diagram explains the differences between these two options: Quadratic Bezier and Cubic Bezier For a quadratic curve, we need to specify one additional point (using the aCPx and aCPy arguments), and the curve is based solely on that point and, of course, the specified end point (from the x and y arguments). For a cubic curve (used by the bezierCurveTo function), you specify two additional points to define the curve. The starting point is the current position of the path.
bezierCurveTo(aCPx1, aCPy1, aCPx2, aCPy2, x, y)	This draws a curve based on the arguments supplied. For an explanation, see the previous table entry. The curve is drawn based on the two coordinates that define the curve (aCPx1, aCPy1, aCPx2, and aCPy2) and the end coordinate (x and y). The start point is the current position of the path.
splineThru(pts)	This function draws a fluid line through the set of coordinates provided (pts). This argument should be an array of THREE.Vector2 objects. The starting point is the current position of the path.
arc(aX, aY, aRadius, aStartAngle, aEndAngle, aClockwise)	This draws a circle (or part of a circle). The circle starts from the current position of the path. Here, aX and aY are used as offsets from the current position. Note that aRadius sets the size of the circle and aStartAngle and aEndAngle define how large a part of the circle is drawn. The Boolean property aClockwise determines whether the circle is drawn clockwise or counterclockwise.
absArc(aX, aY, aRadius, aStartAngle, aEndAngle, AClockwise)	See the description of arc. The position is absolute instead of relative to the current position.

ellipse(aX, aY, xRadius, yRadius, aStartAngle, aEndAngle, aClockwise)	See the description of arc. As an addition, with the ellipse function, we can separately set the x radius and the y radius.
absEllipse(aX, aY, xRadius, yRadius, aStartAngle, aEndAngle, aClockwise)	See the description of ellipse. The position is absolute instead of relative to the current position.
fromPoints(vectors)	If you pass in an array of THREE.Vector2 (or THREE.Vector3) objects into this function, Three.js will create a path using straight lines from the supplied vectors.
holes	The holes property contains an array of THREE.Shape objects. Each of the objects in this array is rendered as a hole. A good example of this is the example we saw at the beginning of this section. In that code fragment, we added three THREE.Shape objects to this array: one for the left eye, one for the right eye, and one for the mouth of our main THREE.Shape object.

Just like for a lot of examples, understanding how the various properties affect the final shape it is easiest way to just enable the wireframe property on the material and play around with the settings. For example, the following screenshot shows what happens when you use a low value for the curveSegments:

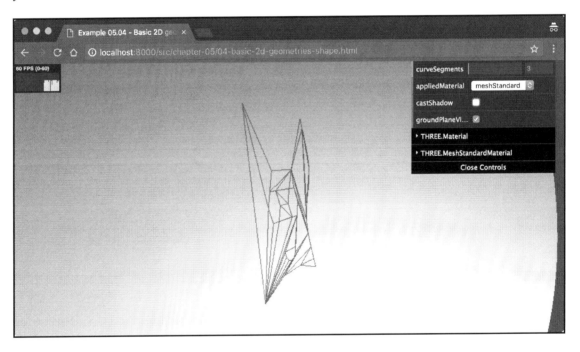

60 FPS (0-60)

As you can see, the shape loses is nice, round edges, but uses a lot less faces in the process. That's it for the 2D shapes. The following sections will show and explain the basic 3D shapes.

3D geometries

In this section on the basic 3D geometries, we'll start with the geometry we've already seen a couple of times: THREE.BoxGeometry.

THREE.BoxGeometry

THREE.BoxGeometry is a very simple 3D geometry that allows you to create a box by specifying its width, height, and depth. We've added an example, 05-basic-3d-geometries-cube.html, where you can play around with these properties. The following screenshot shows this geometry:

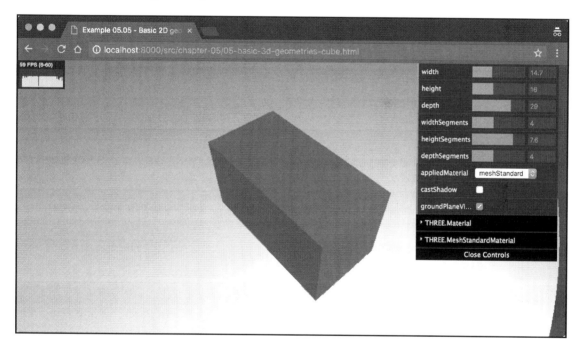

59 FPS(6-60)

As you can see in this example, by changing the `width`, `height`, and `depth` properties of `THREE.BoxGeometry`, you can control the size of the resulting mesh. These three properties are also mandatory when you create a new cube, as follows:

```
new THREE.BoxGeometry(10,10,10);
```

In the example, you can also see a couple of other properties that you can define on the cube. The following table explains all the properties:

Property	Mandatory	Description
width	Yes	This is the width of the cube. This is the length of the vertices of the cube along the *x* axis.
height	Yes	This is the height of the cube. This is the length of the vertices of the cube along the *y* axis.
depth	Yes	This is the depth of the cube. This is the length of the vertices of the cube along the *z* axis.
widthSegments	No	This is the number of segments into which we divide a face along the cube's *x* axis. The default value is 1. The more segments you define, the more faces a side has. If this property and the next two are set to 1, each side of the cube will just have two faces. If this property is set to 2, the face will be divided into two segments, resulting in four faces.
heightSegments	No	This is the number of segments into which we divide a face along the cube's *y* axis. The default value is 1.
depthSegments	No	This is the number of segments into which we divide a face along the cube's *z* axis. The default value is 1.

By increasing the various segment properties, you divide the six main faces of the cube into smaller faces. This is useful if you want to set specific material properties on parts of the cube using `THREE.MeshFaceMaterial`. `THREE.BoxGeometry` is a very simple geometry. Another simple one is `THREE.SphereGeometry`.

THREE.SphereGeometry

With `SphereGeometry`, you can create a 3D sphere. Let's dive straight into the example, `06-basic-3d-geometries-sphere.html`:

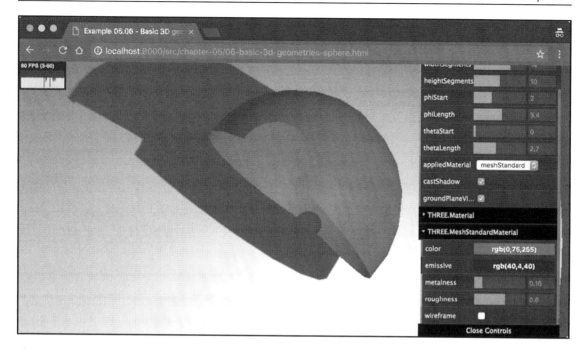

60 FPS (3-60)

In the previous screenshot, we have shown you a half-open sphere that was created based on `THREE.SphereGeometry`. This geometry is a very flexible one and can be used to create all kinds of sphere-related geometries. A basic `THREE.SphereGeometry`, though, can be created as easily as this: `new THREE.SphereGeometry()`. The following properties can be used to tune what the resulting mesh looks like:

Property	Mandatory	Description
radius	No	This is used to set the radius for the sphere. This defines how large the resulting mesh will be. The default value is 50.
widthSegments	No	This is the number of segments to be used vertically. More segments means a smoother surface. The default value is 8 and the minimum value is 3.
heightSegments	No	This is the number of segments to be used horizontally. The more segments, the smoother the surface of the sphere. The default value is 6 and the minimum value is 2.

phiStart	No	This determines where to start drawing the sphere along its *x* axis. This can range from 0 to 2 * PI. The default value is 0.
phiLength	No	This determines how far from phiStart the sphere is to be drawn. 2 * PI will draw a full sphere and 0.5 * PI will draw an open quarter sphere. The default value is 2 * PI.
thetaStart	No	This determines where to start drawing the sphere along its *x* axis. This can range from 0 to 2*PI, and the default value is 0.
thetaLength	No	This determines how far from thetaStart the sphere is drawn. The 2*PI value is a full sphere, whereas PI will draw only half of the sphere. The default value is 2*PI.

The radius, widthSegments, and heightSegments properties should be clear. We've already seen these kinds of properties in other examples. The phiStart, phiLength, thetaStart, and thetaLength properties are a bit harder to understand without looking at an example. Luckily, though, you can experiment with these properties from the menu in the 06-basic-3d-geometries-sphere.html example and create interesting geometries such as these:

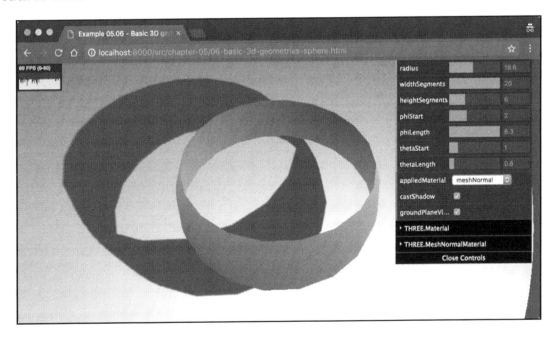

60 FPS(0-60)

The next one on the list is THREE.CylinderGeometry.

THREE.CylinderGeometry

With this geometry, we can create cylinders and cylinder-like objects. As for all the other geometries, we also have an example (07-basic-3d-geometries-cylinder.html) that lets you experiment with the properties of this geometry, the screenshot for which is as follows:

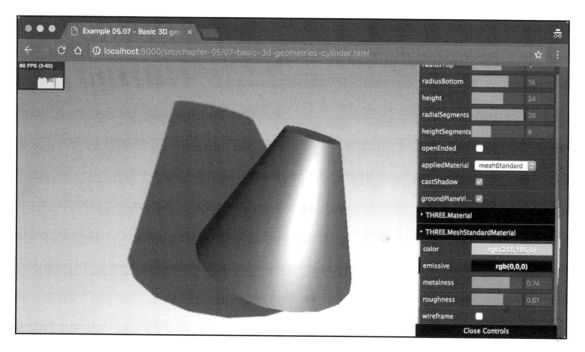

60 FPS (3-60)

When you create `THREE.CylinderGeometry`, there aren't any mandatory argument, so you can create a cylinder by just calling `new THREE.CylinderGeometry()`. You can pass in a number of properties, as you can see in the preceding example, to alter the appearance of this cylinder. The properties are explained in this table:

Property	Mandatory	Description
radiusTop	No	This sets the size this cylinder will be at the top. The default value is `20`.
radiusBottom	No	This sets the size this cylinder will be at the bottom. The default value is `20`.
height	No	This property sets the height of the cylinder. The default height is `100`.
radialSegments	No	This determines the number of segments along the radius of the cylinder. This defaults to `8`. More segments means a smoother cylinder.
heightSegments	No	This determines the number of segments along the height of the cylinder. The default value is `1`. More segments means more faces.
openEnded	No	This determines whether or not the mesh is closed at the top and the bottom. The default value is `false`.
thetaStart	No	This determines where to start drawing the cylinder along its *x* axis. This can range from `0` to `2*PI`, and the default value is `0`.
thetaLength	No	This determines how far from `thetaStart` the cylinder is drawn. The `2*PI` value is a full cylinder, whereas `PI` will draw only half of the cylinder. The default value is `2*PI`.

These are all very basic properties you can use to configure the cylinder. One interesting aspect, though, is when you use a negative radius for the top (or for the bottom). If you do this, you can use this geometry to create an hourglass-like shape, as shown in the following screenshot. One thing to note here, as you can see from the colors, is that the top half in this case is turned inside out. If you use a material that isn't configured with THREE.DoubleSide, you won't see the top half:

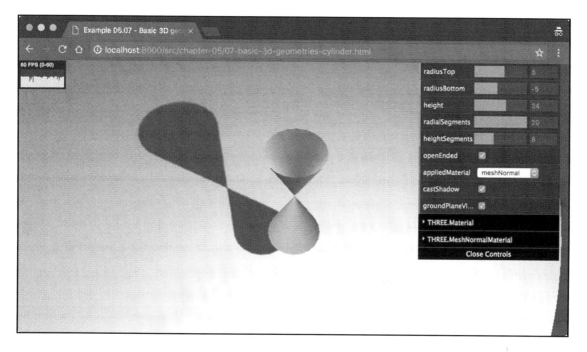

60 FPS (3-60)

The next geometry is THREE.ConeGeometry, which provides the basic functionalities of the THREE.CylinderGeometry, but has the top radius fixed to zero.

THREE.ConeGeometry

The THREE.ConeGeometry is pretty much the same as the THREE.CylinderGeometry. It uses all the same properties, except it only allows you to set the radius instead of a separate radiusTop and radiusBottom:

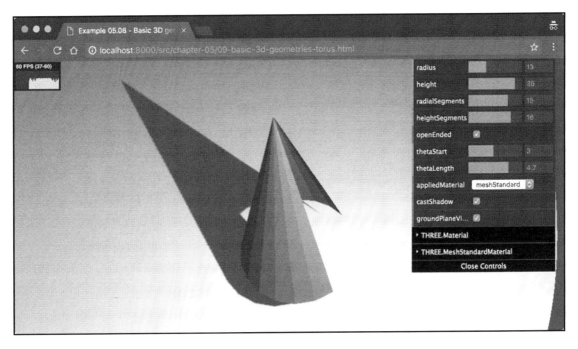

60 FPS (37-60)

The following properties can be set on `THREE.CylinderGeometry`:

Property	Mandatory	Description
radius	No	This sets the size this cylinder will be at the bottom. The default value is `20`.
height	No	This property sets the height of the cylinder. The default height is `100`.
radialSegments	No	This determines the number of segments along the radius of the cylinder. This defaults to `8`. More segments means a smoother cylinder.
heightSegments	No	This determines the number of segments along the height of the cylinder. The default value is `1`. More segments means more faces.
openEnded	No	This determines whether or not the mesh is closed at the top and the bottom. The default value is `false`.
thetaStart	No	This determines where to start drawing the cylinder along its *x* axis. This can range from `0` to `2*PI`, and the default value is `0`.
thetaLength	No	This determines how far from `thetaStart` the cylinder is drawn. The `2*PI` value is a full cylinder, whereas `PI` will draw only half of the cylinder. The default value is `2*PI`.

The next geometry, `THREE.TorusGeometry`, allows you to create a donut-like shaped object.

THREE.TorusGeometry

A torus is a simple shape that looks like a donut. The following screenshot, which you can get yourself by opening the `09-basic-3d-geometries-torus.html` example, shows `THREE.TorusGeometry` in action:

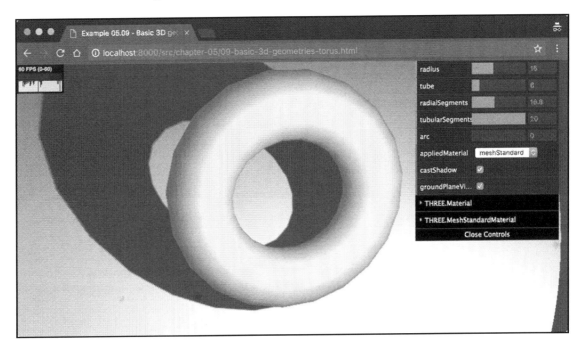

60 FPS (0-60)

Just like most of the simple geometries, there aren't any mandatory arguments when creating `THREE.TorusGeometry`. The following table lists the arguments you can specify when you create this geometry:

Property	Mandatory	Description
radius	No	This sets the size of the complete torus. The default value is 100.
tube	No	This sets the radius of the tube (the actual donut). The default value for this attribute is 40.
radialSegments	No	This determines the number of segments to be used along the length of the torus. The default value is 8. See the effect of changing this value in the demo.

tubularSegments	No	This determines the number of segments to be used along the width of the torus. The default value is 6. See the effect of changing this value in the demo.
arc	No	With this property, you can control whether the torus has drawl a full circle. The default of this value is 2 * PI (a full circle).

Most of these are very basic properties that you've already seen. The arc property, however, is a very interesting one. With this property, you can define whether the donuts makes a full circle or only a partial one. By experimenting with this property, you can create very interesting meshes, such as the following one with an arc set to 0.5 * PI:

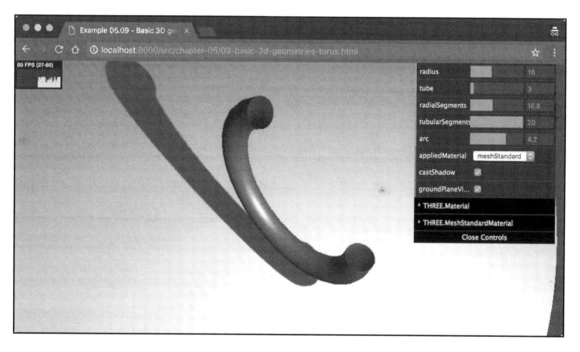

60 FPS (27-60)

THREE.TorusGeometry is a very straightforward geometry. In the next section, we'll look at a geometry that almost shares its name but is much less straightforward: THREE.TorusKnotGeometry.

THREE.TorusKnotGeometry

With `THREE.TorusKnotGeometry`, you can create a torus knot. A torus knot is a special kind of knot that looks like a tube that winds around itself a couple of times. The best way to explain this is by looking at the `10-basic-3d-geometries-torus-knot.html` example. The following screenshot shows this geometry:

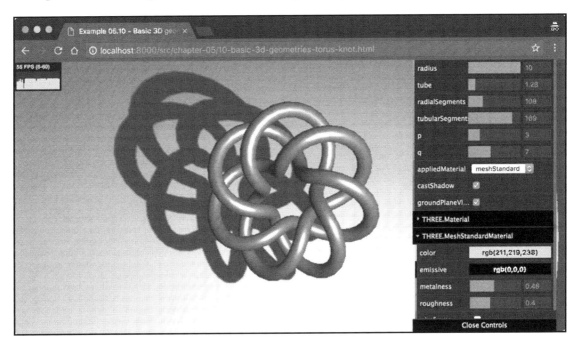

55 FPS (6-60)

If you open this example and play around with the p and q properties, you can create all kinds of beautiful geometries. The p property defines how often the knot winds around its axis, and q defines how much the knot winds around its interior.

If this sounds a bit vague, don't worry. You don't need to understand these properties to create beautiful knots, such as the one shown in the following screenshot (for those interested in the details, Wikipedia has a good article on this subject at `http://en.wikipedia.org/wiki/Torus_knot`):

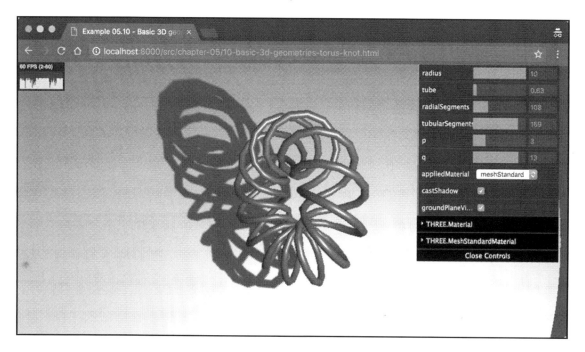

60 FPS (2-60)

With the example for this geometry, you can play around with the following properties and see the effect various combinations of p and q have on this geometry:

Property	Mandatory	Description
radius	No	This sets the size of the complete torus. The default value is 100.
tube	No	This sets the radius of the tube (the actual donut). The default value for this attribute is 40.
radialSegments	No	This determines the number of segments to be used along the length of the torus knot. The default value is 64. See the effect of changing this value in the demo.
tubularSegments	No	This determines the number of segments to be used along the width of the torus knot. The default value is 8. See the effect of changing this value in the demo.
p	No	This defines the shape of the knot, and the default value is 2.
q	No	This defines the shape of the knot, and the default value is 3.
heightScale	No	With this property, you can stretch out the torus knot. The default value is 1.

The next geometry on the list is the last one of the basic geometries: THREE.PolyhedronGeometry.

THREE.PolyhedronGeometry

With this geometry, you can easily create polyhedrons. A polyhedron is a geometry that has only flat faces and straight edges. Most often, though, you won't use this geometry directly. Three.js provides a number of specific polyhedrons you can use directly without having to specify the vertices and the faces of THREE.PolyhedronGeometry. We'll discuss these polyhedrons later on in this section. If you do want to use THREE.PolyhedronGeometry directly, you have to specify the vertices and the faces (just as we did for the cube in Chapter 3, *Working with the Different Light Sources Available in Three.js*). For instance, we can create a simple tetrahedron (also see THREE.TetrahedronGeometry in this chapter) like this:

```
var vertices = [
    1,  1,  1,
   -1, -1,  1,
   -1,  1, -1,
```

```
    1, -1, -1
];

var indices = [
    2, 1, 0,
    0, 3, 2,
    1, 3, 0,
    2, 3, 1
];

polyhedron = createMesh(new THREE.PolyhedronGeometry(vertices, indices,
                    controls.radius, controls.detail));
```

To construct `THREE.PolyhedronGeometry`, **we pass in the** `vertices`, `indices`, `radius`, and `detail` properties. The resulting `THREE.PolyhedronGeometry` object is shown in the `10-basic-3d-geometries-polyhedron.html` **example (set type as Custom in the menu in the top-right corner):**

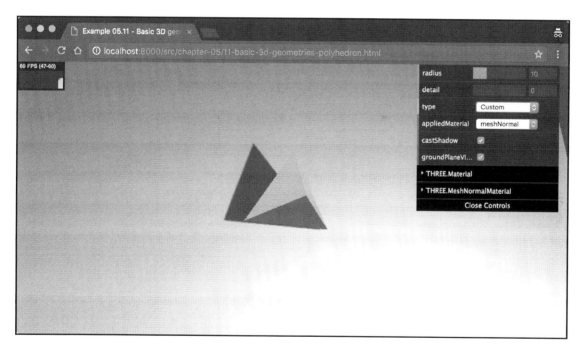

60 FPS (47-60)

When you create a polyhedron, you can pass in the following four properties:

Property	Mandatory	Description
vertices	Yes	These are the points that make up the polyhedron.
indices	Yes	These are the faces that need to be created from the vertices.
radius	No	This is the size of the polyhedron. This defaults to 1.
detail	No	With this property, you can add additional detail to the polyhedron. If you set this to 1, each triangle in the polyhedron will be split into four smaller triangles. If you set this to 2, those four smaller triangles will each be split into four smaller triangles once more, and so on.

The following screenshot shows the same custom mesh, but now with a higher detail:

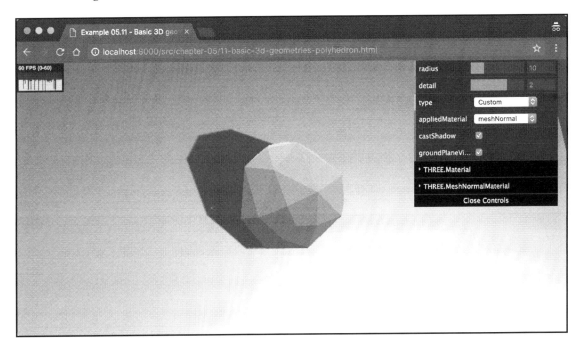

60 FPS (0-60)

At the beginning of this section, we mentioned that Three.js comes with a couple of polyhedrons out of the box. In the following subsections, we'll quickly show you these. All of these polyhedron types can be viewed by looking at the 09-basic-3d-geometries-polyhedron.html example.

THREE.IcosahedronGeometry

THREE.IcosahedronGeometry creates a polyhedron that has 20 identical triangular faces created from 12 vertices. When creating this polyhedron, all you need to specify are the radius and detail levels. This screenshot shows a polyhedron that was created by using THREE.IcosahedronGeometry:

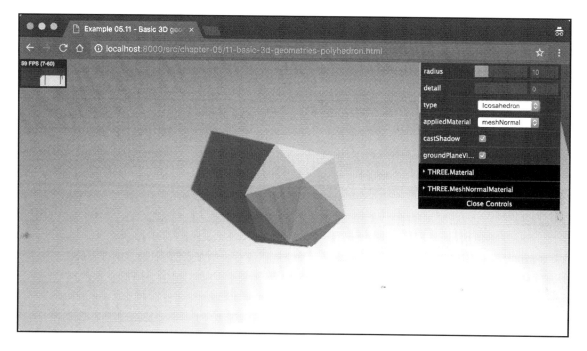

59 FPS (7-60)

THREE.TetrahedronGeometry

The tetrahedron is one of the simplest polyhedrons. This polyhedron only contains four triangular faces that are created from four vertices. You can create `THREE.TetrahedronGeometry` just like the other polyhedrons provided by Three.js, by specifying the `radius` and `detail` levels. Here's a screenshot that shows a tetrahedron that was created by using `THREE.TetrahedronGeometry`:

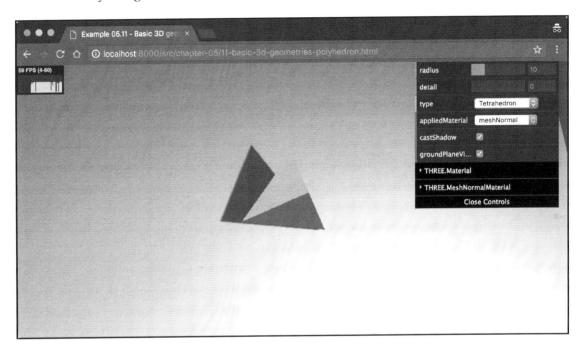

59 FPS (4-60)

THREE.OctahedronGeometry

Three.js also provides an implementation of an octahedron. As the name implies, this polyhedron has eight faces. These faces are created from six vertices. The following screenshot shows this geometry:

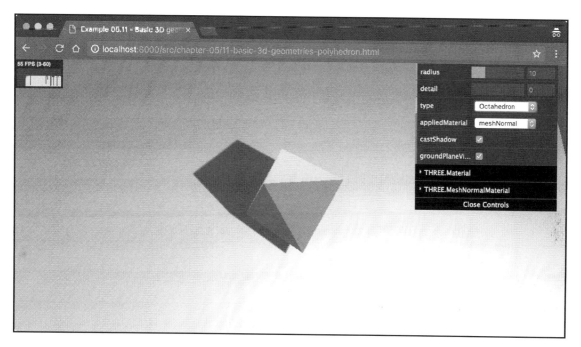

55 FPS (3-60)

THREE.DodecahedronGeometry

The final polyhedron geometry provided by Three.js is `THREE.DodecahedronGeometry`. This polyhedron has 12 faces. The following screenshot shows this geometry:

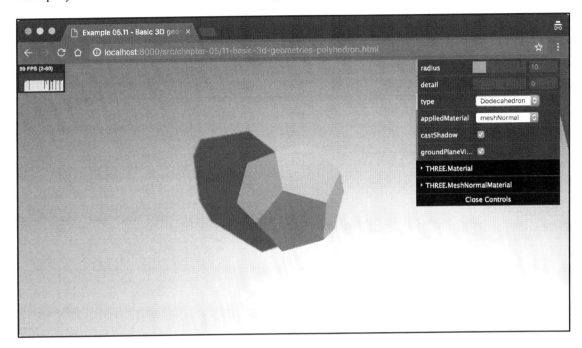

59 FPS (2-60)

Summary

In this chapter, we discussed all of the standard geometries Three.js has to offer. As you saw, there are a whole lot of geometries you can use right out of the box. To best learn how to use the geometries, experiment with these geometries. Use the examples in this chapter to get to know the properties you can use to customize the standard set of geometries available from Three.js. It is also a good thing that when you start with geometries, you can choose a basic material; don't go directly for the complex materials, but start simple with THREE.MeshBasicMaterial with the wireframe set to true, or THREE.MeshNormalMaterial. That way, you'll get a much better picture of the true shape of a geometry. For 2D shapes, it's important to remember that they are placed on the *x-y* plane. If you want to have a 2D shape horizontally, you'll have to rotate the mesh around the *x* axis for $-0.5 * PI$. And finally, take care that if you're rotating a 2D shape, or a 3D shape that is *open* (for example, a cylinder or a tube), remember to set the material to THREE.DoubleSide. If you don't do this, the inside or the back of your geometry won't be shown.

In this chapter, we focused on simple, straightforward meshes. Three.js also provides ways to create complex geometries, which we will cover in Chapter 6, *Advanced Geometries and Binary Operations*.

6

Advanced Geometries and Binary Operations

In Chapter 5, *Learning to Work with Geometries*, we showed you all the basic geometries provided by Three.js. Besides these basic geometries, Three.js also offers a set of more advanced and specialized objects. In this chapter, we'll show you these advanced geometries and cover the following subjects:

- How to use advanced geometries such as THREE.ConvexGeometry, THREE.LatheGeometry, and THREE.TubeGeometry.

- How to create 3D shapes from 2D shapes using THREE.ExtrudeGeometry. We'll do this based on a 2D shape drawn using functionality provided by Three.js, and we'll show an example where we create a 3D shape based on an externally loaded SVG image.

- If you want to create custom shapes yourself, you can easily amend the ones we've discussed in the previous chapters. Three.js, however, also offers a THREE.ParametricGeometry object. With this object, you can create a geometry based on a set of equations.

- Finally, we'll look at how you can create 3D text effects using THREE.TextGeometry.

- Additionally, we'll also show you how you can create new geometries from existing ones using binary operations provided by the Three.js extension, ThreeBSP.

We'll start with the first one from this list, THREE.ConvexGeometry.

THREE.ConvexGeometry

With THREE.ConvexGeometry, we can create a convex hull from a set of points. A convex hull is the minimal shape that encompasses all these points. The easiest way to understand this is by looking at an example. If you open up the 01-advanced-3d-geometries-convex.html example, you'll see the convex hull for a random set of points. The following screenshot shows this geometry:

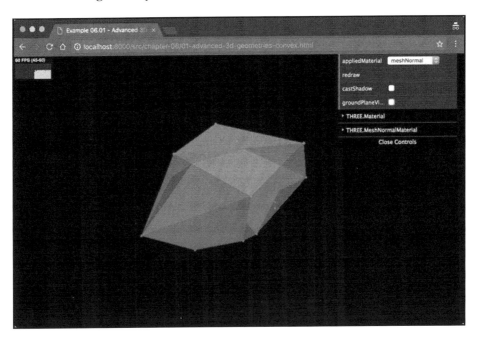

60 FPS (45-60)

In this example, we generate a random set of points, and based on these points, we create THREE.ConvexGeometry. In the example, you can click on **redraw**, which will generate 20 new points and draw the convex hull. If you try this for yourself, enable the material's transparency and set the opacity to a level below 1 to see the points that are used to create this geometry. These points are created as small THREE.SphereGeometry objects. THREE.ConvexGeometry isn't included in the standard Three.js distribution, so you have to include an additional JavaScript file to use this geometry. At the top of your HTML page, add the following:

```
<script src="../../libs/three/geometries/ConvexGeometry.js"></script>
```

To create `THREE.ConvexGeometry`, we need a set of points. The following code fragment shows how we do this:

```
var spGroup;
function generatePoints() {
  if (spGroup) scene.remove(spGroup)
  var points = [];
  for (var i = 0; i < 20; i++) {
    var randomX = -15 + Math.round(Math.random() * 30);
    var randomY = -15 + Math.round(Math.random() * 30);
    var randomZ = -15 + Math.round(Math.random() * 30);
    points.push(new THREE.Vector3(randomX, randomY, randomZ));
  }

  spGroup = new THREE.Object3D();
  var material = new THREE.MeshBasicMaterial({
    color: 0xff0000,
    transparent: false
  });
  points.forEach(function (point) {

    var spGeom = new THREE.SphereGeometry(0.2);
    var spMesh = new THREE.Mesh(spGeom, material);
    spMesh.position.copy(point);
    spGroup.add(spMesh);
  });
  // add the points as a group to the scene
  scene.add(spGroup);
}
```

As you can see in this snippet of code, we create 20 random points (`THREE.Vector3`), which we push into an array. Next, we iterate this array and create `THREE.SphereGeometry`, whose position we set to one of these points (`position.copy(point)`). All the points are added to a group, so we can rotate them easily by just rotating the group.

Once you have this set of points, creating `THREE.ConvexGeometry` from them is very easy, as shown in the following code snippet:

```
// use the same points to create a convexgeometry
var convexGeometry = new THREE.ConvexGeometry(points);

// if we want a smooth rendered object, we have to compute the vertex and
face normals
convexGeometry.computeVertexNormals();
convexGeometry.computeFaceNormals();
convexGeometry.normalsNeedUpdate = true;
```

An array containing vertices (of the `THREE.Vector3` type) is the only argument `THREE.ConvexGeometry` takes. If you look at this code, you can see that we explicitly call `computeVertexNormals` and `computeFaceNormals`. The vertex and face normal vectors help Three.js render the geometries as a smooth object. Most geometries already do this when they are created. For this geometry, however, this isn't done when the object is created so we need to call this explicitly.

The next complex geometry is `THREE.LatheGeometry`, which can be used to create vase-like shapes.

THREE.LatheGeometry

`THREE.LatheGeometry` allows you to create shapes from a smooth curve. This curve is defined by a number of points (also called knots) and is most often called a spline. This spline is rotated around the central z axis of the object and results in vase-like and bell-like shapes. Once again, the easiest way to understand what `THREE.LatheGeometry` looks like is by looking at an example. This geometry is shown in `02-advanced-3d-geometries-lathe.html`. The following screenshot taken from the example shows this geometry:

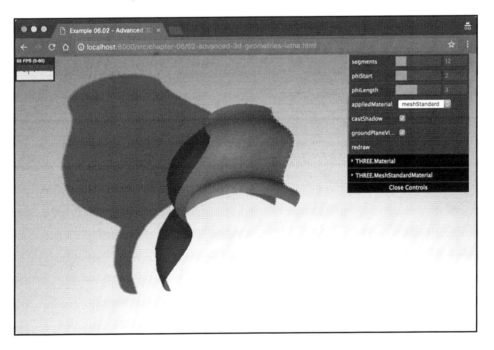

In the preceding screenshot, you can see the points used to create this geometry as a set of small red spheres. The positions of these points are passed in to THREE.LatheGeometry, together with a couple of other arguments. Before we look at all the arguments, let's look at the code used to create the individual points and how THREE.LatheGeometry uses this points:

```
function generatePoints(segments, phiStart, phiLength) {

  var points = [];
  var height = 5;
  var count = 30;
  for (var i = 0; i < count; i++) {
    points.push(new THREE.Vector3((Math.sin(i * 0.2) + Math.cos(i
      * 0.3)) * height + 12, 0, ( i - count ) + count / 2));
  }

  ...

  // use the same points to create a LatheGeometry
  var latheGeometry = new THREE.LatheGeometry (points, segments,
    phiStart, phiLength);
  latheMesh = createMesh(latheGeometry);
  scene.add(latheMesh);
}
```

In this piece of JavaScript, you can see that we generate 30 points whose *x* coordinate is based on a combination of sine and cosine functions, while the *z* coordinate is based on the i and count variables. This creates a spline visualized by the red dots in the preceding screenshot.

Based on these points, we can create THREE.LatheGeometry. Besides the array of vertices, THREE.LatheGeometry takes a couple of other arguments. The following table lists all the arguments:

Property	Mandatory	Description
points	Yes	These are the points that make up the spline used to generate the bell/vase shape.
segments	No	These are the number of segments used when creating the shape. The higher this number, the more *round* and *smooth* the resulting shape will be. The default value for this is 12.
phiStart	No	This determines where to start on a circle when generating the shape. This can range from 0 to 2*PI. The default value is 0.

phiLength	No	This defines how fully generated the shape is. For instance, a quarter shape will be `0.5*PI`. The default value is the full `360` degrees or `2*PI`.

In the next section, we'll look at an alternative way of creating geometries by extracting a 3D geometry from a 2D shape.

Creating a geometry by extruding

Three.js provides a couple of ways in which we can extrude a 2D shape to a 3D shape. By extruding, we mean stretching out a 2D shape along its z axis to convert it to 3D. For instance, if we extrude a `THREE.CircleGeometry`, we get a shape that looks like a cylinder, and if we extrude `THREE.PlaneGeometry`, we get a cube-like shape. The most versatile way of extruding a shape is using the `THREE.ExtrudeGeometry` object.

THREE.ExtrudeGeometry

With `THREE.ExtrudeGeometry`, you can create a 3D object from a 2D shape. Before we dive into the details of this geometry, let's first look at an example: `03-extrude-geometry.html`. The following screenshot taken from the example shows this geometry:

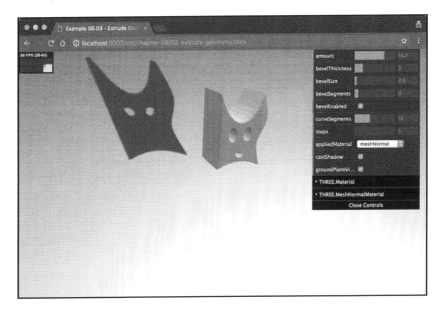

In this example, we took the 2D shape we created in the previous chapter and used `THREE.ExtrudeGeometry` to convert it to 3D. As you can see in this screenshot, the shape is extruded along the z axis, which results in a 3D shape. The code to create `THREE.ExtrudeGeometry` is very easy:

```
var options = {
    amount: controls.amount,
    bevelThickness: controls.bevelThickness,
    bevelSize: controls.bevelSize,
    bevelSegments: controls.bevelSegments,
    bevelEnabled: controls.bevelEnabled,
    curveSegments: controls.curveSegments,
    steps: controls.steps
};

var geom = new THREE.ExtrudeGeometry(drawShape(), options);
```

In this code, we created the shape with the `drawShape()` function just as we did in the previous chapter. This shape is passed on to the `THREE.ExtrudeGeometry` constructor together with an `options` object. With the `options` object, you can define exactly how the shape should be extruded. The following table explains the options you can pass in to `THREE.ExtrudeGeometry`:

Property	Mandatory	Description
shapes	Yes	One or more shapes (`THREE.Shape` objects) are required to extrude the geometry from. See the preceding chapter on how to create such a shape.
amount	No	This determines how far (the depth) the shape should be extruded. The default value is `100`.
bevelThickness	No	This determines the depth of the bevel. The bevel is the rounded corner between the front and back faces and the extrusion. This value defines how deep into the shape the bevel goes. The default value is `6`.
bevelSize	No	This determines the height of the bevel. This is added to the normal height of the shape. The default value is `bevelThickness - 2`.
bevelSegments	No	This defines the number of segments that will be used by the bevel. The more the number of segments used, the smoother the bevel will look. The default value is `3`.
bevelEnabled	No	If this is set to `true`, a bevel is added. The default value is `true`.

curveSegments	No	This determines how many segments will be used when extruding the curves of shapes. The more the number of segments used, the smoother the curves will look. The default value is 12.
steps	No	This defines the number of segments into the extrusion will be divided along its depth. The default value is 1. A higher value will result in more individual faces.
extrudePath	No	This is the path (THREE.CurvePath) along which the shape should be extruded. If this isn't specified, the shape is extruded along the z axis.
uvGenerator	No	When you use a texture with your material, the UV mapping determines what part of a texture is used for a specific face. With the uvGenerator property, you can pass in your own object that will create the UV settings for the faces that are created for the shapes that are passed in. More information on UV settings can be found in Chapter 10, *Loading and Working with Textures*. If none are specified, THREE.ExtrudeGeometry.WorldUVGenerator is used.

If you want to use a different material for the face and the sides, you can pass in an array of materials to the THREE.Mesh. The first material passed in will be applied to the face, and the second material will be used for the sides. You can experiment with these options using the menu from the 03-extrude-geometry.html example. In this example, we extruded the shape along its z axis. As you would have seen in the options, you can also extrude a shape along a path with the extrudePath option. In the following geometry, THREE.TubeGeometry, we'll do just that.

THREE.TubeGeometry

THREE.TubeGeometry creates a tube that extrudes along a 3D spline. You specify the path using a number of vertices, and THREE.TubeGeometry will create the tube. An example that you can experiment with can be found in the sources for this chapter (04-extrude-tube.html). The following screenshot shows this example:

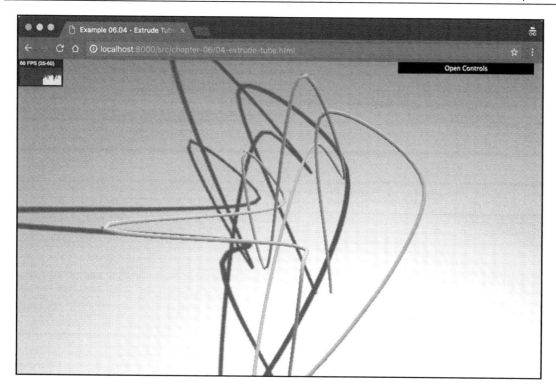

As you can see in this example, we generate a number of random points and use those points to draw the tube. With the controls in the upper-right corner, we can define how the tube looks or generate a new tube by clicking on the **newPoints** button. The code needed to create a tube is very simple, as follows:

```
var points = [];
for (var i = 0 ; i < controls.numberOfPoints ; i++) {
  var randomX = -20 + Math.round(Math.random() * 50);
  var randomY = -15 + Math.round(Math.random() * 40);
  var randomZ = -20 + Math.round(Math.random() * 40);

  points.push(new THREE.Vector3(randomX, randomY, randomZ));
}
var tubeGeometry = new THREE.TubeGeometry(new
THREE.CatmullRomCurve3(points), segments, radius, radiusSegments, closed);

var tubeMesh = createMesh(tubeGeometry);
scene.add(tubeMesh);
```

What we need to do first is get a set of vertices of the `THREE.Vector3` type just like we did for `THREE.ConvexGeometry` and `THREE.LatheGeometry`. Before we can use these points, however, to create the tube, we first need to convert these points to a `THREE.CatmullRomCurve3`. In other words, we need to define a smooth curve through the points we defined. We can do this simply by passing in the array of vertices to the constructor of `THREE.CatmullRomCurve3`. With this curve and the other arguments (which we'll explain in a bit), we can create the tube and add it to the scene. `THREE.TubeGeometry` takes some other arguments besides `THREE.SplineCurve3`. The following table lists all the arguments for `THREE.TubeGeometry`:

Property	Mandatory	Description
path	Yes	This is `THREE.SplineCurve3` that describes the path this tube should follow.
segments	No	These are the segments used to build up the tube. The default value is `64`. The longer the path, the more segments you should specify.
radius	No	This is the radius of the tube. The default value is `1`.
radiusSegments	No	This is the number of segments to be used along the length of the tube. The default value is `8`. The more you use, the more *round* the tube will look.
closed	No	If this is set to `true`, the start of the tube and the end will be connected together. The default value is `false`.

The last extrude example we'll show in this chapter isn't really a different geometry. In the next section, we'll show you how you can use `THREE.ExtrudeGeometry` to create extrusions from existing SVG paths.

Extruding from SVG

When we discussed `THREE.ShapeGeometry`, we mentioned that SVG follows pretty much the same approach of drawing shapes. SVG very closely matches how Three.js handles shapes. In this section, we'll look at how you can use a small library from `https://github.com/asutherland/d3-threeD` to convert SVG paths to a Three.js shape (Three.js also provides a specific `THREE.SVGLoader`, which is explained in `Chapter 8, Creating and Loading Advanced Meshes and Geometries`). For the `05-extrude-svg.html` example, we've taken an SVG drawing of the Batman logo and used `ExtrudeGeometry` to convert it to 3D, as shown in the following screenshot:

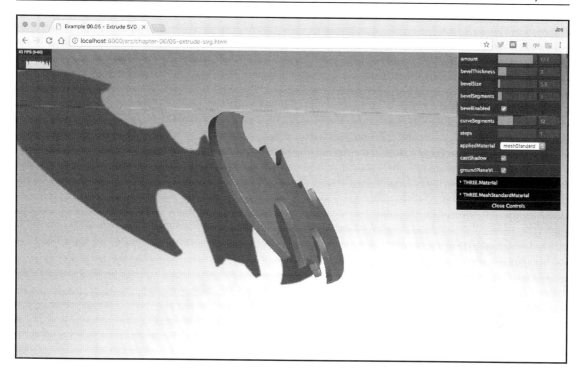

43 FPS (6-60)

First, let's look at what the original SVG code looks like (you can also see this for yourself when looking at the source code for this example):

```
<svg version="1.0" xmlns="http://www.w3.org/2000/svg"
   xmlns:xlink="http://www.w3.org/1999/xlink" x="0px" y="0px"
   width="1152px" height="1152px" xml:space="preserve">
<g>
<path  id="batman-path" style="fill:rgb(0,0,0);" d="M 261.135
   114.535 C 254.906 116.662 247.491 118.825 244.659 119.344 C
   229.433 122.131 177.907 142.565 151.973 156.101 C 111.417
   177.269 78.9808 203.399 49.2992 238.815 C 41.0479 248.66
   26.5057 277.248 21.0148 294.418 C 14.873 313.624 15.3588
   357.341 21.9304 376.806 C 29.244 398.469 39.6107 416.935
   52.0865 430.524 C 58.2431 437.23 63.3085 443.321 63.3431
   444.06 ... 261.135 114.535 "/>
</g>
</svg>
```

Unless you're an SVG guru, this will probably mean nothing to you. Basically though, what you see here are a set of drawing instructions. For instance, C 277.987 119.348 279.673 116.786 279.673 115.867 tells the browser to draw a cubic Bezier curve, and L 489.242 111.787 tells us that we should draw a line to that specific position. Luckily though, we won't have to write the code to interpret this ourselves. With the d3-threeD library, we can convert this automatically. This library was originally created to be used together with the excellent D3.js library, but with some small adaptations, we can also use this specific functionality standalone.

SVG is an XML-based standard that can be used to create vector-based 2D images for the web. This is an open standard that is supported by all of the modern browsers. Directly working with SVG and manipulating it from JavaScript, however, isn't very straightforward. Luckily, there are a couple of open source JavaScript libraries that make working with SVG a lot easier. Paper.js, Snap.js, D3.js, and Raphael.js are some of the best.

The following code fragment shows how we can load in the SVG you saw earlier, convert it to THREE.ExtrudeGeometry, and show it on screen:

```
function drawShape() {
    var svgString = document.querySelector("#batman-path").getAttribute("d");
    var shape = transformSVGPathExposed(svgString);
    return shape;
}

var options = {
    amount: 10,
    bevelThickness: 2,
    bevelSize: 1,
    bevelSegments: 3,
    bevelEnabled: true,
    curveSegments: 12,
    steps: 1
};

shape = createMesh(new THREE.ExtrudeGeometry(drawShape(), options));
```

In this code fragment, you'll see a call to the `transformSVGPathExposed` function. This function is provided by the d3-threeD library and takes an SVG string as an argument. We get this SVG string directly from the SVG element with the following expression: `document.querySelector("#batman-path").getAttribute("d")`. In SVG, the `d` attribute contains the `path` statements used to draw a shape. Add a nice-looking shiny material and a spotlight and you've recreated this example.

The last geometry we'll discuss in this section is `THREE.ParametricGeometry`. With this geometry, you can specify a couple of functions that are used to programmatically create geometries.

THREE.ParametricGeometry

With `THREE.ParametricGeometry`, you can create a geometry based on an equation. Before we dive into our own example, a good thing to start with is to look at the examples already provided by Three.js. When you download the Three.js distribution, you get the `examples/js/ParametricGeometries.js` file. In this file, you can find a couple of examples of equations you can use together with `THREE.ParametricGeometry`. The most basic example is the function to create a plane:

```
plane: function ( width, height ) {
    return function ( u, v, optionalTarget ) {
        var result = optionalTarget || new THREE.Vector3();
        var x = u * width;
        var y = 0;
        var z = v * height;
        return result.set( x, y, z );
    };
}
```

This function is called by `THREE.ParametricGeometry`. The u and v values will range from 0 to 1 and will be called a large number of times for all the values from 0 to 1. In this example, the u value is used to determine the *x* coordinate of the vector and the v value is used to determine the *z* coordinate. When this is run, you'll have a basic plane with a width of `width` and a depth of `depth`.

In our example, we do something similar. However, instead of creating a flat plane, we create a wave-like pattern, as you can see in the `06-parametric-geometries.html` example. The following screenshot shows this example:

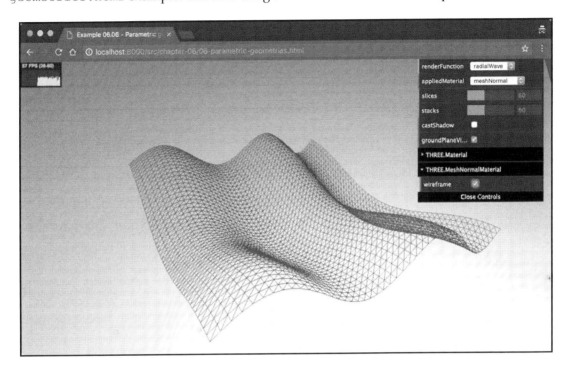

57 FPS (26-60)

To create this shape, we passed the following function to `THREE.ParametricGeometry`:

```
radialWave = function (u, v, optionalTarget) {

    var result = optionalTarget || new THREE.Vector3();
    var r = 50;

    var x = Math.sin(u) * r;
    var z = Math.sin(v / 2) * 2 * r;
    var y = (Math.sin(u * 4 * Math.PI) + Math.cos(v * 2 * Math.PI)) * 2.8;

    return result.set( x, y, z );
};

var mesh = createMesh(new THREE.ParametricGeometry(radialWave, 120, 120,
false));
```

As you can see in this example, with a few lines of code, we can create really interesting geometries. In this example, you can also see the arguments we can pass to THREE.ParametricGeometry. These are explained in the following table:

Property	Mandatory	Description
function	Yes	This is the function that defines the position of each vertex based on the u and v values provided.
slices	Yes	This defines the number of parts the u value should be divided into.
stacks	Yes	This defines the number of parts the v value should be divided into.

By changing the function, we can easily use the exact same approach to render a completely different object:

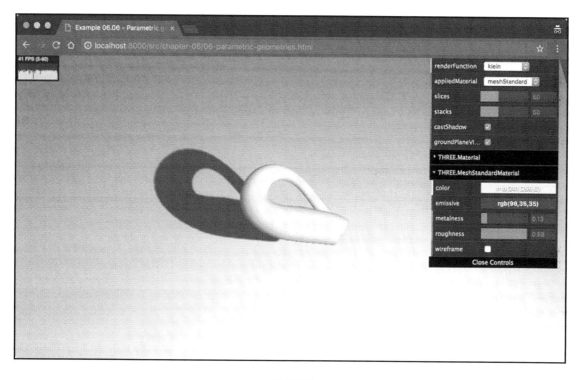

40 FPS (5-60)

A final note on how to use the `slices` and `stacks` properties before moving on to the final part of this chapter. We mentioned that the u and v properties are passed into the `function` argument provided, and that the values of these two properties range from 0 to 1. With the `slices` and `stacks` properties, we can define how often the passed-in function is called. If, for instance, we set `slices` to 5 and `stacks` to 4, the function will be called with the following values:

```
u:0/5,  v:0/4
u:1/5,  v:0/4
u:2/5,  v:0/4
u:3/5,  v:0/4
u:4/5,  v:0/4
u:5/5,  v:0/4
u:0/5,  v:1/4
u:1/5,  v:1/4
...
u:5/5,  v:3/4
u:5/5,  v:4/4
```

So, the higher this value, the more vertices you get to specify and the smoother your created geometry will be. You can use the menu in the top-right corner of the `06-parametric-geometries.html` example to see this effect.

For more examples, you can look at the `examples/js/ParametricGeometries.js` file in the Three.js distribution. This file contains functions to create the following geometries:

- Klein bottle
- Plane
- Flat Mobius strip
- 3D Mobius strip
- Tube
- Torus knot
- Sphere
- Plane

The last part of this section deals with creating 3D text objects.

Creating 3D text

In the next part of this chapter, we'll have a quick look at how you can create 3D text effects. First, we'll look at how to render text using the fonts provided by Three.js, and after that, we'll have a quick look at how you can use your own fonts for this.

Rendering text

Rendering text in Three.js is very easy. All you have to do is define the font you want to use and use the same extrude properties we saw when we discussed `THREE.ExtrudeGeometry`. The following screenshot shows the `07-text-geometry.html` example of how to render text in Three.js:

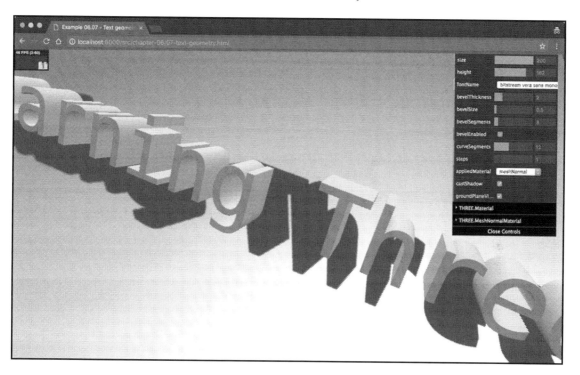

46 FPS (2-60)

The code required to create this 3D text is as follows:

```
var loadedFont;
var fontload = new THREE.FontLoader();
  fontload.load(
'../../assets/fonts/bitstream_vera_sans_mono_roman.typeface.json',
        function ( response ) {
    loadedFont = response;
    render();
});

var options = {
  size: 90,
  height: 90,
  font: loadedFont,
  bevelThickness: 2,
  bevelSize: 4,
  bevelSegments: 3,
  bevelEnabled: true,
  curveSegments: 12,
  steps: 1
};

// the createMesh is the same function we saw earlier
text = createMesh(new THREE.TextGeometry("Learning Three.js", options));
scene.add(text);
```

In this code fragment, you can see that we first have to load the font. For this, Three.js provides THREE.FontLoader(), where we provide the name of the font to load, and once loaded, Three.js will use the callback with the loaded font (response). In this example, we just assign it to a variable, and call the render function. The font that we loaded is also assigned to the options object we use in the constructor of the THREE.TextGeometry. The options we can pass into THREE.TextGeometry match those that we can pass in THREE.ExtrudeGeometry, plus a couple of ones specifically for THREE.TextGeometry.

Let's look at all the options we can specify for `THREE.TextGeometry`:

Property	Mandatory	Description
size	No	This is the size of the text. The default value is `100`.
height	No	This is the length (depth) of the extrusion. The default value is `50`.
font	Yes	The loaded font to use for the text.
bevelThickness	No	This is the depth of the bevel. The bevel is the rounded corner between the front and back faces and the extrusion. The default value is `10`.
bevelSize	No	This is the height of the bevel. The default value is `8`.
bevelSegments	No	This defines the number of segments that will be used by the bevel. The more segments there are, the smoother the bevel will look. The default value is `3`.
bevelEnabled	No	If this is set to `true`, a bevel is added. The default value is `false`.
curveSegments	No	This defines the number of segments used when extruding the curves of shapes. The more segments there are, the smoother the curves will look. The default value is `4`.
steps	No	This defines the number of segments the extrusion will be divided into. The default value is `1`.
extrudePath	No	This is the path along which the shape should be extruded. If this isn't specified, the shape is extruded along the z axis.
uvGenerator	No	When you use a texture with your material, the UV mapping determines what part of a texture is used for a specific face. With the `UVGenerator` property, you can pass in your own object that will create the UV settings for the faces that are created for the passed-in shapes. More information on UV settings can be found in Chapter 10, *Loading and Working with Textures*. If none are specified, `THREE.ExtrudeGeometry.WorldUVGenerator` is used.

The fonts that are included in Three.js are also added to the sources for this book. You can find them in the `assets/fonts` folder. Since `THREE.TextGeometry` is also `THREE.ExtrudeGeometry`, the same approach applies if you want to use different material for the front and the sides of the material. If you pass in an array of two materials when creating `THREE.Mesh`, Three.js will apply the first material to the front of the text, and the second one to the sides.

> If you want to render fonts in 2D, for instance, to use them as a texture for a material, you shouldn't use `THREE.TextGeometry`. `THREE.TextGeometry`, which internally uses `THREE.ExtrudeGeometry` to build the 3D text, and the JavaScript fonts introduce a lot of overhead. Rendering a simple 2D font is better. You can do this by using the HTML5 canvas. With `context.font`, you can set the font to be used, and with `context.fillText`, you can output text to the canvas. You can then use this canvas as input for your texture. We will show you how to do this in `Chapter 10`, *Loading and Working with Textures*.

It's also possible to use other fonts with this geometry, but you first need to convert them to JavaScript. How to do this is shown in the next section.

Adding custom fonts

There are a couple of fonts provided by Three.js that you can use in your scenes. These fonts are based on the fonts provided by the **TypeFace.js** library. TypeFace.js is a library that can convert TrueType and OpenType fonts to JavaScript. The resulting JavaScript file or JSON file can be included in your page, and the font can then be used in Three.js. In older versions, the JavaScript file was used, but in later Three.js versions, Three.js switched to using the JSON file.

To convert an existing OpenType or TrueType font, you can use the web page
at http://gero3.github.io/facetype.js:

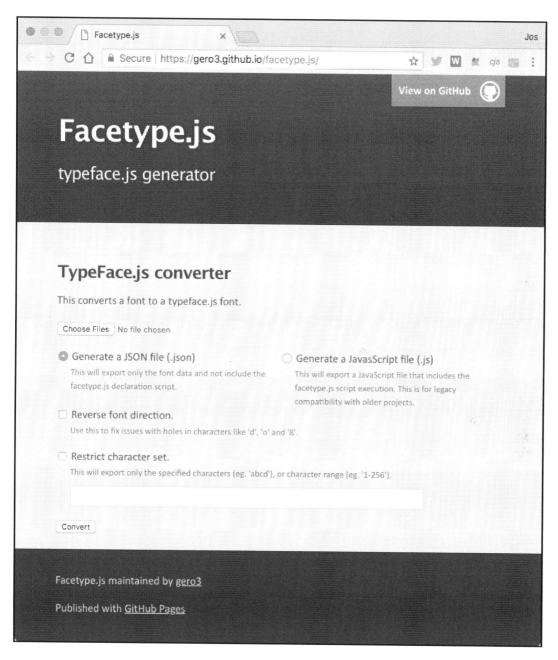

On this page, you can upload a font, and it will be converted to JSON for you. Note that this doesn't work for all types of fonts. The simpler the font (more straight lines), the better the chance that it will be rendered correctly when used in Three.js. The resulting file looks like this, where each of the characters (or glyphs) is described:

```
{"glyphs":{"¦":{"x_min":359,"x_max":474,"ha":836,"o":"m 474 971 l 474 457 l
359 457 l 359 971 l 474 971 m 474 277 l 474 -237 l 359 -237 l 359 277 l 474
277 "},"Ž":{"x_min":106,"x_max":793,"ha":836,"o":"m 121 1013 l 778 1013 l
778 908 l 249 115 l 793 115 l 793 0 l 106 0 l 106 104 l 620 898 l 121 898 l
121 1013 m 353 1109 l 211 1289 l 305 1289 l 417 1168 l 530 1289 l 625 1289
l 482 1109 l 353 1109 "},"Á":{"x_min":25,"x_max":811,"ha":836,"o":"m 417
892 l 27 ....
```

Once you've got the JSON file, you can use the `THREE.FontLoader` (as we've shown previously) to load this font and assign it to the font property of the options you can pass into a `THREE.TextGeometry`. In the next part of this chapter, we'll introduce the ThreeBSP library to create very interesting-looking geometries using binary operations: `intersect`, `subtract`, and `union`.

Using binary operations to combine meshes

In this section, we'll look at a different way of creating geometries. In this chapter so far, and in the previous `Chapter 5`, *Learning to Work with Geometries*, we used the default geometries provided by Three.js to create interesting-looking geometries. With the default set of properties, you can create beautiful models, but you are limited to what Three.js provides. In this section, we'll show you how you can combine these standard geometries to create new ones-a technique known as **Constructive Solid Geometry** (**CSG**). To do this, we use the Three.js extension ThreeBSP, which you can find online at `https://github.com/skalnik/ThreeBSP`. This additional library provides the following three functions:

Name	Description
intersect	This function allows you to create a new geometry based on the intersection of two existing geometries. The area where both geometries overlap will define the shape of this new geometry.
union	The `union` function can be used to combine two geometries and create a new one. You can compare this with the `mergeGeometry` functionality we'll look at in `Chapter 8`, *Creating and Loading Advanced Meshes and Geometries*.
subtract	The `subtract` function is the opposite of the `union` function. You can create a new geometry by removing the overlapping area from the first geometry.

In the following sections, we'll look at each of these functions in more detail. The following screenshot shows an example of what you can create by just using the `union` and `subtract` functionalities one after the other:

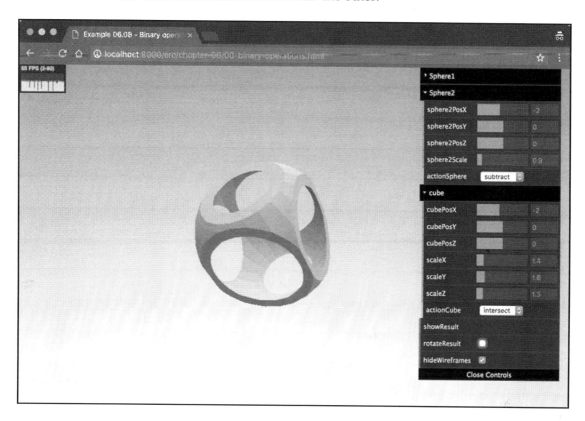

55 FPS (2-60)

To use this library, we need to include it in our page. This library is written in CoffeeScript, a more user-friendly variant of JavaScript. To get this working, we have two options. We can add the CoffeeScript file and compile it on the fly, or we can precompile it to JavaScript and include it directly. For the first approach, we need to do the following:

```
<script type="text/javascript" src="../libs/coffee-script.js">
    </script><script type="text/coffeescript" src="../libs/ThreeBSP.coffee">
    </script>
```

The `ThreeBSP.coffee` file contains the functionality we need for this example, and `coffee-script.js` can interpret the Coffee language used for ThreeBSP. A final step we need to take is make sure the `ThreeBSP.coffee` file has been parsed completely before we start using the ThreeBSP functionality. For this, we add the following to the bottom of the file:

```
<script type="text/coffeescript">
  onReady();
</script>
```

We rename our initial `onload` function to `onReady` like this:

```
function onReady() {
  // Three.js code
}
```

If we precompile CoffeeScript to JavaScript using the CoffeeScript command-line tool, we can include the resulting JavaScript file directly. Before we can do this, though, we need to install CoffeeScript. You can follow the installation instructions on the CoffeeScript website at `http://coffeescript.org/`. Once you've installed CoffeeScript, you can use the following command line to convert the CoffeeScript ThreeBSP file to JavaScript:

```
coffee --compile ThreeBSP.coffee
```

This command creates a `ThreeBSP.js` file that we can include in our example just as we do with the other JavaScript file. In our examples, we use this second approach because it'll load quicker than compiling the CoffeeScript each time we load the page. For this, all we need to do is add the following to the top of our HTML page:

```
<script type="text/javascript" src="../libs/ThreeBSP.js"></script>
```

Now that the ThreeBSP library is loaded, we can use the functions it provides.

The subtract function

Before we start with the `subtract` function, there is one important step you need to keep in mind. These three functions use the absolute position of the mesh for calculations. So, if you group meshes together or use multiple materials before applying these functions, you'll probably get strange results. For the best and most predictable result, make sure you're working with ungrouped meshes.

Let's start by demonstrating the subtract functionality. For this, we've provided an example, 08-binary-operations.html. With this example, you can experiment with the three operations. When you first open the example on binary operations, you'll see something like the following start screen:

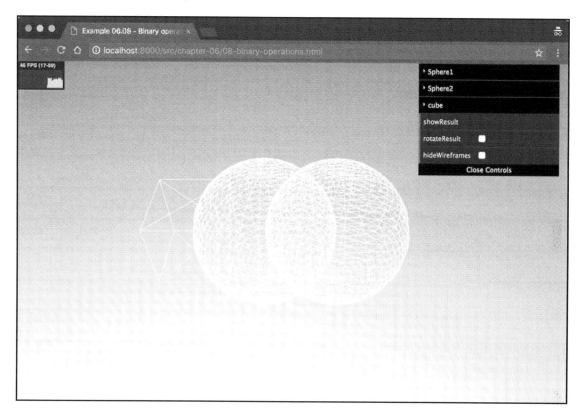

There are three wireframes: a cube and two spheres. **Sphere1**, the center sphere, is the object on which all operations are executed, **Sphere2** is on the right-hand side, and **cube** is on the left-hand side. On **Sphere2** and **cube**, you can define one of four actions: **subtract**, **union**, **intersect**, and **none** (which just resets the scene to the starting point). These actions are applied from the point of view of **Sphere1**. When we set **Sphere2** to subtract and select **showResult** (and hide the wireframes), the result will show **Sphere1** minus the area where **Sphere1** and **Sphere2** overlap.

 A few of these operations might take a couple of seconds to complete after you've pushed the **showResult** button, so be patient while the *busy* indicator is visible.

The following screenshot shows the resulting action of a sphere after subtracting another sphere:

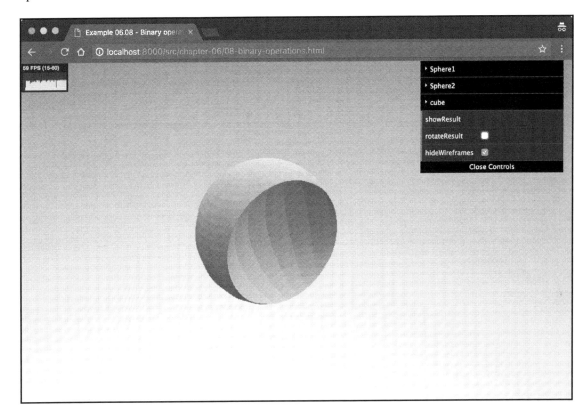

You can see that area where the right sphere overlaps the central sphere is removed (or subtracted). In this example, first the action defined for **Sphere2** is executed, and next, the action for **Cube** is executed. So, if we subtract both **Sphere2** and **Cube** (which we scale a bit along the *x* axis), we get the following result:

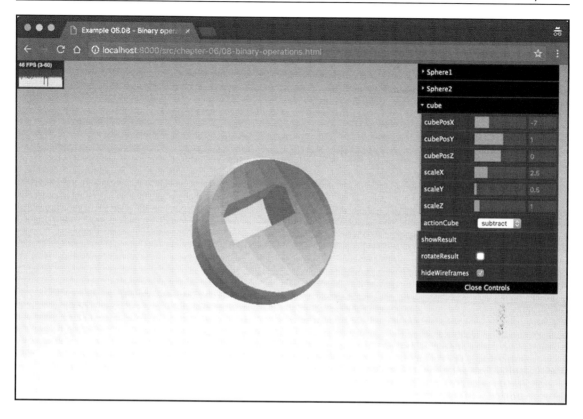

The best way to understand the subtract functionality is to just play around with the example. The ThreeBSP code to accomplish this is very simple and, in this example, is implemented in the redrawResult function, which we call whenever the **showResult** button from the example is clicked on:

```
function redrawResult() {
  scene.remove(result);
  var sphere1BSP = new ThreeBSP(sphere1);
  var sphere2BSP = new ThreeBSP(sphere2);
  var cube2BSP = new ThreeBSP(cube);

  var resultBSP;

  // first do the sphere
  switch (controls.actionSphere) {
    case "subtract":
      resultBSP = sphere1BSP.subtract(sphere2BSP);
    break;
    case "intersect":
```

```
        resultBSP = sphere1BSP.intersect(sphere2BSP);
      break;
      case "union":
        resultBSP = sphere1BSP.union(sphere2BSP);
      break;
      case "none": // noop;
    }

    // next do the cube
    if (!resultBSP) resultBSP = sphere1BSP;
    switch (controls.actionCube) {
      case "subtract":
        resultBSP = resultBSP.subtract(cube2BSP);
      break;
      case "intersect":
        resultBSP = resultBSP.intersect(cube2BSP);
      break;
      case "union":
        resultBSP = resultBSP.union(cube2BSP);
      break;
      case "none": // noop;
    }


    if (controls.actionCube === "none" && controls.actionSphere ===
      "none") {
    // do nothing
    } else {
      result = resultBSP.toMesh();
      result.geometry.computeFaceNormals();
      result.geometry.computeVertexNormals();
      scene.add(result);
    }
  }
```

The first thing we do in this code is wrap our meshes (the wireframes you can see) in a ThreeBSP object. This allows us to apply the subtract, intersect, and union functions on these objects. Now, we can just call the specific function we want on the ThreeBSP object wrapped around the center sphere (sphere1BSP), and the result from this function will contain all the information we need to create a new mesh. To create this mesh, we just call the toMesh() function on the sphere1BSP object. On the resulting object, we have to make sure that all the normals are computed correctly by first calling computeFaceNormals and then calling computeVertexNormals().

These compute functions need to be called since by running one of the binary operations, the vertices and faces of the geometry are changed and this affects the normals of the faces. Explicitly recalculating them will make sure your new object is shaded smoothly (when shading on the material has been set to `THREE.SmoothShading`) and rendered correctly. Finally, we add the result to the scene.

For `intersect` and `union`, we use exactly the same approach.

The intersect function

With everything we explained in the previous section, there isn't much left to explain for the `intersect` function. With this function, only the part of the meshes that overlap is left. The following screenshot is an example where both the sphere and the cube are set to **intersect**:

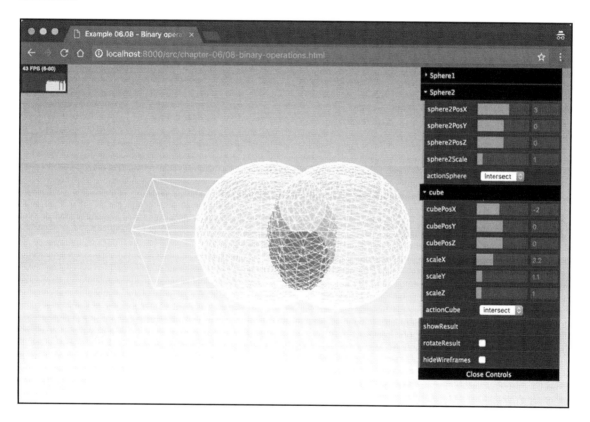

If you look at the example and play around with the settings, you'll see that it's very easy to create these kinds of objects. And remember, this can be applied to every mesh you can create, even the complex ones we saw in this chapter, such as `THREE.ParametricGeometry` and `THREE.TextGeometry`.

The `subtract` and `intersect` functions work well together. The example we showed at the beginning of this section was created by first subtracting a smaller sphere to create a hollow sphere. After that, we used the cube to intersect with this hollow sphere to get the following result (a hollow cube with rounded corners):

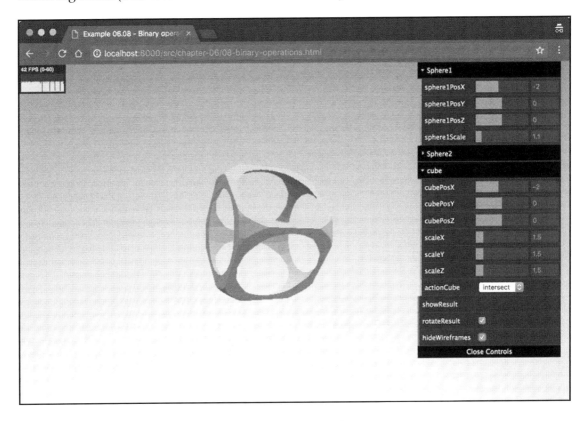

The last function provided by ThreeBSP is the `union` function.

The union function

The final function is the least interesting one of those offered by ThreeBSP. With this function, we can combine two meshes to create a new one. So, when we apply this to the two spheres and the cube, we'll get a single object-a result of the union function:

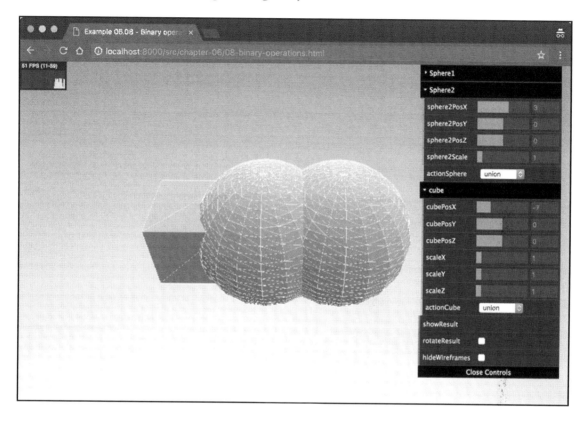

This is not really that useful because this functionality is also provided by Three.js (see Chapter 8, *Creating and Loading Advanced Meshes and Geometries*, where we explain how to use THREE.Geometry.merge), which also offers slightly better performance. If you enable rotation, you can see that this **union** is applied from the perspective of the center sphere since it is rotating around the center of that sphere. The same applies to the other two operations.

Summary

We saw a lot in this chapter. We introduced a couple of advanced geometries and even showed you how you can create interesting-looking geometries using a couple of simple binary operations. We showed you how you can create really beautiful shapes using advanced geometries such as `THREE.ConvexGeometry`, `THREE.TubeGeometry`, and `THREE.LatheGeometry` and how can you experiment with these geometries to get the results you're looking for. A very nice feature is that we can also convert existing SVG paths to Three.js. Remember, though, that you still might need to fine-tune the paths using tools such as GIMP, Adobe Illustrator, or Inkscape.

If you want to create 3D text, Three.js provides the `THREE.TextGeometry`, where you can pass in a font that you want to use. Three.js comes with a couple of fonts, but you can also create your own fonts. However, remember that complex fonts often won't convert correctly. And finally, with ThreeBSP, you have access to three binary operations you can apply to your mesh: `union`, `subtract`, and `intersect`. With `union`, you combine two meshes; with `subtract`, you remove the overlapping part of the meshes from the source mesh; and with `intersect`, only the overlapping part is kept.

Until now, we looked at solid (or wireframe) geometries, where vertices are connected to each other to form faces. In the upcoming chapter, we'll look at an alternative way of visualizing geometries using something called particles. With particles, we don't render complete geometries — we just render the vertices as points in space. This allows you to create great-looking 3D effects that perform well.

7
Points and Sprites

In previous chapters, we discussed the most important concepts, objects, and APIs that Three.js has to offer. In this chapter, we'll look into the only concept we've skipped until now: points and sprites. With `THREE.Points` (sometimes also called sprites), it is very easy to create many small objects that you can use to simulate rain, snow, smoke, and other interesting effects. For instance, you can render individual geometries as a set of points and control these points separately. In this chapter, we'll explore the various point- and sprite-related features provided by Three.js. To be more specific, we'll look at the following subjects in this chapter:

- Creating and styling particles using `THREE.SpriteMaterial`
- Using `THREE.Points` to create a grouped set of points
- Creating a `THREE.Points` object from existing geometries
- Animating `THREE.Points` objects
- Using a texture to style the individual points
- Using the canvas to style a particle with `THREE.SpriteMaterial`

Let's start by exploring what a particle is and how you can create one. Before we get started, though, a quick note on some of the names used in this chapter. In recent versions of Three.js, the names of the objects related to points have changed a number of times. The `THREE.Points` object was previously named `THREE.PointCloud` and, in even older versions, it was called a `THREE.ParticleSystem`. A `THREE.Sprite` used to be called a `THREE.Particle`, and the materials have also undergone a number of name changes. So, if you see online examples using these old names, remember that they are talking about the same concepts. In this chapter, we use the new naming convention introduced in the latest version of Three.js.

Understanding points

As we do with most new concepts, we'll start with an example. In the sources for this chapter, you'll find an example with the name `01-sprites.html`. Open this example and you'll see a grid of very uninteresting-looking colored cubes, as shown in the following screenshot:

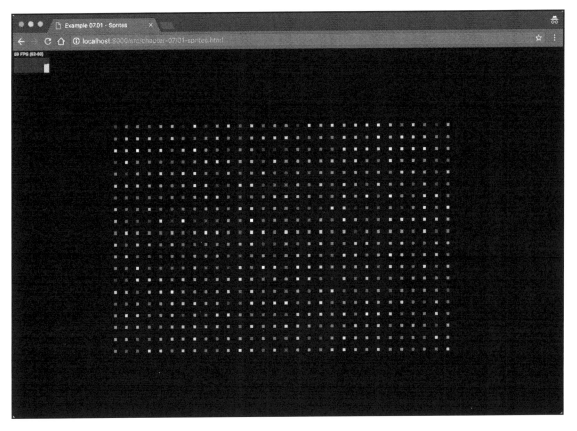

58 FPS (53-60)

We've also enabled the mouse controls for this example, so you can use the mouse or your trackpad to navigate around this scene. One thing you'll notice is that no matter how you look at the squares, they will always look the same. For instance, the following screenshot shows a view of the same scene from a different position:

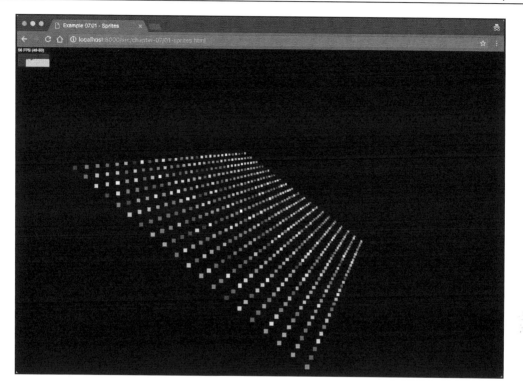

56 FPS (49-60)

What you see in this screenshot are a number of sprites. A sprite is a 2D plane that always faces the camera. If you create a sprite without any properties, they are rendered as small, white, two-dimensional squares. These sprites were created with the following lines of code:

```
function createSprites() {
  for (var x = -15; x < 15; x++) {
    for (var y = -10; y < 10; y++) {
      var material = new THREE.SpriteMaterial({
        color: Math.random() * 0xffffff
      });

      var sprite = new THREE.Sprite(material);
      sprite.position.set(x * 4, y * 4, 0);
      scene.add(sprite);
    }
  }
}
```

In this example, we create the sprites manually using
the `THREE.Sprite(material)` constructor. The only item we pass in is a material. This
has to be either `THREE.SpriteMaterial` or `THREE.SpriteCanvasMaterial`. We'll look
at both of these materials in more depth in the rest of this chapter.

Before we move on to more interesting `THREE.Points` objects, let's look a bit closer at
the `THREE.Sprite` object. A `THREE.Sprite` object extends from
the `THREE.Object3D` object just as `THREE.Mesh` does. This means that most of the
properties and functions you know from `THREE.Mesh` can be used on `THREE.Sprite`. You
can set its position using the `position` attribute, scale it using the `scale` property, and
move it along its axes using the `translate` property.

In older versions of Three.js, you were unable to
use `THREE.Sprite` objects with `THREE.WebGLRenderer` and could use it
only with `THREE.CanvasRenderer`. In the current
version, `THREE.Sprite` objects can be used with both renderers.

With `THREE.Sprite`, you can very easily create a set of objects and move them around the
scene. This works well when you're working with a small number of objects, but you'll
quickly run into performance issues when you want to work with a high number
of `THREE.Sprite` objects because each of the objects needs to be managed separately by
Three.js. Three.js provides an alternative way of handling a large number of sprites (or
particles) using a `THREE.Points` object. With `THREE.Points`, Three.js doesn't have to
manage many individual `THREE.Sprite` objects, just the `THREE.Points` instance. To get
the same result as the screenshot we saw earlier, but this time using `THREE.Points`, we do
the following:

```
function createPoints() {

  var geom = new THREE.Geometry();
  var material = new THREE.PointsMaterial({
    size: 2,
    vertexColors: true,
    color: 0xffffff
  });

  for (var x = -15; x < 15; x++) {
    for (var y = -10; y < 10; y++) {
      var particle = new THREE.Vector3(x * 4, y * 4, 0);
      geom.vertices.push(particle);
      geom.colors.push(new THREE.Color(Math.random() * 0xffffff));
    }
  }
```

```
    var cloud = new THREE.Points(geom, material);
    scene.add(cloud);
}
```

As you can see, for each point, we need to create a vertex (represented by THREE.Vector3), add it to THREE.Geometry, use THREE.Geometry together with THREE.PointsMaterial to create THREE.Points, and add cloud to the scene. An example of THREE.Points in action can be found in the 02-points-webgl.html example. The following screenshot shows this example:

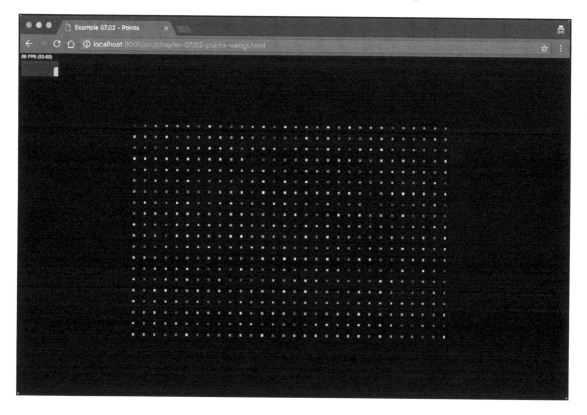

59 FPS (52-60)

In the following sections, we'll explore THREE.Points further.

THREE.Points and THREE.PointsMaterial

At the end of the previous section *Understanding points*, we briefly
introduced `THREE.Points`. The constructor of `THREE.Points` takes two properties: a
geometry and a material. The material is used to color and texture the particles (as we'll see
later on), and the geometry defines where the individual particles are positioned. Each
vertex and each point used to define the geometry is shown as an element on screen. When
we create a `THREE.Point` object based on `THREE.BoxGeometry`, we get eight particles, one
for each corner of the cube. Normally, though, you won't create
a `THREE.Points` object from one of the standard Three.js geometries, but add the vertices
manually to a geometry created from scratch (or use an externally loaded model) just as we
did at the end of the previous section, *Understanding points*. In this section, we'll dive a bit
deeper into this approach and look at how you can use `THREE.PointsMaterial` to style
the individual elements. We'll explore this using the `03-basic-point-`
`cloud.html` example. The following screenshot shows this example:

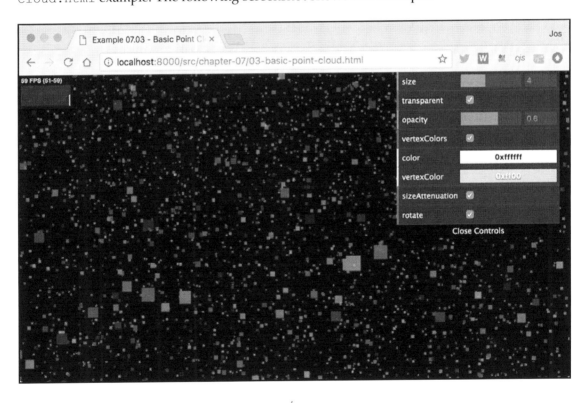

In this example, we create a `THREE.PointCloud`, which we fill with 15,000 particles. All the particles are styled with a `THREE.PointsMaterial`. To create the `THREE.PointCloud` object, we used the following code:

```
function createParticles(size, transparent, opacity, vertexColors,
sizeAttenuation, colorValue, vertexColorValue) {
  var geom = new THREE.Geometry();
  var material = new THREE.PointsMaterial({
    size: size,
    transparent: transparent,
    opacity: opacity,
    vertexColors: vertexColors,
    sizeAttenuation: sizeAttenuation,
    color: new THREE.Color(colorValue)
  });

  var range = 500;
  for (var i = 0; i < 15000; i++) {
    var particle = new THREE.Vector3(
      Math.random() * range - range / 2,
      Math.random() * range - range / 2,
      Math.random() * range - range / 2);
    geom.vertices.push(particle);
    var color = new THREE.Color(vertexColorValue);
    var asHSL = {};
    color.getHSL(asHSL);
    color.setHSL(asHSL.h, asHSL.s, asHSL.l * Math.random());
    geom.colors.push(color);
  }

  cloud = new THREE.Points(geom, material);
  cloud.name = "particles";
  scene.add(cloud);
}
```

In this listing, we first create a `THREE.Geometry` object. We'll add the individual points, represented as `THREE.Vector3`, to this geometry. For this, we've used a simple loop that creates `THREE.Vector3` at a random position and adds it. In this same loop, we also specify the array of colors, `geom.colors`, that are used when we set the `vertexColors` property of `THREE.PointsMaterial` to `true`. The last thing to do is create the `THREE.PointsMaterial` and add it to the scene.

The following table explains all the properties you can set on `THREE.PointsMaterial`:

Name	Description
color	This is the color of all the particles in `ParticleSystem`. Setting the `vertexColors` property to `true` and specifying the colors using the `color` property of the geometry overrides this property (to be more precise, the color of a vertex will be multiplied with this value to determine the final color). The default value is `0xFFFFFF`.
map	With this property, you can apply a texture to the particles. You can, for instance, make them look like snowflakes. This property isn't shown in this example but is explained later on in this chapter.
size	This is the size of the particle. The default value is `1`.
sizeAnnutation	If this is set to false, all the particles will have the same size regardless of how far from the camera they are positioned. If this is set to true, the size is based on the distance from the camera. The default value is `true`.
vertexColors	Normally, all the particles in `THREE.PointCloud` have the same color. If this property is set to `THREE.VertexColors` and the colors array in the geometry has been filled, the colors from that array will be used instead (also see the color entry in this table). The default value is `THREE.NoColors`.
opacity	This, together with the `transparent` property, sets the opacity of the particle. The default value is `1` (no opacity).
transparent	If this is set to true, the particle will be rendered with the opacity set by the opacity property. The default value is `false`.
blending	This is the blend mode to use when rendering the particle.
fog	This determines whether the particles are affected by fog added to the scene. This defaults to `true`.

The previous example provides a simple control menu that you can use to experiment with the properties specific to `THREE.PointsMaterial`.

So far, we've only rendered the particles as small cubes, which is the default behavior. There are, however, a few additional ways you can use to style the particles:

- We can use the THREE.SpriteCanvasMaterial (which only works for THREE.CanvasRenderer) to use the results from an HTML canvas element as a texture.
- Use THREE.SpriteMaterial to render a HTML canvas element with the THREE.WebGLRenderer.
- Load an external image file (or use the HTML5 canvas) with the map property of THREE.PointsMaterial to style all elements of the THREE.Points object.

Next, we look into how you can do this.

Styling particles with the HTML5 canvas

Three.js offers three different ways in which you can use an HTML5 canvas to style your particles. If you use THREE.CanvasRenderer, you can directly reference an HTML5 canvas from THREE.SpriteCanvasMaterial. When you use THREE.WebGLRenderer, you need to take a couple of extra steps to use an HTML5 canvas to style your particles. In the following two sections, we'll show you the different approaches.

Using HTML5 canvas with THREE.CanvasRenderer

With THREE.SpriteCanvasMaterial, you can use the output from an HTML5 canvas as a texture for your particles. This material is specifically created for THREE.CanvasRenderer and only works when you use this specific renderer. Before we look at how to use this material, let's first look at the attributes you can set on this material:

Name	Description
color	This is the color of the particle. Depending on the specified blending mode, this affects the color of the canvas image.
program	This is a function that takes a canvas context as a parameter. This function is called when the particle is rendered. The output from the calls to this 2D drawing context is shown as the particle.
opacity	This determines the opacity of the particle. The default value is 1, and there is no opacity.

transparent	This determines whether the particle is transparent or not. This works together with the `opacity` property.
blending	This is the blend mode to be used.
rotation	This property allows you to rotate the content of the canvas. You'll usually need to set this to PI to correctly align the canvas content. Note that this property can't be passed into the constructor of the material but needs to be set explicitly.

To see `THREE.SpriteCanvasMaterial` in action, you can open the `04-program-based-sprites.html` example. The following screenshot shows this example:

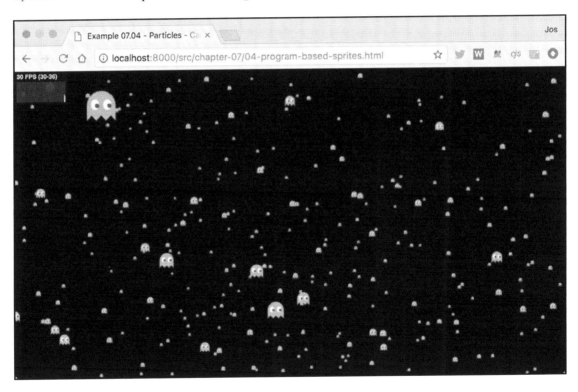

In this example, the particles are created in the `createSprites` function:

```
function createSprites() {

    var material = new THREE.SpriteCanvasMaterial({
        program: getTexture
    });
    material.rotation = Math.PI;

    var range = 500;
    for (var i = 0; i < 1000; i++) {
        var sprite = new THREE.Sprite(material);
        sprite.position = new THREE.Vector3(Math.random() * range -
            range / 2, Math.random() * range - range / 2, Math.random()
            * range - range / 2);
        sprite.scale.set(0.1, 0.1, 0.1);
        scene.add(sprite);
    }
}
```

This code looks a lot like the code we saw in the previous section *Styling particles with the HTML5 canvas*. The main change is that because we're working with `THREE.CanvasRenderer`, we create `THREE.Sprite` objects directly, instead of using `THREE.Points`. In this code, we also define `THREE.SpriteCanvasMaterial` with a `program` attribute that points to the `getTexture` function. This `getTexture` function defines what each vertex will look like (in our case, a ghost from *Pac-Man*):

```
var getTexture = function(ctx) {
    ctx.fillStyle = "orange";
    ...
    // lots of other ctx drawing calls
    ...
    ctx.beginPath();
    ctx.fill();
}
```

We won't dive into the actual canvas code required to draw our shape. What's important here is that we define a function that accepts a 2D canvas context (`ctx`) as its parameter. Everything that is drawn onto that context is used as the shape for `THREE.Sprite`.

Using HTML5 canvas with WebGLRenderer

If we want to use an HTML5 canvas with a THREE.WebGLRenderer, we can take two different approaches. We can use the THREE.PointsMaterial and create a THREE.Points object, or we can use a THREE.Sprite and the map property of THREE.SpriteMaterial.

Let's start with the first approach and create a THREE.Points object. In the attributes for THREE.PointsMaterial, we mentioned the map property. With the map property, we can load a texture for the individual points. With Three.js, this texture can also be the output from an HTML5 canvas. An example showing this concept is 05-program-based-points-webgl.html. The following screenshot shows this example:

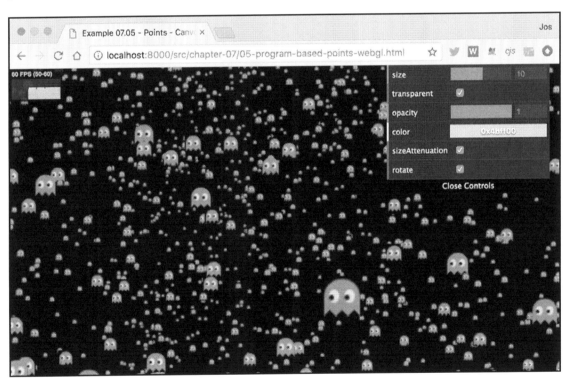

Let's look at the code we wrote to get this effect. Most of the code is the same as our previous WebGL example, so we won't go into too much detail. The important code changes that were made to get this example are shown here:

```
// code can be found in the util.js file
var createGhostTexture = function() {
  var canvas = document.createElement('canvas');
  canvas.width = 32;
  canvas.height = 32;

  var ctx = canvas.getContext('2d');
  ...
  // draw the ghost
  ...
  ctx.fill();
  var texture = new THREE.Texture(canvas);
  texture.needsUpdate = true;
  return texture;
}

function createPoints(size, transparent, opacity,
    sizeAttenuation, color) {

  var geom = new THREE.Geometry();
  var material = new THREE.PointsMaterial ({
      size: size,
      transparent: transparent,
      opacity: opacity,
      map: createGhostTexture(),
      sizeAttenuation: sizeAttenuation,
      color: color});

  var range = 500;
  for (var i = 0; i < 5000; i++) {
    var particle = new THREE.Vector3(Math.random() * range -
        range / 2, Math.random() * range - range / 2,
        Math.random() * range - range / 2);
    geom.vertices.push(particle);
  }

  cloud = new THREE.Points(geom, material);
  scene.add(cloud);
}
```

In `createGhostTexture`, the first of these two JavaScript functions, we create a `THREE.Texture` object based on an HTML5 canvas element. In the second function, `createPoints`, we assign this texture to the `map` property of `THREE.PointsMaterial`.

 In older versions of Three.js it was possible to set the `sortParticles` property of the `THREE.Points` object (then called `THREE.PointsCloud`). With that property, Three.js would sort based on their z-position, relative to the camera, in JavaScript, all the points before sending them to WebGL to be rendered. This was CPU intensive and was removed in later versions of Three.js (as of r70). The result is that when looking at this example, you might see partly overlapping sprites and incorrect transparency. If you still want to make sure that no sprites overlap, you'll have to apply this sorting manually yourself or play around with a material's `alphaTest` or `depthWrite` property. An example of this ordering is shown in example `07-rainy-scene.html`, and the `depthWrite` approach is shown in example `08-snowy-scene.html`.

The result of this is that everything we draw to the canvas in the `createGhostTexture()` method is used for the particles in the `THREE.Points` object. In the following section, we'll look a bit deeper into how this works with textures we load from external files.

 In this example, we only see a very small part of what is possible with textures. In Chapter 10, *Loading and Working with Textures*, we'll dive into the details of what can be done with textures.

At the beginning of this section, we mentioned that we could also use the `THREE.Sprite` together with the `map` property to create a canvas-based particle. For this, we use the same approach to create the `THREE.Texture` variable as we saw in the previous example. This time, however, we assign it to `THREE.Sprite` as follows:

```
function createSprites() {
  var material = new THREE.SpriteMaterial({
    map: getTexture(),
    color: 0xffffff
  });

  var range = 500;
  for (var i = 0; i < 1500; i++) {
    var sprite = new THREE.Sprite(material);
    sprite.position.set(Math.random() * range - range / 2,
      Math.random() * range - range / 2, Math.random() * range -
      range / 2);
    sprite.scale.set(4,4,4);
    scene.add(sprite);
  }
}
```

Using textures to style particles

In the previous example, we saw how you could style `THREE.Points` and individual `THREE.Sprite` objects using an HTML5 canvas. Since you can draw anything you want and even load external images, you can use this approach to add all kinds of styles to the particle system. There is, however, a more direct way to use an image to style your particles. You can use the `THREE.TextureLoader().load()` function to load an image as a `THREE.Texture` object. This `THREE.Texture` object can then be assigned to the `map` property of a material.

In this section, we'll show you two examples and explain how to create them. Both these examples use an image as a texture for your particles. In the first example, we create a simulation of rain, `06-rainy-scene.html`. The following screenshot shows this example:

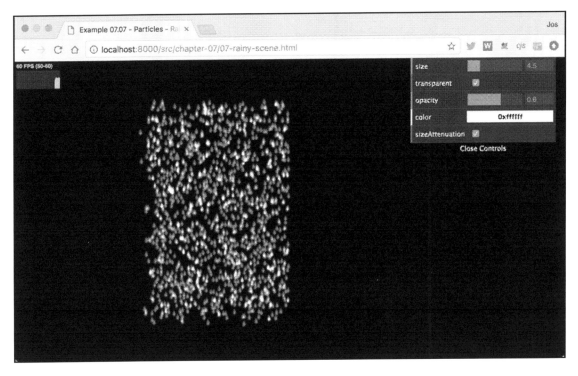

60 FPS (50-60)

The first thing we need to do is get a texture that will represent our raindrop. You can find a couple of examples in the `assets/textures/particles` folder. In the upcoming chapters, we will explain all the details and requirements for textures. For now, all you need to know is that the texture should be square and preferably a power of 2 (for example, 64 x 64, 128 x 128, 256 x 256). For this example, we'll use this texture:

This image uses a black background (needed for correct blending) and shows the shape and color of a raindrop. Before we can use this texture in THREE.PointsMaterial, we first need to load it. This can be done with the following line of code:

```
var texture = new
THREE.TextureLoader().load("../../assets/textures/particles/raindrop-3.png"
);
```

With this line of code, Three.js will load the texture, and we can use it in our material. For this example, we defined the material as follows:

```
var material = new THREE.PointsMaterial({
    size: size,
    transparent: transparent,
    opacity: opacity,
    map: texture,
    blending: THREE.AdditiveBlending,
    sizeAttenuation: sizeAttenuation,
    color: color
});
```

In this chapter, we've discussed all of these properties. The main thing to understand here is that the map property points to the texture we loaded with the THREE.TextureLoader.load function, and we specify THREE.AdditiveBlending as the blending mode. This blending mode means that when a new pixel is drawn, the color of the background pixel is added to the color of this new pixel. For our raindrop texture, this means that the black background won't be shown. We could also have changed the black background to a transparent one, which would have created the same effect.

 In older versions of Three.js, this wasn't possible. In older versions, transparent textures didn't work correctly with WebGL and THREE.Points (or the relevant objects in those versions).

That takes care of styling the THREE.Points object. What you'll also see when you open this example is that the points themselves are moving. In the previous examples, we moved the entire object; this time, we position the individual particles within the THREE.Points object. Doing this is actually very simple. Each point is represented as a vertex that makes up the geometry that was used to create the THREE.Points object. Let's look at how we add the points for this THREE.Points:

```
var range = 40;
for (var i = 0; i < 1500; i++) {
  var particle = new THREE.Vector3(
    Math.random() * range - range / 2,
    Math.random() * range * 1.5,
    Math.random() * range - range / 2);

  particle.velocityX = (Math.random() - 0.5) / 3;
  particle.velocityY = 0.1 + (Math.random() / 5);
  geom.vertices.push(particle);
}
```

This isn't that different than the previous examples we saw. Here, we added two additional properties to each particle (THREE.Vector3): velocityX and velocityY. The first one defines how a particle (a raindrop) moves horizontally, and the second one defines how fast the raindrop falls. The horizontal velocity ranges from -0.16 to $+0.16$, and the vertical speed ranges from 0.1 to 0.3. Now that each raindrop has its own speed, we can move the individual particles inside the render loop:

```
var vertices = system2.geometry.vertices;
vertices.forEach(function (v) {
  v.x = v.x - (v.velocityX);
  v.y = v.y - (v.velocityY);

  if (v.x <= -20 || v.x >= 20) v.velocityX = v.velocityX * -1;
  if (v.y <= 0) v.y = 60;
});
```

In this piece of code, we get all vertices (particles) from the geometry that was used to create THREE.Points. For each of the particles, we take velocityX and velocityY and use them to change the current position of the particle. The last two lines make sure the particles stay within the range we've defined. If the v.y position drops below zero, we add the raindrop back to the top, and if the v.x position reaches any of the edges, we make it bounce back by inverting the horizontal velocity.

If you run this example, with this exact code, you'll probably notice some strange overlapping raindrops:

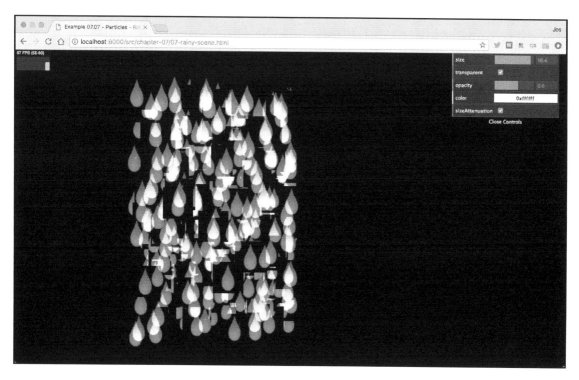

57 FPS (55-60)

This is because the points themselves aren't ordered in their z-position (we used `Math.random() * range - range / 2` to set this position). In older versions, we could solve this by setting `sortParticles` to true, but since that has been removed we have to do this ourselves. To fix this, we just change the position of the z value to `1 + (i/100)`, which makes sure that each subsequent point is positioned on top of the previous one. Now we have the correct output:

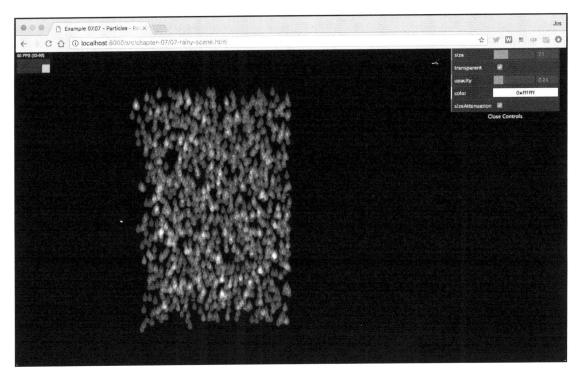

60 FPS (52-60)

Let's look at another example. This time, we won't make rain, but we'll make snow. Additionally, we won't be using just a single texture, but we'll use five separate images (taken from the Three.js examples). Let's start by looking at the result again (see `07-snowy-scene.html`):

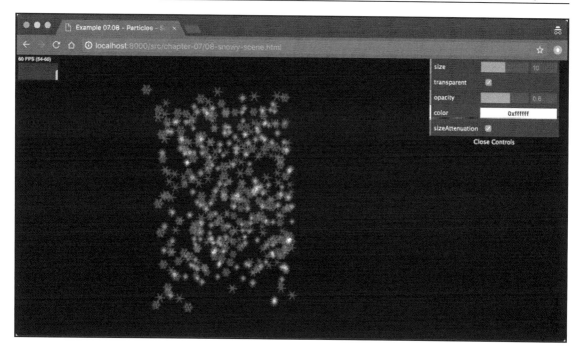

60 FPS (54-60)

In the preceding screenshot, you can see that instead of using just a single image as texture, we've used multiple images, which, instead of having a black background, have a transparent background. You might wonder how we did this. As you probably remember, we can only have a single material for a THREE.Points object. If we want to have multiple materials, we just have to make multiple THREE.Points instances as follows:

```
function createPointInstances(size, transparent, opacity, sizeAttenuation,
color) {

  var loader = new THREE.TextureLoader();

  var texture1 =
loader.load("../../assets/textures/particles/snowflake1_t.png");
  var texture2 =
loader.load("../../assets/textures/particles/snowflake2_t.png");
  var texture3 =
loader.load("../../assets/textures/particles/snowflake3_t.png");
  var texture4 =
loader.load("../../assets/textures/particles/snowflake5_t.png");

  scene.add(createPoints("system1", texture1, size, transparent, opacity,
sizeAttenuation, color));
```

```
  scene.add(createPoints("system2", texture2, size, transparent, opacity,
sizeAttenuation, color));
  scene.add(createPoints("system3", texture3, size, transparent, opacity,
sizeAttenuation, color));
  scene.add(createPoints("system4", texture4, size, transparent, opacity,
sizeAttenuation, color));
}
```

Here, you can see that we load the textures separately and pass all the information on how to create the `THREE.Points` object to the `createPointsInstances` function. This function looks as follows:

```
function createPointCloud(name, texture, size, transparent, opacity,
sizeAttenuation, color) {
  var geom = new THREE.Geometry();

  var color = new THREE.Color(color);
  color.setHSL(color.getHSL().h,
    color.getHSL().s,
    (Math.random()) * color.getHSL().l);

  var material = new THREE.PointsMaterial({
    size: size,
    transparent: transparent,
    opacity: opacity,
    map: texture,
    blending: THREE.AdditiveBlending,
    depthWrite: false,
    sizeAttenuation: sizeAttenuation,
    color: color
  });

  var range = 40;
  for (var i = 0; i < 150; i++) {
    var particle = new THREE.Vector3(
      Math.random() * range - range / 2,
      Math.random() * range * 1.5,
      Math.random() * range - range / 2);
    particle.velocityY = 0.1 + Math.random() / 5;
    particle.velocityX = (Math.random() - 0.5) / 3;
    particle.velocityZ = (Math.random() - 0.5) / 3;
    geom.vertices.push(particle);
  }
```

```
    var system = new THREE.Points(geom, material);
    system.name = name;
    return system;
}
```

The first thing we do in this function is defining the color so that the particles for this specific texture can be rendered. This is done by randomly changing the *lightness* of the passed-in color. Next, the material is created in the same manner we did before. The only change here is that the depthWrite property is set to false. This property defines whether this object affects the WebGL depth buffer. By setting this to false, we make sure that the various point clouds and rendered snowflakes don't interfere with each other. If this property isn't set to false, you'll see that the black background from the texture is sometimes shown when a particle is in front of a particle from another THREE.PointCloud object. The last step taken in this piece of code is randomly placing the particles and adding a random speed to each particle. In the render loop, we can now update the position of all the particles from each THREE.PointCloud object as follows:

```
scene.children.forEach(function (child) {
  if (child instanceof THREE.Points) {
    var vertices = child.geometry.vertices;
    vertices.forEach(function (v) {
      v.y = v.y - (v.velocityY);
      v.x = v.x - (v.velocityX);
      v.z = v.z - (v.velocityZ);

      if (v.y <= 0) v.y = 60;
      if (v.x <= -20 || v.x >= 20) v.velocityX = v.velocityX * -1;
      if (v.z <= -20 || v.z >= 20) v.velocityZ = v.velocityZ * -1;
    });
  }
});
```

With this approach, we can have particles that have different textures. This approach, however, is a bit limited. The greater the variety of textures we want, the more point clouds we'll have to create and manage. If you have a limited set of particles with different styles, you'd better use the THREE.Sprite object we showed at the beginning of this chapter.

Working with sprite maps

At the beginning of this chapter, we used a THREE.Sprite object to render single particles with the THREE.CanvasRenderer and the THREE.WebGLRenderer. These sprites were positioned somewhere in the 3D world, and their size was based on the distance from the camera (this is also sometimes called **billboarding**). In this section, we'll show an alternative use of the THREE.Sprite object. We'll show you how you can use THREE.Sprite to create a layer similar to a **head-up display** (**HUD**) for your 3D content using an extra THREE.OrthographicCamera instance. We will also show you how to select the image for a THREE.Sprite object using a sprite map.

As an example, we're going to create a simple THREE.Sprite object that moves from left to right over the screen. In the background, we'll render a 3D scene with a moving camera to illustrate that the THREE.Sprite object moves independently of the camera. The following screenshot shows what we'll be creating for the first example (09-sprites.html):

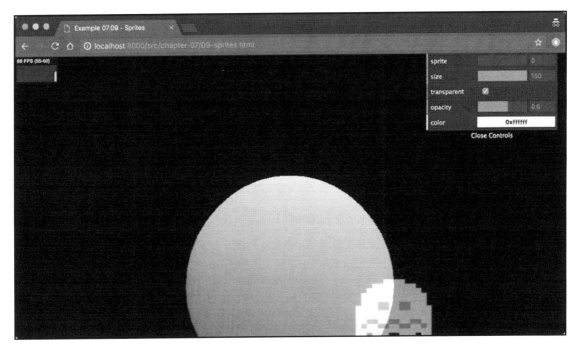

60 FPS (55-60)

If you open this example in your browser, you'll see a Pac-Man ghost-like sprite moving across the screen that changes color and form whenever it hits the right edge. The first thing we'll do is look at how we create `THREE.OrthographicCamera` and a separate scene to render `THREE.Sprite` in:

```
var sceneOrtho = new THREE.Scenc();
var cameraOrtho = new THREE.OrthographicCamera( 0, window.innerWidth,
window.innerHeight, 0, -10, 10 );
```

Next, let's look at the construction of the `THREE.Sprite` object and how the various shapes the sprite can take are loaded:

```
var getTexture = function () {
  return new
THREE.TextureLoader().load("../../assets/textures/particles/sprite-
sheet.png");
};

function createSprite(size, transparent, opacity, color, spriteNumber) {
  var spriteMaterial = new THREE.SpriteMaterial({
    opacity: opacity,
    color: color,
    transparent: transparent,
    map: getTexture()
  });

  // we have 1 row, with five sprites
  spriteMaterial.map.offset = new THREE.Vector2(0.2 * spriteNumber, 0);
  spriteMaterial.map.repeat = new THREE.Vector2(1 / 5, 1);
  spriteMaterial.blending = THREE.AdditiveBlending;
  // make sure the object is always rendered at the front
  spriteMaterial.depthTest = false;
  var sprite = new THREE.Sprite(spriteMaterial);
  sprite.scale.set(size, size, size);
  sprite.position.set(100, 50, -10);
  sprite.velocityX = 5;

  sceneOrtho.add(sprite);
}
```

In the `getTexture()` function, we load a texture. However, instead of loading five different images for each *ghost*, we load a single texture that contains all the sprites (also called a sprite map). The texture appears as follows:

With the `map.offset` and the `map.repeat` properties, we select the correct sprite to show on screen. With the `map.offset` property, we determine the offset for the *x* axis (u) and the *y* axis (v) for the texture we loaded. The scale for these properties runs from 0 to 1. In our example, if we want to select the third ghost, we set the u-offset (*x* axis) to 0.4, and, because we've only got one row, we don't need to change the v-offset (*y* axis). If we only set this property, the texture shows the third, fourth, and fifth ghosts compressed together on screen. To only show one ghost, we need to zoom in. We do this by setting the `map.repeat` property for the u-value to 1/5. This means that we zoom in (only for the *x* axis) to only show 20 percent of the texture, which is exactly one ghost.

The final step we need to take is to update the `render` function:

```
webGLRenderer.render(scene, camera);
webGLRenderer.autoClear = false;
webGLRenderer.render(sceneOrtho, cameraOrtho);
```

We first render the scene with the normal camera and the moving sphere and, after that, we render the scene containing our sprite.

 We need to set the `autoClear` property of the `WebGLRenderer` to `false`. If we don't do this, Three.js will clear the scene before it renders the sprite, and the sphere wouldn't show up.

The following table shows an overview of all the properties of `THREE.SpriteMaterial` we used in the previous examples:

Name	Description
color	This is the color of the sprite.
map	This is the texture to be used for this sprite. This can be a sprite sheet, as shown in the example in this section.

sizeAnnutation	If this is set to `false`, the size of the sprite won't be affected by the distance it's removed from the camera. The default value is `true`.
opacity	This sets the transparency of the sprite. The default value is 1 (no opacity).
blending	This defines the blend mode to be used when rendering the sprite.
fog	This determines whether the sprite is affected by fog added to the scene. This defaults to `true`.

You can also set the `depthTest` and `depthWrite` properties on this material. For more information on these properties, refer to Chapter 4, *Working with Three.js Materials*. We can, of course, also use a sprite map when positioning `THREE.Sprites` in 3D (as we did at the beginning of this chapter). An example (`10-sprites-3D.html`) of this is shown in the following screenshot:

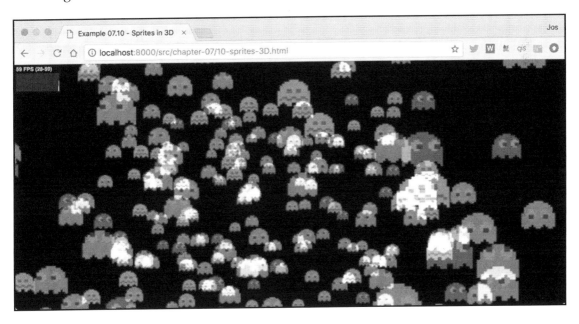

59 FPS (28-59)

With the properties we saw in the previous table, we can very easily create the effect we see in the preceding screenshot:

```
function createSprites() {
    group = new THREE.Object3D();
    var range = 200;
    for (var i = 0; i < 400; i++) {
```

```
        group.add(createSprite(10, false, 0.6, 0xffffff, i % 5, range));
    }
    scene.add(group);
}

function createSprite(size, transparent, opacity, color, spriteNumber,
range) {

    var spriteMaterial = new THREE.SpriteMaterial({
        opacity: opacity,
        color: color,
        transparent: transparent,
        map: getTexture()
    });

    // we have 1 row, with five sprites
    spriteMaterial.map.offset = new THREE.Vector2(0.2 * spriteNumber, 0);
    spriteMaterial.map.repeat = new THREE.Vector2(1 / 5, 1);
    spriteMaterial.depthTest = false;

    spriteMaterial.blending = THREE.AdditiveBlending;

    var sprite = new THREE.Sprite(spriteMaterial);
    sprite.scale.set(size, size, size);
    sprite.position.set(
        Math.random() * range - range / 2,
        Math.random() * range - range / 2,
        Math.random() * range - range / 2);

    return sprite;
}
```

In this example, we create 400 sprites based on the sprite sheet we showed earlier. You'll probably know and understand most of the properties and concepts shown here. As we've added the separate sprites to a group, rotating them is very easy and can be done as follow:

```
group.rotation.x+=0.1;
```

In this chapter, so far, we've mainly looked at creating sprites and point clouds from scratch. An interesting option, though, is to create THREE.Points from an existing geometry.

Creating THREE.Points from an advanced geometry

If you remember, `THREE.Points` renders each particle based on the vertices from the geometry supplied. This means that if we provide a complex geometry (for example, a torus knot or a tube), we can create `THREE.Points` based on the vertices from that specific geometry. In the final section of this chapter, we'll create a torus knot, like the one we saw in Chapter 6, *Advanced Geometries and Binary Operations*, and render it as `THREE.Points`.

We've already explained the torus knot in the previous chapter, so we won't go into much detail here. We're using the exact code from Chapter 6, *Advanced Geometries and Binary Operations*, and we've added a single menu option that you can use to transform the rendered mesh into `THREE.Points`. You can find the example (`11-create-particle-system-from-model.html`) in the sources for this chapter. The following screenshot shows the example:

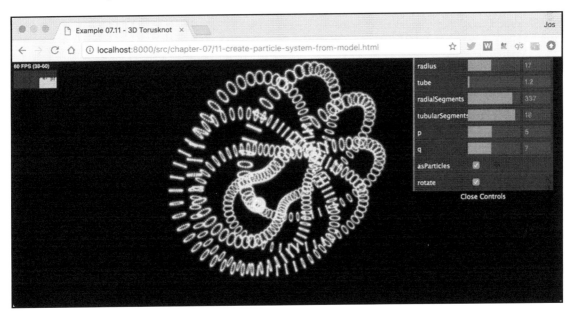

60 FPS (38-60)

As you can see from the preceding screenshot, every vertex used to generate the torus knot is used as a particle. In this example, we've added nice-looking material, based on an HTML canvas, to create this glowing effect. We'll only look at the code to create the material and the particle system as we've already discussed the other properties in this chapter:

```
function generateSprite() {

  var canvas = document.createElement('canvas');
  canvas.width = 16;
  canvas.height = 16;

  var context = canvas.getContext('2d');
  var gradient = context.createRadialGradient(canvas.width / 2,
      canvas.height / 2, 0, canvas.width / 2, canvas.height / 2,
      canvas.width / 2);

  gradient.addColorStop(0, 'rgba(255,255,255,1)');
  gradient.addColorStop(0.2, 'rgba(0,255,255,1)');
  gradient.addColorStop(0.4, 'rgba(0,0,64,1)');
  gradient.addColorStop(1, 'rgba(0,0,0,1)');

  context.fillStyle = gradient;
  context.fillRect(0, 0, canvas.width, canvas.height);

  var texture = new THREE.Texture(canvas);
  texture.needsUpdate = true;
  return texture;
}

function createPoints(geom) {
  var material = new THREE.PointsMaterial({
    color: 0xffffff,
    size: 3,
    transparent: true,
    blending: THREE.AdditiveBlending,
    map: generateSprite(),
    depthWrite: false // instead of sortParticles
  });

  var cloud = new THREE.Points(geom, material);
  return cloud;
}

// use it like this
var geom = new THREE.TorusKnotGeometry(...);
var knot = createPointCloud(geom);
```

In this code fragment, you can see two functions:

`createPoints()` and `generateSprite()`. In the first function, we create a simple `THREE.PointCloud` object directly from the geometry provided (in this example, a torus knot) and set the texture (the `map` property) to a glowing dot (generated on an HTML5 canvas element) with the `generateSprite()` function, which looks like this:

Summary

That's a wrap for this chapter. We've explained what sprites and points are and how you can style these objects with the materials available. In this chapter, you saw how you can use `THREE.Sprite` directly with `THREE.CanvasRenderer` and `THREE.WebGLRenderer`. If you want to create a large number of particles, however, you should use a `THREE.Points` object. With `THREE.Points`, all the elements share the same material, and the only property you can change for an individual particle is their color by setting the `vertexColors` property of the material to `true` and providing a color value in the `colors` array of `THREE.Geometry` used to create `THREE.Points`. We also showed how you can easily animate particles by changing their position. This works the same for an individual `THREE.Sprite` instance and the vertices from the geometry used to create `THREE.Points` objects.

So far, we have created meshes based on geometries provided by Three.js. This works well for simple models such as spheres and cubes but isn't the best approach when you want to create complex 3D models. For those models, you'd usually use a 3D-modeling application such as Blender or 3D Studio Max. In the next chapter, you'll learn how you can load and display models created by such 3D modeling applications.

8
Creating and Loading Advanced Meshes and Geometries

In this chapter, we'll look at a couple of different ways that you can create advanced and complex geometries and meshes. In `Chapter 5`, *Learning to Work with Geometries*, and `Chapter 6`, *Advanced Geometries and Binary Operations*, we showed you how to create a few advanced geometries using the built-in objects from Three.js.

In this chapter, we'll use the following two approaches to create advanced geometries and meshes:

- Grouping and merging
- Loading from external resources

We start with the *group and merge* approach. With this approach, we use the standard Three.js grouping and the `THREE.Geometry.merge()` function to create new objects.

Geometry grouping and merging

In this section, we'll look at two basic features of Three.js: grouping objects together, and merging multiple meshes into a single mesh. We'll start with grouping objects.

Grouping objects together

In some of the previous chapters, you already saw how you can group objects when working with multiple materials. When you create a mesh from a geometry using multiple materials, Three.js creates a group. Multiple copies of your geometry are added to this group, each with their own specific material. This group is returned, so it looks like a mesh that uses multiple materials. In truth, however, it is a group that contains a number of meshes.

Creating groups is very easy. Every mesh you create can contain child elements, which can be added using the add function. The effect of adding a child object to a group is that you can move, scale, rotate, and translate the parent object, and all the child objects will also be affected. Let's look at an example (01-grouping.html). The following screenshot shows this example:

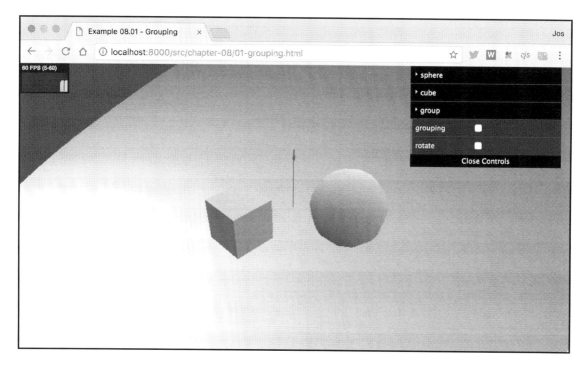

In this example, you can use the menu to move the sphere and the cube around. If you check the **rotate** option, you'll see these two meshes rotating around their center. This isn't anything new and is not very exciting. However, these two objects haven't been added to the scene directly, they have been added as a group. The following code shows how to do this:

```
sphere = createMesh(new THREE.SphereGeometry(5, 10, 10));
cube = createMesh(new THREE.BoxGeometry(6, 6, 6));

group = new THREE.Group();
group.add(sphere);
group.add(cube);

scene.add(group);
```

In this code snippet, you can see that we create THREE.Group. This class is almost identical to a THREE.Object3D, which is the base class of THREE.Mesh and THREE.Scene, but, by itself, it doesn't contain anything or cause anything to be rendered. In this example, we use the add function to add the sphere and cube to this object, and then we add it to the scene. If you look at the example, you can still move the cube and sphere around and scale and rotate these two objects. You can also do these things on the group they are in. If you look at the group menu, you'll see position and scale options. You can use these to scale and move the entire group around. The scale and position of the objects inside this group are relative to the scale and position of the group itself.

Scale and position are very straightforward. One thing to keep in mind, though, is that when you rotate a group, it doesn't rotate the objects inside it separately; it rotates the entire group around its own center (in our example, you rotate the entire group around the center of the group object). In this example, we placed an arrow using the THREE.ArrowHelper object at the center of the group to indicate the rotation point:

```
var arrow = new THREE.ArrowHelper(new THREE.Vector3(0, 1, 0),
group.position, 10, 0x0000ff);
scene.add(arrow);
```

If you check both the **grouping** and **rotate** checkboxes, the group will rotate. You'll see the sphere and cube rotating around the center of the group (indicated by the arrow), as follows:

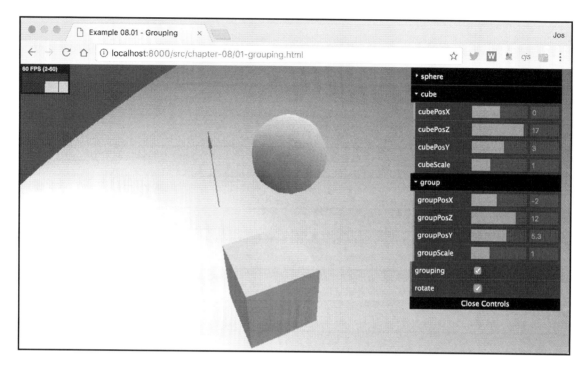

When using a group, you can still refer to, modify, and position the individual geometries. The only thing you need to remember is that all positions, rotations, and translations are done relative to the parent object. In the next section, we'll look at merging, where you'll combine multiple separate geometries and end up with a single THREE.Geometry object.

Merging multiple meshes into a single mesh

In most cases, using groups allows you to easily manipulate and manage a large number of meshes. When you're dealing with a very large number of objects; however, performance will become an issue. With groups, you're still working with individual objects that each need to be handled and rendered separately. With `THREE.Geometry.merge()`, you can merge geometries together and create a combined one. In the following screenshot, you can see how this works and the effect it has on performance. If you open the `02-merging.html` example, you see a scene with a set of randomly distributed semi-transparent cubes. With the slider in the menu, you can set the number of cubes you want in the scene and redraw the scene by clicking on the **redraw** button. Depending on the hardware you're running, you'll see a performance degradation as the number of cubes increases. In our case, as you can see in the following screenshot, this happens at around 6,000 objects, where the refresh rate drops to around 40 **Frames Per Second (fps)** instead of the normal 60 fps:

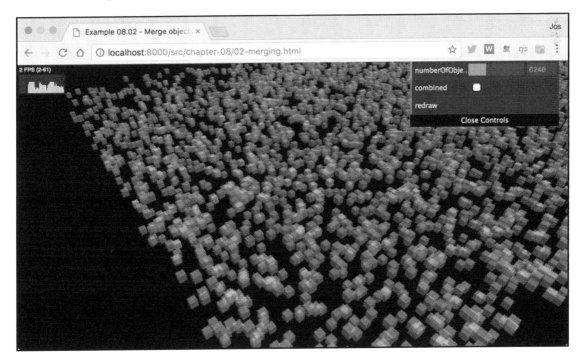

As you can see, there is a certain limit to the number of meshes you can add to the scene. Normally, though, you probably wouldn't need that many meshes, but when creating specific games (for example, something such as *Minecraft*) or advanced visualizations, you might need to manage a large number of individual meshes.

With `THREE.Geometry.merge()`, you can solve this problem. Before we look at the code, let's run this same example but, this time, with the **combined** box checked. With this option flagged, we merge all the cubes into a single `THREE.Geometry` object and add that one instead, as shown in the following screenshot:

As you can see, we can easily render 20,000 cubes without any drop in performance. To do this, we use the following few lines of code:

```
var geometry = new THREE.Geometry();
for (var i = 0; i < controls.numberOfObjects; i++) {
  var cubeMesh = addcube();
  cubeMesh.updateMatrix();
  geometry.merge(cubeMesh.geometry,cubeMesh.matrix);
}
scene.add(new THREE.Mesh(geometry, cubeMaterial));
```

In this code snippet, the addCube() function returns THREE.Mesh. In older versions of Three.js, we could use the THREE.GeometryUtils.merge function to also merge THREE.Mesh objects into THREE.Geometry objects. With the latest version, this functionality has been deprecated in favor of the THREE.Geometry.merge function. To make sure the merged-in THREE.Geometry object is positioned and rotated correctly, we not only provide THREE.Geometry to the merge function, but also its transformation matrix. When we add this matrix to the merge function, the cube we merge it will be positioned correctly.

We do this 20,000 times and are left with a single geometry that we add to the scene. If you look at the code, you can probably see a couple of drawbacks to this approach. Since you're left with a single geometry, you can't apply a material to each individual cube. This, however, can be somewhat solved using THREE.MeshFaceMaterial. The biggest drawback, however, is that you lose control over the individual cubes. If you want to move, rotate, or scale a single cube, you can't (unless you search for the correct faces and vertices and position them individually).

With the grouping and merging approach, you can create large and complex geometries using the basic geometries provided by Three.js. If you want to create more advanced geometries, then using the programmatic approach provided by Three.js isn't always the best and easiest option. Three.js, luckily, offers a couple of other options to create geometries. In the next section, we'll look at how you can load geometries and meshes from external resources.

Loading geometries from external resources

Three.js can read a number of 3D file formats and import geometries and meshes defined in those files. The following table shows the file formats that are supported by Three.js:

Format	Description
JSON	Three.js has its own JSON format that you can use to declaratively define a geometry or a scene. Even though this isn't an official format, it's very easy to use and comes in very handy when you want to reuse complex geometries or scenes.
OBJ or MTL	OBJ is a simple 3D format first developed by Wavefront Technologies. It's one of the most widely adopted 3D file formats and is used to define the geometry of an object. MTL is a companion format to OBJ. In an MTL file, the material of the objects in an OBJ file is specified. Three.js also has a custom OBJ exporter, called OBJExporter.js, should you want to export your models to OBJ from Three.js.
COLLADA	**COLLAborative Design Activity (COLLADA)** is a format for defining *digital assets* in an XML-based format. This is also a widely used format that is supported by pretty much all 3D applications and rendering engines.
STL	**STereoLithography (STL)** is widely used for rapid prototyping. For instance, models for 3D printers are often defined as STL files. Three.js also has a custom STL exporter, called STLExporter.js, should you want to export your models to STL from Three.js.
CTM	CTM is a file format created by openCTM. It's used as a format for storing 3D triangle-based meshes in a compact format.
VTK	**Visualization Toolkit (VTK)** is the file format defined by and used to specify vertices and faces. There are two formats available: a binary one and a text-based ASCII one. Three.js only supports the ASCII-based format.
AWD	AWD is a binary format for 3D scenes and is most often used with http://away3d.com/ engine. Note that this loader doesn't support compressed AWD files.
Assimp	Open asset import library (Assimp) is a standard way to import various 3D model formats. With this loader, you can import models from a large range of 3D formats that have been converted using assimp2json, details of which are available at https://github.com/acgessler/assimp2json.
VRML	**Virtual Reality Modeling Language (VRML)** is a text-based format that allows you to specify 3D objects and worlds. It has been superseded by the X3D file format. Three.js doesn't support loading X3D models, but these models can be easily converted to other formats. More information can be found at http://www.x3dom.org/?page_id=532#.
Babylon	Babylon is a 3D JavaScript game library. It stores models in its own internal format. More information about this can be found at http://www.babylonjs.com/.
PDB	This is a very specialized format, created by **Protein Data Bank (PDB)**, which is used to specify what proteins look like. Three.js can load and visualize proteins specified in this format.
PLY	This format is called the Polygon file format. This is most often used to store information from 3D scanners.
TDS	The Autodesk 3DS format. More information can be found at https://www.autodesk.com/.
3MF	3MF is one of the standards used in 3D printing. Information about this format can be found at the 3FM Consortium homepage: https://3mf.io/
AMF	AMF is another 3D printing standard, but isn't under active development anymore. The following Wikipedia page has additional information on this standard: https://en.wikipedia.org/wiki/Additive_Manufacturing_File_Format

PlayCanvas	PlayCanvas is a really great WebGL-based open source gaming engine. With this loader, you can load PlayCanvas-based models and use them in Three.js. The PlayCanvas website can be found here: `https://playcanvas.com/`
Draco	Draco is a file format for storing geometries and point clouds in a very efficient format. Details about how Draco works can be found on their GitHub page: `https://github.com/google/draco`
PRWM	**Packed Raw WebGL Model** (**PRWM**) is another format focusing on efficient storage and parsing of 3D geometries. More information on this standard and how you can use it is described here: `https://github.com/kchapelier/PRWM`
GCODE	GCode is a standard way of talking to 3D printers or CNC machines. When a model is printed, one of the ways a 3D printer can be controlled is by sending it GCode commands. The details of this standard are described in the following paper: `https://www.nist.gov/publications/nist-rs274ngc-interpreter-version-3?pub_id=823374`
NRRD	NRRD is a file format used to visualize volumetric data. It can, for instance, be used to render CT scans. A lot of information and samples can be found here: `http://teem.sourceforge.net/nrrd/`
SVG	SVG is a standard way to define vector graphics. This loader allows you to load an SVG file and returns a set of `THREE.Path` elements that you can use for extruding or rendering in 2D.

In the `Chapter 9`, *Animations and Moving the Camera*, we'll revisit some of these formats (and look at a number of additional ones) when we look at animations. For now, we start with the first one on the list, the internal format of Three.js.

Saving and loading in Three.js JSON format

You can use the Three.js JSON format for two different scenarios in Three.js. You can use it to save and load a single `THREE.Mesh` object, or you can use it to save and load a complete scene.

Saving and loading THREE.Mesh

To demonstrate saving and loading, we created a simple example based on `THREE.TorusKnotGeometry`. With this example, you can create a torus knot, just as we did in `Chapter 5`, *Learning to Work with Geometries*, and, using the **Save** button from the **Save & Load** menu, you can save the current geometry. For this example, we save using the HTML5 local storage API. This API allows us to easily store persistent information in the client's browser and retrieve it at a later time (even after the browser has been shut down and restarted).

We will look at the `03-load-save-json-object.html` example. This example is demonstrated in the following screenshot:

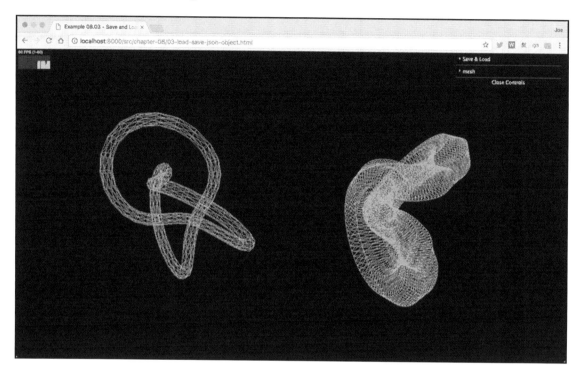

Exporting in JSON from Three.js is very easy and doesn't require you to include any additional libraries. The only thing you need to do to export `THREE.Mesh` as JSON is the following:

```
var result = knot.toJSON();
localStorage.setItem("json", JSON.stringify(result));
```

Before saving it, we first convert the result from the `toJSON` function, a JavaScript object, to a string using the `JSON.stringify` function. This results in a JSON string that looks as follows:

```
{
  "metadata": {
    "version": 4.5,
    "type": "Object",
    "generator": "Object3D.toJSON"
  },
  "geometries": [
    {
```

```
      "uuid": "8EEBC72A-C436-4431-89F0-175D3EA0A04E",
      "type": "TorusKnotGeometry",
      "radius": 10,
      "tube": 1,
      "tubularSegments": 64,
      "radialSegments": 8,
      "p": 2,
      "q": 3
    }
  ],
  "materials": [
    {
      "uuid": "9609BC46-EB00-47B3-AD62-3424D12821D9",
      "type": "MeshBasicMaterial",
      "color": 11184810,
      "side": 2,
      "vertexColors": 2,
      "depthFunc": 3,
      "depthTest": true,
      "depthWrite": true,
      "wireframe": true,
      "wireframeLinewidth": 2
    }
  ],
  "object": {
    "uuid": "64B07BE0-8EC0-4CC4-BCA5-0A1DD29E07B2",
    "type": "Mesh",
    "matrix": [
      0.8560666518372149,
      0,
      0.5168654443974957,
      0,
      0,
      1,
      0,
      0,
      -0.5168654443974957,
      0,
      0.8560666518372149,
      0,
      20,
      0,
      0,
      1
    ],
    "geometry": "8EEBC72A-C436-4431-89F0-175D3EA0A04E",
```

```
        "material": "9609BC46-EB00-47B3-AD62-3424D12821D9"
    }
}
```

As you can see, Three.js saves all the information about the `THREE.Mesh` object. To save this information using the HTML5 local storage API, all we have to do is call the `localStorage.setItem` function. The first argument is the key value (`json`) that we can later use to retrieve the information we passed in as the second argument.

Loading `THREE.Mesh` back into Three.js also requires just a couple of lines of code, as follows:

```
var json = localStorage.getItem("json");

if (json) {
  var loadedGeometry = JSON.parse(json);
  var loader = new THREE.ObjectLoader();

  loadedMesh = loader.parse(loadedGeometry);
  loadedMesh.position.x -= 40;
  scene.add(loadedMesh);
}
```

Here, we first get the JSON from local storage using the name we saved it with (`json` in this case). For this, we use the `localStorage.getItem` function provided by the HTML5 local storage API. Next, we need to convert the string back to a JavaScript object (`JSON.parse`) and convert the JSON object back to `THREE.Mesh`. Three.js provides a `helper` object called `THREE.ObjectLoader`, which you can use to convert JSON to `THREE.Mesh`. In this example, we used the `parse` method on the loader to directly parse a JSON string. The loader also provides a `load` function, where you can pass in the URL to a file containing the JSON definition.

As you can see here, we only saved a `THREE.Mesh` object. We lose everything else. If you want to save the complete scene, including the lights and the cameras, you can use `THREE.SceneExporter`.

Saving and loading a scene

If you want to save a complete scene, you use the same approach as we saw in the previous section for the geometry. `04-load-save-json-scene.html` is a working example showing this. The following screenshot shows this example:

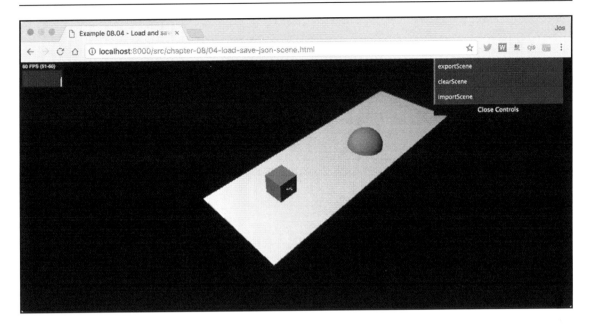

60 FPS (51-60)

In this example, you've got three options: **exportScene**, **clearScene**, and **importScene**. With **exportScene**, the current state of the scene will be saved in the browser's local storage. To test the `import` functionality, you can remove the scene by clicking on the **clearScene** button and loading it from local storage with the **importScene** button. The JavaScript needed for this is trivial:

```
localStorage.setItem('scene', JSON.stringify(scene.toJSON()));
```

This approach is exactly the same as we used in the previous section, only this time we export the `THREE.Scene` object, instead of the individual mesh:

```
{
  "metadata": {
    "version": 4.5,
    "type": "Object",
    "generator": "Object3D.toJSON"
  },
  "geometries": [
    {
      "uuid": "C13443D6-3BE2-4E78-BD8E-C07D5279AA59",
      "type": "PlaneGeometry",
      "width": 60,
      "height": 20,
      "widthSegments": 1,
```

```
            "heightSegments": 1
        },
        ...
    ],
    "materials": [
        {
            "uuid": "B57ED003-B65A-480A-81AC-FAA63A912F73",
            "type": "MeshLambertMaterial",
            "color": 16777215,
            "emissive": 0,
            "depthFunc": 3,
            "depthTest": true,
            "depthWrite": true
        },
        ...
    ],
    "object": {
        "uuid": "245E4001-CB51-47D8-BC35-6D767B68B15F",
        "type": "Scene",
        "matrix": [
            1,
            0,
            0,
            0,
            0,
            1,
            0,
            0,
            0,
            0,
            1,
            0,
            0,
            0,
            0,
            1
        ],
        "children": [
            {
                "uuid": "12129DB6-48E2-4409-A015-5421F445D9DE",
                "type": "Mesh",
                "matrix": [
                    1,
                    0,
                    0,
                    0,
                    0,
                    2.220446049250313e-16,
```

```
          -1,
          0,
          0,
          1,
          2.220446049250313e-16,
          0,
          15,
          0,
          0,
          1
      ],
      "geometry": "C13443D6-3BE2-4E78-BD8E-C07D5279AA59",
      "material": "B57ED003-B65A-480A-81AC-FAA63A912F73"
  },
  ...
  {
      "uuid": "6CC1F6E5-86CF-41FB-9F33-D38870F009C7",
      "type": "PointLight",
      "matrix": [
          1,
          0,
          0,
          0,
          0,
          1,
          0,
          0,
          0,
          0,
          1,
          0,
          -40,
          60,
          -10,
          1
      ],
      "color": 16777215,
      "intensity": 1,
      "distance": 0,
      "decay": 1,
      "shadow": {
        "camera": {
          "uuid": "65C7746B-8896-4469-A2C5-97C9CDD5D483",
          "type": "PerspectiveCamera",
          "fov": 90,
          "zoom": 1,
          "near": 0.5,
          "far": 500,
```

```
                    "focus": 10,
                    "aspect": 1,
                    "filmGauge": 35,
                    "filmOffset": 0
                }
            }
        }
    ]
  }
}
```

When you load this JSON again, Three.js just recreates the objects exactly as they were exported. Loading a scene is executed as follows:

```
var loadedSceneAsJson = JSON.parse(json);
var loader = new THREE.ObjectLoader();
var scene = loader.parse(loadedSceneAsJson);
```

If you run into older material on Three.js, you might see a reference to a THREE.SceneLoader. This was the old way of storing and loading scenes but has been superseded by the approach shown earlier.

There are many different 3D programs you can use to create complex meshes. A popular open source one is Blender (www.blender.org). Three.js has an exporter for Blender (and for Maya and 3D Studio Max) that directly exports to the JSON format of Three.js. In the next section, we'll walk you through getting Blender configured to use this exporter and show you how you can export a complex model in Blender and show it in Three.js.

Working with Blender

Before we get started with the configuration, we'll show the result that we'll be aiming for. In the following screenshot, you can see a simple Blender model that we exported with the Three.js plugin and imported into Three.js with `THREE.JSONLoader`:

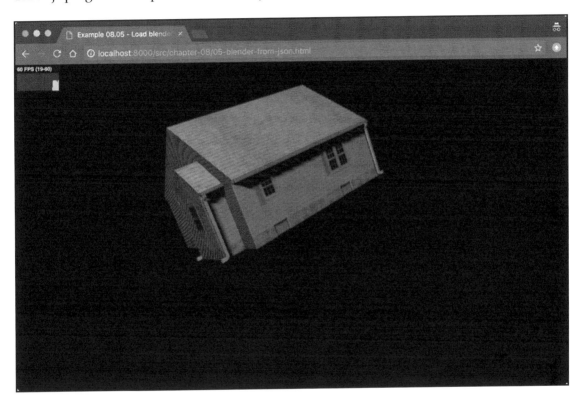

Installing the Three.js exporter in Blender

To get Blender to export Three.js models, we first need to add the Three.js exporter to Blender. The following steps are for Mac OS X but are pretty much the same on Windows and Linux. You can download Blender from `www.blender.org` and follow the platform-specific installation instructions. After installation, you can add the Three.js plugin. First, locate the `addons` directory from your Blender installation using a terminal window:

```
6. jos@Joss-MBP-3: ~/Downloads/blender-2.79-macOS-10.6/blender.app/Contents/Resourc...
➜ addons ls -l | head
total 4176
drwxr-xr-x@ 20 jos   staff      680 Sep 11  2017 add_advanced_objects_menu
drwxr-xr-x@ 10 jos   staff      340 Sep 11  2017 add_advanced_objects_panels
drwxr-xr-x@ 13 jos   staff      442 Sep 11  2017 add_curve_extra_objects
-rw-r--r--@  1 jos   staff    26581 Aug 18  2017 add_curve_ivygen.py
drwxr-xr-x@  5 jos   staff      170 Sep 11  2017 add_curve_sapling
drwxr-xr-x@  5 jos   staff      170 Sep 11  2017 add_mesh_BoltFactory
drwxr-xr-x@ 26 jos   staff      884 Sep 11  2017 add_mesh_extra_objects
-rw-r--r--@  1 jos   staff    13097 Aug 18  2017 animation_add_corrective_shape_key.py
-rw-r--r--@  1 jos   staff    17700 Aug 18  2017 animation_animall.py
➜ addons []
```

- On my Mac, it's located here: `./blender.app/Contents/MacOS/2.79/scripts/addons`
- For Windows, this directory can be found at the following location: `C:/Users/USERNAME/AppData/Roaming/Blender Foundation/Blender/2.79/scripts/addons`
- For Linux, you can find this directory here: `/home/USERNAME/.config/blender/2.79/scripts/addons`

Next, you need to get the Three.js distribution and unpack it locally. In this distribution, you can find the following folder: `utils/exporters/blender/addons/`. In this directory, there is a single subdirectory with the name `io_three`. Copy this directory to the `addons` folder of your Blender installation.

Now all we need to do is start Blender and enable the exporter. In Blender, open **Blender User Preferences (File | User Preferences)**. In the window that opens, select the **Addons** tab, and, in the **Search** box, type `three`. This will show the following screen:

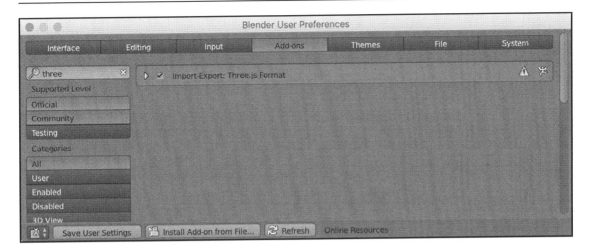

When you open this for the first time, the Three.js plugin is still disabled. Check the small checkbox to the right, and the Three.js exporter will be enabled. As a final check to see whether everything is working correctly, open the **File | Export** menu option, and you'll see Three.js listed as an **Export** option. This is shown in the following screenshot:

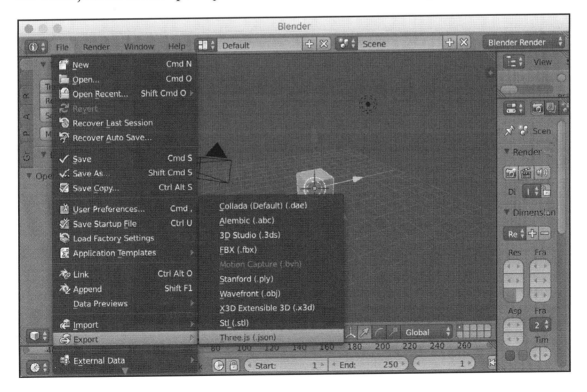

With the plugin installed, we can load our first model and export it to Three.js's JSON format.

Loading and exporting a model from Blender

As an example, we've added a simple Blender model named `hjmediastudios_house_dist.blend` in the `assets/models` folder, which you can find in the sources for this book. In this section, we'll load this model and show the minimal steps it takes to export this model to Three.js.

First, we need to load this model in Blender. Use **File** | **Open** and navigate to the folder containing the `hjmediastudios_house_dist.blend` file. Select this file and click on **Open**. This will bring up a screen that looks somewhat like this:

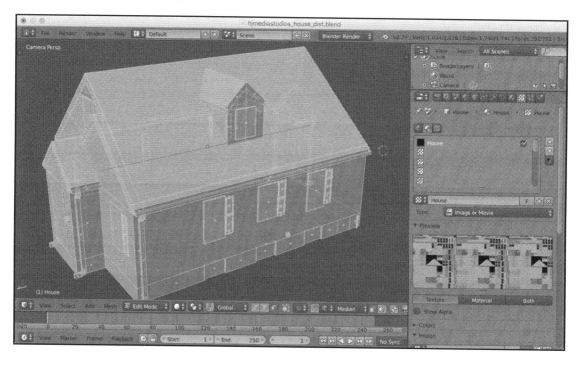

Exporting this model to the Three.js JSON format is pretty straightforward. From the **File** menu, open **Export | Three.js**, and type in the name of the export file and select **Export Three.js**. You're now presented with a list of options that can be used to fine-tune the export to Three.js. For this example, we'll use the defaults, but make sure to check that the **Textures** and **Export textures** flags are checked. In the folder you selected, this will create two files:

- `hjmediastudios_house_dist.json`: This is the JSON file in a Three.js format that describes the model.
- `Lightmap.png`: This is the exported texture, which is used by the material applied to the model.

Part of the content of the JSON file is shown next:

```
...
    "metadata":{
        "version":3,
        "type":"Geometry",
        "uvs":1,
        "faces":782,
        "vertices":1036,
        "materials":1,
        "normals":280,
        "generator":"io_three"
    }
...
```

If you look deeper into the JSON file, you can also find the material definition. If everything went OK, then you should see a reference to the `Lightmap.png` texture:

```
    "materials":[{
        "DbgColor":15658734,
        "transparent":false,
        "mapDiffuseAnisotropy":1,
        "mapDiffuseWrap":["repeat","repeat"],
        "DbgIndex":0,
        "wireframe":false,
        "mapDiffuse":"Lightmap.png",
        "depthTest":true,
        "DbgName":"House",
        "colorDiffuse":[0.64,0.64,0.64],
        "depthWrite":true,
        "blending":1,
        "mapDiffuseRepeat":[1,1],
        "visible":true,
        "colorEmissive":[0,0,0],
```

```
        "shading":"lambert",
        "opacity":1,
        "doubleSided":true
    }]
```

As you can see, the `Lightmap.png` is referenced from this material. At this point, we're ready to load the model into Three.js. The code to load this into Three.js at this point looks as follow:

```
var loader = new THREE.JSONLoader();
loader.load('../../assets/models/house/house.json', function (geometry,
mat) {

    var mesh = new THREE.Mesh(geometry, mat[0]);
    mesh.castShadow = true;
    mesh.receiveShadow = true;

    // call the default render loop.
    loaderScene.render(mesh, camera);
});
```

We've already seen `JSONLoader` before, but, this time, we use the `load` function instead of the `parse` function. In this function, we specify the URL we want to load (points to the exported JSON file), a `callback` that is called when the object is loaded. This `callback` takes two parameters: `geometry` and `mat`. The `geometry` parameter contains the model, and the `mat` parameter contains an array of material objects. We know that there is only one material, so when we create `THREE.Mesh`, we directly reference that material. Note that in this example, as in most of the others exploring the various loaders, we use the `loaderScene.render` function to show the model. This is a custom function that renders the provided mesh in a simple scene, with a couple of lights, and mouse controls to rotate the scene. If you open the `05-blender-from-json.html` example, you'll see the house we just exported from Blender.

Using the Three.js exporter isn't the only way of loading models from Blender into Three.js. Three.js understands a number of 3D file formats, and Blender can export in a couple of those formats. Using the Three.js format, however, is very easy, and if things go wrong, they are often detected quickly. In the following section, we'll look at a couple of the formats Three.js supports and also show a Blender-based example for the OBJ and MTL file formats.

Importing from 3D file formats

At the beginning of this chapter, we listed a number of formats that are supported by Three.js. In this section, we'll quickly walk through a couple of examples for those formats.

For all these formats, an additional JavaScript file needs to be included. You can find all these files in the Three.js distribution in the `examples/js/loaders` directory.

The OBJ and MTL formats

OBJ and MTL are companion formats and often used together. The OBJ file defines the geometry, and the MTL file defines the materials that are used. Both OBJ and MTL are text-based formats. A part of an OBJ file looks as follow:

```
v −0.032442 0.010796 0.025935
v −0.028519 0.013697 0.026201
v −0.029086 0.014533 0.021409
usemtl Material
s 1
f 2731 2735 2736 2732
f 2732 2736 3043 3044
```

The MTL file defines materials as follows:

```
newmtl Material
Ns 56.862745
Ka 0.000000 0.000000 0.000000
Kd 0.360725 0.227524 0.127497
Ks 0.010000 0.010000 0.010000
Ni 1.000000
d 1.000000
illum 2
```

The OBJ and MTL formats by Three.js are understood well and are also supported by Blender. So, as an alternative, you could choose to export models from Blender in the OBJ/MTL format instead of the Three.js JSON format. Three.js has two different loaders you can use. If you only want to load the geometry, you can use OBJLoader. We used this loader for our example (06-load-obj.html). The following screenshot shows this example:

To import this in Three.js, you have to add the OBJLoader JavaScript file:

```
<script type="text/javascript" src="../libs/OBJLoader.js"></script>
```

Import the model as follow:

```
var loader = new THREE.OBJLoader();
loader.load('../../assets/models/pinecone/pinecone.obj', function (mesh)
{

  var material = new THREE.MeshLambertMaterial({
    color: 0x5C3A21
  });

  // loadedMesh is a group of meshes. For
  // each mesh set the material, and compute the information
  // three.js needs for rendering.
  mesh.children.forEach(function (child) {
    child.material = material;
    child.geometry.computeVertexNormals();
    child.geometry.computeFaceNormals();
  });

  mesh.scale.set(120,120,120)

  // call the default render loop.
  loaderScene.render(mesh, camera);
});
```

In this code, we use `OBJLoader` to load the model from a URL. Once the model is loaded, the `callback` we provide is called, and we can customize the loaded mesh.

Usually, a good first step is to print out the response from the `callback` to the console to understand how the loaded object is built up. Often, with these loaders, the geometry or mesh is returned as a hierarchy of groups. Understanding this makes it much easier to place and apply the correct material and take any other additional steps. Also, look at the position of a couple of vertices to determine whether you need to scale the model up or down and where to position the camera. In this example, we've also made the calls to `computeFaceNormals` and `computeVertexNormals`. This is required to ensure that the material used (`THREE.MeshLambertMaterial`) is rendered correctly.

The next example (`07-load-obj-mtl.html`) uses the `OBJLoader`, together with the `MTLLoader`, to load a model and directly assign a material. The following screenshot shows this example:

First, we need to add the correct loaders to the page:

```
<script type="text/javascript" charset="UTF-8"
src="../../libs/three/loaders/MTLLoader.js"></script>
<script type="text/javascript" charset="UTF-8"
src="../../libs/three/loaders/OBJLoader.js"></script>
```

We can load the model from the OBJ and MTL files as follows:

```
var mtlLoader = new THREE.MTLLoader();
  mtlLoader.setPath("../../assets/models/butterfly/")
  mtlLoader.load('butterfly.mtl', function (materials) {
    materials.preload();

    var objLoader = new THREE.OBJLoader();
    objLoader.setMaterials(materials);
    objLoader.load('../../assets/models/butterfly/butterfly.obj', function
(object) {
```

```
    // move wings to more horizontal position
    [0, 2, 4, 6].forEach(function (i) {
      object.children[i].rotation.z = 0.3 * Math.PI
    });

    [1, 3, 5, 7].forEach(function (i) {
      object.children[i].rotation.z = -0.3 * Math.PI
    });

    // configure the wings,
    var wing2 = object.children[5];
    var wing1 = object.children[4];

    wing1.material.opacity = 0.9;
    wing1.material.transparent = true;
    wing1.material.depthTest = false;
    wing1.material.side = THREE.DoubleSide;

    wing2.material.opacity = 0.9;
    wing2.material.depthTest = false;
    wing2.material.transparent = true;
    wing2.material.side = THREE.DoubleSide;

    object.scale.set(140, 140, 140);
    mesh = object;

    object.rotation.x = 0.2;
    object.rotation.y = -1.3;

    loaderScene.render(mesh, camera);
  });
});
```

The first thing to mention before we look at the code is that if you receive an OBJ file, an MTL file, and the required texture files, you'll have to check how the MTL file references the textures. These should be referenced relative to the MTL file and not as an absolute path. The code itself isn't that different than the one we saw for THREE.ObjLoader. The first thing we do is to load the MTL file with a THREE.MTLLoader and the loaded materials are set in THREE.ObjLoader through the setMaterials function.

The model we've used as an example, in this case, is a complex model. So, we set some specific properties in the callback to fix a number of rendering issues, as follows:

- The opacity in the source files was set incorrectly, which caused the wings to be invisible. So, to fix that, we set the `opacity` and `transparent` properties ourselves.

- By default, Three.js only renders one side of an object. Since we look at the wings from two sides, we need to set the `side` property to the `THREE.DoubleSide` value.

- The wings caused some unwanted artifacts when they needed to be rendered on top of one another. We've fixed that by setting the `depthTest` property to `false`. This has a slight impact on performance, but it can often solve some strange rendering artifacts.

But, as you can see, you can easily load complex models directly into Three.js and render them in real time in your browser. You might need to fine-tune various material properties though.

Loading a COLLADA model

COLLADA models (the extension is `.dae`) are another very common format for defining scenes and models (and animations, as we'll see in the following chapter). In a COLLADA model, it is not just the geometry that is defined but also the materials. It's even possible to define light sources. To load COLLADA models, you have to take pretty much the same steps as for the OBJ and MTL models. You start by including the correct loader:

```
<script type="text/javascript" src="../libs/ColladaLoader.js"></script>
```

For this example, we'll load the following model:

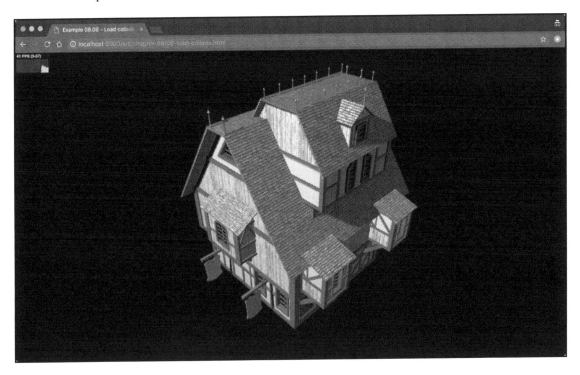

Loading this model is once again pretty simple:

```
// load the model
  var loader = new THREE.ColladaLoader();
  loader.load("../../assets/models/medieval/Medieval_building.DAE",
function (result) {
    var sceneGroup = result.scene;

    sceneGroup.children.forEach(function (child) {
      if (child instanceof THREE.Mesh) {
        child.receiveShadow = true;
        child.castShadow = true;
      } else {
        // remove any lighting sources from the model
        sceneGroup.remove(child);
      }
    });

    // correctly scale and position the model
    sceneGroup.rotation.z = 0.5 * Math.PI;
    sceneGroup.scale.set(8, 8, 8);
```

```
    // call the default render loop.
    loaderScene.render(sceneGroup, camera);
});
```

The main difference here is the result of the object that is returned to the `callback`. The `result` object has the following structure:

```
var result = {
  scene: scene,
  animations: [...],
  kinematic: {...},
  library: {...},
};
```

In this chapter, we're interested in the objects that are in the `scene` parameter. To get a good idea of what's in there, you can print out the scene object to the console first. In this case, we remove all the non `THREE.Mesh` objects and enable shadows on the `THREE.Mesh` objects.

As you can see, for most complex models, including materials, you often have to take a number of additional steps to get the desired results. By looking closely at how the materials are configured (using `console.log()`), or replacing them with test materials, problems are often easy to spot and solve.

Loading models from other supported formats

We're going to quickly skim over these file formats as they all follow the same principles:

1. Include `[NameOfFormat]Loader.js` in your web page.
2. Use `[NameOfFormat]Loader.load()` to load a URL.
3. Check what the response format for the `callback` function looks like and render the result.

We have included an example for all these formats:

Name	Example	Screenshot
STL	09-load-STL.html	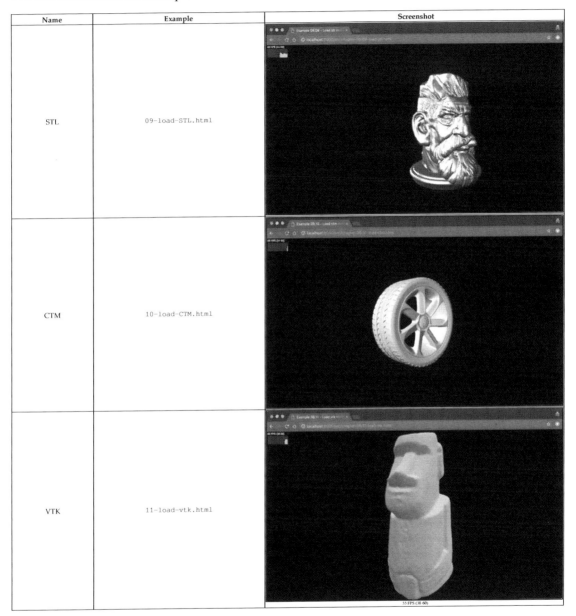
CTM	10-load-CTM.html	
VTK	11-load-vtk.html	

AWD	14-load-awd.html	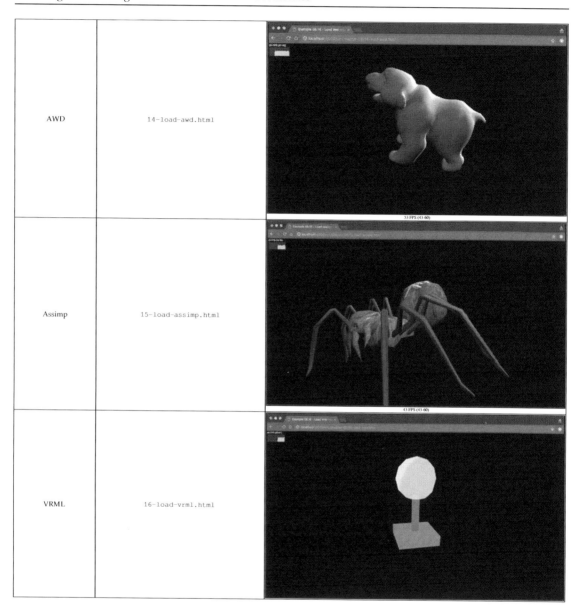
Assimp	15-load-assimp.html	
VRML	16-load-vrml.html	

Babylon	The Babylon loader is slightly different to the other loaders in this table. With this loader, you don't load a single `THREE.Mesh` or `THREE.Geometry` instance, but, with this loader, you load a complete scene, including lights. `17-load-babylon.html`	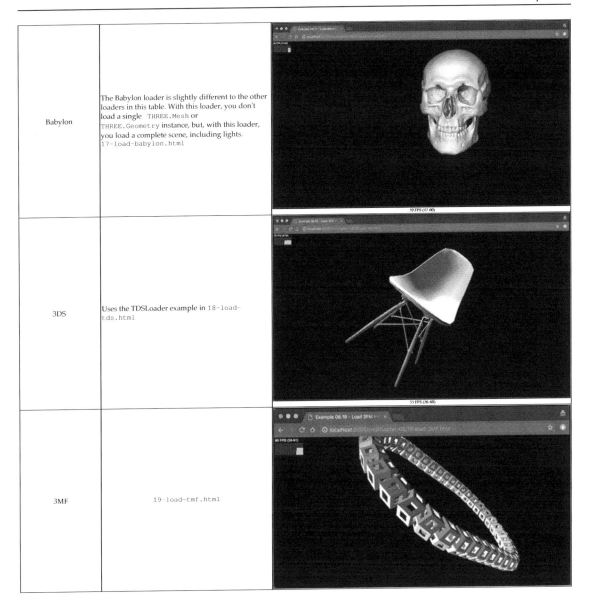
3DS	Uses the TDSLoader example in `18-load-tds.html`	
3MF	`19-load-tmf.html`	

AMF	`20-load-amf.html`	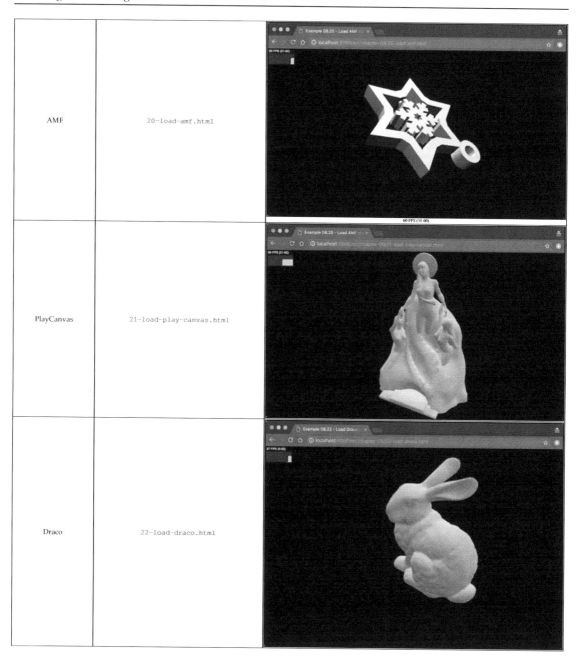
PlayCanvas	`21-load-play-canvas.html`	
Draco	`22-load-draco.html`	

PRWM	23-load-prwm.html	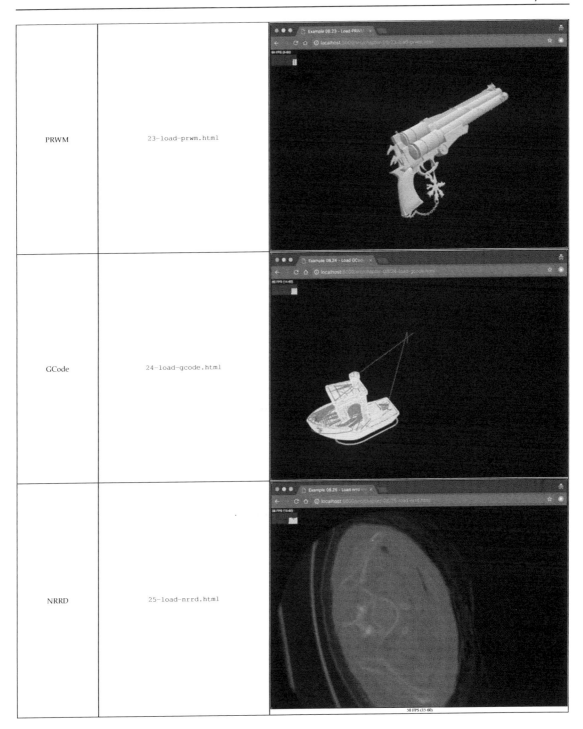
GCode	24-load-gcode.html	
NRRD	25-load-nrrd.html	

SVG	`26-load-svg.html`	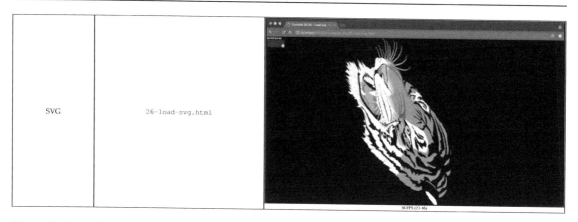

If you look at the source code for these examples, you might see that for some of them, we need to change a number of `material` properties or do some scaling before the model is rendered correctly. The reason we need to do this is because of the way the model is created in its external application, giving it different dimensions and grouping. When rendering in Three.js, we need to take that into account.

We've almost shown all the supported file formats. In the next two sections, we'll look at two different kinds of a loader. First, we'll look at how to render proteins from PDB format, and finally, we'll use a model defined in PLY format to create a particle system.

Show proteins from PDB

PDB (`www.rcsb.org`) contains detailed information about many different molecules and proteins. Besides the explanation of these proteins, they also provide a way to download the structure of these molecules in PDB format. Three.js provides a loader for files specified in the PDB format. In this section, we'll give an example of how you can parse PDB files and visualize them with Three.js.

The first thing we always need to do to load in a new file format is to include the correct loader in Three.js, as follows:

```
<script type="text/javascript" src="../libs/PDBLoader.js"></script>
```

With this loader included, we're going to create the following 3D model of the molecule description provided (see the 12-load-pdb.html example):

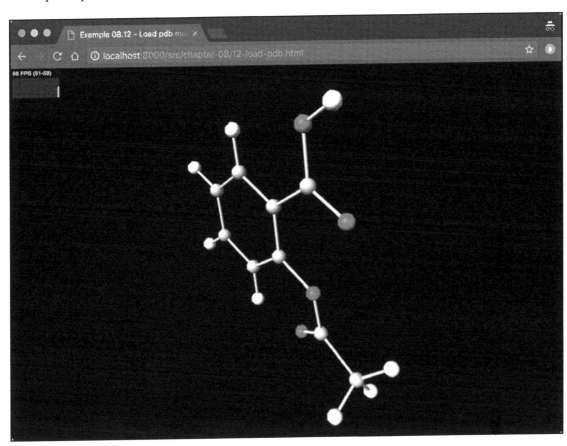

Loading a PDB file is done in the same manner as the previous formats, as follows:

```
loader.load("../../assets/models/molecules/aspirin.pdb", function
(geometries) {

    var group = new THREE.Object3D();

    // create the atoms
    var geometryAtoms = geometries.geometryAtoms;

    for (i = 0; i < geometryAtoms.attributes.position.count; i++) {
        var startPosition = new THREE.Vector3();
        startPosition.x = geometryAtoms.attributes.position.getX(i);
        startPosition.y = geometryAtoms.attributes.position.getY(i);
```

```
        startPosition.z = geometryAtoms.attributes.position.getZ(i);

        var color = new THREE.Color();
        color.r = geometryAtoms.attributes.color.getX(i);
        color.g = geometryAtoms.attributes.color.getY(i);
        color.b = geometryAtoms.attributes.color.getZ(i);

        var material = new THREE.MeshPhongMaterial({
          color: color
        });

        var sphere = new THREE.SphereGeometry(0.2);
        var mesh = new THREE.Mesh(sphere, material);
        mesh.position.copy(startPosition);
        group.add(mesh);
    }

    // create the bindings
    var geometryBonds = geometries.geometryBonds;

    for (var j = 0; j < geometryBonds.attributes.position.count; j += 2) {
      var startPosition = new THREE.Vector3();
      startPosition.x = geometryBonds.attributes.position.getX(j);
      startPosition.y = geometryBonds.attributes.position.getY(j);
      startPosition.z = geometryBonds.attributes.position.getZ(j);

      var endPosition = new THREE.Vector3();
      endPosition.x = geometryBonds.attributes.position.getX(j + 1);
      endPosition.y = geometryBonds.attributes.position.getY(j + 1);
      endPosition.z = geometryBonds.attributes.position.getZ(j + 1);

      // use the start and end to create a curve, and use the curve to draw
      // a tube, which connects the atoms
      var path = new THREE.CatmullRomCurve3([startPosition, endPosition]);
      var tube = new THREE.TubeGeometry(path, 1, 0.04);
      var material = new THREE.MeshPhongMaterial({
        color: 0xcccccc
      });
      var mesh = new THREE.Mesh(tube, material);
      group.add(mesh);
    }

    loaderScene.render(group, camera);
```

As you can see from this example code, we instantiate THREE.PDBLoader, pass in the model file we want to load, and provide a callback that is called when the model is loaded. For this specific loader, the callback function is called with a JavaScript object that contains two properties: geometryAtoms and geometryBonds. The position attributes from the geometryAtoms argument supplied contain the positions of the individual atoms, and the color attributes can be used to color the individual atoms. For the link between the atoms, geometryBounds is used.

Based on the position and color, we create a THREE.Mesh object and add it to a group:

```
var material = new THREE.MeshPhongMaterial({
  color: color
});

var sphere = new THREE.SphereGeometry(0.2);
var mesh = new THREE.Mesh(sphere, material);
mesh.position.copy(startPosition);
group.add(mesh);
```

With regard to the connection between the atoms, we follow the same approach. We get the start and end position of the connection and use that to draw the connection:

```
var path = new THREE.CatmullRomCurve3([startPosition, endPosition]);
var tube = new THREE.TubeGeometry(path, 1, 0.04);
var material = new THREE.MeshPhongMaterial({
  color: 0xcccccc
});
var mesh = new THREE.Mesh(tube, material);
group.add(mesh);
```

For the connection, we first create a 3D path using the `THREE.CatmullRomCurve3`. This path is used as input for `THREE.Tube` and is used to create the connection between the atoms. All the connections and atoms are added to a group, and this group is added to the scene. There are many models you can download from PDB. For instance, the following screenshot shows the structure of a diamond:

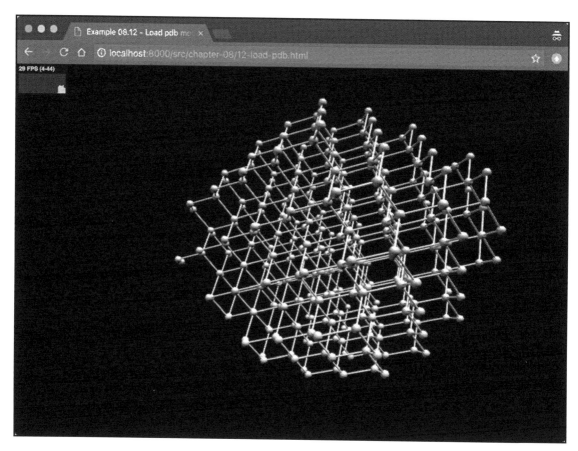

Creating a particle system from a PLY model

Working with the PLY format isn't that much different than the other formats. You include the loader, provide a `callback` function, and visualize the model. For this last example, however, we're going to do something different. Instead of rendering the model as a mesh, we'll use the information from this model to create a particle system (see the `15-load-ply.html` example). The following screenshot shows this example:

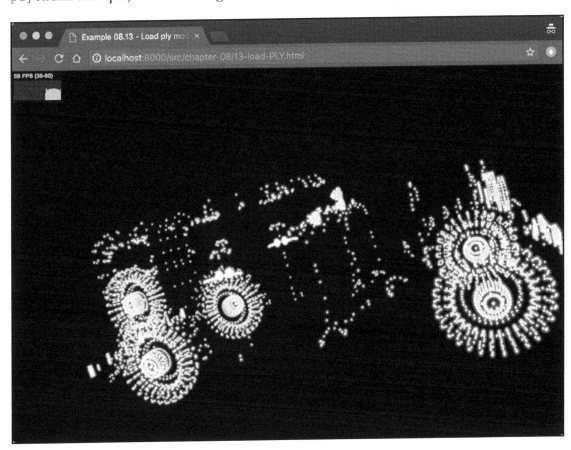

The JavaScript code to render the preceding screenshot is actually very simple; it is as follows:

```
loader.load("../../assets/models/carcloud/carcloud.ply", function
(geometry) {
    var material = new THREE.PointsMaterial({
      color: 0xffffff,
      size: 1,
```

```
      opacity: 0.6,
      transparent: true,
      blending: THREE.AdditiveBlending,
      depthWrite: false,
      map: generateSprite()
    });

    var group = new THREE.Points(geometry, material);
    group.scale.set(2.5, 2.5, 2.5);

    loaderScene.render(group, camera);
  });
```

As you can see, we use `THREE.PLYLoader` to load the model. The `callback` function returns `geometry`, and we use this geometry as input for `THREE.Points`. The material we use is the same as what we used for the last example in Chapter 7, *Points and Sprites*. As you can see, with Three.js, it is very easy to combine models from various sources and render them in different ways, all with a few lines of code.

Summary

Using models from external sources isn't that hard to do in Three.js. Especially for simple models, you only have to take a few simple steps. When working with external models, or creating them using grouping and merging, it is good to keep a couple of things in mind. The first thing you need to remember is that when you group objects, they still remain available as individual objects. Transformations applied to the parent also affect the children, but you can still transform the children individually. Besides grouping, you can also merge geometries together. With this approach, you lose the individual geometries and get a single new geometry. This is especially useful when you're dealing with thousands of geometries you need to render and you're running into performance issues.

Three.js supports a large number of external formats. When using these format loaders, it's a good idea to look through the source code and log out the information received in the callback. This will help you to understand the steps you need to take to get the correct mesh and set it to the correct position and scale. Often, when the model doesn't show correctly, this is caused by its material settings. It could be that incompatible texture formats are used, opacity is incorrectly defined, or the format contains incorrect links to the texture images. It is usually a good idea to use a test material to determine whether the model itself is loaded correctly and log the loaded material to the JavaScript console to check for unexpected values. It is also possible to export meshes and scenes by just calling the `asJson` function and load them again with the `JSONLoader`.

The models you worked within this chapter, and in the previous chapters, are mostly static models. They aren't animated, don't move around, and don't change shape. In `Chapter 9`, *Animations and Moving the Camera*, you'll learn how you can animate your models to make them come to life. Besides animations, the following chapter will also explain the various camera controls provided by Three.js. With a camera control, you can move, pan, and rotate the camera around your scene.

9
Animations and Moving the Camera

In the previous chapters, we have seen some simple animations, but nothing too complex. In `Chapter 1`, *Creating Your First 3D Scene with Three.js*, we introduced the basic rendering loop, and in the chapters following that, we used that to rotate some simple objects and show a couple of other basic animation concepts. In this chapter, we're going to look in more detail at how animation is supported by Three.js. We will look in detail at the following four subjects:

- Basic animation
- Moving the camera
- Morphing and skinning
- Loading external animations

We start with the basic concepts behind animations.

Basic animations

Before we look at the examples, let's do a quick recap of what was shown in `Chapter 1`, *Creating Your First 3D Scene with Three.js* on the render loop. To support animations, we need to tell Three.js to render the scene every so often. For this, we use the standard HTML5 `requestAnimationFrame` functionality, as follows:

```
render();

function render() {

  // render the scene
  renderer.render(scene, camera);
  // schedule the next rendering using requestAnimationFrame
```

```
    requestAnimationFrame(render);
}
```

With this code, we only need to call the `render()` function once when we're done initializing the scene. In the `render()` function itself, we use `requestAnimationFrame` to schedule the next rendering. This way, the browser will make sure the `render()` function is called at the correct interval (usually around 60 times a second). Before `requestAnimationFrame` was added to browsers, `setInterval(function, interval)` or `setTimeout(function, interval)` were used. These would call the specified function once every set interval. The problem with this approach is that it doesn't take into account what else is going on. Even if your animation isn't shown or is in a hidden tab, it is still called and is still using resources. Another issue is that these functions update the screen whenever they are called, not when it is the best time for the browser, which would result in higher CPU usage. With `requestAnimationFrame`, we don't tell the browser when it needs to update the screen; we ask the browser to run the supplied function when it's most opportune. Usually, this results in a frame rate of about 60 fps. With `requestAnimationFrame`, your animations will run more smoothly and will be more CPU- and GPU-friendly, and you don't have to worry about timing issues yourself.

Simple animations

With this approach, we can very easily animate objects by changing their rotation, scale, position, material, vertices, faces, and anything else you can imagine. In the next render loop, Three.js will render the changed properties. A very simple example, based on the one we already saw in Chapter 1, *Creating Your First 3D Scene with Three.js*, is available in `01-basic-animation.html`. The following screenshot shows this example:

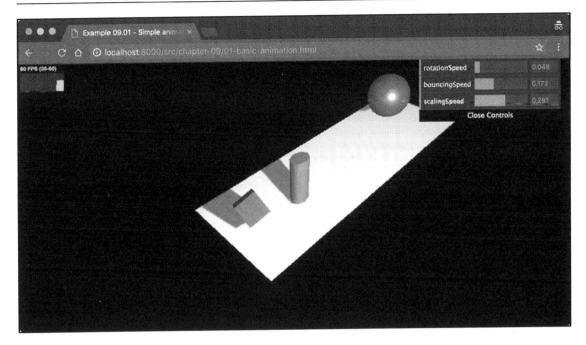

60 FPS (35-60)

The `render` loop for this is very simple. Just change the properties of the involved meshes, and Three.js handles the rest. Here's how we do this:

```
function render() {
  cube.rotation.x += controls.rotationSpeed;
  cube.rotation.y += controls.rotationSpeed;
  cube.rotation.z += controls.rotationSpeed;

  step += controls.bouncingSpeed;
  sphere.position.x = 20 + ( 10 * (Math.cos(step)));
  sphere.position.y = 2 + ( 10 * Math.abs(Math.sin(step)));

  scalingStep += controls.scalingSpeed;
  var scaleX = Math.abs(Math.sin(scalingStep / 4));
  var scaleY = Math.abs(Math.cos(scalingStep / 5));
  var scaleZ = Math.abs(Math.sin(scalingStep / 7));
  cylinder.scale.set(scaleX, scaleY, scaleZ);

  renderer.render(scene, camera);
  requestAnimationFrame(render);
}
```

Nothing spectacular here, but it nicely shows the concept behind the basic animations we discuss in this book. In the next section, we'll take a quick sidestep. Besides animations, an important aspect, which you'll quickly run into when working with Three.js in more complex scenes, is the ability to select objects on screen using the mouse.

Selecting objects

Even though not directly related to animations, since we'll be looking into cameras and animations in this chapter, it is a nice addition to the subjects explained in this chapter. What we'll show here is how you can select an object from a scene using the mouse. We'll first look at the code required for this before we look at the example:

```
var projector = new THREE.Projector();
function onDocumentMouseDown(event) {

    var vector = new THREE.Vector3((event.clientX / window.innerWidth) * 2
 - 1, -(event.clientY / window.innerHeight) * 2 + 1, 0.5);
    vector = vector.unproject(camera);

    var raycaster = new THREE.Raycaster(camera.position,
vector.sub(camera.position).normalize());
    var intersects = raycaster.intersectObjects([sphere, cylinder, cube]);

    if (intersects.length > 0) {
        console.log(intersects[0]);
        intersects[0].object.material.transparent = true;
        intersects[0].object.material.opacity = 0.1;
    }
}
```

In this code, we use `THREE.Projector` together with `THREE.Raycaster` to determine whether we've clicked on a specific object. What happens when we click on the screen is the following:

1. First, `THREE.Vector3` is created based on the position where we've clicked on the screen.

2. Next, with the `vector.unproject` function, we convert the clicked position on screen to coordinates in our Three.js scene. In other words, we unproject from screen coordinates to 3D-world coordinates.

3. Next, we create `THREE.Raycaster`. With `THREE.Raycaster`, we can cast rays into our scene. In this case, we emit a ray from the position of the camera (`camera.position`) to the position we clicked on in the scene.

4. Finally, we use the `raycaster.intersectObjects` function to determine whether any of the supplied objects are hit by this ray.

The result from this final step contains information on any object that is hit by this ray. The following information is provided:

```
09-02.js:123
▼ {distance: 62.06043252608528, point: Vector3, object: Mesh, uv: Vector2, face: Face3, …}
    distance: 62.06043252608528
  ▶ face: Face3 {a: 14, b: 15, c: 7, normal: Vector3, vertexNormals: Array(3), …}
    faceIndex: 13
  ▶ object: Mesh {uuid: "19E6C6A6-5DA3-436C-B42E-63A87568E680", name: "", type: "Mesh", parent: Scene, children: Array(0), …}
  ▶ point: Vector3 {x: -0.2910410329675761, y: -6.669043305314233, z: 1.8774922991090282}
  ▶ uv: Vector2 {x: 0.8281414821798634, y: 0.03480514310623093}
  ▶ __proto__: Object
```

The mesh that was clicked on is the `Object`, `face`, and `faceIndex` point to the face of the mesh that was selected. The `distance` value is measured from the camera to the clicked object, and `point` is the exact position on the mesh where it was clicked. Finally, we have the `uv` value, which determines, when using textures, where the point clicks appear on the 2D texture (in a range from 0 to 1; more information on `uv` can be found in Chapter 10, *Loading and Working with Textures*). You can test this out in the `02-selecting-objects.html` example. Any object you click on will become transparent, and the details of the selection will be printed to the console.

If you want to see the path of the ray that is cast, you can enable the showRay property from the menu. The following screenshot shows the ray that was used to select the blue sphere:

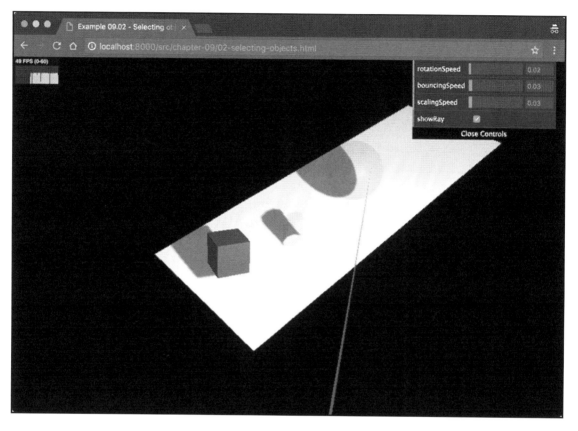

49 FPS (0-60)

Now that we've finished this small intermission, let's get back to our animations. Until now, we've changed the properties in our render loop to animate an object. In the next section, we'll look at a small library that makes defining animations a lot easier.

Animating with Tween.js

Tween.js is a small JavaScript library that you can download
from `https://github.com/sole/tween.js/` and that you can use to easily define the
transition of a property between two values. All the intermediate points between the start
and end values are calculated for you. This process is called **tweening**. For instance, you
can use this library to change the x position of a mesh from 10 to 3 in 10 seconds, as
follows:

```
var tween = new TWEEN.Tween({x: 10}).to({x: 3}, 10000)
    .easing(TWEEN.Easing.Elastic.InOut)
    .onUpdate( function () {
        // update the mesh
    })
```

In this example, we've created `TWEEN.Tween`. This tween will make sure that the x property
is changed from 10 to 3 over a period of 10000 milliseconds. Tween.js also allows you to
define how this property is changed over time. This can be done using linear, quadratic, or
any of the other possibilities
(see `http://sole.github.io/tween.js/examples/03_graphs.html` for a complete
overview). The way the value is changed over time is called **easing**. With Tween.js, you
configure this using the `easing()` function.

Using this library together with Three.js is very simple. If you open the `03-animation-tween.html` example, you can see the Tween.js library in action. The following screenshot shows a still image of the example:

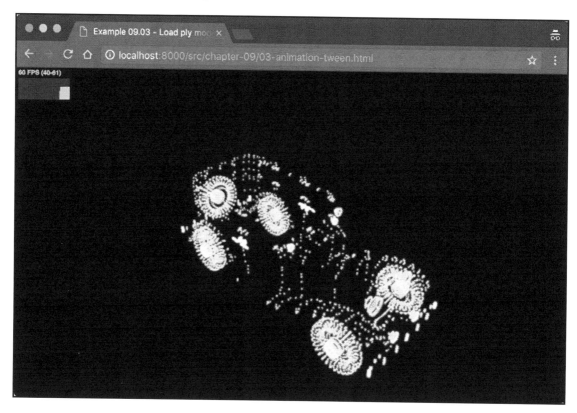

And we'll use the Tween.js library to move this to a single point using a specific easing(), which at a certain point looks as follows:

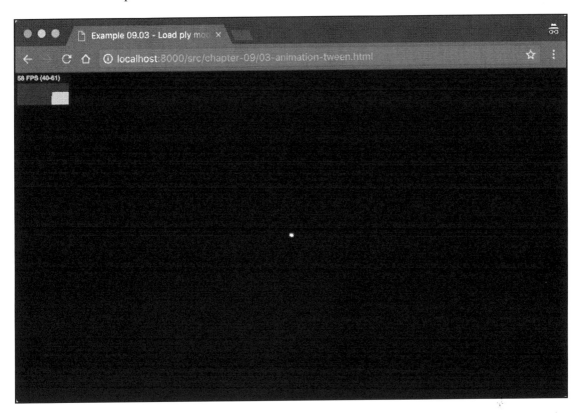

In this example, we've taken a particle cloud from Chapter 7, *Points and Sprites*, and created an animation where all the points slowly move down to the ground. The position of these particles is set by using on a tween created with the Tween.js library, as follows:

```
var posSrc = { pos: 1}
var tween = new TWEEN.Tween(posSrc).to({pos: 0}, 2000);
tween.easing(TWEEN.Easing.Bounce.InOut);

var tweenBack = new TWEEN.Tween(posSrc).to({pos: 1}, 2000);
tweenBack.easing(TWEEN.Easing.Bounce.InOut);
tweenBack.chain(tween);
tween.chain(tweenBack);
tween.start();

var onUpdate = function () {
  var count = 0;
```

```
var pos = this.pos;

loadedGeometry.vertices.forEach(function (e) {
  var newY = ((e.y + 3.22544) * pos) - 3.22544;
  particleCloud.geometry.vertices[count++].set(e.x, newY, e.z);
});

particleCloud.sortParticles = true;
};
```

With this piece of code, we create two tweens: `tween` and `tweenBack`. The first one defines how the `position` property transitions from 1 to 0, and the second one does the opposite. With the `chain()` function, we chain these two tweens to each other, so these tweens will start looping when started. To use the value from the tween, we have two different options. We can use the `onUpdate` function provided by this library to call a function with the updated values, whenever the `tween` is updated (which is done by calling `TWEEN.update()`), or we can directly access the updated values. In this example, we use the latter approach. Before we look at the changes we need to make in the `render` function, we first take one additional step after we load the model. We want to tween between the original values to zero and back again. For this, we need to store the original positions of the vertices somewhere. We do this by adding this to the `callback` when we load the model:

```
// copy the original position, so we can referene that when tweening
var origPosition = geometry.attributes['position'].clone()
geometry.origPosition = origPosition
```

Now, whenever we want to access the original position, we can look at the `origPosition` variable on the geometry.

The loader in this example uses `BufferGeometry`; we don't copy the vertices array, but we need to copy the `'position'` attribute.

Now that we've got a reference to the original array, we can simply use that value to calculate the new positions based on the value of the `tween`. In the `render` function, we add the following:

```
TWEEN.update();

var positionArray = mesh.geometry.attributes['position']
var origPosition = mesh.geometry.origPosition

for (i = 0; i < positionArray.count ; i++) {
```

```
    var oldPosX = origPosition.getX(i);
    var oldPosY = origPosition.getY(i);
    var oldPosZ = origPosition.getZ(i);
    positionArray.setX(i, oldPosX * posSrc.pos);
    positionArray.setY(i, oldPosY * posSrc.pos);
    positionArray.setZ(i, oldPosZ * posSrc.pos);
  }
  positionArray.needsUpdate = true;
```

In this `render` function, we first call `TWEEN.Update`, which calculates the new value of the tweened variable (from 1 to 0 and back again). Remember that we used the `posSrc.pos` variable for this. Now we iterate over all the vertices, and update their positions.

With these steps in place, the `tween` library will take care of positioning the various points on the screen. As you can see, using this library is much easier than having to manage the transitions yourself. Besides animating and changing objects, we can also animate a scene by moving the camera around. In the previous chapters, we already did this a couple of times by manually updating the position of the camera. Three.js also provides a number of additional ways of updating the camera.

Working with the camera

Three.js has a number of camera controls you can use to control the camera throughout a scene. These controls are located in the Three.js distribution and can be found in the `examples/js/controls` directory. In this section, we'll look in more detail at the following controls:

Name	Description
FirstPersonControls	These are controls that behave like those in first-person shooters. Move around with the keyboard and look around with the mouse.
FlyControls	These are flight simulator-like controls. Move and steer with the keyboard and the mouse.
TrackBallControls	These are the most-used controls, allowing you to use the mouse (or the trackball) to easily move, pan, and zoom around the scene. Note that if you use `OrtographicCamera`, you can use `OrtographicTrackBallControls`, which are specifically made to work with this camera type.
OrbitControls	This simulates a satellite in orbit around a specific scene. This allows you to move around with the mouse and keyboard.

These controls are the most useful controls available. Besides these, Three.js also provides a number of additional controls you can use (but that aren't explained in this book). Using these controls, however, is done in the same manner as the ones explained in the previous table:

Name	Description
DeviceOrientationControls	This controls the movement of the camera based on the orientation of the device. It internally uses the HTML device orientation API: http://www.w3.org/TR/orientation-event/.
EditorControls	These are controls that are specifically created for online 3D editors. This is used by the Three.js online editor, which you can find at http://threejs.org/editor/.
OculusControls	These are controls that allow you to use an Oculus Rift device to look around your scene.
OrthographicTrackballControls	This is the same control as TrackBallControls but specifically created to be used with THREE.OrthographicCamera.
PointerLockControls	This is a simple control that locks the mouse using the DOM element on which the scene is rendered. This provides basic functionality for a simple 3D game.
TransformControls	This is an internal control used by the Three.js editor.
VRControls	This is a control that uses the PositionSensorVRDevice API to control the scene. More information on this standard can be found at https://developer.mozilla.org/en-US/docs/Web/API/Navigator.getVRDevices.

If you look through the example code, you might notice the DragControls class. While it is called a control, it is different than the ones we're discussing in this chapter. With the DragControls object, instead of moving the camera around, you can move an object around in the scene.

Besides using these camera controls, you can of course also move the camera yourself by setting position and change where it is pointed to using the lookAt() function.

If you've worked with an older version of Three.js, you might be missing a specific camera control named THREE.PathControls. With this control, it was possible to define a path (for example, using THREE.Spline) and move the camera along that path. In the last version of Three.js, this control was removed because of code complexity. The people behind Three.js are currently working on a replacement, but one isn't available yet.

Another one of the controls that has been removed is THREE.RollControls. This control provided a subset of the functionality provided by THREE.FlyControls, so it has been removed. You can configure THREE.FlyControls to behave just like the old THREE.RollControls, should you want to.

The first of the controls we'll look at is `TrackballControls`.

TrackballControls

Before you can use `TrackballControls`, you first need to include the correct JavaScript file in your page:

```
<script type="text/javascript" src="../libs/TrackballControls.js"></script>
```

With this included, we can create the controls and attach them to the camera, as follows:

```
var trackballControls = new THREE.TrackballControls(camera);
trackballControls.rotateSpeed = 1.0;
trackballControls.zoomSpeed = 1.0;
trackballControls.panSpeed = 1.0;
```

Updating the position of the camera is something we do in the `render` loop, as follows:

```
var clock = new THREE.Clock();
function render() {
  var delta = clock.getDelta();
  trackballControls.update(delta);
  requestAnimationFrame(render);
  webGLRenderer.render(scene, camera);
}
```

In the preceding code snippet, we see a new Three.js object, `THREE.Clock`. The `THREE.Clock` object can be used to exactly calculate the elapsed time that a specific invocation or rendering loop takes to complete. You can do this by calling the `clock.getDelta()` function. This function will return the elapsed time between this call and the previous call to `getDelta()`. To update the position of the camera, we call the `trackballControls.update()` function. In this function, we need to provide the time that has passed since the last time this update function was called. For this, we use the `getDelta()` function from the `THREE.Clock` object. You might wonder why we don't just pass in the frame rate (1/60 seconds) to the `update` function. The reason is that with `requestAnimationFrame`, we can expect 60 fps, but this isn't guaranteed. Depending on all kinds of external factors, the frame rate might change. To make sure the camera turns and rotates smoothly, we need to pass in the exact elapsed time.

A working example for this can be found in `04-trackball-controls-camera.html`. The following screenshot shows a still image of this example:

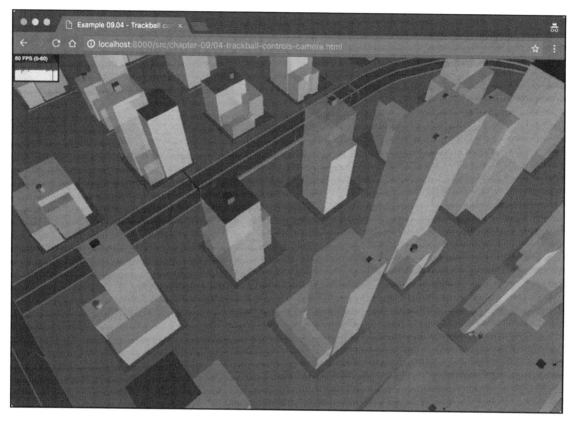

60 FPS (0-60)

You can control the camera in the following manner:

Control	Action
Left mouse button and move	Rotate and roll the camera around the scene
Scroll wheel	Zoom in and zoom out
Middle mouse button and move	Zoom in and zoom out
Right mouse button and move	Pan around the scene

There are a couple of properties that you can use to fine-tune how the camera acts. For instance, you can set how fast the camera rotates with the `rotateSpeed` property and disable zooming by setting the `noZoom` property to `true`. In this chapter, we won't go into detail on what each property does as they are pretty much self-explanatory. For a complete overview of what is possible, look at the source of the `TrackballControls.js` file, where these properties are listed.

FlyControls

The next control we'll look at is `FlyControls`. With `FlyControls`, you can fly around a scene using controls also found in flight simulators. An example can be found in `05-fly-controls-camera.html`. The following screenshot shows a still image of this example:

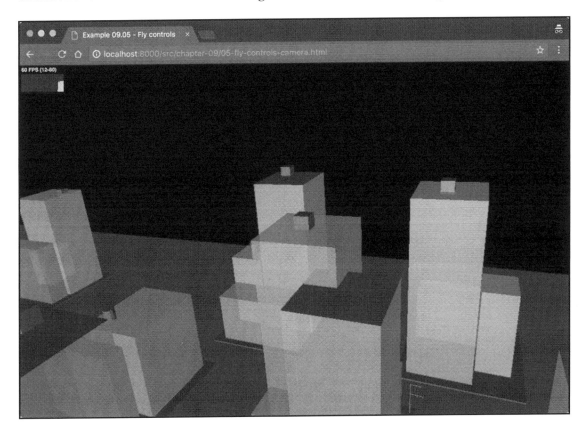

60 FPS (12-60)

Enabling `FlyControls` works in the same manner as `TrackballControls`. First, load the correct JavaScript file:

```
<script type="text/javascript" src="../libs/FlyControls.js"></script>
```

Next, we configure the controls and attach them to the camera, as follows:

```
var flyControls = new THREE.FlyControls(camera);
flyControls.movementSpeed = 25;
flyControls.domElement = document.querySelector('#WebGL-output');
flyControls.rollSpeed = Math.PI / 24;
flyControls.autoForward = true;
flyControls.dragToLook = false;
```

Once again, we won't look into all the specific properties. Look at the source of the `FlyControls.js` file for that. Let's just pick out the properties you need to configure to get this control working. The property that needs to be set correctly is the `domElement` property. This property should point to the element in which we render the scene. For the examples in this book, we use the following element for our output:

```
<div id="webgl-output"></div>
```

We set the property like this:

```
flyControls.domElement = document.querySelector('#webgl-output');
```

If we don't set this property correctly, moving the mouse around will result in strange behavior. You can control the camera with `THREE.FlyControls` in the following manner:

Control	Action
Left and middle mouse button	Start moving forward
Right mouse button	Move backward
Mouse movement	Look around
W	Start moving forward
S	Move backward
A	Move left
D	Move right
R	Move up
F	Move down
Left, right, up, and down arrows	Look left, right, up, and down
G	Roll left
E	Roll right

The next control we'll look at is THREE.FirstPersonControls.

FirstPersonControls

As the name implies, FirstPersonControls allows you to control the camera just like in a first-person shooter. The mouse is used to look around, and the keyboard is used to walk around. You can find an example in 07-first-person-camera.html. The following screenshot shows a still image of this example:

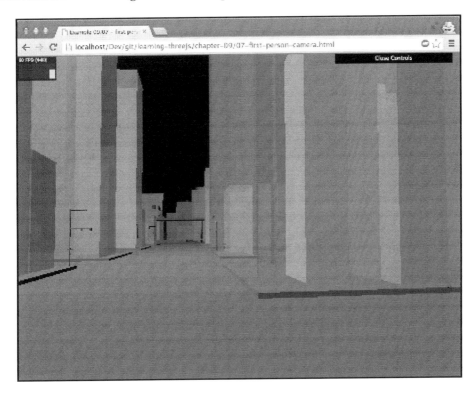

Creating these controls follows the same principles as the ones followed for other controls we've seen until now. The example we've just shown uses the following configuration:

```
var fpControls = new THREE.FirstPersonControls(camera);
fpControls.lookSpeed = 0.4;
fpControls.movementSpeed = 20;
fpControls.lookVertical = true;
fpControls.constrainVertical = true;
fpControls.verticalMin = 1.0;
fpControls.verticalMax = 2.0;
fpControls.lon = -150;
fpControls.lat = 120;
```

The only properties that you should carefully look at when using this control for yourself are the last two: the `lon` and `lat` properties. These two properties define where the camera is pointed at when the scene is rendered for the first time.

The controls for this control are pretty straightforward:

Control	Action
Mouse movement	Look around
Left, right, up, and down arrows	Move left, right, forward, and backward
W	Move forward
A	Move left
S	Move backward
D	Move right
R	Move up
F	Move down
Q	Stop all movement

For the final control, we'll move on from this first-person perspective to the perspective from space.

OrbitControl

The OrbitControl control is a great way to rotate and pan around an object in the center of the scene. With 08-controls-orbit.html, we've included an example that shows how this control works. The following screenshot shows a still image of this example:

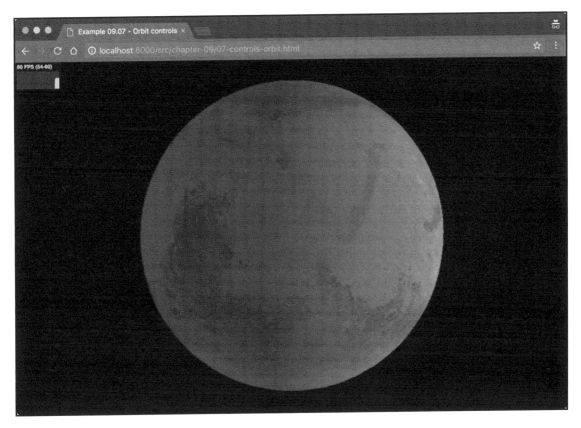

60 FPS (54-60)

Using `OrbitControl` is just as simple as using the other controls. Include the correct JavaScript file, set up the control with the camera, and use `THREE.Clock` again to update the control:

```
<script type="text/javascript" src="../libs/OrbitControls.js"></script>
...
var orbitControls = new THREE.OrbitControls(camera);
orbitControls.autoRotate = true;
var clock = new THREE.Clock();
...
var delta = clock.getDelta();
orbitControls.update(delta);
```

The controls for `THREE.OrbitControls` are focused on using the mouse, as shown in the following table:

Control	Action
Left mouse click + move	Rotate the camera around the center of the scene
Scroll wheel or middle mouse click + move	Zoom in and zoom out
Right mouse click + move	Pan around the scene
Left, right, up, and down arrows	Pan around the scene

That's it for the camera and moving it around. In this part, we've seen a lot of controls that allow you to easily interact with and move through the scene by changing the camera properties. In the next section, we'll look at more advanced methods of animation: morphing and skinning.

Morphing and skeletal animation

When you create animations in external programs (for instance, Blender), you usually have two main options to define animations:

- **Morph targets**: With morph targets, you define a deformed version, that is, a key position, of the mesh. For this deformed target, all vertex positions are stored. All you need to do to animate the shape is move all the vertices from one position to another key position and repeat that process. The following screenshot shows various morph targets used to show facial expressions (the screenshot has been provided by the Blender Foundation):

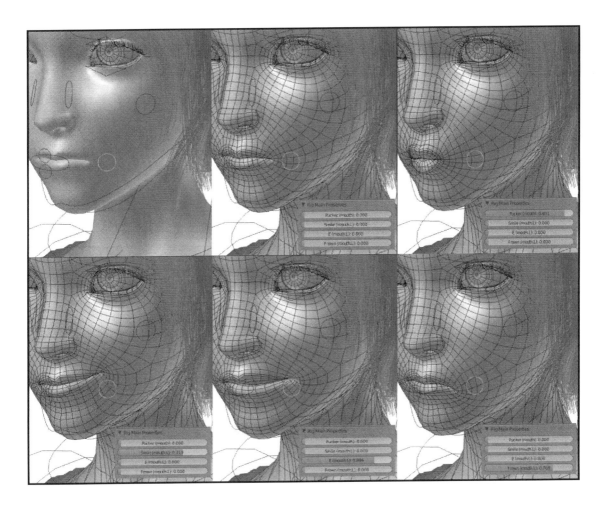

- **Skeletal animation**: An alternative is using skeletal animation. With skeletal animation, you define the skeleton, that is, the bones, of the mesh and attach vertices to the specific bones. Now, when you move a bone, any connected bone is also moved appropriately, and the attached vertices are moved and deformed based on the position, movement, and scaling of the bone. The following screenshot, once again provided by the Blender foundation, shows an example of how bones can be used to move and deform an object:

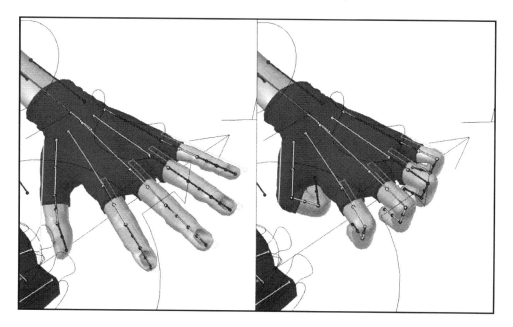

Three.js supports both modes, but, generally, you'll probably get better results with morph targets. The main problem with skeletal animation is getting a good export from a 3D program such as Blender that can be animated in Three.js. It's much easier to get a good working model with morph targets than it is with bones and skins. On the other hand, working with skeletons provides many more options and much more flexibility.

In this section, we'll look at both options and additionally look at a couple of external formats supported by Three.js in which animations can be defined.

Animation with morph targets

Morph targets are the most straightforward way of defining an animation. You define all the vertices for each important position (also called keyframes) and tell Three.js to move the vertices from one position to the other. The disadvantage of this approach, though, is that for large meshes and large animations, the model files will become very large. The reason is that for each key position, all the vertex positions are repeated.

We'll show you how to work with morph targets using two examples. In the first example, we'll let Three.js handle the transition between the various keyframes (or morph targets as we'll call them from now on), and in the second one, we'll do this manually. Keep in mind that we only scratch the surface of what is possible with animations in Three.js. As you'll see in this section, Three.js has excellent support to control animations, supports syncing of animations, and provides ways to smoothly transition from one animation to another, warranting a book just on this subject. So, in the next couple of sections, we'll provide you with the basics of animations in Three.js, which should provide enough information to get started and explore the more complex subjects.

Animation with a mixer and morph targets

Before we dive into the examples, first we'll look at the three core classes that you use to animate with Three.js. Further on in this chapter, we'll show you all the functions and properties provided by these objects:

- THREE.AnimationClip: When you load a model that contains animations, you can look in the response object for a field usually called animations. This field will contain a list of THREE.AnimationClip objects.
  A THREE.AnimationClip most often holds the data for a certain animation or activity the model you loaded can perform. For instance, if you loaded a model of a bird, one THREE.AnimationClip would contain the information needed to flap the wings, and another one might be opening and closing its beak.
- THREE.AnimationMixer: THREE.AnimationMixer is used to control a number of THREE.AnimationClip objects. It makes sure the timing of the animation is correct, and makes it possible to sync animations together, or cleanly move from one animation to another.
- THREE.AnimationAction: THREE.AnimationMixer itself doesn't expose a large number of functions to control the animation, though. This is done through THREE.AnimationAction objects, which are returned when you add a THREE.AnimationClip to a THREE.AnimationMixer (or you can get them at a later time, by using functions provided by THREE.AnimationMixer).

In the following example, you can control a `THREE.AnimationMixer` and a `THREE.AnimationAction`, which were created using a `THREE.AnimationClip` from the model. The `THREE.AnimationClip` represents the horse galloping.

For this first morphing example, we use a model that is also available from the Three.js distribution: the horse. The easiest way to understand how a morph targets-based animation works is by opening up the `10-morph-targets.html` example. The following screenshot shows a still image of this example:

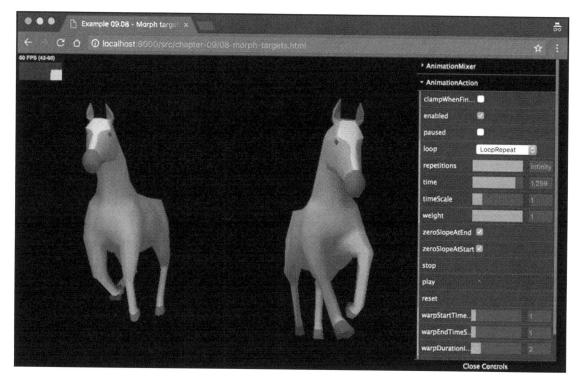

60 FPS (42-60)

In this example, the horse on the right-hand side is animated and running, and the horse on the left-hand side is standing still. This second horse (the left-hand-side one) is rendered from the basic model, that is, the original set of vertices. With the menu in the top-right corner, you can browse through all the morph targets that are available and see the different positions the left-hand side horse can take. We've also added controls for the `THREE.AnimationMixer` and `THREE.AnimationAction` (for more details on all these options, look at the tables shown later in this chapter).

In older versions of Three.js, we had to use specific meshes (for example
`THREE.MorphAnimMesh` or `THREE.MorphBlendMesh`) to work with animations. In the later
versions of Three.js, you can use the normal `THREE.Mesh` objects to create your meshes and
place them in a scene. To run an animation, we now use the `THREE.AnimationMixer`:

```
var loader = new THREE.JSONLoader();
loader.load('../../assets/models/horse/horse.js', function (geometry, mat)
{

  geometry.computeVertexNormals();
  geometry.computeMorphNormals();

  var mat = new THREE.MeshLambertMaterial({morphTargets: true,
vertexColors: THREE.FaceColors});
  mesh = new THREE.Mesh(geometry, mat);
  mesh.scale.set(0.15,0.15,0.15);
  mesh.translateY(-10);
  mesh.translateX(10);

  mixer = new THREE.AnimationMixer( mesh );
  // or create a custom clip from the set of morphtargets
  // var clip = THREE.AnimationClip.CreateFromMorphTargetSequence(
'gallop', geometry.morphTargets, 30 );
  mixer.clipAction( geometry.animations[0] ).setDuration( 1 ).play();
  scene.add(mesh)
})
```

With a `THREE.AnimationMixer`, we can control the animations of a single object
(although, if you want, you can have a single `THREE.AnimationMixer` control multiple
objects). In this example, we create a `THREE.AnimationMixer` for the loaded
`geometry` and then tell the `mixer` to play the first animation that was defined on the model
using the `mixer.clipAction` function. This function, which takes a
`THREE.AnimationClip` as its argument, returns a `THREE.AnimationAction`. On this
`THREE.AnimationAction`, we set the `duration` of the clip to 1 second, and call `play`.

If you want to know which animations are supported on a loaded model,
the best approach is to print out the geometry or the mesh to the console
and explore the properties. Different loaders can have the animations
defined in different ways; it is always good to first look at what the model
looks like that you've loaded, before setting up animations.

At this point, though, when we render the scene, the animation won't play yet. For this, we have to make a small change to our `render` loop:

```
function render() {
  stats.update();
  var delta = clock.getDelta();
  trackballControls.update(delta);
  requestAnimationFrame(render);
  renderer.render(scene, camera)

  if (mixer) {
    mixer.update( delta );
  }
}
```

As you can see, we have to call `mixer.update(delta)` to inform our mixer how much time has passed between this `render` loop and the previous one. This information is used by the mixer to determine how far it should morph the vertices to the next morph target (keyframe).

The `THREE.AnimationMixer` and the `THREE.AnimationClip` provides a number of other functions that you can use to control the animation or create new `THREE.AnimationClip` objects. We start with the `THREE.AnimationClip`:

Name	Description
duration	The duration of this track (in seconds).
name	The name of this clip. In the case of our horse, this might be `"gallop"`.
tracks	The internal property used to keep track of how certain properties of the model are animated.
uuid	This unique ID of this clip. This is assigned automatically.
optimize()	This optimizes the `THREE.AnimationClip`.
resetDuration()	This determines the correct `duration` of this clip.
trim()	This trims all the internal tracks to the duration set on this clip.

`CreateClipsFromMorphTargetSequences(`
`    name, morphTargetSequences,`
`        fps,`
`        noLoop)`
	This used internally by the `THREE.JsonLoader` to create a list of `THREE.AnimationClip` instances based on a set of morph-target sequences.

`CreateFromMorphTargetSequences(`
`    name, morphTargetSequence,`
`        fps,`
`        noLoop)`
	This creates a single `THREE.AnimationClip` from a sequence of morph-targets.

`findByName(objectOrClipArray, name)`	Searches for `THREE.AnimationClip` by name.
`parse` and `toJson`	Allows you to restore and save a `Three.AnimationClip` as JSON.
`parseAnimation`	Used internally to create a `THREE.AnimationClip`.

Once you've got a `THREE.AnimationClip`, you can pass it into `THREE.AnimationMixer` object, which provides the following functionality:

Name	Description
`AnimationMixer(rootObject)`	The constructor for this object. This constructor takes a `THREE.Object3D` as an argument (for example, a `THREE.Mesh` of a `THREE.Group`).
`.time`	The global time for this mixer; this starts at `0`, at the time when this mixer is created.
`.timeScale`	The timescale can be used to speed up or slow down all the animations managed by this mixer. If the value of this property is set to `0`, all the animations are effectively paused.
`.clipAction(animationClip,` `    optionalRoot)`	This creates a `THREE.AnimationAction` that can be used to control the passed-in `THREE.AnimationClip`. If the animation clip is for a different root object, you can pass that in as well.

.existingAction(animationClip, optionalRoot)	This returns the THREE.AnimationAction that can be used to control the passed-in THREE.AnimationClip. Once again, if the THREE.AnimationClip is for a different rootObject, you can also pass that in.

When you get back the THREE.AnimationClip, you can use it to control the animation:

Name	Description
clampWhenFinished	When set to true, this will cause the animation to be paused when it reaches its last frame. The default is false.
enabled	When set to false, this will disable the current action so that it has no effect on the model. When the action is re-enabled, the animation will continue where it left off.
loop	The looping mode of this action (which can be set using the setLoop function). This can be set to the following: • THREE.LoopOnce: Plays the clip only one time. • THREE.LoopRepeat: Repeats the clip based on the number of repetitions that have been set. • THREE.LoopPingPong: Plays the clip based on the number of repetitions, but alternates between playing the clip forward and backward.
paused	Setting this property to true will pause the execution of this clip.
repetitions	Number of times to repeat the animation. Used by the loop property. The default is Infinity.
time	The time this action has been running; this is wrapped from 0 to the duration of the clip.
timeScale	The timescale can be used to speed up or slow down this animation. If the value of this property is set to 0, this animation is effectively paused.
weight	The effect this animation has on the model from a scale of 0 to 1. When set to 0, you won't see any transformation of the model from this animation, and when set to 1, you see the full effect of this animation.
zeroSlopeAtEnd	When set to true (which is the default), this will make sure there is a smooth transition between separate clips.
zeroSlopeAtStart	When set to true (which is the default), this will make sure there is a smooth transition between separate clips.

crossFadeFrom(fadeOutAction, durationInSeconds, warpBoolean)	Causes this action to fade in, while the fadeOutAction is faded out. The total fade takes durationInSeconds time. This allows for smooth transitions between animations. With the warpBoolean set to true, it will apply additional smoothing of timescales as well.
crossFadeTo(fadeInAction, durationInSeconds, warpBoolean)	Same as crossFadeFrom, but this time fades in the provided action, and fades out this action.
fadeIn(durationInSeconds)	Increases the weight property slowly from 0 to 1, within the passed time interval.
fadeOut(durationInSeconds)	Decreases the weight property slowly from 0 to 1 within the passed time interval.
getEffectiveTimeScale()	Returns the effective timescale based on the currently running warp.
getEffectiveWeight()	Returns the effective weight based on the current running fade.
getClip()	Returns the THREE.AnimationClip this action is managing.
getMixer()	Returns the mixer that is playing this action.
getRoot()	Gets the root object which is controlled by this action.
halt(durationInSeconds)	Gradually decreases the timeScale to 0 within the durationInSeconds.
isRunning()	Checks whether the animation is currently running.
isScheduled()	Checks whether this action is currently active in the mixer.
play()	Starts running this action (starting the animation).
reset()	Resets this action. This will result in setting paused to false, enabled to true, and time to 0.
setDuration(durationInSeconds)	Sets the duration of a single loop. This will change the timeScale so that the complete animation can play within the durationInSeconds.
setEffectiveTimeScale(timeScale)	Sets the timeScale to the provided value.
setEffectiveWeight()	Sets the weight to the provided value.
setLoop(loopMode, repetitions)	Sets the loopMode and the number of repetitions. See the loop property for the options and their effect.
startAt(startTimeInSeconds)	Delays starting the animation for startTimeInSeconds.
stop()	Stops this action, and reset is applied.
stopFading()	Stops any scheduled fading.
stopWarping()	Stops any schedule warping.
syncWith(otherAction)	Syncs this action with the passed-in action. This will set this actions time and timeScale value to the passed-in action.
warp(startTimeScale, endTimeScale, durationInSeconds)	Changes the timeScale property from the startTimeScale to the endTimeScale within the specified durationInSeconds.

Besides all the functions and properties you can use to control the animation, the `THREE.AnimationMixer` also provides two events you can listen to by calling `addEventListener` on the mixer. The event with type `"loop"` is sent when a single loop is finished, and the `"finished"` event is sent when the complete action has finished.

If you look back at the code fragment where we loaded our model, you might have noticed these two lines:

```
geometry.computeVertexNormals();
geometry.computeMorphNormals();
```

If we don't add the `computeMorphNormals` (which depends on correct vertex normals), our model would look like it used a material that had flat shading enabled. When calling `computeMorphNormals`, Three.js will make sure that when animating the model, it has the correct information to render the model smoothly. If not, the result will look something like this:

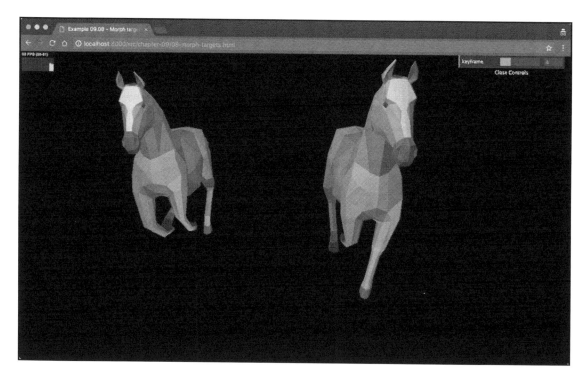

53 FPS (50-61)

The approach shown here is the easiest way to get animations up and running and allows you to quickly set up an animation from a model that has morph targets defined. An alternative approach is to set up the animation manually, as we will show in the next section.

Using multiple THREE.AnimationClip objects

In the previous section, we used a model that included the animations, so we could directly load them. That example, though, only had a single `THREE.AnimationClip`. In this example, we'll create a very simple animation using two `THREE.AnimationClip` objects. The first clip will morph the cube from a size of (2, 2, 2) to a size of (2, 20, 2), and the other clip will animate the cube to a size of (40, 2, 2). You can find the example in `09-morph-targets-manually.html`:

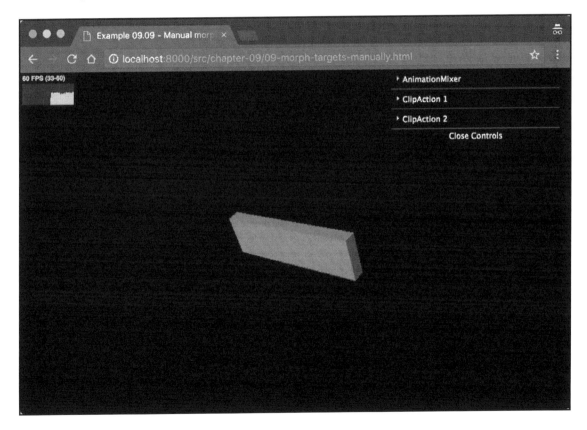

In this example, you've got a menu on the right to control the first THREE.AnimationClip and another one that you can use to control the second THREE.AnimationClip. When you don't change anything, you can see from the size of the cube that both of the morph targets are applied simultaneously. The width grows to 40 and the height grows to 20. Before we look at how the options we saw in the previous section affect the animation, we'll first look at how we created this animation from scratch:

```
// initial cube
var cubeGeometry = new THREE.BoxGeometry(2, 2, 2);
var cubeMaterial = new THREE.MeshLambertMaterial({morphTargets: true,
color: 0xff0000});

// define morphtargets, we'll use the vertices from these geometries
var cubeTarget1 = new THREE.BoxGeometry(2, 20, 2);
var cubeTarget2 = new THREE.BoxGeometry(40, 2, 2);

// define morphtargets and compute the morphnormal
cubeGeometry.morphTargets[0] = {name: 't1', vertices:
cubeGeometry.vertices};
cubeGeometry.morphTargets[1] = {name: 't2', vertices:
cubeTarget2.vertices};
cubeGeometry.morphTargets[2] = {name: 't3', vertices:
cubeTarget1.vertices};
cubeGeometry.computeMorphNormals();

// create a mesh
var mesh = new THREE.Mesh(cubeGeometry, cubeMaterial);

// position the cube
mesh.position.x = 0;
mesh.position.y = 3;
mesh.position.z = 0;

// add the cube to the scene
scene.add(mesh);
mixer = new THREE.AnimationMixer( mesh );

animationClip = THREE.AnimationClip.CreateFromMorphTargetSequence('first',
            [cubeGeometry.morphTargets[0],
cubeGeometry.morphTargets[1]], 1);
animationClip2 =
THREE.AnimationClip.CreateFromMorphTargetSequence('second',
            [cubeGeometry.morphTargets[0],
cubeGeometry.morphTargets[2]], 1);
clipAction = mixer.clipAction( animationClip ).play();
clipAction2 = mixer.clipAction( animationClip2 ).play();
```

As you look through this code, you can see that we define three `morphTargets`. The first one is the vertices of the initial geometry with a size of `(2, 2, 2)`; next, we take the vertices of two larger geometries and add those as well to the `morphTargets` property of our geometry. Next, we do the standard stuff to add the `THREE.Mesh` to the scene, and then define our two animation clips: `animationClip` and `animationClip2`. The first animation moves from the initial state (`morphTargets[0]`) to the size defined in `morpTargets[1]`, and the second animation also starts with the initial state, but moves to the size defined in `morphTargets[2]`. To create an `animationClip`, we use the `CreateFromMorphTargetSequence` function. Finally, we set them to `play` and you see the result when you open the example in your browser.

Now that we've got two `THREE.AnimationClip` objects running at the same time, we can play around with the settings to see what the effect is. The best approach is for you to play around with it, but we'll have a closer look at the two properties that are most important: `weight` and `timeScale`. First, the `weight` property. As we explained earlier, the weight determines how much the model is affected by this clip. If you set one of the two to `0.5`, you'll immediately see that the effect of that clip is reduced, and if you drop it to `0`, you won't see any effect at all:

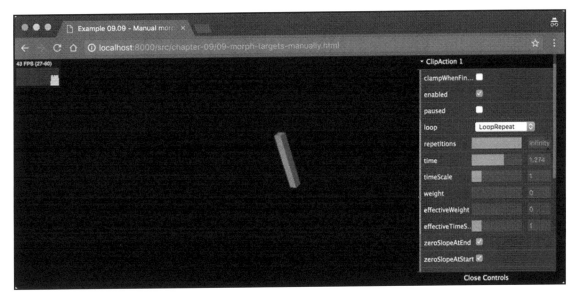

43 FPS (47-60)

This is very useful if you want to slowly transition from one animation to another (for which Three.js provides helper functions such as `fadeIn`, `fadeOut`, `crossFadeFrom`, and `crossFradeTo`). We can also play around with the `timeScale`. The `timeScale` property controls how fast a clip is running. If we set this to 2, that clip will play twice as fast, if we set it to 0, it will pause in the state it is in.

In the next couple of sections, we'll provide you with the same UI when we show an animation, so you can always experiment with the different properties provided by a `THREE.ClipAction`.

Animation using bones and skinning

Morph animations are very straightforward. Three.js knows all the target vertex positions and only needs to transition each vertex from one position to the next. For bones and skinning, it becomes a bit more complex. When you use bones for animation, you move the bone, and Three.js has to determine how to translate the attached skin (a set of vertices) accordingly. For this example, we use a model that was exported from Blender to the Three.js format (`hand-1.js` in the `models/hand` folder). This is a model of a hand, complete with a set of bones. By moving the bones around, we can animate the complete model. Let's first look at how we loaded the model:

```
loader.load('../../assets/models/hand/hand-1.js', function (geometry,
mat) {
    var mat = new THREE.MeshLambertMaterial({color: 0xF0C8C9, skinning:
true});
    mesh = new THREE.SkinnedMesh(geometry, mat);
    mesh.scale.set(15,15,15);
    mesh.position.x = -5;
    mesh.rotateX(0.5*Math.PI);
    mesh.rotateZ(0.3*Math.PI);
    scene.add(mesh);
    startAnimation();
});
```

Loading a model for bone animation isn't that different than any of the other models. We just specify the model file, which contains the definition of vertices, faces, and also bones, and, based on that geometry, we create a mesh. Three.js provides a specific mesh for skinned geometries such as these, called THREE.SkinnedMesh. The one thing you need to specify to make sure the model is updated is set the skinning property of the material you use to true. If you don't set this to true, you won't see any bone movement. In this example, we'll use a tween object to handle the animation, which is created in the startAnimation() function. This tween instance is defined as follows:

```
function startAnimation() {
  tween = new TWEEN.Tween({pos: -1.5})
  .to({pos: 0}, 3000)
  .easing(TWEEN.Easing.Cubic.InOut)
  .yoyo(true)
  .repeat(Infinity)
  .onUpdate(onUpdate);

  tween.start();
}
```

With this tween, we transition the pos variable from -1.5 to 0. We've also set the yoyo property to true, which causes our animation to run in reverse the next time it is run, and, to make sure our animation keeps running, we set repeat to Infinity. You can also see that we specify an onUpdate method. This method is used to position the individual bones, and we'll look at that next. Before we move the bones, let's look at the 10-bones-manually.html example.

The following screenshot shows a still image of this example:

When you open this example, you see the hand making a grab-like motion. We did this by setting the *z* rotation of the finger bones in the `onUpdate` method that is called from our `tween` **animation**, as follows:

```
var onUpdate = function () {
  var pos = this.pos;

  // rotate the fingers
  mesh.skeleton.bones[5].rotation.set(0, 0, pos);
  mesh.skeleton.bones[6].rotation.set(0, 0, pos);
  mesh.skeleton.bones[10].rotation.set(0, 0, pos);
  mesh.skeleton.bones[11].rotation.set(0, 0, pos);
  mesh.skeleton.bones[15].rotation.set(0, 0, pos);
  mesh.skeleton.bones[16].rotation.set(0, 0, pos);
  mesh.skeleton.bones[20].rotation.set(0, 0, pos);
  mesh.skeleton.bones[21].rotation.set(0, 0, pos);

  // rotate the wrist
  mesh.skeleton.bones[1].rotation.set(pos, 0, 0);
};
```

Whenever this update method is called, the relevant bones are set to the pos position. To determine which bone you need to move, it is a good idea to print out the mesh.skeleton property to the console. This will list all the bones and their names.

Three.js provides a simple helper you can use to show the bones of the models. Add the following to the code:

```
helper = new THREE.SkeletonHelper( mesh );
helper.material.linewidth = 2;
helper.visible = false;
scene.add( helper );
```
You can see an example of this by enabling the showHelper property shown in the 10-bones-manually.html example.

If you enable the THREE.SkeletonHelper, you'll see the skeleton that is used to control this hand:

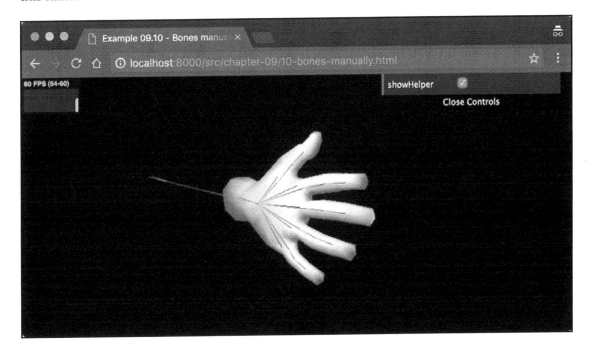

As you can see, working with bones takes a bit more effort but is much more flexible than the fixed morph targets. In this example, we've only moved the rotation of the bones; you can also move the position or change the scale. In the next section, we look at loading animations from external models. In that section, we'll revisit this example, but now, we'll run a predefined animation from the model instead of manually moving the bones around.

Creating animations using external models

In Chapter 8, *Creating and Loading Advanced Meshes and Geometries*, we looked at a number of 3D formats that are supported by Three.js. A couple of those formats also support animations. In this chapter, we'll look at the following examples:

- **Blender with the JSON exporter**: We'll start with an animation created in Blender and exported to the Three.js JSON format.
- **COLLADA model**: The COLLADA format has support for animations. For this example, we'll load an animation from a COLLADA file and render it with Three.js.
- **MD2 model**: The MD2 model is a simple format used in the older Quake engines. Even though the format is a bit dated, it is still a very good format for storing character animations.
- **glTF models**: The **GL Transmission (glTF)** format is a format specifically designed for storing 3D scenes and models. It focuses on minimizing the size of the assets, and tries to be as efficient as possible in unpacking the models.
- **FBX model**: FBX is a format produced by the mixamo tooling available at https://www.mixamo.com. With mixamo, you can easily rig and animate models, without needing to have lots of modeling experience.

- **DirectX models**: DirectX used to have its own format for storing geometries, materials, and animations. While it is hard to find models for this, Three.js does support this format through the XLoader. This loader does follow a kind of different approach, since animations and models are stored in separate files and need to be combined.
- **BVH model**: The **Biovision (BVH)** format is a slightly different one when compared to the other loaders. With this loader, you don't load a geometry with a skeleton or a set of animations. With this format, which is used by Autodesk MotionBuilder, you just load a skeleton, which you can visualize or even attach to your own geometry.
- **SEA model**: SEA3D is a format for containing 3D scenes, animations, and sounds. You can create these using the SEA3D editor. The SEA3D importer for Three.js supports more than just animations; it also supports sounds and physics. In this chapter, though, we will focus on how to load and use the provided animations.

 There is another loader that supports animations, which we haven't included in this chapter. This is the MMDLoader, which allows you to render MikuMikuDance models. The approach to load and animate these models is the same as we saw for the other loaders, but most, if not all, models can't be used for commercial purposes. As such, we can't include an example for this specific loader in this book.

We'll start with the Blender model.

Creating a bones animation using Blender

To get started with animations from Blender, you can load the example we've included in the `models` folder. You can find the `hand.blend` file there, which you can load into Blender. The following screenshot shows a still image of this example:

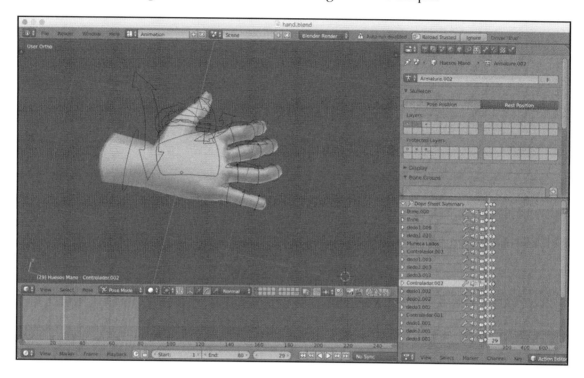

There isn't room in this book to go into much detail on how to create animations in Blender, but there are a few things you need to keep in mind:

- Every vertex from your model must at least be assigned to a vertex group.
- The name of the vertex groups you use in Blender must correspond to the name of the bone that controls it. That way, Three.js can determine which vertices it needs to modify when moving the bones.
- Only the first *action* is exported. So, make sure the animation you want to export is the first one.
- When creating keyframes, it is a good idea to select all the bones even if they don't change.

- When exporting the model, make sure the model is in its rest pose and is selected. If this is not the case, you'll see a very deformed animation.
- It is preferred to just export a single object together with its animation, instead of exporting the complete scene.

When you've created the animation in Blender, you can export the file using the Three.js exporter we used in `Chapter 10`, *Loading and Working with Textures*. When exporting the file using the Three.js exporter, you have to make sure that the following properties are checked:

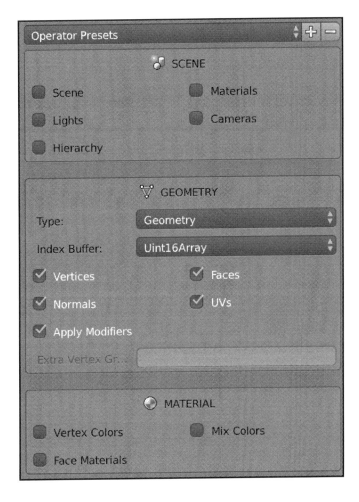

Also:

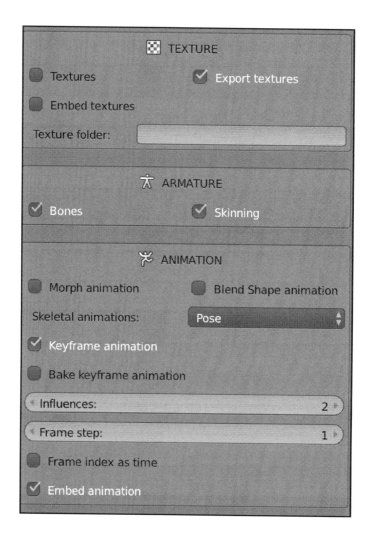

This will export the animation you've specified in Blender as a skeletal animation instead of a morph animation. With a skeletal animation, the movements of the bones are exported, which we can replay in Three.js, as follows:

```
var loader = new THREE.JSONLoader();
loader.load('../../assets/models/hand/hand-8.json', function (result) {
    var mesh = new THREE.SkinnedMesh(result, new
THREE.MeshNormalMaterial({skinning: true}));
    mesh.scale.set(18, 18, 18)
```

```
        scene.add(mesh);

        // setup the mixer
        mixer = new THREE.AnimationMixer( mesh );
        animationClip = mesh.geometry.animations[0];
        clipAction = mixer.clipAction( animationClip ).play();
        animationClip = clipAction.getClip();
    });

    function render() {
        ..
        var delta = clock.getDelta();
        mixer.update( delta );
        ..
    }
```

To run this animation, all we have to do is create a `THREE.SkinnedMesh` and, just like we did for the previous examples, use a `THREE.AnimationMixer`, a `THREE.AnimationClip`, and a `THREE.ClipAction` together to tell Three.js how to play the exported animation. Always remember that you have to call the `mixer.update()` function in the render loop as well. The result of this example (`13-animation-from-blender.html`) is a simple waving hand:

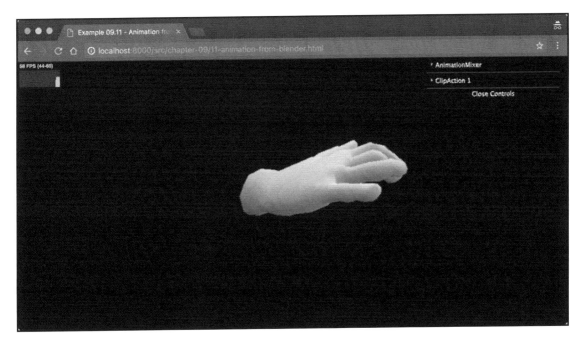

58 FPS (44-60)

Besides the Three.js format, we can use a couple of other formats to define animations. The first one we'll look at is loading a COLLADA model.

Loading an animation from a COLLADA model

Loading a model from a COLLADA file works in the same manner as for the other formats. First, you have to include the correct loader JavaScript file:

```
<script type="text/javascript" src="../libs/ColladaLoader.js"></script>
```

While the normal COLLADA models aren't compressed (and they can get quite large) there is also a KMZLoader available in Three.js. This is basically a compressed COLLADA model, so if you run into **Keyhole Markup language Zipped (KMZ)** models, you can follow the steps here, and use the KMZLoader instead of the ColladaLoader.

Now we create a loader and use it to load the model file:

```
var loader = new THREE.ColladaLoader();
loader.load('../../assets/models/monster/monster.dae', function (result)
{

    scene.add(result.scene);
    result.scene.rotateZ(-0.2*Math.PI)
    result.scene.translateX(-20)
    result.scene.translateY(-20)

    // setup the mixer
    mixer = new THREE.AnimationMixer(result.scene);
    animationClip = result.animations[0];
    clipAction = mixer.clipAction( animationClip ).play();
    animationClip = clipAction.getClip();

    // add the animation controls
    enableControls();
});
```

A COLLADA file can contain much more than just a single mode: it can store complete scenes, including cameras, lights, animations, and more. A good way to work with a COLLADA model is to print out the result from the `loader.load` function to the console and determine which components you want to use. In this case, the result looks something like this:

```
▼ {animations: Array(1), kinematics: {…}, library: {…}, scene: Group}
  ▶ animations: [AnimationClip]
  ▶ kinematics: {}
  ▶ library: {animations: {…}, clips: {…}, controllers: {…}, images: {…}, effects: {…}, …}
  ▼ scene: Group
      castShadow: false
    ▼ children: Array(2)
      ▶ 0: Bone {uuid: "C265DD0E-9956-46A1-8A7E-06794B2658FF", name: "Bone1", type: "Bone", paren
      ▼ 1: SkinnedMesh
        ▶ bindMatrix: Matrix4 {elements: Array(16)}
        ▶ bindMatrixInverse: Matrix4 {elements: Array(16)}
          bindMode: "attached"
          castShadow: false
        ▶ children: []
          drawMode: 0
          frustumCulled: true
```

In Three.js, we can add `THREE.Group` elements to a `THREE.Scene`, so, for now, we just add the complete scene. If your COLLADA file contains elements you want to exclude, you can just select the ones from the `scene` property to add. To render and animate this model, all we have to do is set up the animation just as we did for the Blender-based model; even the render loop stays the same. And the result for this specific COLLADA file looks as follows:

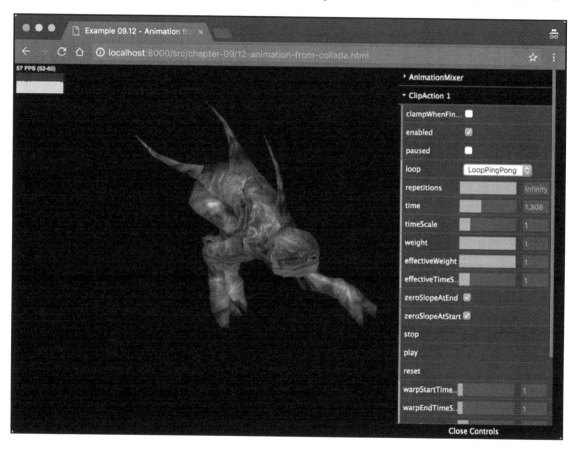

57 FPS (52-60)

Another example of an external model, one that uses morph targets, is the MD2 file format.

Animation loaded from a Quake model

The MD2 format was created to model characters from Quake, a great game from 1996. Even though the newer engines use a different format, you can still find a lot of interesting models in the MD2 format. Using an MD2 file works the same as any of the others we've seen so far. When you load an MD2 model, you get a geometry, so you have to make sure that you create a material first and assign a skin:

```
var textureLoader = new THREE.TextureLoader();
var loader = new THREE.MD2Loader();
loader.load('../../assets/models/ogre/ogro.md2', function (result) {

  var mat = new THREE.MeshStandardMaterial(
    { morphTargets: true,
      color: 0xffffff,
      metalness: 0,
      map: textureLoader.load('../../assets/models/ogre/skins/skin.jpg')
  })

  var mat2 = new THREE.MeshNormalMaterial();
  var mesh = new THREE.Mesh(result, mat);
  scene.add(mesh);

  // // setup the mixer
  mixer = new THREE.AnimationMixer(mesh);
  animationClip1 = result.animations[7];
  clipAction1 = mixer.clipAction( animationClip1 ).play();
  animationClip2 = result.animations[9];
  clipAction2 = mixer.clipAction( animationClip2 );
  animationClip3 = result.animations[10];
  clipAction3 = mixer.clipAction( animationClip3 );

  // add the animation controls
  enableControls(result);
});
```

In the preceding code, you can see that we use a THREE.MeshStandardMaterial for the skin of the model. We also create three animations based on the information from the loaded model. Since we don't have bones in this model, we have to set the morphTargets property to true to see the animations. If you look at 15-animation-from-md2.html, you can see and control the animations. We've also added a drop-down menu, where you can switch between all the animations provided by the model:

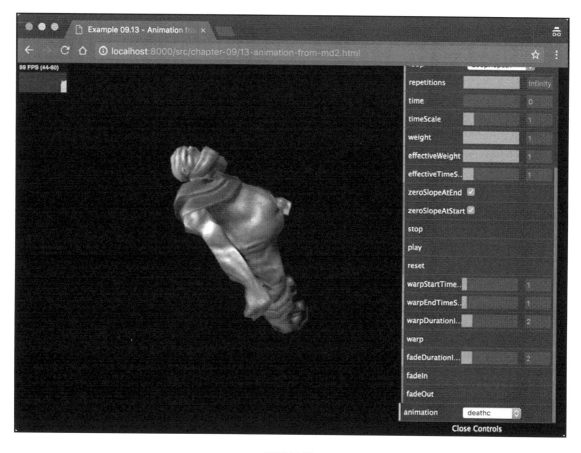

60 FPS (44-60)

Using the gltfLoader

A format which is getting more and more attention lately is the glTF format. This format, for which you can find a very extensive explanation at `https://github.com/KhronosGroup/glTF`, focuses on optimizing size and resource usage. Using the `glTFLoader` is similar to the other loaders. Note that besides the `THREE.GLTFLoader`, there is also a `THREE.LegacyGLTFLoader`. The first one should normally be used, since it supports glTF Versions 2.0 and up (which is the current standard). Should you run into older versions, then you can use the `THREE.LegacyGLTFLoader`. To use this loader, include the correct JavaScript file:

```
<script type="text/javascript" charset="UTF-8"
src="../../libs/three/loaders/GLTFLoader.js"></script>
```

Use the `THREE.GLTFLoader` as follows:

```
var loader = new THREE.GLTFLoader();
loader.load('../../assets/models/CesiumMan/CesiumMan.gltf', function
(result) {
    // correctly position the scene
    result.scene.scale.set(6, 6, 6);
    result.scene.translateY(-3);
    result.scene.rotateY(-0.3*Math.PI);
    scene.add(result.scene)

    // setup the mixer
    mixer = new THREE.AnimationMixer( result.scene );
    animationClip = result.animations[0];
    clipAction = mixer.clipAction( animationClip ).play();
    animationClip = clipAction.getClip();

    // add the animation controls
    enableControls();
});
```

This loader also loads a complete scene, so you can either add everything in the group, or select child elements. For this example, you can view the results by opening `14-animation-from-gltf.html`:

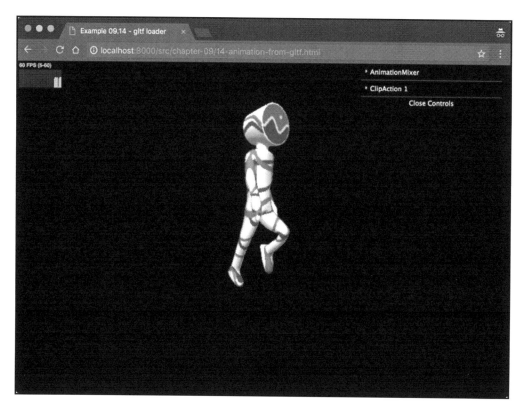

60 FPS (5-60)

The next loader on the list is for the Autodesk **Filmbox (FBX)** format.

Visualize motions captured models using the fbxLoader

The Autodesk FBX format has been around for a while, and is very easy to use. There is a great resource online where you can find many animations that you can download in this format: `https://www.mixamo.com/`. This site provides 2,500 animations that you can use and customize:

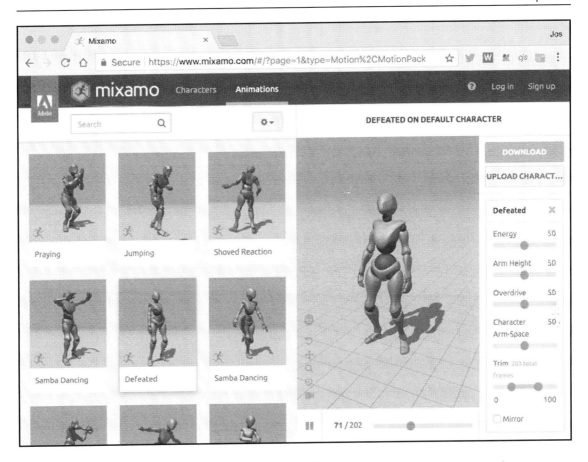

After downloading an animation, using it from Three.js is easy:

```
var loader = new THREE.FBXLoader();
loader.load('../../assets/models/salsa/salsa.fbx', function (result) {

    result.scale.set(0.2, 0.2, 0.2);
    result.translateY(-13);
    scene.add(result)
    // setup the mixer
    mixer = new THREE.AnimationMixer( result );
    animationClip = result.animations[0];
    clipAction = mixer.clipAction( animationClip ).play();
    animationClip = clipAction.getClip();

    enableControls();
});
```

And the resulting animation, as you can see in `15-animation-from-fbx.html`, looks great:

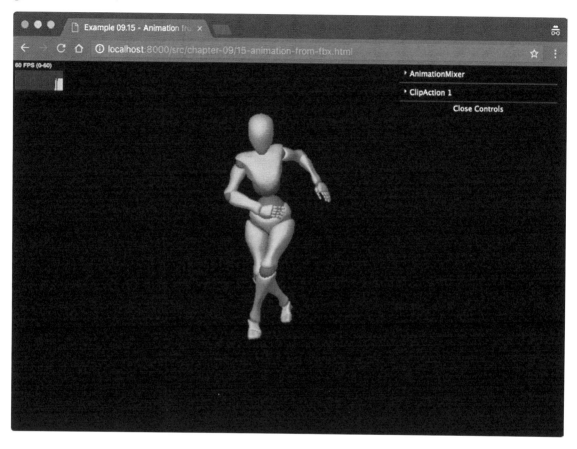

60 FPS (0-60)

Loading legacy DirectX models through the xLoader

Microsoft's DirectX used to have a specific format (in old versions) to store 3D models and animations. Though it is hard to find models in this format, with the `THREE.XLoader`, we can use the models in Three.js. An example on how to do this can be found in `16-animation-from-x.html`:

To see the animation, you need to set the `timeScale` to a high value. If you don't do this, the animation moves very slowly:

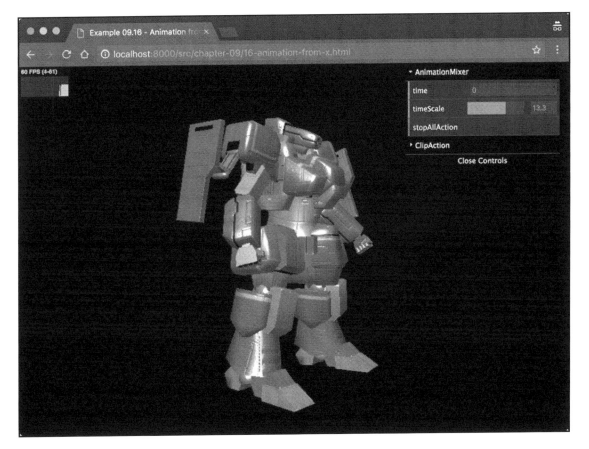

60 FPS (4-61)

Loading these kinds of models follows a slightly different approach since in this format the model and the animations are stored in separate files. The following code fragment shows how you can load and animate these models:

```
var manager = new THREE.LoadingManager();
var textureLoader = new THREE.TextureLoader();
var loader = new THREE.XLoader( manager, textureLoader );
var animLoader = new THREE.XLoader( manager, textureLoader );

// we could also queue this or use promises
loader.load(["../../assets/models/x/SSR06_model.x"], function (result) {
  var mesh = result.models[0];
  animLoader.load(["../../assets/models/x/stand.x", { putPos: false,
putScl: false }], function (anim) {
    animLoader.assignAnimation(mesh);
    // at this point we've got a normal mesh, and can get the mixer and
clipaction
    mixer = mesh.animationMixer;
    clipAction = mixer.clipAction( "stand" ).play();
    var clip = clipAction.getClip();

    mesh.translateY(-6)
    mesh.rotateY(-0.7*Math.PI);
    scene.add(mesh)
  });
});
```

To work with the THREE.XLoader, we first use a THREE.XLoader to load the model, then a THREE.XLoader to load the animation, and finally, we have to call assignAnimation to connect the animation to the loaded model. Once that is done, we can follow the standard way of animating the model.

Visualizing a skeleton with the BVHLoader

The BVHLoader is a slightly different loader than the once we have we've seen so far. This loader doesn't return meshes or geometries with animations but just returns a skeleton and an animation. An example of this is shown in 17-animation-from-bvh.html:

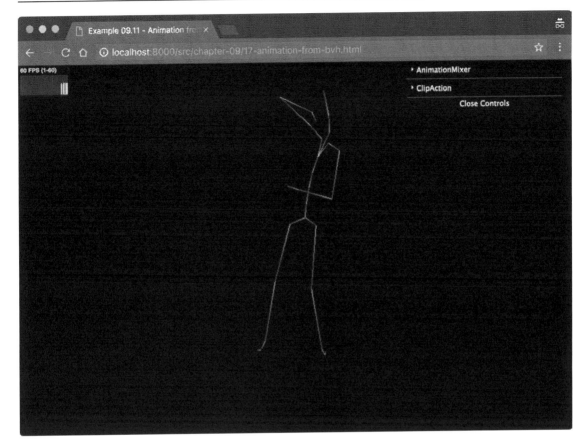

60 FPS (1-60)

To visualize this, we can reuse the THREE.SkeletonHelper, as seen here:

```
var loader = new THREE.BVHLoader();
loader.load('../../assets/models/amelia-dance/DanceNightClub7_t1.bvh',
function (result, mat) {

    skeletonHelper = new THREE.SkeletonHelper( result.skeleton.bones[ 0 ]
);
    // allow animation mixer to bind to SkeletonHelper directly
    skeletonHelper.skeleton = result.skeleton;
    var boneContainer = new THREE.Object3D();
    boneContainer.translateY(-70);
    boneContainer.translateX(-100);
    boneContainer.add( result.skeleton.bones[ 0 ] );
    scene.add( skeletonHelper );
    scene.add( boneContainer );
```

```
        mixer = new THREE.AnimationMixer( skeletonHelper );
        clipAction = mixer.clipAction( result.clip ).setEffectiveWeight( 1.0
).play();
    })
```

For the final animation, we're going to show how to load and animate a model from the open source SEA3D project.

Reusing models from the SEA3D project

SEA3D is an open source project that can be used to create games, make models, add animations, and much more. For now, we'll just show you how you can use the models from this project and visualize them in Three.js. The approach is a little bit different than we've seen so far, but not by much:

```
var sceneContainer = new THREE.Scene();

var loader = new THREE.SEA3D({
  container: sceneContainer
});

loader.load('../../assets/models/mascot/mascot.sea');
loader.onComplete = function( e ) {
  var skinnedMesh = sceneContainer.children[0];
  skinnedMesh.scale.set(0.1, 0.1, 0.1);
  skinnedMesh.translateX(-40);
  skinnedMesh.translateY(-20);
  skinnedMesh.rotateY(-0.2*Math.PI);
  scene.add(skinnedMesh);

  // and set up the animation
  mixer = new THREE.AnimationMixer( skinnedMesh );
  animationClip = skinnedMesh.animations[0].clip;
  clipAction = mixer.clipAction( animationClip ).play();
  animationClip = clipAction.getClip();
  enableControls();
};
```

The main difference, as you can see from the code, is that we have provided the THREE.Scene that we want to models loaded into when we create the loader (which is called THREE.SEA3D). Something else that is different compared to the other loaders is that instead of specifying the callback in the load call, we have to specify the callback through the onComplete function. Once the scene has been loaded, though, we process it just as we do for other animations.

The result of this loader can be seen by opening `chapter-09/18-animation-from-sea.html`:

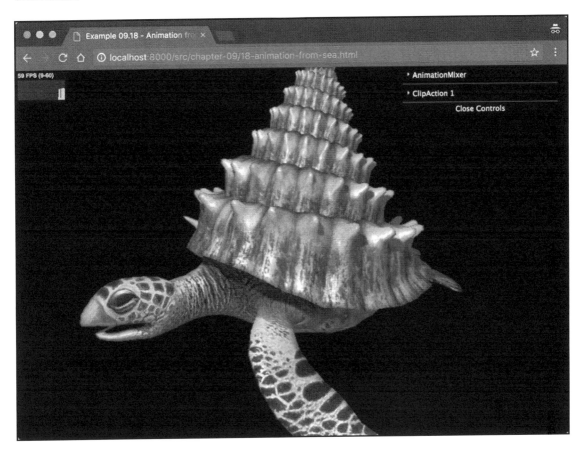

59 FPS (9-60)

This concludes the sections on loading animations from external formats.

Summary

In this chapter, we looked at different ways that you can animate your scene. We started with some basic animation tricks, moved on to camera movement and control, and ended with animation models using morph targets, and skeleton/bones animations. When you have the `render` loop in place, adding simple animations is very easy. Just change a property of the mesh, and in the next rendering step, Three.js will render the updated mesh. For the more complex animations, you would usually model them in external programs and load them through one the loaders provided by Three.js.

In previous chapters, we looked at the various materials you can use to skin your objects. For instance, we saw how you can change the color, shininess, and opacity of these materials. What we haven't discussed in detail yet, however, is how you can use external images (also called textures) together with these materials. With textures, you can easily create objects that look as if they are made of wood, metal, stone, and much more. In Chapter 10, *Loading and Working with Textures*, we'll explore all the different aspects of textures and how they are used in Three.js.

10
Loading and Working with Textures

In `Chapter 4`, *Working with Three.js Materials*, we introduced you to the various materials that are available in Three.js. However, we didn't discuss applying textures to meshes. In this chapter, we'll look at that subject. Specifically, we'll discuss the following topics:

- Loading textures in Three.js and applying them to a mesh
- Using bump, normal, and displacement maps to apply depth and detail to a mesh
- Creating fake shadows using a lightmap and an ambient occlusion map
- Using specular, metalness, and roughness maps to set the *shininess* of specific parts of a mesh
- Applying an alpha map for partial transparency of an object
- Adding detailed reflections to a material using an environment map
- Fine-tuning and customizing the UV mapping of a mesh
- Using the HTML5 canvas and video element as input for a texture

Let's start with the most basic example, where we will show you how to load and apply a texture.

Using textures in materials

There are different ways that textures can be used in Three.js. You can use them to define the colors of the mesh, but you can also use them to define shininess, bumps, and reflections. The first example we will look at, though, is the most basic approach, where we use a texture to define the colors of the individual pixels of a mesh.

Loading a texture and applying it to a mesh

The most basic usage of a texture is when it's set as a map on a material. When you use this material to create a mesh, the mesh will be colored based on the supplied texture.

Loading a texture and using it on a mesh can be done in the following manner:

```
var textureLoader = new THREE.TextureLoader();
textureLoader.load("'../../assets/textures/general/metal-rust.jpg")
```

In this code sample, we use an instance of the `THREE.TextureLoader` function to load an image file from a specific location. Using this loader, you can use PNG, GIF, or JPEG images as input for a texture (further on in this chapter, we'll show you how to load other texture formats). Note that loading textures is done asynchronously: if it is a large texture and you render the scene before the texture is completely loaded, you'll see your meshes without a texture applied for a short time. If you want to wait until a texture is loaded, you can provide a `callback` to the `textureLoader.load()` function:

```
var textureLoader = new THREE.TextureLoader();
textureLoader.load("'../../assets/textures/general/metal-rust.jpg",
                        onLoadFunction, onProgressFunction,
onErrorFunction)
```

As you can see, the `load` function takes three additional functions as parameters: the `onLoadFunction` is called when the texture is loaded, the `onProgressFunction` can be used to track how much of the texture is loaded, and the `onErrorFunction` is called when something goes wrong while loading or parsing the texture.

You can use pretty much any image you'd like as a texture. The best results, however, come through using a square texture whose dimensions are a power of 2. So, dimensions such as 256 x 256, 512 x 512, 1024 x 1024, and so on, work the best. If the texture isn't a power of two, Three.js will scale down the image to the closest power of two value. For instance, one of the textures that we're using in the examples in this chapter as follows:

The pixels of a texture (also called **texels**) usually don't map one-to-one on the pixels of the face. If the camera is very close, we need to magnify the texture, and if we're zoomed out, we probably need to shrink the texture. For this purpose, WebGL and Three.js offer a couple of different options. You can specify how the texture is magnified by setting the `magFilter` property, and how it is minified with the `minFilter` property. These properties can be set to the following two basic values:

Name	Description
THREE.NearestFilter	This filter uses the color of the nearest texel that it can find. When used for magnification, this will result in blockiness, and when used for minification, the result will lose a lot of detail.
THREE.LinearFilter	This filter is more advanced, it and uses the color values of the four neighboring texels to determine the correct color. You'll still lose a lot of detail in minification, but the magnification will be much smoother and less blocky.

Aside from these basic values, we can also use an **MIP** map. A MIP map is a set of texture images, each half the size of the previous one. These are created when you load the texture and allow for much smoother filtering. So, when you have a square texture (as a power of 2), you can use a couple of additional approaches for better filtering. The properties can be set using the following values:

Name	Description
THREE.NearestMipMapNearestFilter	This property selects the MIP map that best maps the required resolution and applies the nearest filter principle, which we discussed in the previous table. Magnification is still blocky, but minification looks much better.
THREE.NearestMipMapLinearFilter	This property selects not just a single MIP map but the two nearest MIP map levels. On both of these levels, the nearest filter is applied, to get two intermediate results. These two results are passed through a linear filter to get the final result.
THREE.LinearMipMapNearestFilter	This property selects the MIP map that best maps the required resolution and applies the linear filter principle, which discussed in the previous table.

THREE.LinearMipMapLinearFilter	This property selects not a single MIP map, but the two nearest MIP map levels. On both of these levels, a linear filter is applied, to get two intermediate results. These two results are passed through a linear filter to get the final result.

If you don't specify the magFilter and minFilter properties explicitly, Three.js uses THREE.LinearFilter as the default for the magFilter property and THREE.LinearMipMapLinearFilter as the default for the minFilter property. In our examples, we'll just use these default properties. An example of the basic texture can be found in 01-basic-texture.html. The following screenshot shows this example:

In this example, we load a couple of textures (using the code that you saw earlier) and apply them to various shapes. You can use the menu on the right to change any of the material properties.

In this example, you can see that the textures nicely wrap around the shapes. When you create geometries in Three.js, it makes sure that any texture that is used is applied correctly. This is done through something called **UV mapping**. With UV mapping, we can tell the renderer which part of a texture should be applied to a specific face. We'll get into the details of UV mapping later in this chapter.

Aside from the standard image formats, that we can load with THREE.TextureLoader, Three.js also provides a couple of custom loaders you can use to load textures provided in different formats. The following table shows the additional loaders you can use, and shows an example of how they look:

Name	Description
THREE.DDSLoader	With this loader, you can load textures that are provided in the DirectDraw Surface format. This format is a proprietary Microsoft format to store compressed textures. Using this loader is very easy. First, include the DDSLoader.js file in your HTML page, and then use the following to use a texture: `var textureLoader = new THREE.DDSLoader();` `var texture = textureLoader.load('../../assets/textures/dds/test-dxt1.dds');` You can see an example of this loader in the sources for this chapter in 02-basic-texture-dds.html. Internally, this loader uses THREE.CompressedTextureLoader:

	Power VR is another proprietary file format to store compressed textures. Three.js supports the Power VR 3.0 file format, and can use textures provided in this format. To use this loader, include the `PVRLoader.js` file in your HTML page and then use the following to use a texture:
	`var textureLoader = new THREE.PVRLoader();`
	`var texture = textureLoader.load('../../assets/textures/pvr/tex_base.pvr');`
	Note that not all devices can use PVR compressed textures. When running Chrome on a desktop, you get an error message in the console, stating something like this: `WEBGL_compressed_texture_pvrtc extension not supported`. PVR textures, however, are often used in iOS; so, if you open the `03-basic-texture-pvr.html` example on an iOS device, you'll see the correct result. The following screenshot was taken on an iPhone:

	Targa is a raster graphics file format that is still used by a large number of 3D software programs. With the `THREE.TGALoader` object, you can use textures provided in this format with your 3D models. To use these image files, you first have to include the `TGALoader.js` file in your HTML, and then, you can use the following to load a TGA texture:
	`var loader = new THREE.TGALoader();`
	`var texture =  loader.load( '../../assets/textures/tga/dried_grass.tga' );`
	An example of this loader is provided in the sources of this chapter. You can view this example by opening `04-basic-texture-tga.html` in your browser:

	Khronos Texture (KTX) is a file format from the Khronos group (the organization behind the standardization of WebGL). This file format aims for a set of efficiently compressed textures that can be directly processed by WebGL, with minimal processing overhead. Textures in KTX format usually come in the different encoding, and based on the support from a device, a different encoding can be loaded. To use this loader, you first have to include the following in your HTML file: `XTXLoader.js`. A general approach is to first check the support from WebGL, and then, based on that, load the correct KTX file:

```
function determineFormat() {

    if ( renderer.extensions.get ( 'WEBGL_compressed_texture_astc' ) !== null) return
"astc";
    if ( renderer.extensions.get ( 'WEBGL_compressed_texture_etc1' ) !== null) return
"etc1";
    if ( renderer.extensions.get ( 'WEBGL_compressed_texture_s3tc' ) !== null) return
"s3tc";
    if ( renderer.extensions.get ( 'WEBGL_compressed_texture_pvrtc' ) !== null) return
"pvrtc";
}

var ktxTextureLoader = new THREE.KTXLoader();
var texture

switch (determineFormat()) {
    case "astc":
    texture = ktxTextureLoader.load('../../assets/textures/ktx/disturb_ASTC4x4.ktx');
    break;
    case "etc1":
    texture = ktxTextureLoader.load('../../assets/textures/ktx/disturb_ETC1.ktx');
    break;
    case "s3tc":
    texture = ktxTextureLoader.load('../../assets/textures/ktx/disturb_BC1.ktx');
    break;
    case "pvrtc":
    texture = ktxTextureLoader.load('../../assets/textures/ktx/disturb_PVR2bpp.ktx');
    break;
}
```

`THREE.KTXLoader`

You can see KTX being used by opening `06-basic-texture-ktx.html`:

The preceding textures were seen are just normal (or compressed) images. Aside for these normal images Three.js also supports HDR images. An HDR image captures a higher range of luminance levels than standard images, and can more closely match what we see with the human eye. Three.js supports the EXR and RGBE formats. In the following examples, you can also fine-tune how Three.js renders the HDR image, since an HDR image contains more luminance information than can be shown on a display. This is done by setting the following properties in the THREE.WebGLRenderer:

Property	Description
toneMapping	This property defines how to map the colors from the HDR image to the display. Three.js provides the following options: • THREE.NoToneMapping • THREE.LinearToneMapping • THREE.ReinhardToneMapping • THREE.Uncharted2ToneMapping • THREE.CineonToneMapping In the examples of the HDR loaders, you can switch between the tone mappings to see how they affect the rendering of HDR textures. The default is THREE.LinearToneMapping.
toneMappingExposure	This is exposure level of the toneMapping. This can be used to fine-tune the colors of the rendered texture.
toneMappingWhitePoint	This is the white point used for the toneMapping. This can also be used to fine-tune the colors of the rendered texture.

The following table shows how to use `THREE.EXRLoader` and `THREE.RGBELoader`, and how to change the `toneMapping`, `toneMappingExposure`, and `toneMappingWhitePoint`:

Name	Description

`THREE.EXRLoader`	The EXR file format is an HDR image file format developed by *Industrial Light & Magic*. To use textures in this format, load them by including the EXRLoader.js in your page, and use the `THREE.EXRLoader` as follows:
	`var loader = new THREE.EXRLoader();`
	`exrTextureLoader.load('../../assets/textures/exr/Rec709.exr'`
	An example of EXR can be found in `06-basic-texture-exr.html`:
	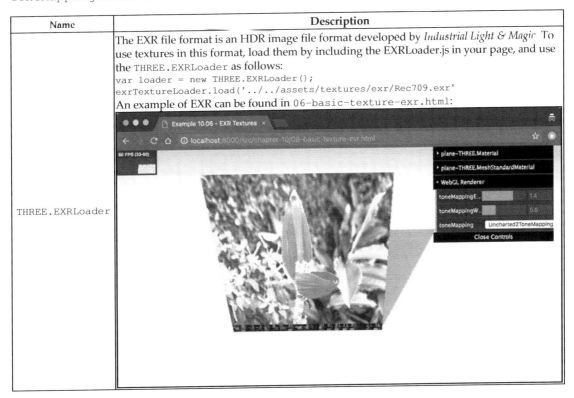

THREE.RGBELoader	RGBE is the Radiance HDR format, and it is used and supported by many applications. Using it from Three.js works in the same way as the other texture loaders. Include `RGBELoader.js` in your HTML page, and load it like this:
	
	``
	var hdrTextureLoader = new THREE.RGBELoader();
	hdrTextureLoader.load('../../assets/textures/hdr/dani_cathedral_oBBC.hdr',
	  function(texture, metadata) {
	    texture.encoding = THREE.RGBEEncoding;
	    texture.flipY = true;
	    ... and use the texture
	}
	``
	
	To use RGBE images, make sure to set the texture's encoding to `THREE.RGBEEncoding`, or else the colors will look wrong. Often, when you use RGBE images, you will notice that they are rendered upside down. To correct this, you can use the `flipY` property. When you open `07-basic-texture-rgbe.html`, you can see how an RGBE image is rendered:
	
	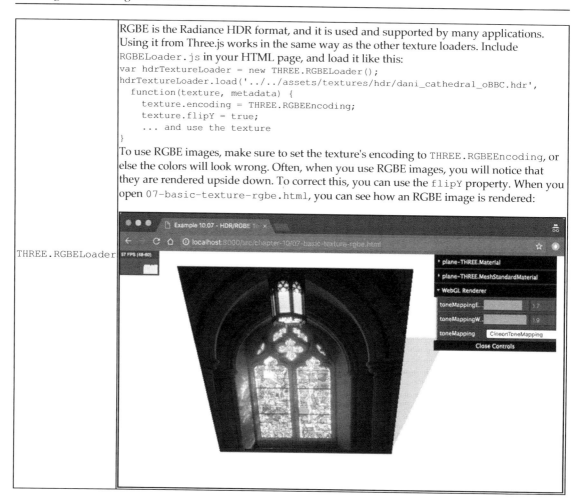

In these examples, we've used textures to define the colors in the pixels of our mesh. We can also use textures for other purposes. The following examples are used to illustrate how shading is applied to a material. You use shading to create bumps and wrinkles on the surface of a mesh.

Using a bump map to create wrinkles

A **bump map** is used to add more depth to a material. You can see this in action by opening the `02-bump-map.html` example:

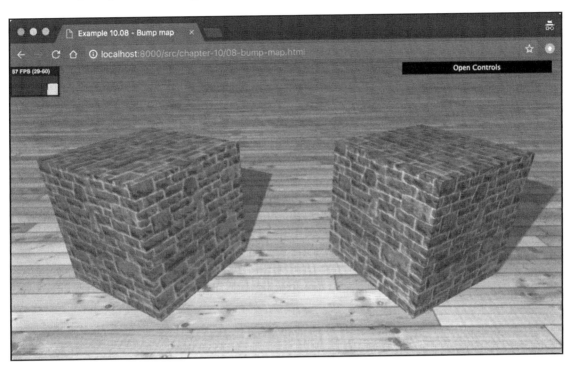

In this example, you can see that the right-hand side wall looks much more detailed, and seems to have more depth as compared to the wall on the left-hand side. This is done by setting an additional texture, a so-called bump map, on the material:

```
var cubeMaterial = new THREE.MeshStandardMaterial({
    map: textureLoader.load("../../assets/textures/stone/stone.jpg"),
    bumpMap = textureLoader.load("../../assets/textures/stone/stone-
bump.jpg"),
    metalness: 0.2,
    roughness: 0.07
});
```

In this code, you can see that aside from setting the `map` property, we have also set the `bumpMap` property to a texture. Additionally, with the `bumpScale` property, which is available through the menu in the previous example, we can set the height (or depth, if set to a negative value) of the bumps. The textures used in this example are shown as follows:

The bump map is a grayscale image, but you can also use a color image. The intensity of the pixel defines the height of the bump. A bump map only contains the relative height of a pixel. It doesn't say anything about the direction of the slope. So, the level of detail and perception of depth that you can reach with a bump map are limited. For more detail, you can use a normal map.

Achieving more detailed bumps and wrinkles with a normal map

In a normal map, the height (displacement) is not stored, but the direction of the normal for each picture is stored. Without going into too much detail, with normal maps, you can create very detailed-looking models that use only a small number of vertices and faces. For instance, take a look at the `09-normal-map.html` example:

In preceding screenshot, you can see a very detailed plastered cube on the right. The light source moves around the cubes, and you can see that the texture responds to the light source. This provides a very realistic-looking model, naturally and only requires a very simple model and a couple of textures. The following code fragment shows how to use a normal map in Three.js:

```
var cubeMaterial = new THREE.MeshStandardMaterial({
    map: textureLoader.load("../../assets/textures/general/plaster.jpg"),
    normalMap: textureLoader.load("../../assets/textures/general/plaster-
normal.jpg"),
    metalness: 0.2,
    roughness: 0.07
});
```

This involves the same approach as that used for the bump map. This time, though, we set the `normalMap` property to the normal texture. We can also define how pronounced the bumps look by setting the `normalScale` property `mat.normalScale.set(1,1)`. With this property, you can scale along the *x* and *y* axes. The best approach, though, is to keep these values the same.

Once again: when these values are below zero, the heights inverse.

The following screenshot shows both of the textures used in this example:

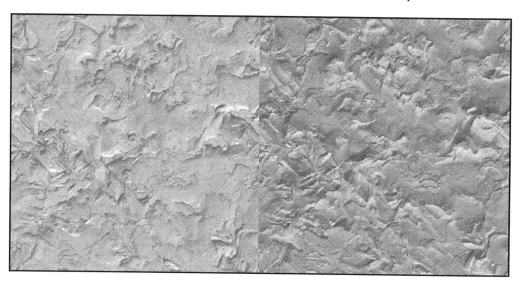

The problem with normal maps, however, is that they aren't very easy to create. You need to use specialized tools, such as Blender or Photoshop. These programs can use high-resolution renderings or textures as input, and can create normal maps from them.

With a normal or bump map, you don't change the shape of the model; all of the vertices stay in the exact same location. These maps just use the lights from the scene to create fake depth and details. Three.js provides a third method that you can use to add details to a model using a map, which does change the positions of the vertices. This is done through a displacement map.

Using a displacement map to alter the position of vertices

Three.js also provides a texture that you can use to change the positions of the vertices of your model. While the bump map and the normal map give an illusion of depth, with a displacement map, we really change the model's shape, based on the information from the texture. Using a displacement map is done in the same way as we use other maps:

```
var textureLoader = new THREE.TextureLoader();
var sphere = new THREE.SphereGeometry(8, 180, 180)
var sphereMaterial = new THREE.MeshStandardMaterial({
    map: textureLoader.load("../../assets/textures/w_c.jpg"),
    displacementMap: textureLoader.load("../../assets/textures/w_d.png"),
    metalness: 0.02,
    roughness: 0.07,
    color: 0xffffff
});
```

In the preceding code fragment, we load a displacement map, which looks as follows:

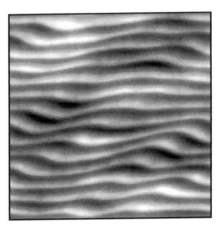

The brighter the color, the more a vertex is displaced. When you run example 10-displacement-map.html, you will see that the result of the displacement map is a model where the shape of the model is changed based on the information from the map:

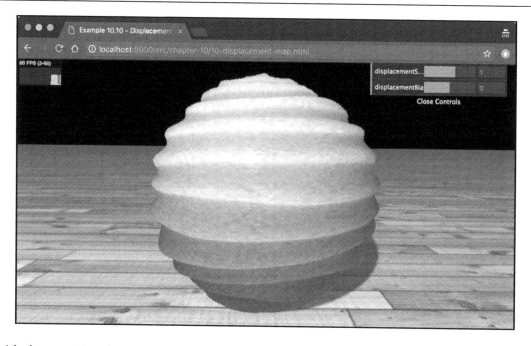

Aside from setting the `displacementMap` texture, we can also use the `displacementScale` and the `displacementOffset` to control how pronounced the displacement is. One final thing to mention about using a displacement map is that it will only have good results if your mesh contains a large number of vertices. If not, the displacement won't look like the provided texture, since there are too few vertices to represent the required displacement.

Adding subtle shadows with an ambient occlusion map

In the previous chapters, you learned how you can use shadows in Three.js. If you set the `castShadow` and `receiveShadow` properties of the correct meshes, add a couple of lights, and configure the shadow camera of the lights correctly, Three.js will render shadows. Rendering shadows, however, is a rather expensive operation that is repeated for each and every `render` loop. If you have lights or objects that are moving around, this is necessary; but often, some of the lights or models are fixed, so it would be great if we could calculate the shadows once, and then reuse them. To accomplish this, Three.js offers two different maps: the ambient occlusion map and a lightmap. In this section, we'll look at the ambient occlusion map, and in the next section, we'll look at the lightmap.

Ambient occlusion is a technique to determine how much each part of a model is exposed to the ambient lighting in a scene. In tools such as Blender, ambient light is often modeled through a hemisphere light or a directional light, such as the sun. While most parts of a model will receive some of this ambient lighting, not all of the parts will receive the same. If, for instance, you model a person, the top of the head will receive more ambient lighting than the bottoms of the arms. This difference in lighting, the shadows, can be rendered (baked, as shown in the following screenshot) into a texture, and we can then apply that texture to our models to give them shadows, without having to calculate the shadows each and every time:

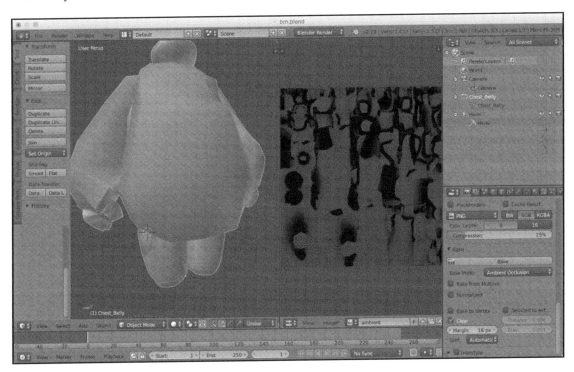

Once you have an ambient occlusion map, you can assign it to the `aoMap` property of the material, and Three.js will take this information into account when applying and calculating how much the `THREE.AmbientLight` objects in the scene should be applied to that specific part of the model. The following code fragment shows how to set the `aoMap` property:

```
var textureLoader = new THREE.TextureLoader();
var material = new THREE.MeshStandardMaterial({
    aoMap: textureLoader.load("../../assets/models/baymax/ambient.png"),
    aoMapIntensity: 2,
```

```
color: 0xffffff,
metalness: 0,
roughness: 1
});
```

Just like the other kinds of texture maps, we just use the `THREE.TextureLoader` to load the texture and assign it to the correct property of the material. And like with many of the other maps, we can also tune how much the map affects the lighting of the model by setting the `aoMapIntenisty` property. To make this work, we will need one additional step. We have already mentioned UV mappings. These define which part of a texture is mapped to a specific face of the model. For the ambient occlusion map, and also for the lightmap in the next example, Three.js uses a separate set of UV mappings, because often, the other textures need to be applied differently than the shadow and lightmap textures. For our example, we just copy the UV mappings from the model; remember that when we are using the `aoMap` property or the `lightMap` property, Three.js will use the value of `faceVertexUvs[1]` for mapping the texture:

```
geometry.faceVertexUvs.push(geometry.faceVertexUvs[0]);
```

An example that uses an ambient occlusion map can be found by opening `11-ao-map.html`:

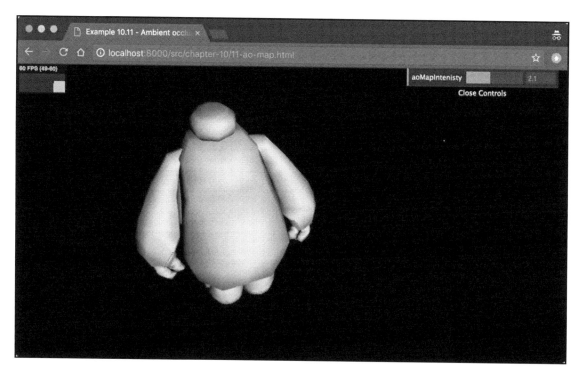

The model that you can see in the preceding screenshot has shadows applied to it. All of these shadows come from the ambient occlusion map. The lights in this example don't cast any shadows themselves.

While an ambient occlusion map changes the amount of light received by certain parts of the model, Three.js also supports a lightmap, which does the opposite (approximately), by specifying a map that adds extra lighting to certain parts of the model.

Creating fake shadows using a lightmap

In this section, we'll use a lightmap. A lightmap is a texture that contains information about how much the lights in the scene will affect the model. In other words, the effect of the lights is baked into a texture. Lightmaps are baked in 3D software, such as Blender, and contain the light value for each part of the model:

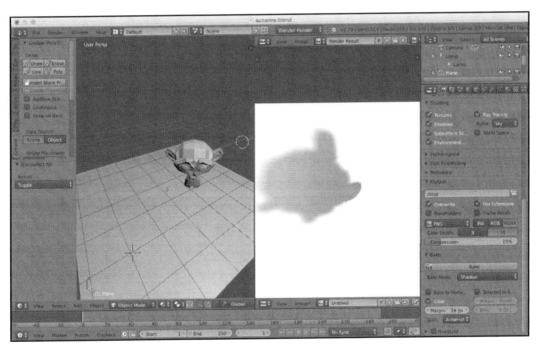

The lightmap that we'll use in this example is shown in the previous Blender screenshot. The right part of the edit window shows a baked lightmap for the ground plane. You can see that the whole ground plane is illuminated with a white light, and parts of it receive less light, because there is also a model in the scene. The code for using a lightmap is similar to that of an ambient occlusion map:

```
plane.geometry.faceVertexUvs.push(plane.geometry.faceVertexUvs[0]);
plane.material = new THREE.MeshBasicMaterial({
  map: textureLoader.load("../../assets/textures/general/floor-wood.jpg"),
  lightMap:
textureLoader.load("../../assets/textures/lightmap/lightmap.png"),
});
```

Once again, we provide Three.js with an additional set of `faceVertexUvs`, and we use `THREE.TextureLoader` to load the textures; in this case, a simple texture is used for the colors of the floor and the lightmap created for this example in Blender. The result looks as follows (`12-light-map.html`):

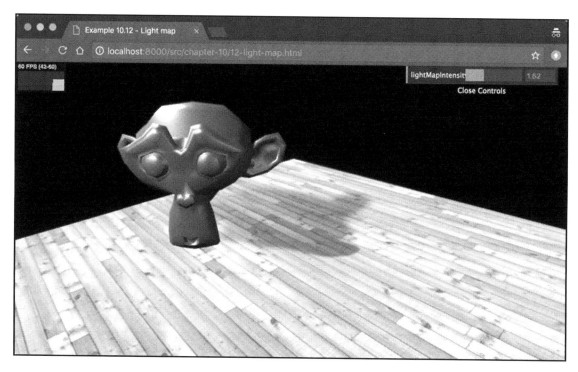

If you look at the preceding example, you can see that the information from the lightmap is used to create a very nice-looking shadow, which seems to be cast by the model. It is important to remember that baking shadows, lights, and ambient occlusion only affects work in static scenes, for static objects. As soon as objects or light sources change or start to move, you will have to calculate the shadows in real time.

Metalness and roughness maps

When discussing the materials available in Three.js, we mentioned that a good default material to use is `THREE.MeshStandardMaterial`. You can use this to create shiny, metal-like materials, but also to apply a roughness, to make it look more like wood or plastic. By using the `metalness` and `roughness` properties of the material, we can configure the material to represent the material that we want. Aside from these two properties, you can also configure these properties by using a texture. So, if we have a rough object and we want to specify that a certain part of that object is shiny, we can set the `metalnessMap` property of the `THREE.MeshStandardMaterial` and, if we want to indicate that some parts of the mesh should be seen as scratched or rougher, we can set the `roughnessMap` property. When you use these maps, the value of the texture for a specific part of the model is multiplied with either the `roughness` property or the `metalness` property, and that determines how that specific pixel should be rendered. These properties are best demonstrated by opening `example 13-metal-roughness-map.html`:

In this example, we've skipped ahead a bit and have also used an environment map, which allows us to render reflections from the environment on top of the objects. An object with a high `metalness` reflects more, and an object with a high `roughness` diffuses the reflection more. For the sphere on the right, we've used a `roughnessMap`, and you can see that the certain parts of the sphere look a bit rusted, and for the sphere on the left, we've used the same texture, but this time, we applied it to the `metalnessMap` property. There, you can see the inverse, where the object itself is rough, with a couple of parts that still reflect the environment. The texture that we've used looks as follows:

For the `metalnessMap`, the value of the material is multiplied with the `metalness` property of the material; for the `roughnessMap`, the same applies, but in that case, the value is multiplied with the `roughness` property. Loading this texture and setting it to the material is done in a familiar way:

```
mat1.metalnessMap =
textureLoader.load("../../assets/textures/engraved/roughness-map.jpg")
mat2.roughnessMap =
textureLoader.load("../../assets/textures/engraved/roughness-map.jpg")
```

Next up is the alpha map. With the alpha map, we can use a texture to change the transparency of parts of the model.

Alpha map

The alpha map is a way to control the opacity of the surface. If the value of the map is black, that part of the model will be fully transparent, and if it is white, it will be fully opaque. Before we look at the texture and how to apply it, we'll first look at the example (`14-alpha-map.html`):

In this example, we've rendered a sphere and set the `alphaMap` property of the material. If you open this example, you'll notice that you can only see the front-facing part of the sphere, unlike the preceding example, where you can look through the sphere and see the other side. The reason is that by default, the `side` property of the used material is set to `THREE.FrontSide`. To render the side that is normally hidden, we have to set the **side** property of the material to `THREE.BothSides`, and you see the sphere rendered as is shown in the previous screenshot.

The texture that we used in this example is a very simple one as follows:

To load it, we use the same approach as that of the other textures:

```
var sphereMaterial = new THREE.MeshStandardMaterial({
    alphaMap: textureLoader.load("../../assets/textures/alpha/partial-
transparency.png"),
    envMap: alternativeMap,
    metalness: 0.02,
    roughness: 0.07,
    color: 0xffffff,
    alphaTest: 0.5
});

sphereMaterial.alphaMap.wrapS = THREE.RepeatWrapping;
sphereMaterial.alphaMap.wrapT = THREE.RepeatWrapping;
sphereMaterial.alphaMap.repeat.set(8, 8);
```

When you look at the material that we've used for this, you can see that we've set the alphaTest property to 0.5. This is done to avoid rendering artifacts when working with transparency. If you see strange artifacts when using multiple transparent objects, or when working with alphaMap properties, experimenting with this property can often solve the problem. In this same code fragment, you can also see that we've set the wrapS, wrapT, and repeat properties of the texture. We'll explain these properties in more detail later in this chapter, but these properties can be used to determine how often we want to repeat the texture on the mesh. If set to (1, 1), the whole texture won't be repeated when applied to the mesh, and, if set to higher values, the texture will shrink and will be repeated multiple times. In this case, we repeat it in both directions 8 times.

Emissive map

The emissive map is a texture that can be used to make certain parts of the model glow, just like the emissive property does for the whole model. This is easier to understand by looking at an example. If you open up the 15-emissive-map.html example in the browser, you will see two lava-like objects. With the controls, you can limit the light emitted from the lights, and you can see that even with low lighting, the objects still glow:

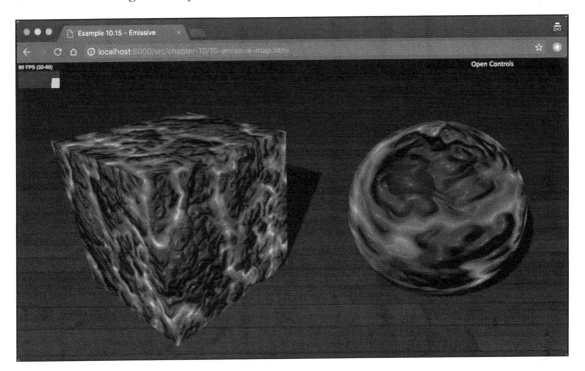

When you look really closely, though, you might see that while the objects seem to glow, the objects themselves don't emit light. This means that you can use this to enhance objects, but the objects themselves don't contribute to the lighting of the scene. For this example, we used an emissive map that looks as follows:

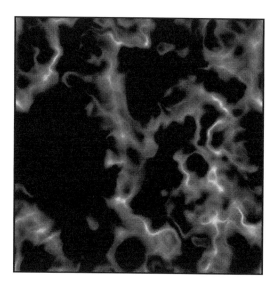

To load and use an emissive map, we use a THREE.TextureLoader to load the emissive map and assign it to the emissiveMap property:

```
var cubeMaterial = new THREE.MeshStandardMaterial({
    emissive: 0xffffff,
    emissiveMap:
textureLoader.load("../../assets/textures/emissive/lava.png"),
    normalMap: textureLoader.load("../../assets/textures/emissive/lava-
normals.png"),
    metalnessMap:
textureLoader.load("../../assets/textures/emissive/lava-smoothness.png"),
    metalness: 1,
    roughness: 0.4,
    normalScale: new THREE.Vector2(4,4)
});
```

Since the color from the emissiveMap is modulated with the emissive property, make sure that you set the emissive property of the material to something other than black.

Specular map

In the previous examples, we mostly used THREE.MeshStandardMaterial, and the different maps supported by that material. THREE.MeshStandardMaterial is often your best choice if you need a material, since it can be easily configured to represent a large number of different types of real-world materials. In older Versions of Three.js, you had to use THREE.MeshPhongMaterial for shiny materials and THREE.MeshLambertMaterial for non-shiny materials. The specular map used in this section can only be used together with the THREE.MeshPhongMaterial. With a specular map, you can define which parts of the model should be shiny, and which parts of them should be rough (similar to the metalnessMap and roughnessMap that we saw earlier). In the 16-specular-map.html example, we've rendered the earth and used a specular map to make the oceans shinier than the landmasses:

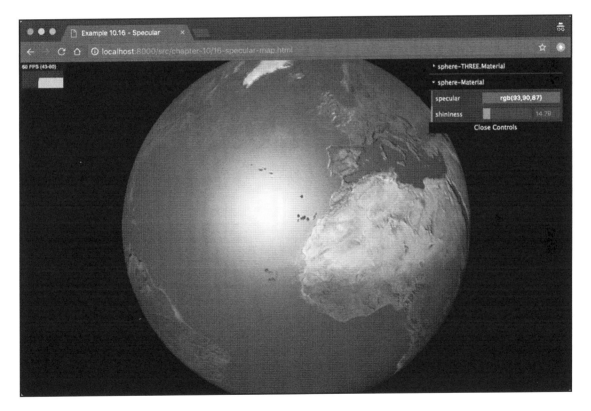

By using the menu in the top right, you can play around with the specular color and the shininess. As you can see, these two properties affect how the oceans reflect light, but they don't change the landmasses' shininess. This is because that we've used the following specular map:

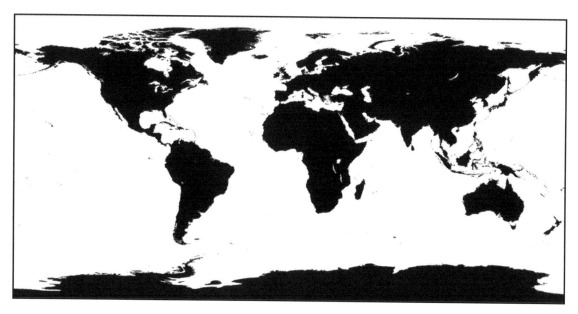

In this map, the black color means that those parts of the map have a shininess of zero percent, and the white parts a shininess of 100 percent.

To use a specular map, we use THREE.TextureLoader to load the map and assign it to the specularMap property of a THREE.MathPhongMaterial:

```
var earthMaterial = new THREE.MeshPhongMaterial({
    map: textureLoader.load("../../assets/textures/earth/Earth.png"),
    normalMap:
textureLoader.load("../../assets/textures/earth/EarthNormal.png"),
    specularMap:
textureLoader.load("../../assets/textures/earth/EarthSpec.png"),
    normalScale: new THREE.Vector2(6,6)
});
```

With the specular map, we've discussed most of the basic textures that you can use to add depth, color, transparency, or additional light effects to your model. In the next two sections, we'll look at one more type of map, which will allow you to add environment reflections to your model.

Creating fake reflections using an environment map

Calculating environment reflections is very CPU-intensive, and it usually requires a ray tracer approach. If you want to use reflections in Three.js, you can still do that, but you'll have to fake it. You can do so by creating a texture of the environment the object is in and applying it to the specific object. First, we'll show you the result that we're aiming for (see `17-env-map-static.html`, which is also shown in the following screenshot):

In the preceding screenshot, you can see that the sphere and cube reflect the environment. If you move your mouse around, you can also see that the reflection corresponds with the camera angle, in relation to the environment you see. To create this example, we perform the following steps:

1. Create a `CubeMap` object. A `CubeMap` is a set of six textures that can be applied to each side of a cube.

2. Set the skybox. When we have a `CubeMap`, we can set it as the background of the scene. If we do this, we effectively create a very large box, inside of which the cameras and objects are placed, so that when we move the camera around, the background of the scene also changes correctly. Alternatively, we can create a very large cube, apply the `CubeMap`, and add it to the scene ourselves.

3. Apply the `CubeMap` object as a texture. The same `CubeMap` object that we used to simulate the environment can be used as a texture on the meshes. Three.js will make sure it looks like a reflection of the environment.

Creating a `CubeMap` is pretty easy, once you have the source material. What you will need six images that together make up a complete environment. So, you will need the following pictures: looking forward (`posz`), looking backward (`negz`), looking up (`posy`), looking down (`negy`), looking right (`posx`), and looking left (`negx`). Three.js will patch these together to create a seamless environment map. There are a number of sites where you can download panoramic images, but they are often in a spherical equirectangular format, which looks as follows:

The easiest way to use this as a CubeMap is to use one of the online tools to split the texture into separate files. Two sites that allow you to do this are the following:

- https://jaxry.github.io/panorama-to-cubemap/
- https://www.360toolkit.co/convert-spherical-equirectangular-to-cubemap.html

Aside from converting them before you use them, Three.js has support for using spherical equirectangular images as a CubeMap, but you have to take a couple of additional steps to use them.

For loading, we can use the standard texture loader, but we have to inform Three.js that we want to use a specific mapping:

```
var textureLoader = new THREE.TextureLoader();
var cubeMap = textureLoader.load(
"textures/2294472375_24a3b8ef46_o.jpg" );
cubeMap.mapping = THREE.EquirectangularReflectionMapping;
cubeMap.magFilter = THREE.LinearFilter;
cubeMap.minFilter = THREE.LinearMipMapLinearFilter;
```

Now, we can assign the CubeMap to the envMap property for our models. We can't set the loaded texture as background for the scene, however. For that, we will need to create a skybox ourselves:

```
var equirectShader = THREE.ShaderLib[ "equirect" ];
var equirectMaterial = new THREE.ShaderMaterial( {
fragmentShader: equirectShader.fragmentShader,
vertexShader: equirectShader.vertexShader,
uniforms: equirectShader.uniforms,
depthWrite: false,
side: THREE.BackSide
});
equirectMaterial.uniforms[ "tEquirect" ].value = cubeMap;

// create the skybox
var skybox = new THREE.Mesh(new THREE.BoxGeometry(10000,
10000, 10000), material);
scene.add(skybox);
```

As you can see, there are a couple of additional steps to get these kinds of panorama images working, but it is possible to do so if you don't want to convert the images before using them. For the rest of this section, we're going to assume that we are working with separate images, instead of a single spherical equirectangular one.

Once you have the six separate pictures, you can load them, as shown in the following code fragment:

```
var urls = [
    '../../assets/textures/cubemap/flowers/right.png',
    '../../assets/textures/cubemap/flowers/left.png',
    '../../assets/textures/cubemap/flowers/top.png',
    '../../assets/textures/cubemap/flowers/bottom.png',
    '../../assets/textures/cubemap/flowers/front.png',
    '../../assets/textures/cubemap/flowers/back.png'
];

var cubeLoader = new THREE.CubeTextureLoader();
var cubeMap = cubeLoader.load(urls);
```

Instead of using the `THREE.TextureLoader`, we use a `THREE.CubeTextureLoader`, and, in the `load` function, we pass in the URLs of the images that we want to load (take care that you add them in the correct order). The result is a `CubeMap` that we can use for the skybox and for the environment map of our models. The next step, which isn't mandatory but usually looks better, is to add the `CubeMap` as a skybox. All we need to do is the following:

```
scene.background = cubeMap
```

The last step is setting the loaded `CubeMap` as the `envMap` property of the material we're using for our meshes:

```
var sphereMaterial = new THREE.MeshStandardMaterial({
    envMap: cubeMap,
    color: 0xffffff,
    metalness: 1,
    roughness: 0,
});
```

The result is a scene where it looks like we're standing in a wide, outdoor environment, where the meshes reflect the environment. The menu at the side allows you to set the properties of the material. You can see that if you increase the `metalness` of an object, it will reflect more of the environment, and if the roughness is increased, the reflections will look more `diffused`. For instance, in the following screenshot, the metalness and diffuseness are both set to a high value:

Aside from reflection, Three.js also allows you to use a `CubeMap` object for refraction (glass-like objects). The following screenshot shows this (you can test this yourself by using the menu on the right):

To get this effect, we only need to set the mapping property of the `cubeMap` to `THREE.CubeRefractionMapping` (the default is the reflection, which can also be set manually by specifying `THREE.CubeReflectionMapping`):

```
cubeMap.mapping = THREE.CubeRefractionMapping
```

The amount of refraction is determined by the `metalness` and `roughness` properties of the material.

In this example, we used a static environment map for the meshes. In other words, we only saw the environment reflection, and not the other meshes in the environment. In the following screenshot (which you can see in action by opening `18-env-map-dynamic.html` in your browser), we'll show you how you can create a reflection that also shows the other objects in the scene:

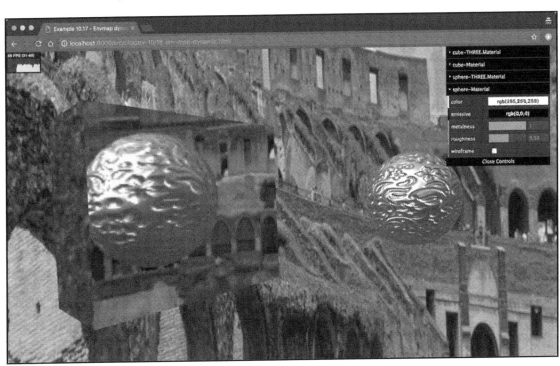

To also show reflections from the other objects in the scene, we need to use some other Three.js components. The first of them is an additional camera called `THREE.CubeCamera`:

```
var cubeCamera = new THREE.CubeCamera(0.1, 10, 512);
cubeCamera.position.copy(cubeMesh.position);
scene.add(cubeCamera);
```

We will use THREE.CubeCamera to take a snapshot of the scene with all of the objects rendered, and will use that to set up CubeMap. The first two arguments define the near and far properties of the camera. So, in this case, the camera only renders what it can see from 0.1 to 1.0. The last property is the size of the texture that will be created. The higher the value, the more detailed the reflection will look. You need to make sure that you position this camera at the exact location of the THREE.Mesh on which you want to show the dynamic reflections. In this example, we copy the position from the cube, so that the camera is positioned correctly.

Now that we have the CubeCamera set up correctly, we need to make sure that what the CubeCamera sees is applied as a texture to the cube in our example. To do this, we set the envMap property to cubeCamera.renderTarget:

```
cubeMaterial.envMap = cubeCamera.renderTarget;
```

Now, we have to make sure that cubeCamera renders the scene, so we can use that output as input for the cube. For this, we update the render loop as follows:

```
function render() {
    ...

    cube1.visible = false;
    cubeCamera.updateCubeMap(renderer, scene);
    cube1.visible = true;

    requestAnimationFrame(render);
    renderer.render(scene, camera);
    ....
}
```

As you can see, we first disable the visibility of the cube1 mesh. We do this because we only want to see reflections from the sphere. Next, we render the scene using cubeCamera, by calling the updateCubeMap function. After that, we make the sphere visible again and render the scene as normal. The result is that in the reflection of the cube, you can see a sphere. You can play around with the settings of the sphere material, and you can see that they are updated in real time, in the reflection on the cube.

Advanced usage of textures

In the previous section, you saw some basic texture usages. Three.js also provides options for more advanced texture usage. In this section, we'll look at a couple of options that Three.js provides.

Custom UV mapping

We'll start with a deeper look at UV mappings. Earlier we explained that with UV mapping, you can specify what part of a texture is shown on a specific face. When you create a geometry in Three.js, these mappings will also automatically be created, based on the type of geometry that you created. In most cases, you don't really need to change the default UV mapping. A good way to understand how UV mapping works is to look at an example from Blender, which is shown in the following screenshot:

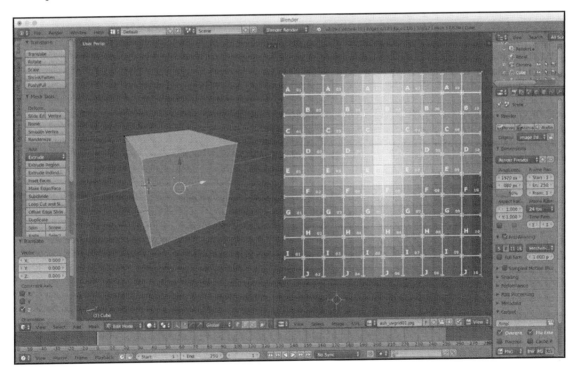

In this example, you can see two windows. The window on the left-hand side contains a cube geometry. The window on the right-hand side is the UV mapping, where we've loaded an example texture to show how the mapping is. In this example, we've selected a single face for the window on the left-hand side, and the window on the right-hand side shows the UV mapping for this face. As you can see, each vertex of the face is positioned in one of the corners of the UV mapping on the right (the small circles). This means that the complete texture will be used for that face. All of the other faces of this cube are mapped in the same manner, so the result will show a cube where each face shows the complete texture; see `19-uv-mapping.html`, which is also shown in the following screenshot:

This is the default for a cube in Blender (and also in Three.js). Let's change the UV by mapping each face to a different part of the texture as follows:

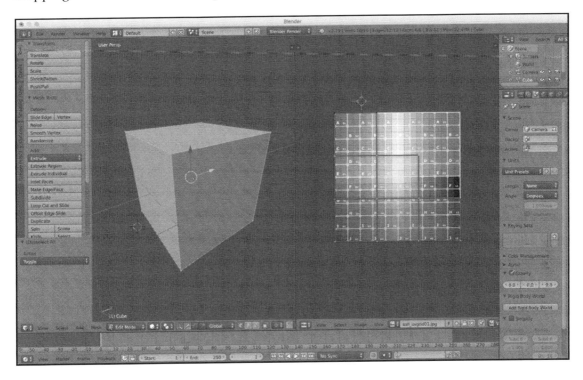

If we show this in Three.js, you will see that the texture is applied differently, as shown in the following screenshot:

Customizing UV mappings is normally done from programs such as Blender, especially when the models become more complex. The most important thing to remember here is that UV mappings run in two dimensions, u and v, from 0 to 1. To customize the UV mapping, you need to define, for each face, what part of the texture should be shown. You do this by defining u and v coordinates for each of the vertices that make up the face. You can use the following code to set u and v values:

```
geom.faceVertexUvs[0][0][0].x = 0.5;
geom.faceVertexUvs[0][0][0].y = 0.7;
geom.faceVertexUvs[0][0][1].x = 0.4;
geom.faceVertexUvs[0][0][1].y = 0.1;
geom.faceVertexUvs[0][0][2].x = 0.4;
geom.faceVertexUvs[0][0][2].y = 0.5;
```

This code snippet will set the uv properties of the first face to the specified value. Remember that each face is defined by three vertices; so, to set all of the uv values for a face, we will need to set six properties. If you open the 20-uv-mapping-manual.html example, you can see what happens when you change the uv mappings manually. The following screenshot shows the example, where you can modify the UV mappings of a single face and see the result directly:

Next, we'll look at how textures can be repeated, which is done by some internal UV mapping tricks.

Repeat wrapping

When you apply a texture to a geometry created by Three.js, Three.js will try to apply the texture as optimally as possible. For instance, for cubes, this means that each side will show the complete texture, and for spheres, the complete texture is wrapped around the sphere. There are, however, situations where you won't want the texture to spread around a complete face or the complete geometry, but rather have the texture repeat itself. Three.js provides functionality that allows you to control this. An example where you can play around with the repeat properties is provided in `21-repeat-wrapping.html`. The following screenshot shows this example:

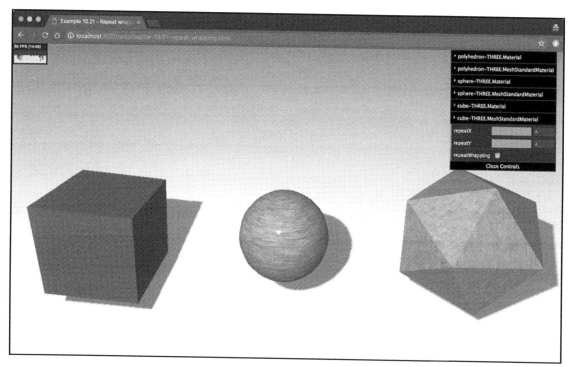

Before this property will have the desired effect, you need to make sure that you set the wrapping of the texture to `THREE.RepeatWrapping`, as shown in the following code snippet:

```
cube.material.map.wrapS = THREE.RepeatWrapping;
cube.material.map.wrapT = THREE.RepeatWrapping;
```

The `wrapS` property defines how you want the texture to behave along its *x* axis, and the `wrapT` property defines how the texture should behave along its *y* axis. Three.js provides two options for this, which are as follows:

- `THREE.RepeatWrapping` allows the texture to repeat itself.
- `THREE.ClampToEdgeWrapping` is a default setting.
  With `THREE.ClampToEdgeWrapping`, the texture doesn't repeat as a whole; only the pixels at the edge are repeated.

If you disable the **repeatWrapping** menu option, the `THREE.ClampToEdgeWrapping` option is used, which looks as follows:

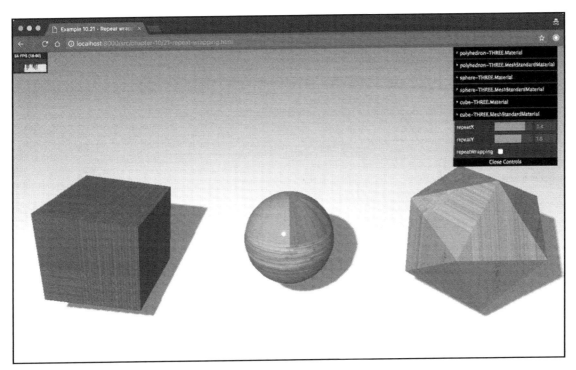

If we use `THREE.RepeatWrapping`, we can set the `repeat` property, as shown in the following code fragment:

```
cube.material.map.repeat.set(repeatX, repeatY);
```

The `repeatX` variable defines how often the texture is repeated along its x axis, and the `repeatY` variable defines the same for the y axis. If these values are set to 1, the texture won't repeat itself; if they are set to a higher value, you'll see that the texture will start to repeat. You can also use values lower than one. In that case, you'll zoom in on the texture. If you set the repeat value to a negative value, the texture will be mirrored.

When you change the `repeat` property, Three.js will automatically update the textures and render them with this new setting. If you change from `THREE.RepeatWrapping` to `THREE.ClampToEdgeWrapping`, you will have to explicitly update the texture:

```
cube.material.map.needsUpdate = true;
```

Until now, we've only used static images for our textures. However, Three.js also has the option to use the HTML5 canvas as a texture.

Rendering to a canvas and using it as a texture

In this section, we will look at two different examples. First, we will look at how you can use the canvas to create a simple texture and apply it to a mesh, and after that, we'll go one step further and create a canvas that can be used as a bump map, using a randomly generated pattern.

Using the canvas as a texture

In the first example, we will use the Literally library (from `http://literallycanvas.com/`) to create an interactive canvas that you can draw on; see the bottom-left corner in the following screenshot. You can view this example at `09-canvas-texture`. The following screenshot shows the example:

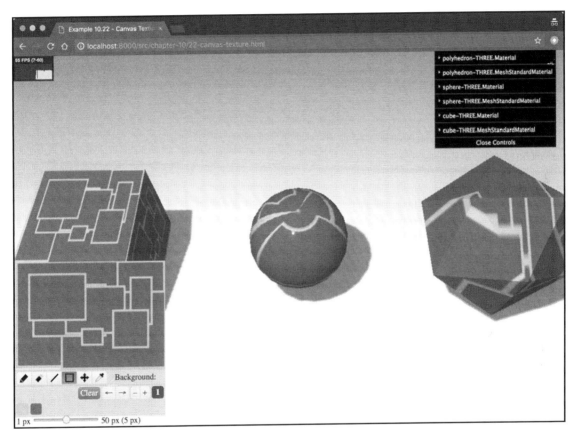

Anything that you draw on this canvas is directly rendered on the cube as a texture. Accomplishing this in Three.js is really simple, and it only takes a couple of steps. The first thing that we need to do is create a canvas element, and, for this specific example, configure it to be used with the Literally library, as follows:

```
<div class="fs-container">
  <div id="canvas-output" style="float:left">
  </div>
</div>
```

```
...
var canvas = document.createElement("canvas");
document.getElementById('canvas-output').appendChild(canvas);
$('#canvas-output').literallycanvas({imageURLPrefix:
'../../libs/other/literally/img'});
```

We just create a `canvas` element from JavaScript and add it to a specific `div` element. With the `literallycanvas` call, we can create the drawing tools that you can use to draw directly on the canvas. Next, we need to create a texture that uses the canvas drawing as its input:

```
var texture = new THREE.Texture(canvas);
```

As the preceding code shows, the only thing that you need to do is pass in the reference to the canvas element when you create a new texture, `new THREE.Texture(canvas)`. This will create a texture that uses the canvas element as its material. All that is left to do is update the material whenever we render, so that the latest Version of the canvas drawing is shown on the cube, as follows:

```
function render() {
    renderer.render(scene, camera);

    polyhedronMesh.rotation.x += 0.01;
    sphereMesh.rotation.x += 0.01;
    cubeMesh.rotation.x += 0.01;

    polyhedronMesh.material.map.needsUpdate = true;
    sphereMesh.material.map.needsUpdate = true;
    cubeMesh.material.map.needsUpdate = true;
}
```

To inform Three.js that we want to update the texture, we just set the `needsUpdate` property of the texture to `true`. In this example, we've used the canvas element as input for the most simple of textures. We can, of course, use this same idea for all of the different types of maps that we've seen so far. In the next example, we'll use it as a bump map.

Using the canvas as a bump map

As you saw earlier in this chapter, we can create a simple wrinkled texture with a bump map. The higher the intensity of a pixel in this map, the higher the wrinkling. Since a bump map is just a simple black and white image, nothing keeps us from creating it on a canvas and using that canvas as an input for the bump map.

In the following example, we use a canvas to generate a random grayscale image, and we use that image as an input for the bump map that we apply to the cube. See the `23-canvas-texture-bumpmap.html` example. The following screenshot shows the example:

The JavaScript code required for this is not that different from the previous example. We need to create a canvas element and fill that canvas with some random noise. To do so, we use **Perlin noise**. Perlin noise (`http://en.wikipedia.org/wiki/Perlin_noise`) generates a very natural-looking random texture, as you can see in the preceding screenshot. We use the Perlin noise function from `https://github.com/wwwtyro/perlin.js`, as follows:

```
var ctx = canvas.getContext("2d");
function fillWithPerlin(perlin, ctx) {

    for (var x = 0; x < 512; x++) {
```

```
for (var y = 0; y < 512; y++) {
    var base = new THREE.Color(0xffffff);
    var value = perlin.noise(x / 10, y / 10, 0);
    base.multiplyScalar(value);
    ctx.fillStyle = "#" + base.getHexString();
    ctx.fillRect(x, y, 1, 1);
  }
 }
}
```

We use the `perlin.noise` function to create a value from 0 to 1, based on the *x* and *y* coordinates of the canvas element. This value is used to draw a single pixel on the canvas element. Doing this for all the pixels creates the random map that you can see in the bottom-left corner of the previous screenshot. This map can then be used as a bump map. The following shows how the random map can be created:

```
var cube = new THREE.CubeGeometry(23, 10, 16)
var cubeMaterial = new THREE.MeshStandardMaterial({
    bumpMap: new THREE.Texture(canvas),
    metalness: 0,
    roughness: 1,
    color: 0xffffff,
    bumpScale: 3,
    map: textureLoader.load('../../assets/textures/general/wood-2.jpg')
});
```

In this example, we rendered Perlin noise using an HTML canvas element. Three.js also provides an alternative way to dynamically create a texture. You can create a `THREE.DataTexture` texture where you can pass in a `Uint8Array` where you can directly set the RGB values.

The final input that we use for the texture is another HTML element: the HTML5 video element.

Using the output from a video as a texture

If you read the preceding section on rendering to a canvas, you may have thought about rendering video to canvas and using that as input for a texture. That's one way to do it, but Three.js already has direct support to use the HTML5 video element (through WebGL). Check out `24-video-texture.html`. Refer to the following screenshot for a still image of this example:

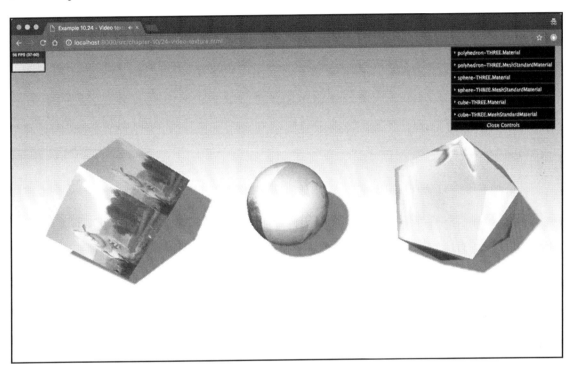

Using video as input for a texture is easily, just like using the canvas element. First we need a video element to play the video:

```
<video
    id="video"
    style="display: none; position: absolute; left: 15px; top: 75px;"
    src="../../../assets/movies/Big_Buck_Bunny_small.ogv"
    controls="true"
    autoplay="true">
</video>
```

This is just a basic HTML5 video element that we set to play automatically. Next, we can configure Three.js to use the video as an input for a texture, as follows:

```
var video = document.getElementById( 'video' );
var texture = new THREE.VideoTexture(video);
texture.minFilter = THREE.LinearFilter;
texture.magFilter = THREE.LinearFilter;
texture.format = THREE.RGBFormat;
```

Since our video isn't square, we need to make sure that we disable the MIP map generation on the material. We also set some simple, high-performance filters, as the material changes very often. That's it. Now, we can create materials, and add the texture to the map property. The result is as can be seen in the 24-video-texture.html example.

Summary

We will now end this chapter on textures. As you've seen, there are a lot of different kinds of textures available in Three.js, each with a different use. You can use any image in the PNG, JPG, GIF, TGA, DDS, PVR, TGA, KTX, EXR, or RGBE format as a texture. Loading these images is done asynchronously, so remember to either use a rendering loop or add a callback when you load a texture. With the different types of textures available, you can create great-looking objects from low-poly models.

With Three.js, it is also easy to create dynamic textures, using either the HTML5 canvas element or the video element. Just define a texture with these elements as the input, and set the needsUpdate property to true whenever you want the texture to be updated.

With this chapter out of the way, we've pretty much covered all of the important concepts of Three.js. However, we haven't, looked at an interesting feature that Three.js offers: postprocessing. With postprocessing, you can add effects to your scene after it is rendered. You can, for instance, blur or colorize your scene, or add a TV-like effect using scan lines. In Chapter 11, *Render Postprocessing*, we'll look at postprocessing and how you can apply it to your scene.

11
Render Postprocessing

We're approaching the end of the book, and, in this chapter, we'll look at one of the main features of Three.js that we haven't touched upon yet: render postprocessing.

The main points we'll discuss in this chapter are as follows:

- Setting up Three.js for postprocessing
- The basic postprocessing passes provided by Three.js, such as `THREE.BloomPass` and `THREE.FilmPass`
- Applying effects to part of a scene using masks
- Using `THREE.ShaderPass` to add even more basic postprocessing effects, such as sepia filters, mirror effects, and color adjustments
- Using `THREE.ShaderPass` for various blurring effects and more advanced filters
- Creating a custom postprocessing effect by writing a simple shader

In *Chapter 1, Creating Your First 3D Scene with Three.js*, in the *Introducing requestAnimationFrame* section, we set up a `rendering` loop that we've used throughout the book, in order to render and animate our scenes. For postprocessing, we need to make a couple of changes to this setup, to allow Three.js to postprocess the final rendering. In the first section, we'll look at how to do this.

Setting up Three.js for postprocessing

To set up Three.js for postprocessing, we have to make a couple of changes to our current setup, as follows:

1. Create `THREE.EffectComposer`, which can be used to add postprocessing passes.
2. Configure `THREE.EffectComposer` so that it renders our scene and applies any additional postprocessing steps.
3. In the `render` loop, use `THREE.EffectComposer` to render the scene, apply for the passes, and show the output.

As always, we will illustrate an example that you can use to experiment with and can adapt for your own purposes. The first example in this chapter can be accessed from `01-basic-effect-composer.html`. You can use the menu in the top-right corner to modify the properties of the postprocessing step used in this example. In this example, we render a simple globe and add an old television-like effect to it, as follows:

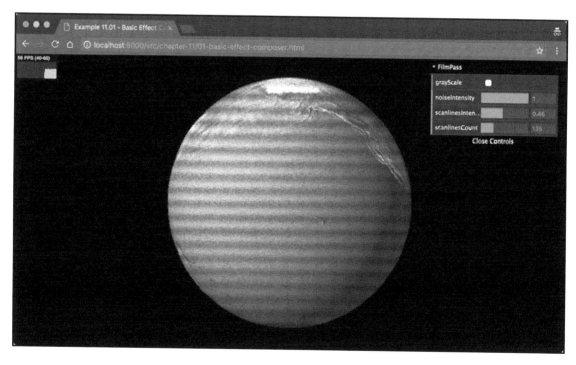

This television effect is added after the scene is rendered by using `THREE.FilmPass`, together with `THREE.EffectComposer`.

Creating THREE.EffectComposer

First, let's look at the additional JavaScript files that you need to include. These files can be found in the Three.js distribution, in the `examples/js/postprocessing` and `examples/js/shaders` directories. For the `THREE.FilmPass` example, we need to include the following:

```
    <script type="text/javascript"
 src="../../libs/three/postprocessing/EffectComposer.js"></script>
    <script type="text/javascript"
 src="../../libs/three/postprocessing/ShaderPass.js"></script>
    <script type="text/javascript"
 src="../../libs/three/postprocessing/MaskPass.js"></script>
    <script type="text/javascript"
 src="../../libs/three/postprocessing/RenderPass.js"></script>
    <script type="text/javascript"
 src="../../libs/three/shaders/CopyShader.js"></script>
```

The `EffectComposer.js` file provides the `THREE.EffectComposer` object that allows us to add postprocessing steps. `MaskPass.js`, `ShaderPass.js`, and `CopyShader.js` are used by `THREE.EffectComposer` internally, and `RenderPass.js` allows us to add a rendering pass to `THREE.EffectComposer`. Without that pass, our scene won't be rendered at all.

In this example, we will add two additional JavaScript files, to add a film-like effect to our scene:

```
    <script type="text/javascript"
 src="../../libs/three/shaders/FilmShader.js"></script>
    <script type="text/javascript"
 src="../../libs/three/postprocessing/FilmPass.js"></script>
```

The first thing that we need to do is create a `THREE.EffectComposer`. You can do this by passing in a `THREE.WebGLRenderer` to its constructor:

```
var renderer = new THREE.WebGLRenderer();
var composer = new THREE.EffectComposer(renderer);
```

Next, we will add various passes to this composer.

Configuring THREE.EffectComposer for postprocessing

Each pass is executed in the sequence it is added to `THREE.EffectComposer`. The first pass that we add is `THREE.RenderPass`. This pass renders our `scene` using the `camera` provided, but doesn't output it to the screen yet:

```
var renderPass = new THREE.RenderPass(scene, camera);
composer.addPass(renderPass);
```

With the `addPass` function, we add a `THREE.RenderPass` to `THREE.EffectComposer`. The next step is to add another pass that will output its result to the screen. Not all the available passes allow for this (more on that later), but `THREE.FilmPass`, which is used in this example, allows us to output the result of its pass to the screen. To add `THREE.FilmPass`, we need to first create it and add it to the composer. The resulting code looks as follows:

```
var renderPass = new THREE.RenderPass(scene, camera);
var effectFilm = new THREE.FilmPass(0.8, 0.325, 256, false);
effectFilm.renderToScreen = true;

var composer = new THREE.EffectComposer(renderer);
composer.addPass(renderPass);
composer.addPass(effectFilm);
```

As you can see, we created `THREE.FilmPass` and set the `renderToScreen` property to `true`. This pass is added to `THREE.EffectComposer` after `renderPass`; so, when this composer is used, the scene is rendered first and is then passed through a `THREE.FilmPass`, and finally, we can see the output on the screen.

Updating the render loop

Now, we just need to make a small modification to our `render` loop, to use the composer instead of a `THREE.WebGLRenderer`:

```
function render() {
  stats.update();
  var delta = clock.getDelta();
  trackballControls.update(delta);
```

```
    earth.rotation.y += 0.001;
    pivot.rotation.y += -0.0003;

    // request next and render using composer
    requestAnimationFrame(render);
    composer.render(delta);
}
```

The only modification that we made is that we removed `renderer.render(scene, camera)` and replaced it with `composer.render(delta)`. This will call the render function on `EffectComposer`, which, in turn, uses the passed-in `THREE.WebGLRenderer`; and, since we set the `renderToScreen` of `FilmPass` to `true`, the result from `FilmPass` is shown on the screen. Now, when you run this example, it'll show the Earth with the `THREE.FilmPass` applied:

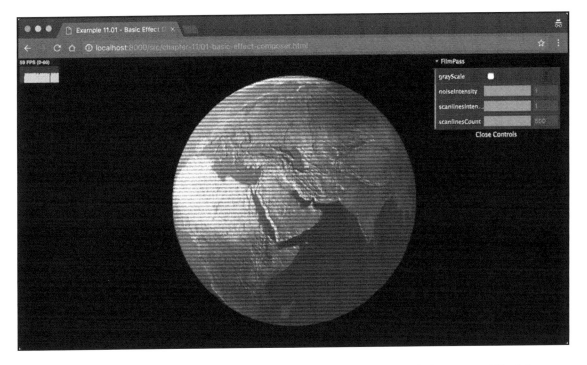

You can still use the normal controls to move around the scene. All of the effects that you will see in this chapter are applied after the scene is rendered. With this basic setup, we'll look at the available postprocessing passes in the next couple of sections.

Postprocessing passes

Three.js comes with a number of postprocessing passes that you can use directly with `THREE.EffectComposer`.

 Most of the shaders and passes shown in this chapter can be configured. When you want to apply one yourself, it is usually easiest to just add a simple UI that allows you to play around with the properties. That way, you can see what is a good setting for your specific scenario.

The following table gives an overview of all of the passes that are available:

Pass name	Description
THREE.AdaptiveToneMappingPass	This render pass adapts the luminosity of the scene, based on the amount of light available in the scene.
THREE.BloomPass	This is an effect that makes lighter areas bleed into darker areas. This simulates an effect wherein the camera is overwhelmed by extremely bright light.
THREE.BokehPass	This adds a Bokeh effect to the scene. With a Bokeh effect, the foreground of the scene is in focus, while the rest is out of focus.
THREE.ClearPass	This spill pass clears the current texture buffer.
THREE.CubeTexturePass	This can be used to render a skybox in the scene.
THREE.DotScreenPass	This applies a layer of black dots, representing the original image across the screen.
THREE.FilmPass	This simulates a TV screen by applying scanlines and distortions.
THREE.GlitchPass	This shows an electronic glitch on the screen at a random time interval.
THREE.HalfTonePass	This adds a halftone effect to the scene. With a halftone effect, the scene is rendered as a set of colored glyphs (circles, squares, and so on) of various sizes.
THREE.MaskPass	This allows you to apply a mask to the current image. Subsequent passes are only applied to the masked area.
THREE.OutlinePass	This renders the outline of the objects in the scene.
THREE.RenderPass	This renders a scene based on the scene and camera supplied.

THREE.SAOPass	This provides runtime ambient occlusion.
THREE.SMAAPass	This adds an anti-aliasing effect to the scene.
THREE.SSAARenderPass	This adds an anti-aliasing to the scene.
THREE.SSAOPass	This provides an alternative way to perform runtime ambient occlusion.
THREE.SavePass	When this pass is executed, it makes a copy of the current rendering step that you can use later. This pass isn't that useful in practice, and we won't use it in any of our examples.
THREE.ShaderPass	This allows you to pass in custom shaders for advanced or custom postprocessing passes.
THREE.TAARenderPass	This adds an anti-aliasing effect to the scene.
THREE.TexturePass	This stores the current state of the composer in a texture that you can use as input for other EffectComposer instances.
THREE.UnrealBloomPass	This is the same as THREE.BloomPass, but with an effect similar to the effect used in the Unreal 3D engine.

Three.js also provides an alternative way to use the Bokeh effect. You can use THREE.BokehShader2 and THREE.DOFMipMapShader, together with THREE.ShaderPass. Using these shaders requires a rather complex setup. An example of these shaders in action can be found on the Three.js website, at http://threejs.org/examples/webgl_postprocessing_dof2.html.

Let's start a number of simple passes.

Simple postprocessing passes

For simple passes, we'll look at what we can do with
THREE.FilmPass, THREE.BloomPass, and THREE.DotScreenPass. For these passes, an example is available, (02-post-processing-simple), which will allow you to experiment with these passes and see how they affect the original output differently. The following screenshot shows the example:

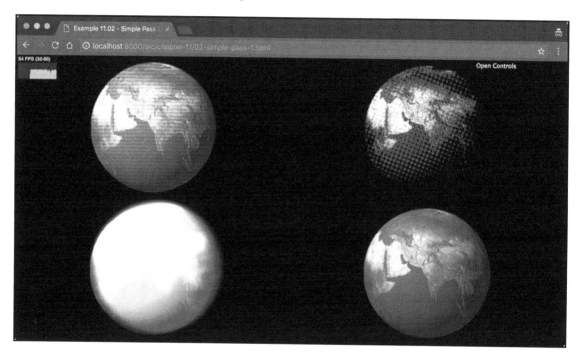

In this example, you can see four scenes at the same time, and, in each scene, a different postprocessing pass is added. The one in the top-left corner shows THREE.FilmPass, the one in the top-right corner shows THREE.DotScreenPass, and the one in the bottom-left corner shows THREE.BloomPass. The scene in the bottom-right corner shows the original render.

In this example, we also use `THREE.ShaderPass` and `THREE.TexturePass`, to reuse the output from the original rendering as input for the other three scenes. That way, we only need to render the scene once. So, before we look at the individual passes, let's look at these two passes, as follows:

```
var renderPass = new THREE.RenderPass(scene, camera);
var effectCopy = new THREE.ShaderPass(THREE.CopyShader);
effectCopy.renderToScreen = true;

var composer = new THREE.EffectComposer(renderer);
composer.addPass(renderPass);
composer.addPass(effectCopy);

// reuse the rendered scene from the composer
var renderedScene = new THREE.TexturePass(composer.renderTarget2);
```

In this piece of code, we set up `THREE.EffectComposer`, which will output the default scene (the one in the bottom-right corner). This composer has two passes. `THREE.RenderPass` renders the scene, and `THREE.ShaderPass`, when configured with `THREE.CopyShader`, renders the output (without any further postprocessing to the screen, if we set the `renderToScreen` property to `true`). If you look at the example, you can see that we show the same scene four times, but with a different effect applied each time. We can also render the scene from scratch by using `THREE.RenderPass` four times, but that would be a bit of a waste, since we can just reuse the output from the first composer. To do this, we create a `THREE.TexturePass` and pass in the `composer.renderTarget2` value. This property contains the rendered scene as a texture, which we can pass into the `THREE.TexturePass`. We can now use the `renderedScene` variable as input for our other composers, without having to render the scene from scratch. Let's revisit `THREE.FilmPass` first, and look at how we can use `THREE.TexturePass` as input.

Using THREE.FilmPass to create a TV-like effect

We already looked at how to create `THREE.FilmPass` in the first section of this chapter, so let's look at how to use this effect with, `THREE.TexturePass` from the previous section:

```
var effectFilm = new THREE.FilmPass(0.8, 0.325, 256, false);
effectFilm.renderToScreen = true;

var effectFilmComposer = new THREE.EffectComposer(renderer);
effectFilmComposer.addPass(renderedScene);
effectFilmComposer.addPass(effectFilm);
effectFilmComposer.addPass(effectCopy);
```

The only step that we need to take to use `THREE.TexturePass` is to add it as the first pass in your composer. Next, we can just add `THREE.FilmPass`, and the effect will be applied. `THREE.FilmPass` takes four parameters, as shown in the following table:

Property	Description
`noiseIntensity`	This property allows you to control how grainy the scene looks.
`scanlinesIntensity`	`THREE.FilmPass` adds a number of scanlines to the scene. With this property, you can define how prominently these scanlines are shown.
`scanLinesCount`	The number of scanlines that are shown can be controlled with this property.
`grayscale`	If this is set to `true`, the output will be converted to grayscale.

There are actually two ways that you can pass in these parameters. In this example, we passed them in as arguments to the constructor, but you can also set them directly, as follows:

```
effectFilm.uniforms.grayscale.value = controls.grayscale;
effectFilm.uniforms.nIntensity.value = controls.noiseIntensity;
effectFilm.uniforms.sIntensity.value = controls.scanlinesIntensity;
effectFilm.uniforms.sCount.value = controls.scanlinesCount;
```

In this approach, we use the `uniforms` property, which communicates directly with WebGL. In the section where we talk about creating a custom shader (later in this chapter), we'll get a bit deeper into `uniforms`; for now, all you need to know is that this way, you can update the configuration of postprocessing passes and shaders, and see the results directly.

Adding a bloom effect to the scene with THREE.BloomPass

The effect, that you see in the lower-left corner is called the bloom effect. When you apply the bloom effect, the bright areas of a scene will be made more prominent and will bleed into the darker areas. The code to create `THREE.BloomPass` is as follows:

```
var bloomPass = new THREE.BloomPass();
var effectCopy = new THREE.ShaderPass(THREE.CopyShader);
effectCopy.renderToScreen = true;

var bloomComposer = new THREE.EffectComposer(renderer);
bloomComposer.addPass(renderedScene);
```

```
bloomComposer.addPass(bloomPass);
bloomComposer.addPass(effectCopy);
```

If you compare this with `THREE.EffectComposer`, which we used with `THREE.FilmPass`, you'll notice that we add an additional pass, `effectCopy`. This step, which we also used for the normal output, doesn't add any special effect, but just copies the output from the last pass to the screen. We need to add this step, since `THREE.BloomPass` doesn't render directly to the screen.

The following table lists the properties that you can set on `THREE.BloomPass`:

Property	Description
strength	This is the strength of the bloom effect. The higher this is, the more bright the brighter areas are, and the more they will bleed to the darker areas.
kernelSize	This property controls the offset of the bloom effect.
sigma	With the `sigma` property, you can control the sharpness of the bloom effect. The higher the value, the more blurred the bloom effect will look.
Resolution	The `Resolution` property defines how precisely the bloom effect is created. If you make this too low, the result will look blocky.

A better way to understand these properties is to just experiment with them by using the example mentioned previously: `02-post-processing-simple`. The following screenshot shows the bloom effect with a high sigma size and high strength:

The next simple effects that we'll look at are the `THREE.DotScreenPass` effects.

Output the scene as a set of dots

Using THREE.DotScreenPass is very similar to using THREE.BloomPass. We just saw THREE.BloomPass in action. Now, let's look at the code for THREE.DotScreenPass:

```
var dotScreenPass = new THREE.DotScreenPass();

var dotScreenComposer = new THREE.EffectComposer(renderer);
dotScreenComposer.addPass(renderedScene);
dotScreenComposer.addPass(dotScreenPass);
dotScreenComposer.addPass(effectCopy);
```

With this effect, we have to once again add effectCopy, to output the result to the screen. THREE.DotScreenPass can also be configured with a number of properties, as follows:

Property	Description
center	With the center property, you can fine-tune the way the dots are offset.
angle	The dots are aligned in a certain manner. With the angle properties, you can change this alignment.
Scale	With this, we can set the sizes of the dots to use. The lower the scale, the larger the dots.

What applies to the other shaders also applies to this shader. It's much easier to get the right settings with experimentation, as indicated by the following image:

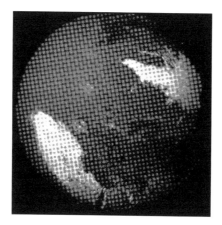

Before we move on to the next set of simple shaders, we'll first look at how we've rendered multiple scenes on the same screen.

Showing the output of multiple renderers on the same screen

This section won't go into detail on how to use postprocessing effects, but will explain how to get the output of all four `THREE.EffectComposer` instances on the same screen. First, let's look at the `render` loop used for this example:

```
renderer.autoClear = false;
function render() {
  stats.update();
  var delta = clock.getDelta();
  trackballControls.update(delta);

  renderer.clear();
  renderer.setViewport(0, 0, halfWidth, halfHeight);
  effectFilmComposer.render(delta);

  renderer.setViewport(0, halfHeight, halfWidth, halfHeight);
  bloomComposer.render(delta);
  renderer.setViewport(halfWidth, 0, halfWidth, halfHeight);
  dotScreenComposer.render(delta);
  renderer.setViewport(halfWidth, halfHeight, halfWidth, halfHeight);
  composer.render(delta);

  requestAnimationFrame(render);
}
```

The first thing to notice is that we set the `renderer.autoClear` property to `false` and then explicitly call the `clear()` function in the `render` loop. If we don't do this each time we call the `render()` function on a composer, the previously rendered scenes will be cleared. With this approach, we only clear everything at the beginning of our `render` loop.

To avoid having all of our composers render in the same space, we set the viewport of the `renderer`, which is used by our composers, to a different part of the screen. This function takes four arguments: `x`, `y`, `width`, and `height`. As you can see in the code sample, we use this function to divide the screen into four areas and make the composers render to their individual areas. Note that you can also use this approach with multiple scenes, cameras, and `WebGLRenderer` instances, if you want.

With this setup, the `render` loop will render each of the four `THREE.EffectComposer` objects to their own parts of the screen. Besides the passes shown in `02-simple-pass-1.html`, we also show a number of additional simple passes the example `03-simple-pass-2.html`.

Additional simple passes

If you open example `03-simple-pass-2.html` in your browser, you will see a number of additional passes in action:

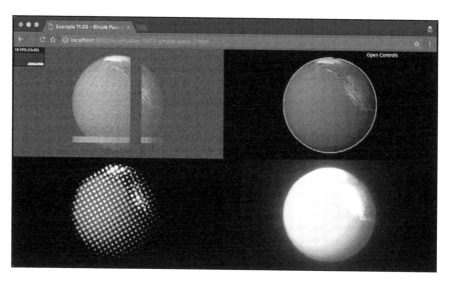

We won't go into too much detail here, since these passes are configured in the same way as those in the previous sections. In this example, you can see the following:

- In the top-right corner, you can see the `THREE.OutlinePass`. The outline pass can be used to draw an outline on top, for a `THREE.Mesh` object.
- In the top-left corner, the `THREE.GlitchPass` is shown. As the name implies, this pass provides a technical rendering glitch effect.
- In the bottom-right corner, the `THREE.UnrealBloom` effect is shown.
- In the bottom-left corner, the `THREE.HalftonePass` is used to convert the rendering to a set of dots.

As is the case for all of the examples in this chapter, you can configure the individual properties of these passes by using the menu on the right.

Advanced EffectComposer flows using masks

In the previous examples, we applied the postprocessing pass to the complete screen. However, Three.js, also has the ability to apply passes only to a specific area. In this section, we will perform the following steps:

1. Create a scene to serve as a background image.
2. Create a scene containing a sphere that looks like Earth.
3. Create a scene containing a sphere that looks like Mars.
4. Create `EffectComposer`, which renders these three scenes into a single image.
5. Apply a colorify effect to the sphere rendered as Mars.
6. Apply a sepia effect to the sphere rendered as Earth.

This might sound complex, but it is actually surprisingly easy to accomplish. First, let's look at the result that we're aiming for in the `03-post-processing-masks.html` example. The following screenshot shows the results of these steps:

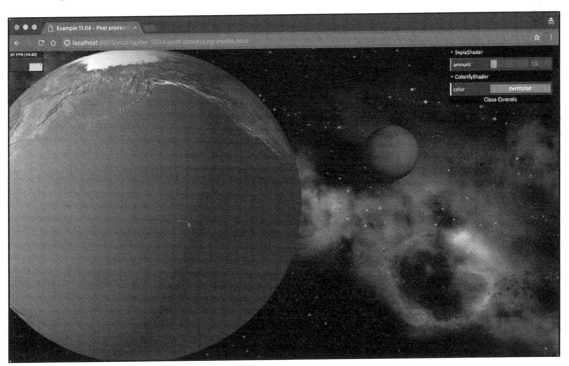

The first thing that we need to do is set up the various scenes that we'll be rendering:

```
var sceneEarth = new THREE.Scene();
var sceneMars = new THREE.Scene();
var sceneBG = new THREE.Scene();
```

To create the Earth and Mars spheres, we just create the spheres with the correct material and textures, and add them to their specific scenes, as shown in the following code (addEarth and addMars are just helper functions, to keep the code clear, they create a simple THREE.Mesh from a THREE.SphereGeometry creates some lights and adds them all to the THREE.Scene):

```
sceneBG.background = textureLoader.load("../../assets/textures/bg/starry-
deep-outer-space-galaxy.jpg");
var earthAndLight = addEarth(sceneEarth);
sceneEarth.translateX(-16);
sceneEarth.scale.set(1.2, 1.2, 1.2);
var marsAndLight = addMars(sceneMars);
sceneMars.translateX(12);
sceneMars.translateY(6);
sceneMars.scale.set(0.2, 0.2, 0.2);
```

In this example, we use the background property of a scene to add the starry background. There is also an alternative way to create a background. We can use THREE.OrhoGraphicCamera. With THREE.OrthoGraphicCamera, the size of the rendered object doesn't change when it is closer or further away from the camera; so, by positioning a THREE.PlaneGeometry variable directly in front of a THREE.rhoGraphicCamera variable, we can create a background, as well.

We now have got our three scenes, and we can start to set up our passes and THREE.EffectComposer. Let's start by looking at the complete chain of passes, after which we'll look at the individual passes:

```
var composer = new THREE.EffectComposer(renderer);
composer.renderTarget1.stencilBuffer = true;
composer.renderTarget2.stencilBuffer = true;
composer.addPass(bgRenderPass);
composer.addPass(earthRenderPass);
composer.addPass(marsRenderPass);
composer.addPass(marsMask);
composer.addPass(effectColorify);
composer.addPass(clearMask);
composer.addPass(earthMask);
composer.addPass(effectSepia);
```

```
composer.addPass(clearMask);
composer.addPass(effectCopy);
```

To work with masks, we need to create `THREE.EffectComposer` in a slightly different manner. We need to set the `stencilBuffer` property of the internally used render targets to `true`. A stencil buffer, a special type of buffer and is used to limit the area of rendering. So, by enabling the stencil buffer, we can use our masks. Let's look at the first three passes that are added. These three passes render the background, the Earth scene, and the Mars scene, as follows:

```
var bgRenderPass = new THREE.RenderPass(sceneBG, camera);
var earthRenderPass = new THREE.RenderPass(sceneEarth, camera);
earthRenderPass.clear = false;
var marsRenderPass = new THREE.RenderPass(sceneMars, camera);
marsRenderPass.clear = false;
```

There's nothing new here, except that we set the `clear` property of two of these passes to `false`. If we don't do this, we'll only see the output from `renderPass2`, since it will clear everything before it starts rendering. If you look back at the code for `THREE.EffectComposer`, the next three passes are `marsMask`, `effectColorify`, and `clearMask`. First, we'll look at how these three passes are defined:

```
var marsMask = new THREE.MaskPass(sceneMars, camera );
var clearMask = new THREE.ClearMaskPass();
var effectColorify = new THREE.ShaderPass(THREE.ColorifyShader );
effectColorify.uniforms['color'].value.setRGB(0.5, 0.5, 1);
```

The first of these three passes is `THREE.MaskPass`. When creating a `THREE.MaskPass` object, you pass in a scene and a camera, just as you did for `THREE.RenderPass`. `THREE.MaskPass` will render this scene internally, but instead of showing this on screen, it will use this information to create a mask. When a `THREE.MaskPass` object is added to `THREE.EffectComposer`, all of the subsequent passes will be applied only to the mask defined by `THREE.MaskPass`, until a `THREE.ClearMaskPass` object is encountered. In this example, this means that the `effectColorify` pass, which adds a blue glow, is only applied to the objects rendered in `sceneMars`.

We use the same approach to apply a sepia filter to the `Earth` object. We first create a mask based on the `Earth` scene, and use this mask in `THREE.EffectComposer`. After using `THREE.MaskPass`, we add the effect that we want to apply (`effectSepia` in this case), and, once we're done with that, we add `THREE.ClearMaskPass` to remove the mask again. The last step for this specific `THREE.EffectComposer` is one that we've already seen. We need to copy the final result to the screen, and we once again use the `effectCopy` pass for that. With this setup, we can apply the effects that we want to be a part of the total screen. Be aware, though, that these effects are applied to a part of the rendered image, if the Mars scene and the `Earth` scene overlap.

The effects of both will be applied to that part of the screen:

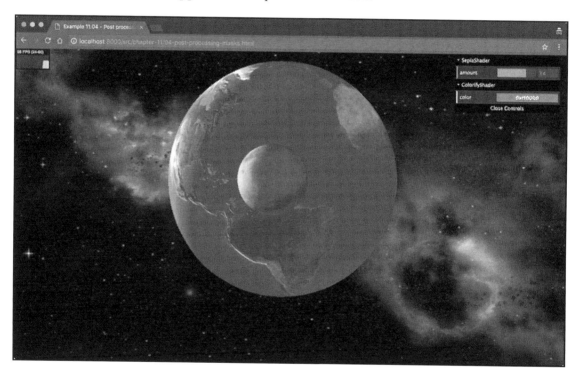

There is one additional property that's interesting when working with THREE.MaskPass, and that's the inverse property. If this property is set to true, the mask is inversed. In other words, the effect is applied to everything but the scene passed into THREE.MaskPass. This is shown in the following screenshot, where we set the inverse property of the earthMask to true:

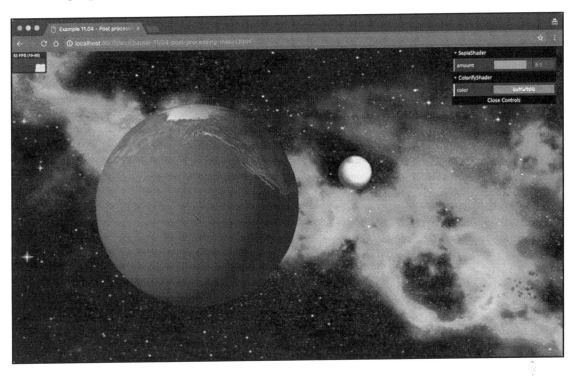

Before we move on to a discussion of the THREE.ShaderPass, we're going to look at two passes that provide a more advanced effect: THREE.BokehPass and THREE.SSAOPass.

Advanced pass - Bokeh

With the `THREE.BokehPass`, you can add a Bokeh effect to your scene. In a Bokeh effect, only part of the scene is in focus, and the rest of the scene looks blurry. To see this effect in action, you can open `example 05-bokeh.html`:

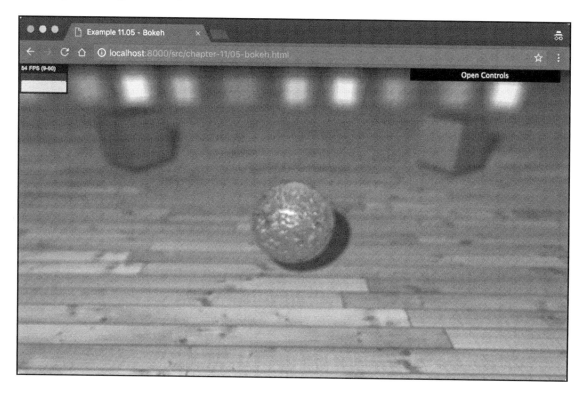

When you open it, initially, the whole seen will look blurry. With the Bokeh controls on the right, you can set the `focus` value to the part of the scene that you want to have in focus, and play around with the aperture property to determine the size of the area that should be in focus. By sliding the focus, you can have the sphere in the foreground in focus, as follows:

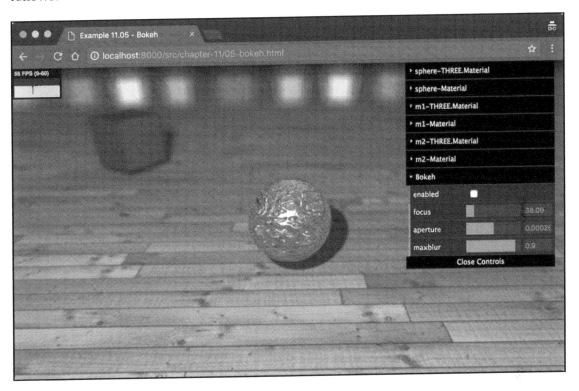

Or, if we slide it further, we can focus on the blue cubes:

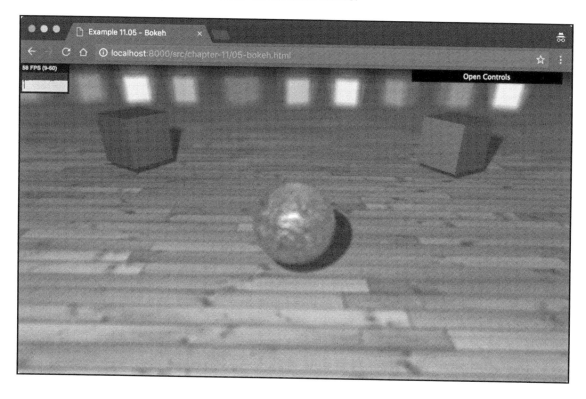

And, if we slide it even further, we can focus on the set of green cubes at the far end of the scene:

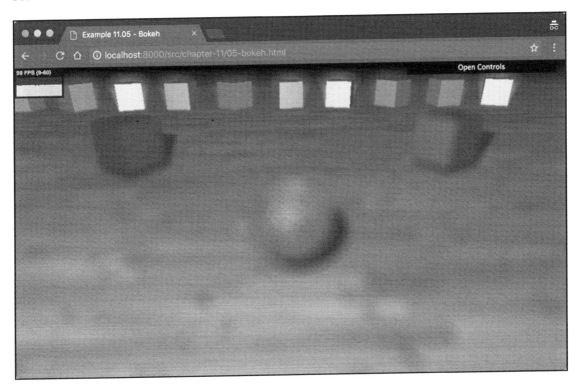

`THREE.BokehPass` can be used just like the other passes we've seen so far:

```
var params = {
  focus: 10,
  aspect: camera.aspect,
  aperture: 0.0002,
  maxblur: 1,
};

var renderPass = new THREE.RenderPass(scene, camera);
var bokehPass = new THREE.BokehPass(scene, camera, params)
bokehPass.renderToScreen = true;
var composer = new THREE.EffectComposer(renderer);
composer.addPass(renderPass);
composer.addPass(bokehPass);
```

Achieving the desired result might require some fine-tuning of the properties.

Advance pass - ambient occlusion

In `Chapter 10`, *Loading and Working with Textures*, we discussed using a pre-baked ambient occlusion map (an `aoMap`) to directly apply shadows, based on the ambient lighting. Ambient occlusion involves the shadows and light intensity variations that you see on objects, since not all parts of an object receive the same amount of ambient light. Besides using an `aoMap`, it is also possible to use a pass on `THREE.EffectComposer`, to get this same effect. If you open example `06-ambient-occlusion.html`, you will see the result of using `THREE.SSAOPass`, which is one of the two available passes that provide ambient occlusion:

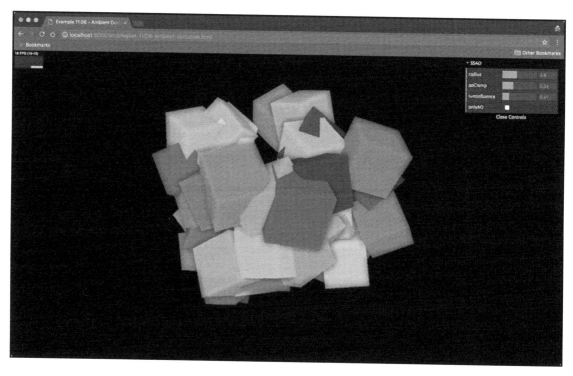

A similar scene, without the application of an ambient occlusion filter, appears to be really flat, as follows:

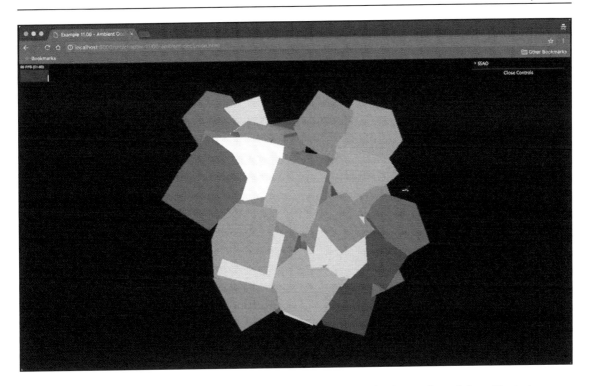

You can use the controls on the right-hand side to change the intensity of the effect. As you can see from the frame rate in the top-left corner, this is a very expensive render step. While it shouldn't be a problem to apply this to static scenes (or to static parts of the scene), applying it to the dynamic parts of the scene is usually overly GPU intensive.

Until now, we've used the standard passes provided by Three.js for our effects. Three.js also provides THREE.ShaderPass, which can be used for custom effects, and which comes with a large number of shaders that you can use and experiment with.

Using THREE.ShaderPass for custom effects

With THREE.ShaderPass, we can apply a large number of additional effects to our scene by passing in a custom shader. Three.js comes with a set of shaders that can be used together with this THREE.ShaderPass. They will be listed in this section. We've divided this section into three parts. The first set involves simple shaders. All of these shaders can be viewed and configured by opening up the example 07-shaderpass-simple.html:

Name	Description
THREE.BleachBypassShader	This creates a bleach bypass effect. With this effect, a silver-like overlay will be applied to the image.
THREE.BlendShader	The THREE.BlendShader isn't a shader that you apply as a single postprocessing step, but this shader allows you to blend two textures together. You can, for instance, use this shader to smoothly blend the rendering of one scene into another (not shown in 07-shaderpass-simple.html).
THREE.BrightnessContrastShader	This allows you to change the brightness and contrast of an image.
THREE.ColorifyShader	This applies a color overlay to the screen. We've seen this one already, in the mask example.
THREE.ColorCorrectionShader	With this shader, you can change the color distribution.
THREE.FreiChenShader	This shader provides edge detection.
THREE.GammaCorrectionShader	This applies a gamma correction to the rendered scene. This uses a fixed gamma factor of 2. Note that you can also set the gamma correction directly on THREE.WebGLRenderer by using the gammaFactor, gammaInput, and gammaOutput properties.
THREE.HueSaturationShader	This allows you to change the *hue* and *saturation* of the colors.
THREE.KaleidoShader	This adds a kaleidoscope effect to the scene, which provides radial reflection around the center of the scene.
THREE.LuminosityShader and THREE.LuminostyHighPassShader	This provides a luminosity effect, where the luminosity of the scene is shown.
THREE.MirrorShader	This creates a mirror effect for part of the screen.
THREE.PixelShader	This creates a pixelated effect.
THREE.RGBShiftShader	This shader separates the red, green, and blue components of a color.
THREE.SepiaShader	This creates a sepia-like effect on the screen.
THREE.SobelOperatorShader	This provides edge detection.

`THREE.VignetteShader`	This applies a vignette effect. This effect shows dark borders around the center of the image.

Next, we'll look at the shaders that provide a couple of blur-related effects. These effects can be experimented with through the `08-shaderpass-blurs.html` example:

Name	Description
`THREE.HorizontalBlurShader` and `THREE.VerticalBlurShader`	These apply a blur effect to the complete scene.
`THREE.HorizontalTiltShiftShader` and `THREE.VerticalTiltShiftShader`	These recreate the tilt shift effect. With the tilt shift effect, it is possible to create scenes that look like a miniature, by making sure that only part of the image is sharp.
`THREE.TriangleBlurShader`	This applies a blur effect, using a triangle-based approach.
`THREE.FocusShader`	This is a simple shader that results in a sharply rendered center area with blurring along its borders.

Finally, there are a number of shaders that we won't look at in detail; we are listing them simply for the sake of completeness. These shaders are mostly used internally, by either other shader, or the shader passes that we discussed at the beginning of this chapter:

Name	Description
`THREE.FXAAShader`	This shader applies an anti-aliasing effect during the postprocessing phase. Use this if applying anti-aliasing during rendering is too expensive.
`THREE.ConvolutionShader`	This shader is used internally, by the `THREE.BloomPass` render pass.
`THREE.DepthLimitedBlurShader`	This is used internally by `THREE.SAOPass`, for ambient occlusion.
`THREE.HalftoneShader`	This is used internally by `THREE.HalftonePass`.
`THREE.SAOShader`	This provides ambient occlusion in shader form.
`THREE.SSAOShader`	This provides ambient occlusion in shader form.
`THREE.SMAAShader`	This provides anti-aliasing to the rendered scene.
`THREE.ToneMapShader`	This is used internally by `THREE.AdaptiveToneMappingPass`.

`THREE.UnpackDepthRGBAShader`	This can be used to visualize encoded depth values from an RGBA texture as a visual color.

If you look through the Shaders Directory of the Three.js distribution, you might notice a couple of other shaders that we haven't listed in this chapter. These shaders - the FresnelShader, OceanShader, ParallaxShader, and WaterRefractionShader - aren't shaders that can be used for postprocessing, but should be used from the `THREE.ShaderMaterial` object that we discussed in the chapter on materials.

We will start with a couple of the simple shaders.

Simple shaders

To experiment with the basic shaders, we've created an example where you can play around with most of the shaders and see the effects directly in the scene. You can find this example at `07-shaderpass-simple.html`. The following screenshots show some of the effects.

The `THREE.BrigthnessContrastShader` effect is as follows:

The `THREE.FreiChenShader` effect is as follows:

The `THREE.KaleidoShader` effect is as follows:

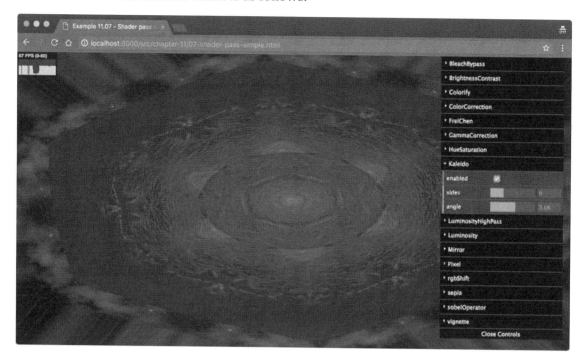

The `THREE.MirrorShader` effect is as follows:

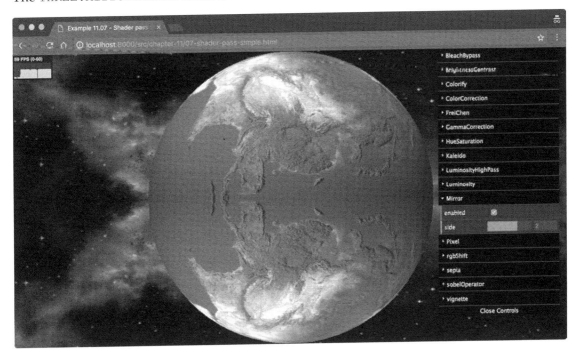

The THREE.RGBShiftShader effect is as follows:

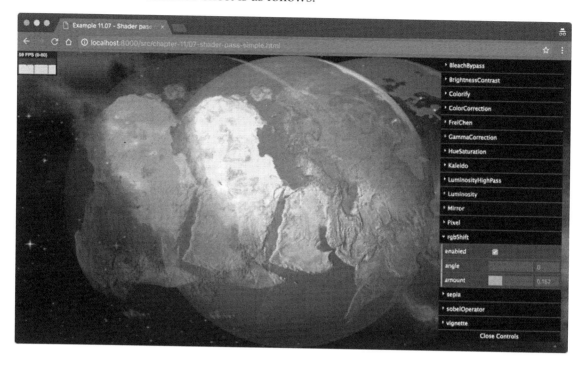

The `THREE.SobelOperatorShader` effect is as follows:

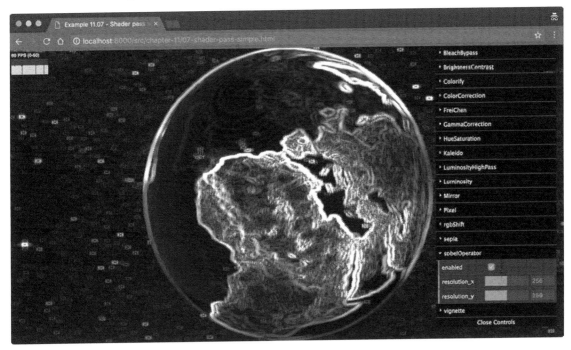

Three.js also provides a couple of shaders that are specifically used to add blurring effects. Those are shown in the next section.

Blurring shaders

Again in this section, we won't dive into the code; we'll just show you the results of the various blur shaders. You can experiment with these by using the `08-shaderpass-blur.html` example:

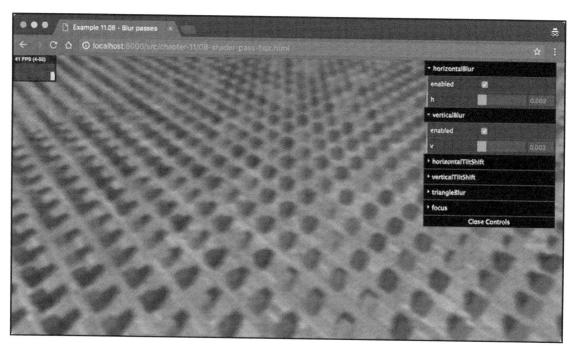

The preceding image shows
`THREE.HorizontalBlurShader` and `THREE.VerticalBlurShader`. You can see that the effect is a blurred scene.

Besides these two blur effects, Three.js provides an additional shader that blurs an image, THREE.TriangleShader, which is shown here. As an example, you can use this shader to depict motion blur, as shown in the following screenshot:

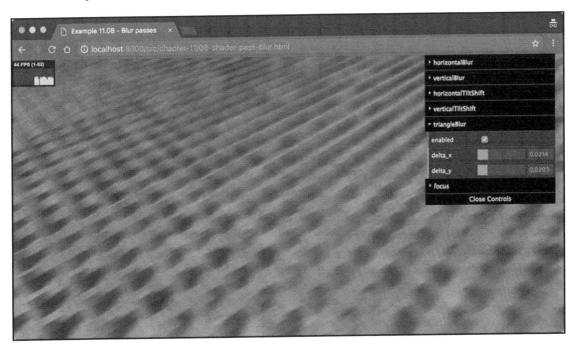

Another blur-like effect is provided by
`THREE.HorizontalTiltShiftShader` and `THREE.VerticalTiltShiftShader`. This
shader doesn't blur the complete scene, but only a small area. This provides an effect
called tilt shift. This is often used to create miniature-like scenes from normal photographs.
The following screenshot shows this effect:

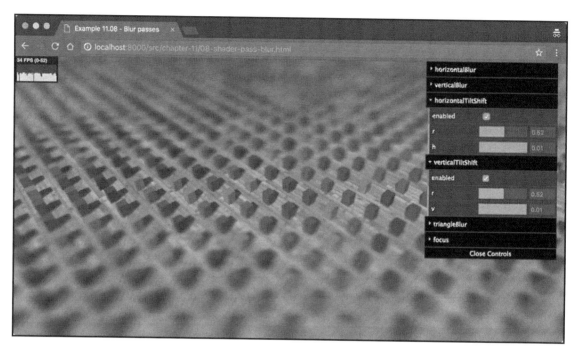

The final blur-like effect is the THREE.FocusShader, as follows:

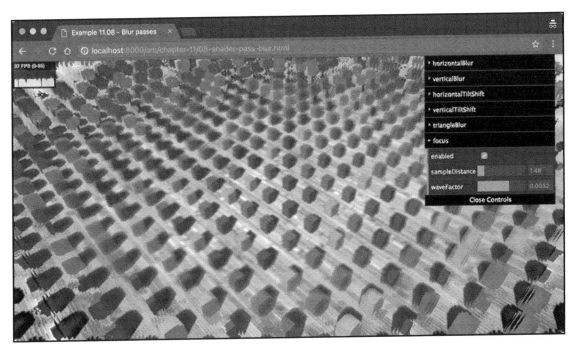

So far, we've used the shaders provided by Three.js. However, it is also possible to write your own shaders for use in `THREE.EffectComposer`.

Creating custom postprocessing shaders

In this section, you'll learn how to create a custom shader that you can use in postprocessing. We'll create two different shaders. The first one will convert the current image to a grayscale image, and the second one will convert the image to an 8-bit image by reducing the number of colors that are available.

 Creating vertex and fragment shaders is a very broad subject. In this section, we will only touch the surface of what can be done by these shaders, and how they work. For more in-depth information, you can find the WebGL specification at http://www.khronos.org/webgl/. An additional resource, full of examples, is Shadertoy, available at https://www.shadertoy.com/.

Custom grayscale shader

To create a custom shader for Three.js (and also for other WebGL libraries), you have to create two components: a vertex shader and a fragment shader. The vertex shader can be used to change the position of individual vertices, and the fragment shader can be used to determine the colors of individual pixels. For a postprocessing shader, we only need to implement a fragment shader, and we can keep the default vertex shader provided by Three.js. An important point to make before looking at the code is that GPUs support multiple shader pipelines. This means that the vertex shaders run in parallel on multiple vertices at the same time, and the same goes for the fragment shaders.

Let's start by looking at the complete source code for the shader that applies a grayscale effect to our image (`custom-shader.js`):

```
THREE.CustomGrayScaleShader = {

  uniforms: {
    "tDiffuse": { type: "t", value: null },
    "rPower":   { type: "f", value: 0.2126 },
    "gPower":   { type: "f", value: 0.7152 },
    "bPower":   { type: "f", value: 0.0722 }
  },

  vertexShader: [
```

```
    "varying vec2 vUv;",
    "void main() {",
      "vUv = uv;",
      "gl_Position = projectionMatrix * modelViewMatrix * vec4(
        position, 1.0 );",
    "}"
  ].join("n"),

  fragmentShader: [

    "uniform float rPower;",
    "uniform float gPower;",
    "uniform float bPower;",
    "uniform sampler2D tDiffuse;",

    "varying vec2 vUv;",

    "void main() {",
      "vec4 texel = texture2D( tDiffuse, vUv );",
      "float gray = texel.r*rPower + texel.g*gPower
        + texel.b*bPower;",
      "gl_FragColor = vec4( vec3(gray), texel.w );",
    "}"
  ].join("n")
};
```

As you can see, this isn't JavaScript. When you write shaders, you write them in the **OpenGL Shading Language (GLSL)**, which looks a lot like the C programming language. More information on GLSL can be found at http://www.khronos.org/opengles/sdk/docs/manglsl/.

First, let's look at the vertex shader:

```
"varying vec2 vUv;","void main() {",
  "vUv = uv;",
  "gl_Position = projectionMatrix * modelViewMatrix * vec4(position, 1.0
);",
  "}"
```

For postprocessing, this shader doesn't really need to do anything. The preceding code that is the standard way that Three.js implements a vertex shader. It uses `projectionMatrix`, which is the projection from the camera, together with `modelViewMatrix`, which maps an object's position into the world position, in order to determine where to render an object on screen. For postprocessing, the only interesting thing in this piece of code is that the `uv` value, which indicates which texel to read from a texture, is passed on to the fragment shader using the `varyingvec2vUv` variable.

This can be used to get the pixel to modify in the fragment shader.

Now, let's look at the fragment shader and see what the code is doing. We will start with the following variable declaration:

```
"uniform float rPower;",
"uniform float gPower;",
"uniform float bPower;",
"uniform sampler2D tDiffuse;",

"varying vec2 vUv;",
```

Here, we can see four instances of the `uniforms` property. The instances of the `uniforms` property have values that are passed in from JavaScript to the shader, which are the same for each fragment that is processed. In this case, we pass in three floats, identified by type `f` (which are used to determine the ratio of a color to include in the final grayscale image), and a texture (`tDiffuse`) is also passed in, identified by type `t`. This texture contains the image from the previous pass from `THREE.EffectComposer`. Three.js makes sure it gets passed to this shader appropriately when `tDiffuse` is used as the name of this texture. We can also set the other instances of the `uniforms` property from JavaScript by ourselves. Before we can use these uniforms from JavaScript, we have to define which `uniforms` properties we want to expose to JavaScript. This is done as follows, at the top of the shader file:

```
uniforms: {

  "tDiffuse": { type: "t", value: null },
  "rPower":   { type: "f", value: 0.2126 },
  "gPower":   { type: "f", value: 0.7152 },
  "bPower":   { type: "f", value: 0.0722 }

},
```

At this point, we can receive configuration parameters from Three.js, and Three.js will provide the output of the current rendering. Let's look at the code that will convert each pixel to a gray pixel:

```
"void main() {",
  "vec4 texel = texture2D( tDiffuse, vUv );",
  "float gray = texel.r*rPower + texel.g*gPower + texel.b*bPower;",
  "gl_FragColor = vec4( vec3(gray), texel.w );"
```

What happens here is that we get the correct pixel from the passed-in texture. We do this by using the `texture2D` function, where we pass in our current image (`tDiffuse`) and the location of the pixel (`vUv`) that we want to analyze. The result is a texel (a pixel from a texture) that contains a color and an opacity (`texel.w`).

Next, we use the `r`, `g`, and `b` properties of this texel to calculate a gray value. This gray value is set to the `gl_FragColor` variable, which is eventually shown on the screen. And, with that, we have our own custom shader. This shader is used in the same way that we've already seen a couple of times in this chapter. First, we just need to set up `THREE.EffectComposer`, as follows:

```
var renderPass = new THREE.RenderPass(scene, camera);
var effectCopy = new THREE.ShaderPass(THREE.CopyShader);
effectCopy.renderToScreen = true;

var shaderPass = new THREE.ShaderPass(THREE.CustomGrayScaleShader);

var composer = new THREE.EffectComposer(renderer);
composer.addPass(renderPass);
composer.addPass(shaderPass);
composer.addPass(effectCopy);
```

We call `composer.render(delta)` in the `render` loop. If we want to change the properties of this shader at runtime, we can just update the `uniforms` property that we've defined, as follows:

```
shaderPass.enabled = controls.grayScale;
shaderPass.uniforms.rPower.value = controls.rPower;
shaderPass.uniforms.gPower.value = controls.gPower;
shaderPass.uniforms.bPower.value = controls.bPower;
```

The result can be seen in `09-shaderpass-custom.html`. The following screenshot shows this example:

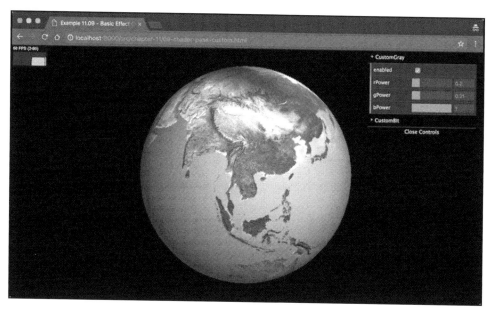

Let's create another custom shader. This time, we'll reduce the 24-bit output to a lower bit count.

Creating a custom bit shader

Normally, colors are represented as a 24-bit value, which gives us about 16 million different colors. In the early days of computing, this wasn't possible, and the colors where often represented as 8 or 16-bit colors. With this shader, we'll automatically transform our 24-bit output to a color depth of 4 bits (or anything that you want).

Since it hasn't changed with regard to our previous example, we'll skip the vertex shader and directly list the instances of the `uniforms` property, as follows:

```
uniforms: {

  "tDiffuse": { type: "t", value: null },
  "bitSize":  { type: "i", value: 4 }

}
```

The `fragmentShader` code is as follows:

```
fragmentShader: [

  "uniform int bitSize;",

  "uniform sampler2D tDiffuse;",

  "varying vec2 vUv;",

  "void main() {",

    "vec4 texel = texture2D( tDiffuse, vUv );",
    "float n = pow(float(bitSize),2.0);",
    "float newR = floor(texel.r*n)/n;",
    "float newG = floor(texel.g*n)/n;",
    "float newB = floor(texel.b*n)/n;",

    "gl_FragColor = vec4(newR, newG, newB, texel.w );",

  "}"

].join("n")
```

We define two instances of the `uniforms` property, which can be used to configure this shader. The first one is the one Three.js uses to pass in the current screen, and the second one that is defined by us as an integer (`type:"i"`), and serves as the color depth that we want to render the result in. The code itself is very straightforward:

- First, we get `texel` from the texture and `tDiffuse`, based on the passed-in `vUv` location of the pixel.

- We calculate the number of colors that we can have, based on the `bitSize` property, by calculating 2 to the power of `bitSize` (`pow(float(bitSize),2.0))`).

- Next, we calculate the new value of the color of `texel` by multiplying this value by n, rounding it off, (`floor(texel.r*n)`), and dividing it again by n.

- The result is set to `gl_FragColor` (red, green, and blue values and the opacity), and is shown on the screen.

You can view the result for this custom shader in the same example as our previous custom shader, `07-shaderpass-custom.html`. The following screenshot shows this example:

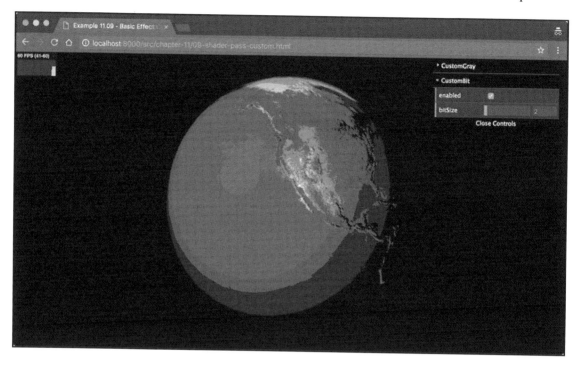

That's it for this chapter on postprocessing.

Summary

We discussed many different postprocessing options in this chapter. As you saw, creating THREE.EffectComposer and chaining passes together is actually very easy. You just have to keep a few things in mind. Not all passes will have an output on the screen. If you want to output to the screen, you can always use THREE.ShaderPass with THREE.CopyShader. The sequence in which you add passes to a composer is important. The effects are applied in that sequence. If you want to reuse the result from a specific THREE.EffectComposer instance, you can do so by using THREE.TexturePass. When you have more than one THREE.RenderPass in your THREE.EffectComposer, make sure to set the clear property to false. If not, you'll only see the output from the last THREE.RenderPass step. If you want to only apply an effect to a specific object, you can use THREE.MaskPass. When you're done with the mask, clear the mask with THREE.ClearMaskPass. Besides the standard passes provided by Three.js, there are also many standard shaders available. You can use these together with THREE.ShaderPass. Creating custom shaders for postprocessing is very easy, using the standard approach from Three.js. You only have to create a fragment shader.

We have now covered pretty much everything there is to know about Three.js. In Chapter 12, *Adding Physics and Sounds to Your Scene*, the last chapter, we'll look at a library called Physijs, which you can use to extend Three.js with physics, in order to apply collisions, gravity, and constraints.

Adding Physics and Sounds to Your Scene

12

In this final chapter, we'll look at Physijs, another library you can use to extend the basic functionality of Three.js. Physijs is a library that allows you to introduce physics into your 3D scene. By physics, we mean that your objects are subject to gravity, they can collide with one another, can be moved by applying impulses, and can be constrained in their movement through hinges and sliders. This library internally makes use of another well-known physics engine called ammo.js. Besides physics, we'll also look at how Three.js can help you with adding spatial sounds to your scene.

In this chapter, we'll discuss the following topics:

- Creating a Physijs scene where your objects are subject to gravity and can collide with one another
- Showing how to change the friction and restitution (bounciness) of the objects in the scene
- Explaining the various shapes supported by Physijs and how to use them
- Showing how to create compound shapes by combining simple shapes together
- Showing how a height field allows you to simulate a complex shape
- Limiting the movement of an object by applying a point, hinge, slider, and cone twist, and the degree of freedom constraint
- Adding sound sources to your scene, whose sound volume and direction is based on the distance to the camera.

There are a number of different open source JavaScript physics engines available. Most of them, though, are not under active development. The same applies to Physijs, which hasn't seen an update in a couple of years. After looking at the other libraries, we decided to keep with Physijs, since it is a stable, well-tested library that nicely shows how physics can be added to your scene. Should you choose to use any of the other libraries out there, the information in this chapter is still useful, since most of the libraries use the same approach as demonstrated in this chapter. So, while the implementation and used classes and functions might be different, the concepts and setup shown in this chapter will, for the most part, be applicable, regardless of the Physijs library.

The first thing we will do is create a Three.js scene that can be used with Physijs. We'll do that in our first example.

Creating a basic Three.js scene with physics

Setting up a Three.js scene for Physijs is very simple and only takes a couple of steps. The first thing we need to do is include the correct JavaScript file, which you can get from the GitHub repository at http://chandlerprall.github.io/Physijs/. Add the Physijs library to your HTML page like this:

```
<script type="text/javascript" src="../libs/physi.js"></script>
```

We've also included the necessary libraries in the sources of this book. Note that there is a bug in the Physijs code, which causes issues when using the point constraint. The Physijs library provided with the book contains a patch to make the code work correctly even with this specific constraint.

Simulating a scene is rather processor-intensive. If we run all the simulation computations on the render thread (since JavaScript is single threaded in nature), it will seriously affect the frame rate of our scene. To compensate for that, Physijs does its calculations in a background thread. This background thread is provided through the *web workers* specification that is implemented by most modern browsers. With this specification, you can run CPU-intensive tasks in a separate thread, thus not affecting the rendering. More information on web workers can be found at http://www.w3.org/TR/workers/.

For Physijs, this means we have to configure the JavaScript file that contains this worker task and also tell Physijs where it can find the ammo.js file needed to simulate our scene. The reason we need to include the ammo.js file is that Physijs is a wrapper around ammo.js to make it easy to use. Ammo.js (which you can find at https://github.com/kripken/ammo.js/) is the library that implements the physics engine; Physijs just provides an easy-to-use interface with this physics library. Since Physijs is just a wrapper, we can also use other physics engines together with Physijs. On the Physijs repository, you can also find a branch that uses Cannon.js, a different physics engine.

To configure Physijs, we have to set the following two properties in our script:

```
Physijs.scripts.worker = '../../libs/other/physijs/physijs_worker.js';
Physijs.scripts.ammo = './ammo.js';
```

The first property points to the worker tasks we want to execute, and the second property points to the ammo.js library that is used internally. The next step we need to perform is to create a scene. Physijs provides a wrapper around the Three.js normal scene, so, in your code, you do the following to create a scene:

```
var scene = new Physijs.Scene();
scene.setGravity(new THREE.Vector3(0, -10, 0));
```

This creates a new scene where physics is applied, and we set the gravity. In this case, we set the gravity on the *y* axis to be −10. In other words, objects fall straight down. You can set, or change at runtime, the gravity for the various axes to any value you see fit, and the scene will respond accordingly.

Before we can start simulating the physics in the scene, we need to add some objects. For this, we can use the normal way Three.js specifies objects, but we have to wrap them inside a specific Physijs object so that they can be managed by the Physijs library, as you can see from the following code fragment:

```
var stoneGeom = new THREE.BoxGeometry(0.6, 6, 2);
var stone = new Physijs.BoxMesh(stoneGeom, Physijs.createMaterial(new
THREE.MeshStandardMaterial({
  color: colors[index % colors.length], transparent: true, opacity: 0.8
}})));
scene.add(stone)
```

In this example, we create a simple `THREE.BoxGeometry` object. Instead of creating `THREE.Mesh`, we create a `Physijs.BoxMesh`, which tells Physijs to treat the shape of the geometry as a box when simulating physics and detecting collisions. Physijs provides a number of meshes you can use for the various shapes. More information on the shapes available can be found later in this chapter.

Now that `THREE.BoxMesh` has been added to the scene, we have all the ingredients for the first Physijs scene. All that is left to do is to tell `Phyijs.js` to simulate the physics and update the position and rotation of the objects in our scene. We can do this by calling the `simulate` method on the scene we just created. So, for this, we change our basic `render` loop to the following:

```
render = function() {
  requestAnimationFrame(render);
  renderer.render(scene, camera);
  scene.simulate();
}
```

And with that final step, by calling `scene.simulate()`, we have our basic setup for a Physijs scene. If we were to run this example, though, we wouldn't see much. We would just see a single cube in the middle of the screen that starts falling down as soon as the scene renders. So, let's look at a more complex example, where we'll simulate dominos falling down.

For this example, we're going to create the following scene:

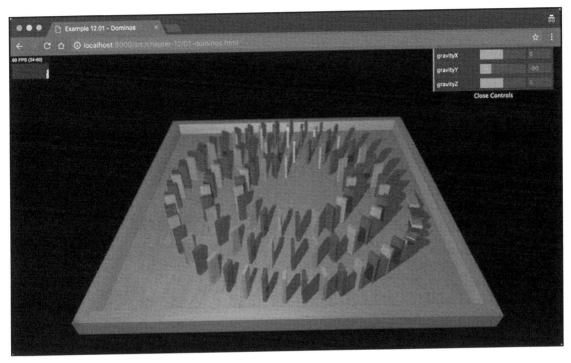

If you open the `01-dominos.html` example in your browser, you'll see a set of domino tiles that start falling down as soon as the scene is loaded. The first one will tip over the second one, and so on. The complete physics of this scene is managed by Physijs. The only thing we did to start this animation was to tip over the first domino. Creating this scene is actually very easy and only takes a few steps, which are as follows:

1. Define a Physijs scene
2. Define the ground area that holds the stones
3. Place the stones
4. Tip over the first stone

Let's skip this first step since we've already seen how to do this and go directly to the second step, where we define the sandbox that contains all the stones. This sandbox is constructed out of a couple of boxes that are grouped together. The following is the code required to accomplish this:

```
function createGroundAndWalls(scene) {
  var textureLoader = new THREE.TextureLoader();
```

```
    var ground_material = Physijs.createMaterial(
    new THREE.MeshStandardMaterial(
    {map: textureLoader.load('../../assets/textures/general/wood-2.jpg')}
            ),
            .9, .3);

    var ground = new Physijs.BoxMesh(new THREE.BoxGeometry(60, 1, 60),
    ground_material, 0);
    ground.castShadow = true;
    ground.receiveShadow = true;

    var borderLeft = new Physijs.BoxMesh(new THREE.BoxGeometry(2, 3, 60),
    ground_material, 0);
    borderLeft.position.x = -31;
    borderLeft.position.y = 2;
    borderLeft.castShadow = true;
    borderLeft.receiveShadow = true;

    ground.add(borderLeft);

    var borderRight = new Physijs.BoxMesh(new THREE.BoxGeometry(2, 3, 60),
    ground_material, 0);
    borderRight.position.x = 31;
    borderRight.position.y = 2;
    borderRight.castShadow = true;
    borderRight.receiveShadow = true;

    ground.add(borderRight);

    var borderBottom = new Physijs.BoxMesh(new THREE.BoxGeometry(64, 3, 2),
    ground_material, 0);
    borderBottom.position.z = 30;
    borderBottom.position.y = 2;
    borderBottom.castShadow = true;
    borderBottom.receiveShadow = true;

    ground.add(borderBottom);

    var borderTop = new Physijs.BoxMesh(new THREE.BoxGeometry(64, 3, 2),
    ground_material, 0);
    borderTop.position.z = -30;
    borderTop.position.y = 2;
    borderTop.castShadow = true;
    borderTop.receiveShadow = true;

    ground.add(borderTop);
    scene.add(ground);
}
```

This code isn't very complicated. First, we create a simple box that serves as the ground plane, and next we add a couple of borders to prevent objects falling off this ground plane. We add these borders to the ground object to create a compound object. This is an object that is treated by Physijs as a single object. There are a couple of other new things in this code that we'll explain in more depth in the following sections. The first one is `ground_material`, which we create. We use the `Physijs.createMaterial` function to create this material. This function wraps a standard Three.js material but allows us to set the `friction` and `restitution` (bounciness) of the material. More on this can be found in the next section. Another new aspect is the final parameter we add to the `Physijs.BoxMesh` constructor. For all the `BoxMesh` objects, we create in this section, we add 0 as the final parameter. With this parameter, we set the weight of the object. We do this to prevent the ground from being subject to the gravity in the scene so that it doesn't fall down.

Now that we have the ground, we can place the dominos. For this, we create simple `Three.BoxGeometry` instances that we wrap inside `BoxMesh` and place them at a specific position on top of the ground mesh, as follows:

```
var stoneGeom = new THREE.BoxGeometry(0.6, 6, 2);
var stone = new Physijs.BoxMesh(stoneGeom, Physijs.createMaterial(new
THREE.MeshStandardMaterial({
  color: colors[index % colors.length], transparent: true, opacity: 0.8
}))); 
stone.position.copy(point);  // point is the location where to position the
stone
stone.lookAt(scene.position);
stone.__dirtyRotation = true;
stone.position.y=3.5;
scene.add(stone);
```

We don't show the code where the position of each domino is calculated (see the `getPoints()` function in the source code of the example for this); this code just shows how the dominoes are positioned. What you can see here is that we once again create `BoxMesh`, which wraps `THREE.BoxGeometry`. To make sure the dominos are aligned correctly, we use the `lookAt` function to set their correct rotation. If we don't do this, they'll all face the same way and won't fall down. We have to make sure that after we manually update the rotation (or the position) of a Physijs wrapped object, we tell Physijs that something has changed so that Physijs can update its own internal representation of all the objects in the scene. For the rotation, we can do this with the internal `__dirtyRotation` property, and for the position, we can set `__dirtyPosition` to true.

Now, all that is left to do is to tip the first domino. We do this by just setting the rotation on the x axis to 0.2, which tips it slightly. The gravity in the scene will do the rest and completely tip over the first domino. Here's how we tip the first domino:

```
stones[0].rotation.x = 0.2;
stones[0].__dirtyRotation = true;
```

When you open the example, you can see that the first stone is slightly tilted and, after a short time, will fall over, hit the next one, and start the domino effect. This completes the first example, which already shows a lot of features from Physijs.

If you want to play around with the gravity, you can change it through the menu in the top-right corner. For example, by adding gravity on the x-axes, you see an effect such as this:

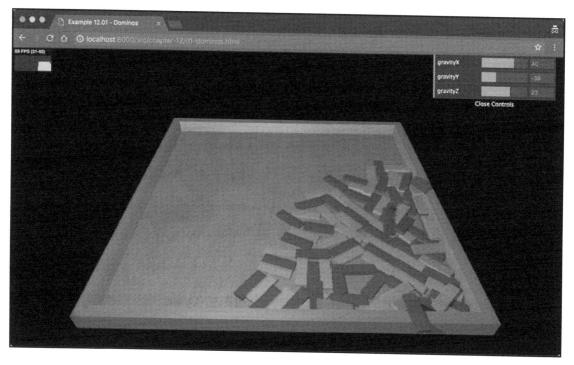

In the next section, we'll have a closer look at how the Physijs material properties affect the objects.

Physi.js material properties

Let's begin with an explanation of the example. When you open the 02-material-properties.html example, you'll see an empty box somewhat similar to the previous example. This box is rotating up and down around its x axis. In the menu, in the top-right corner, you have several sliders that can be used to change some of the material properties of Physijs. These properties apply to the cubes and spheres you can add with the **addCubes** and **addSpheres** buttons. When you press the **addSpheres** button, five spheres will be added to the scene, and when you press the **addCubes** button, five cubes will be added. The following screenshot is an example demonstrating friction and restitution:

This example allows you to play around with the `restitution` (bounciness) and `friction` properties that you can set when you create a Physijs material. If, for example, you set **cubeFriction** all the way to 1 and add some cubes, you'll see that, even though the ground is moving, the cubes barely move. If you set **cubeFriction** to 0, you'll notice the cubes sliding around as soon as the ground stops being level. The following screenshot shows that high friction allows cubes to resist gravity:

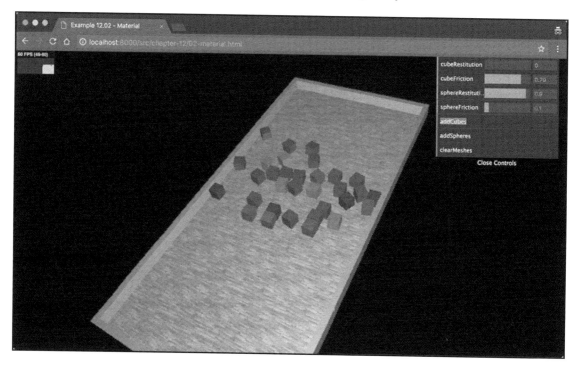

The other property you can set in this example is the `restitution` property. The `restitution` property defines how much of the energy that an object possesses is restituted when it collides. In other words, high restitution creates a bouncy object, and low restitution results in an object that stops immediately when it hits another object.

When you use a physics engine, you normally don't have to worry about detecting collisions. The engine will take care of that. It is, however, sometimes very useful to be informed when a collision between two objects occurs. For instance, you might want to create a sound effect, or, when creating a game, deduct a life. With Physijs, you can add an event listener to a Physijs mesh, as shown in the following code:

```
mesh.addEventListener( 'collision', function(
other_object, relative_velocity, relative_rotation,
contact_normal ) {
});
```

A good way to demonstrate this is by using spheres, setting the `restitution` to 1, and clicking on the **addSpheres** button a couple of times. This will create a number of spheres that bounce everywhere:

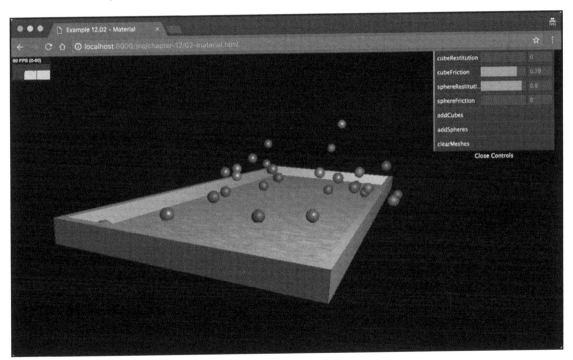

Before we move on to the next section, let's look at a bit of code used in this example:

```
var sphere = new Physijs.SphereMesh(new THREE.SphereGeometry(2, 20),
  Physijs.createMaterial(
  new THREE.MeshStandardMaterial({ color: colorSphere }),
```

```
controls.sphereFriction, controls.sphereRestitution));

sphere.position.set(Math.random() * 50 - 25, 20 + Math.random() * 5,
Math.random() * 50 - 25);
meshes.push(sphere);
scene.add(sphere);
```

This is the code that gets executed when we add spheres to the scene. This time, we use a different Physijs mesh: `Physijs.SphereMesh`. We're creating `THREE.SphereGeometry`, and the best match from the set of meshes provided is, logically, `Physijs.SphereMesh` (more on this in the next section). When we create `Physijs.SphereMesh`, we pass in our geometry and use `Physijs.createMaterial` to create a Physijs-specific material. We do this so that we can set `friction` and `restitution` for this object.

Until now, we've seen `BoxMesh` and `SphereMesh`. In the next section, we'll explain and show the different types of meshes provided by Physijs that you can use to wrap your geometries.

Physi.js supported shapes

Physijs provides a number of shapes you can use to wrap your geometries. In this section, we'll walk you through all the available Physijs meshes and demonstrate these meshes through an example. Remember that all you have to do to use these meshes is replace the `THREE.Mesh` constructor with one of these meshes.

The following table provides an overview of the meshes that are available in Physijs:

Name	Description
`Physijs.PlaneMesh`	This mesh can be used to create a zero-thickness plane. You could also use `BoxMesh` for this, together with `THREE.BoxGeometry` with low height.
`Physijs.BoxMesh`	If you have geometries that look like cubes, use this mesh. For instance, this is a good match for `THREE.BoxGeometry`.
`Physijs.SphereMesh`	For sphere shapes, use this geometry. This geometry is a good match for `THREE.SphereGeometry`.

Physijs.CylinderMesh	With THREE.Cylinder, you can create various cylinder-like shapes. Physijs provides multiple meshes depending on the shape of the cylinder. Physijs.CylinderMesh should be used for a normal cylinder with the same top radius and bottom radius.
Physijs.ConeMesh	If you specify the top radius as 0 and use a positive value for the bottom radius, you can use THREE.Cylinder to create a cone. If you want to apply physics to such an object, the best fit from Physijs is ConeMesh.
Physijs.CapsuleMesh	A capsule is just like THREE.Cylinder, but with a rounded top and a rounded bottom. We'll show you how to create a capsule in Three.js later on in this section.
Physijs.ConvexMesh	hysijs.ConvexMesh is a rough shape you can use for more complex objects. It creates a convex (just like THREE.ConvexGeometry) to approximate the shape of complex objects.
Physijs.ConcaveMesh	While ConvexMesh is a rough shape, ConcaveMesh is a more detailed representation of your complex geometry. Note that the performance penalty of using ConcaveMesh is very high. Usually, it is better to either create separate geometries with their own specific Physijs meshes or group them together (as we do with the floors shown in the previous examples).
Physijs.HeightfieldMesh	This mesh is very specialized. With this mesh, you can create a height field from THREE.PlaneGeometry. Look at the 03-shapes.html example for this mesh.

We'll quickly walk you through these shapes using 03-shapes.html as a reference. We won't explain Physijs.ConcaveMesh any further since its usage is very limited. Before we look at the example, we'll first have a quick look at Physijs.PlaneMesh. This mesh creates a simple plane based on THREE.PlaneGeometry, as follows:

```
var plane = new Physijs.PlaneMesh(new THREE.PlaneGeometry(5,5,10,10),
material);
scene.add( plane );
```

In this function, you can see that we just pass in a simple THREE.PlaneGeometry to create this mesh. If you add this to the scene, you'll notice something strange. The mesh you just created doesn't respond to gravity. The reason is that Physijs.PlaneMesh has a fixed weight of 0, so it won't respond to gravity or be moved by collisions with other objects. Besides this mesh, all the other meshes respond to gravity and collisions, as you'd expect. The following screenshot shows a height field on which the various supported shapes can be dropped:

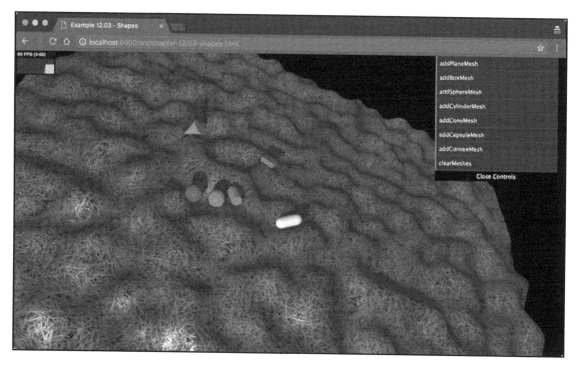

The previous screenshot shows the 03-shapes.html example. In this example, we've created a random height field (more on that later) and have a menu in the top-right corner that you can use to drop objects of various shapes. If you play around with this example, you'll see how different shapes respond differently to the height map and in collisions with other objects.

Let's look at the construction of some of these shapes:

```
new Physijs.SphereMesh(new THREE.SphereGeometry(3,20),mat);
new Physijs.BoxMesh(new THREE.BoxGeometry(4,2,6),mat);
new Physijs.CylinderMesh(new THREE.CylinderGeometry(2,2,6),mat);
new Physijs.ConeMesh(new THREE.CylinderGeometry(0,3,7,20,10),mat);
```

There's nothing special here; we create a geometry and use the best matching mesh from Physijs to create the object we add to the scene. However, what if we want to use `Physijs.CapsuleMesh`? Three.js doesn't contain a capsule-like geometry, so we have to create one ourselves. Here's the code we use for this purpose:

```
var merged = new THREE.Geometry(); var cyl = new THREE.CylinderGeometry(2,
2, 6); var top = new THREE.SphereGeometry(2); var bot = new
THREE.SphereGeometry(2); var matrix = new THREE.Matrix4();
matrix.makeTranslation(0, 3, 0); top.applyMatrix(matrix); var matrix = new
THREE.Matrix4(); matrix.makeTranslation(0, -3, 0); bot.applyMatrix(matrix);
// merge to create a capsule merged.merge(top); merged.merge(bot);
merged.merge(cyl); // create a physijs capsule mesh var capsule = new
Physijs.CapsuleMesh(merged, getMaterial());
```

`Phyijs.CapsuleMesh` looks like a cylinder but has a rounded top and bottom. We can easily recreate this in Three.js by creating a cylinder (`cyl`) and two spheres (`top` and `bot`) and merging them together using the `merge()` function. The following screenshot shows a number of capsules rolling down the heightmap:

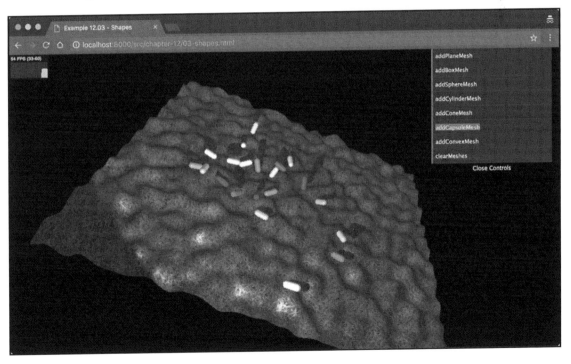

Before we look at the height map, let's look at the last of the shapes you can add to this example, `Physijs.ConvexMesh`. A convex is the minimal shape that wraps all the vertices of a geometry. The resulting shape will only have angles smaller than 180 degrees. You would use this mesh for complex shapes such as torus knots, as shown in the following code:

```
var convex = new Physijs.ConvexMesh(new
    THREE.TorusKnotGeometry(0.5,0.3,64,8,2,3,10), material);
```

In this case, for physics simulation and collisions, the convex of the torus knot will be used. This is a very good way to apply physics and detect collisions for complex objects, while still minimizing the performance impact. The last mesh from Physijs to be discussed is `Physijs.HeightMap`. The following screenshot shows a height map created with Physijs:

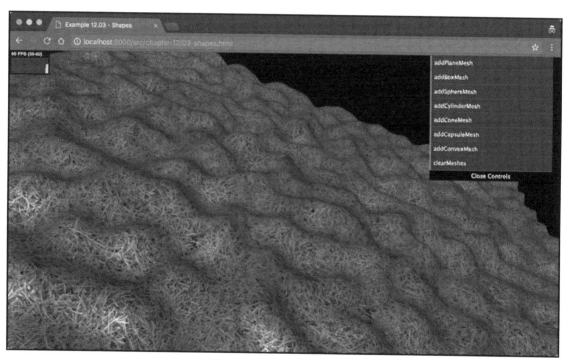

With a height map, you can very easily create a terrain that contains bumps and shallows. Using `Physijs.Heightmap`, we make sure all the objects respond correctly to the height differences of this terrain. Let's look at the code required to accomplish this:

```
var date = new Date();
var pn = new Perlin('rnd' + date.getTime());

function createHeightMap(pn) {

  var ground_material = Physijs.createMaterial(
    new THREE.MeshLambertMaterial({
      map: textureLoader.load('../assets/textures/ground/grasslight-
big.jpg')}),
      0.3, // high friction
      0.8 // low restitution
  );

  var ground_geometry = new THREE.PlaneGeometry(120, 100, 100,
      100);
  for (var i = 0; i < ground_geometry.vertices.length; i++) {
    var vertex = ground_geometry.vertices[i];
    var value = pn.noise(vertex.x / 10, vertex.y / 10, 0);
    vertex.z = value * 10;
  }
  ground_geometry.computeFaceNormals();
  ground_geometry.computeVertexNormals();

  var ground = new Physijs.HeightfieldMesh(
    ground_geometry,
    ground_material,
    0, // mass
    100,
    100
  );
  ground.rotation.x = Math.PI / -2;
  ground.rotation.y = 0.4;
  ground.receiveShadow = true;

  return ground;
}
```

In this code fragment, we take a couple of steps to create the height map you can see in the example. First we create the Physijs material and a simple `PlaneGeometry` object. To create a bumpy terrain from `PlaneGeometry`, we walk through each of the vertices of this geometry and randomly set the z property. For this, we use a Perlin noise generator to create a bump map just as we used in the *Using the canvas as a bumpmap* section of `Chapter 10`, *Loading and Working with Textures*. We need to call `computeFaceNormals` and `computeVertexNormals` to make sure the texture, lighting, and shadows are rendered correctly. At this point, we have `PlaneGeometry`, which contains the correct height information. With `PlaneGeometry`, we can create `Physijs.HeightFieldMesh`. The last two parameters for the constructor take the number of horizontal and vertical segments of `PlaneGeometry` and should match the last two properties used to construct `PlaneGeometry`. Finally, we rotate `HeightFieldMesh` to the position we want and add it to the scene. All other Physijs objects will now interact correctly with this height map.

Using constraints to limit the movement of objects

Until now, we've seen some basic physics in action. We've seen how the various shapes respond to gravity, friction, and restitution, and how they affect collisions. Physijs also provides advanced constructs that allow you to limit the movement of your objects. In Physijs, these objects are called constraints. The following table gives an overview of the constraints that are available in Physijs:

Constraint	Description
`PointConstraint`	This allows you to fix the position of one object to the position of another object. If one object moves, the other will move with it, keeping the distance between them the same.
`HingeConstraint`	`HingeConstraint` allows you to limit the movement of an object as if it were on a hinge, such as a door.
`SliderConstraint`	This constraint, as the name implies, allows you to limit the movement of an object to a single axis, for instance, a sliding door.
`ConeTwistConstraint`	With this constraint, you can limit the rotation and the movement of one object to another. This constraint functions like a ball-and-socket joint; for instance, the way your arm moves in your shoulder socket.

DOFConstraint	DOFConstraint allows you to specify the limit of movement around any of the three axes, and it allows you to set the minimum and maximum angle that is allowed. This is the most versatile of the constraints available.

The easiest way to understand these constraints is to see them in action and play around with them. For this, we've provided a couple of examples where these constraints are used. The first one we look at is PointConstraint.

Using PointConstraint to limit movement between two points

If you open the 04-point-contstraint.html example, you see the following:

In this example, we rendered a horizontal bar on which a chain of beads is dropped. When you open this example, you can see that the beads curl themselves around the bar, before falling out of the screen. This happens because each bead uses a `PointConstraint` to keep a certain distance to its neighbor. So, as soon as one side is heavier then the other, gravity and this constraint will make sure the chain slides over the horizontal bar.

The `PointConstraint` objects in this example are created as follows:

```
function createPointToPoint(scene) {

  var beads = [];
  var rangeMin = -10;
  var rangeMax = 10;
  var count = 20;
  var scale = chroma.scale(['red', 'yellow']);

  for (var i = 0 ; i < count ; i++) {
    var bead = new THREE.SphereGeometry(0.5);
    var physBead = new Physijs.SphereMesh(bead, Physijs.createMaterial(
                      new THREE.MeshStandardMaterial({color:
scale(Math.random()).hex()}), 0, 0));
    physBead.position.set(i * (-rangeMin + rangeMax)/count + rangeMin, 10,
Math.random()/2);
    scene.add(physBead);
    if (i != 0) {
       var beadConstraint = new Physijs.PointConstraint(beads[i-1],
physBead, physBead.position);
       scene.addConstraint(beadConstraint);
    }
    physBead.castShadow = true;
    beads.push(physBead);
  }
}
```

Here, you can see that we create objects using a Physijs-specific mesh (`SphereMesh` in this case) and add them to the scene. We also connect each bead to the previous one using a `Physijs.PointConstraint`. To create this constraint, we have to define three parameters:

- The first two arguments define which objects you want to connect to one another. In this case, we connect two spheres to each other.
- The third argument defines to what position the constraint is bound. For instance, if you bind the first object to a very large object, you can set this position, to the right-hand side of that object. Usually, if you just want to connect two objects together, a good choice is to just set it to the position of the second object (which is the center of the sphere).

If you don't want to fix an object to another one, but to a static position in the scene, you can omit the second parameter. In that case, the first object keeps the same distance to the position you specified, while complying with gravity and other aspects of physics, of course.

Once the constraint is created, we can enable it by adding it to the scene with the `addConstraint` function. As you start experimenting with constraints, you'll likely run into some strange issues. To make debugging easier, you can pass in `true` to the `addConstraint` function. If you do this, the constraint point and orientation are shown in the scene. This can help you get the rotation and position of your constraint correct.

Hinge constraints

HingeConstraint, as the name implies, allows you to create an object that behaves like a hinge. It rotates around a specific axis, limiting the movement to a specified angle. In our example, HingeConstraint is shown with two green flippers at the bottom of the scene (example, 05-sliders-hinges.html):

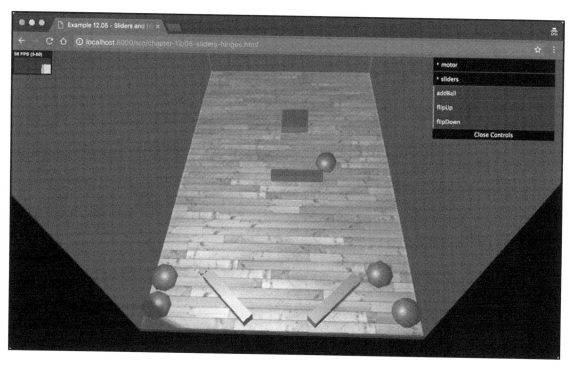

These flippers are constrained to the small cubes and can rotate around them. If you want to play around with these hinges, you can enable them by clicking the flipUp and flipDown buttons in the menu. This will accelerate the flippers to the velocity specified in the **motor** menu.

Let's take a closer look at how we created one of these flippers:

```
function createLeftFlipper(scene, mat) {
    var flipperLeft = new Physijs.BoxMesh(new THREE.BoxGeometry(12, 2, 2),
mat, 10);
    flipperLeft.position.x = -8;
    flipperLeft.position.y = 2;
    flipperLeft.position.z = 30;
    flipperLeft.castShadow = true;
```

```
    scene.add(flipperLeft);

    var flipperLeftPivot = new Physijs.SphereMesh(new THREE.BoxGeometry(1, 1,
1), mat, 0);
    flipperLeftPivot.position.y = 2;
    flipperLeftPivot.position.x = -15;
    flipperLeftPivot.position.z = 30;
    flipperLeftPivot.rotation.y = 1.4;
    flipperLeftPivot.castShadow = true;

    scene.add(flipperLeftPivot);

    var constraint = new Physijs.HingeConstraint(flipperLeft,
flipperLeftPivot, flipperLeftPivot.position,
                                    new THREE.Vector3(0, 1, 0));

    scene.addConstraint(constraint);

    constraint.setLimits(-2.2, -0.6, 0.3, 0.5);
    return constraint;
}
```

This constraint takes four parameters. Let's look at each one in a bit more detail:

Parameter	Description
mesh_a	The first object passed into the function is the object that is to be constrained. In this example, the first object is the white cube that serves as the flipper. This is the object that is constrained in its movements.
mesh_b	The second object defines to which object mesh_a is constrained. In this example, mesh_a is constrained to the small, brown cube. If we move this mesh around, mesh_a would follow it around, still keeping HingeConstraint in place. You'll see that all constraints have this option. You could, for instance, use this if you've created a car that moves around and want to create a constraint for opening a door. If this second parameter is omitted, the hinge will be constrained to the scene (and never be able to move around).
position	This is the point where the constraint is applied. In this case, it's the hinge point around which mesh_a rotates. If you've specified mesh_b, this hinge point will move around with the position and rotation of mesh_b.
axis	This is the axis around which the hinge should rotate. In this example, we've set the hinge horizontally (0,1,0).

Adding `HingeConstraint` to the scene works in the same way as we've seen with `PointConstraint`. You use the `addConstraint` method, specify the constraint to add, and optionally add `true` to show the exact location and orientation of the constraint for debugging purposes. For `HingeConstraint`, however, we also need to define the range of movement that is allowed. We do this with the `setLimits` function.

This function takes the following four parameters:

Parameter	Description
low	This is the minimum angle, in radians, of motion.
high	This is the maximum angle, in radians, of motion.
bias_factor	This property defines the rate at which the constraint corrects itself after an error in position. For instance, when the hinge is pushed out of its constraints by a different object, it will move itself to its correct position. The higher this value, the faster it will correct its position. It is best to keep it below `0.5`.
relaxation_factor	This defines the rate at which the velocity is changed by the constraint. If this is set to a high value, the object will bounce when it reaches its minimum or maximum angle of motion.

You can change these properties at runtime if you want. If you add `HingeConstraint` with these properties, you won't see much movement. The mesh will only move when hit by another object or based on gravity. This constraint, as with many others, however, can also be moved by an internal motor. This is what you see when you click on the `flipperUp` button:

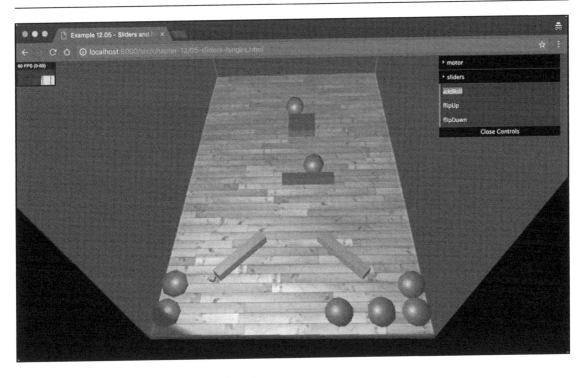

The following code is used to enable this motor:

```
constraint.enableAngularMotor( controls.velocity, controls.acceleration );
```

This will speed up the mesh (in our case, the flipper) to the specified velocity using the acceleration provided. If we want to move the flipper the other way, we just specify a negative velocity. If we didn't have any limits, this would cause our flipper to rotate as long as our motor kept running. To disable a motor, we can just call the following code:

```
flipperLeftConstraint.disableMotor();
```

Now, the mesh will slow down as a result of friction, collisions, gravity, and other aspects of physics.

Limiting movement to a single axis with SliderConstraint

The next constraint is `SliderConstraint`. With this constraint, you can limit the movement of an object to any one of its axes. The blue sliders in the `05-sliders-hinges.html` example can be controlled from the **sliders** submenu. The sliders can only move on their defined axis. The top one will move up and down, and the bottom one can move from left to right:

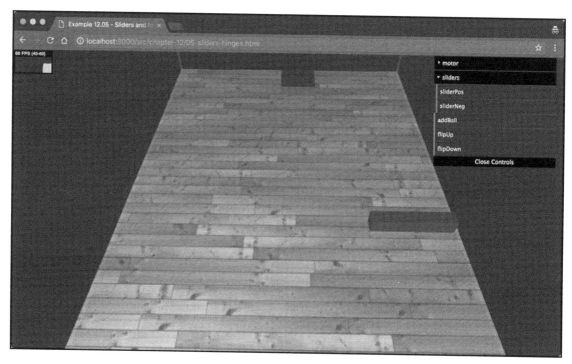

With the **sliderPos** button, the sliders will move to the left-hand side (their lower limit), and with the **sliderNeg** button, they will move to the right-hand side (their upper limit). Creating these constraints from code is very easy:

```
function createSliderTop(scene, mat) {
  var sliderSphere = new THREE.BoxGeometry(7, 2, 7);
  var sliderMesh = new Physijs.BoxMesh(sliderSphere, mat, 100);
  sliderMesh.position.z = -15;
  sliderMesh.position.x = 2;
  sliderMesh.position.y = 1.5;
  scene.add(sliderMesh);
```

```
//position is the position of the axis, relative to the ref, based on the
current position
var constraint = new Physijs.SliderConstraint(sliderMesh,
                            new THREE.Vector3(-15, 2, 1.5),
                            new THREE.Vector3(Math.PI / 2, 0, 0));
scene.addConstraint(constraint);
constraint.setLimits(-18, 18, 0.5, -0, 5);
constraint.setRestitution(0.1, 0.1);

return constraint;
}
```

As you can see from the code, this constraint takes three arguments (or four if you want to constrain an object to another object). The following table explains the arguments for this constraint:

Parameter	Description
mesh_a	The first object passed into the function is the object that is to be constrained. In this example, the first object is the green cube that serves as the slider. This is the object that will be constrained in its movements.
mesh_b	This is the second object, which defines to which object mesh_a is constrained. This is an optional argument and omitted in this example. If omitted, the mesh will be constrained to the scene. If it is specified, the slider will move around when this mesh moves around or when its orientation changes.
position	This is the point where the constraint is applied. This is especially important when you constrain mesh_a to mesh_b.
axis	This is the axis on which mesh_a will slide. Note that this is relative to the orientation of mesh_b if it is specified. In the current version of Physijs, there seems to be a strange offset to this axis when using a linear motor with linear limits. The following works for this version if you want to slide along: • The *x* axis: newTHREE.Vector3(0,1,0) • The *y* axis: newTHREE.Vector3(0,0,Math.PI/2) • The *z* axis: newTHREE.Vector3(Math.PI/2,0,0)

After you've created the constraint and added it to the scene using `scene.addConstraint`, you can set the `constraint.setLimits(-10,10,0,0)` limits for this constraint to specify how far the slider may slide. You can set the following limits on `SliderConstraint`:

Parameter	Description
linear_lower	This is the lower linear limit of the object
linear_upper	This is the upper linear limit of the object
angular_lower	This is the lower angular limit of the object
angular_higher	This is the upper angular limit of the object

Finally, you can set the restitution (the bounce) that'll occur when you hit one of these limits. You do this with `constraint.setRestitution(res_linear, res_angular)`, where the first parameter sets the amount of bounce when you hit the linear limit and the second one sets the amount of bounce when you hit the angular limit.

Now the complete constraint has been configured, and we can wait until collisions occur that slide the object around (you can use the `addBall` button to add additional meshes) or use a motor. For `SlideConstraint`, we have two options: we can use an angular motor to accelerate along the axis we specified, complying with the angular limits we set, or use a linear motor to accelerate along the axis we specified, complying with the linear limits. In this example, we used a linear motor. For using an angular motor, take a look at `DOFConstraint`, which is explained next.

Creating a ball-and-socket-joint-like constraint with ConeTwistConstraint

With `ConeTwistConstraint`, it is possible to create a constraint where the movement is limited to a set of angles. We can specify what the minimum and maximum angle is from one object to the other for the *x*, *y*, and *z* axes. We don't show this in an example, but using and creating this constraint works similar to the other ones discussed in this chapter. The easiest way to understand `ConeTwistConstraint` is by looking at the code required to create one. The code required to accomplish this is as follows:

```
var baseMesh = new THREE.SphereGeometry(1);
var armMesh = new THREE.BoxGeometry(2, 12, 3);

var objectOne = new Physijs.BoxMesh(baseMesh,
    Physijs.createMaterial(new THREE.MeshPhongMaterial({color:
    0x4444ff, transparent: true, opacity:0.7}), 0, 0), 0);
```

```
objectOne.position.z = 0;
objectOne.position.x = 20;
objectOne.position.y = 15.5;
objectOne.castShadow = true;
scene.add(objectOne);

var objectTwo = new Physijs.SphereMesh
    (armMesh,Physijs.createMaterial(new THREE.MeshPhong
    Material({color: 0x4444ff, transparent: true, opacity:0.7}), 0,
    0), 10);
objectTwo.position.z = 0;
objectTwo.position.x = 20;
objectTwo.position.y = 7.5;
scene.add(objectTwo);
objectTwo.castShadow = true;

var constraint = new Physijs.ConeTwistConstraint(objectOne,
    objectTwo, objectOne.position);

scene.addConstraint(constraint);

constraint.setLimit(0.5*Math.PI, 0.5*Math.PI, 0.5*Math.PI);
constraint.setMaxMotorImpulse(1);
constraint.setMotorTarget(new THREE.Vector3(0, 0, 0));
```

In this piece of JavaScript, you'll probably already recognize a number of concepts we discussed earlier. We start by creating the objects that we connect to each other with the following constraint: objectOne (a sphere) and objectTwo (a box). We position these objects so that objectTwo hangs below objectOne. Now we can create ConeTwistConstraint. The arguments this constraint takes aren't anything new if you've already looked at the other constraints. The first parameter is the object to constrain, the second parameter is the object to which the first object is constrained, and the last parameter is the location where the constraint is constructed (in this case, it's the point around which objectOne rotates). After adding the constraint to the scene, we can set its limits with the setLimit function. This function takes three radian values that specify the maximum angle for each of the axes.

Just as with most of the other constraints, we can move objectOne using the motor provided by the constraint. For ConeTwistConstraint, we set MaxMotorImpulse (how much force the motor can apply), and we set the target angles the motor should move objectOne to.

Creating detailed control with DOFConstraint

`DOFConstraint`, also called the degree of freedom constraint, allows you to exactly control an object's linear and angular movement. We'll demonstrate how to use this constraint by creating an example where you can drive around a simple, car-like shape. This shape consists of a single rectangle that serves as the body and four spheres that serve as the wheels. Let's start by creating the wheels:

```
function createWheel(position) {
  var wheel_material = Physijs.createMaterial(
    new THREE.MeshLambertMaterial({
      color: 0x444444,
      opacity: 0.9,
      transparent: true
    }),
    1.0, // high friction
    0.5 // medium restitution
  );

  var wheel_geometry = new THREE.CylinderGeometry(4, 4, 2, 10);
  var wheel = new Physijs.CylinderMesh(
    wheel_geometry,
    wheel_material,
    100
  );

  wheel.rotation.x = Math.PI / 2;
  wheel.castShadow = true;
  wheel.position = position;
  return wheel;
}
```

In this piece of code, we just created a simple `CylinderGeometry` and `CylinderMesh` object that can be used as the wheels for our car. The following screenshot depicts the result of the preceding code:

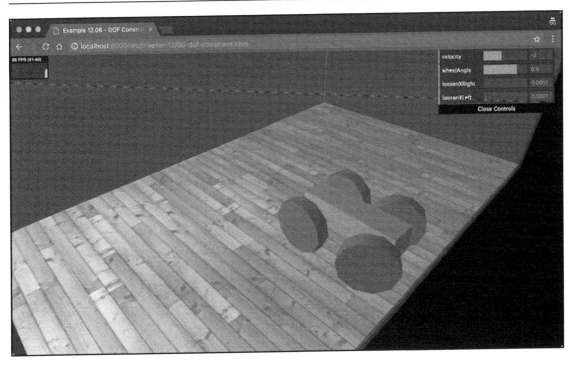

Next, we need to create the body of the car and add everything to the scene:

```
var car = {};
var car_material = Physijs.createMaterial(new THREE.
    MeshLambertMaterial({
      color: 0xff4444,
      opacity: 0.9, transparent: true
    }),    0.5, 0.5
);

var geom = new THREE.BoxGeometry(15, 4, 4);
var body = new Physijs.BoxMesh(geom, car_material, 500);
body.position.set(5, 5, 5);
body.castShadow = true;
scene.add(body);

var fr = createWheel(new THREE.Vector3(0, 4, 10));
var fl = createWheel(new THREE.Vector3(0, 4, 0));
var rr = createWheel(new THREE.Vector3(10, 4, 10));
var rl = createWheel(new THREE.Vector3(10, 4, 0));

scene.add(fr);
scene.add(fl);
```

```
scene.add(rr);
scene.add(rl);
```

Until now, we just created the separate components that will have to make up our car. To tie everything together, we're going to create constraints. Each wheel will be constrained to body. The constraints are created as follows:

```
var frConstraint = new Physijs.DOFConstraint(fr,body, new
THREE.Vector3(0,4,8));
scene.addConstraint(frConstraint);
var flConstraint = new Physijs.DOFConstraint (fl,body, new
THREE.Vector3(0,4,2));
scene.addConstraint(flConstraint);
var rrConstraint = new Physijs.DOFConstraint (rr,body, new
THREE.Vector3(10,4,8));
scene.addConstraint(rrConstraint);
var rlConstraint = new Physijs.DOFConstraint (rl,body, new
THREE.Vector3(10,4,2));
scene.addConstraint(rlConstraint);
```

Each wheel (the first argument) has its own constraint, and the position where it is attached to the car (the second argument) is specified with the last argument. If we ran with this configuration, we'd see that the four wheels hold up the body of the car. We need to do two more things to get the car moving: we need to set up the constraints for the wheels (along which axis they can move), and we need to configure the correct motors. First, we set up the constraints for the two front wheels; what we want for these front wheels is just to be able to rotate along the z axis so that they can power the car, and they shouldn't be allowed to move along the other axes.

The code required to accomplish this is as follows:

```
frConstraint.setAngularLowerLimit({ x: 0, y: 0, z: 0 });
frConstraint.setAngularUpperLimit({ x: 0, y: 0, z: 0 });
flConstraint.setAngularLowerLimit({ x: 0, y: 0, z: 0 });
flConstraint.setAngularUpperLimit({ x: 0, y: 0, z: 0 });
```

At first glance, this might seem weird. By setting the lower and upper limits to the same value, we make sure that no rotation is possible in the specified direction. This would also mean that the wheels can't rotate around their *z* axis. The reason
we specify it like this is that when you enable a motor for a specific axis, these limits are ignored. So, setting limits on the *z* axis at this point doesn't have any effect on our front wheels.

We're going to steer with our rear wheels, and to make sure they don't fall over, we need to fix the *x* axis. With the following code, we fix the *x* axis (set upper and lower limits to 0), fix the *y* axis so that these wheels are already initially turned, and disable any limit on the *z* axis:

```
rrConstraint.setAngularLowerLimit({ x: 0, y: 0.5, z: 0.1 });
rrConstraint.setAngularUpperLimit({ x: 0, y: 0.5, z: 0 });
rlConstraint.setAngularLowerLimit({ x: 0, y: 0.5, z: 0.1 });
rlConstraint.setAngularUpperLimit({ x: 0, y: 0.5, z: 0 });
```

As you can see, to disable the limits, we have to set the lower limit of that specific axis higher than the upper limit. This will allow free rotation around that axis. If we don't set this for the *z* axis, these two wheels will just be dragged along. In this case, they'll turn together with the other wheels because of the friction with the ground. All that is left to do is to set up the motors for the front wheels, which can be done as follows:

```
flConstraint.configureAngularMotor(2, 0.1, 0, -2, 1500);
frConstraint.conAngularMotor(2, 0.1, 0, -2, 1500);
```

Since there are three axes we can create a motor for, we need to specify the axis the motor works on: 0 is the *x* axis, 1 is the *y* axis, and 2 is the *z* axis. The second and third arguments define the angular limits for the motor. Here, we once again set the lower limit (0.1) higher than the upper limit (0) to allow free rotation. The third argument specifies the velocity we want to reach, and the last argument specifies the force this motor can apply. If this last one is too little, the car won't move; if it's too high, the rear wheels will lift off from the ground. Enable them with the following code:

```
flConstraint.enableAngularMotor(2);
frConstraint.enableAngularMotor(2);
```

If you open the `06-dof-constraint.html` example, you can play around with the various constraints and motors and drive the car around. The following screenshot shows this example:

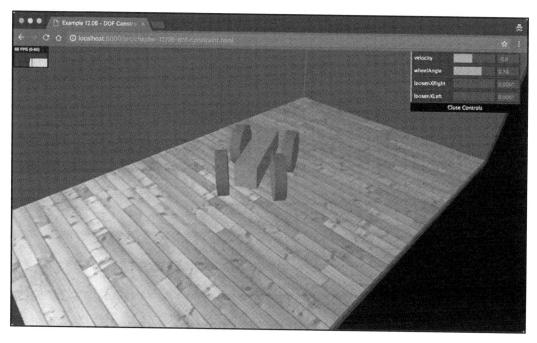

In the next section, we'll look at the last subject we'll discuss in this book, and that is how to add sounds to your Three.js scene.

Add sound sources to your scene

With the subjects discussed until now, we have a lot of the ingredients in place to create beautiful scenes, games, and other 3D visualizations. What we haven't shown, however, is how to add sounds to your Three.js scene. In this section, we'll look at two Three.js objects that allow you to add sources of sound to your scene. This is especially interesting since these sound sources respond to the position of the camera:

- The distance between the sound source and the camera determines the volume of the sound source
- The positions to the left-hand side and the right-hand side of the camera determine the sound volume of the left-hand side speaker and the right-hand side speaker, respectively

The best way to explain this is to see this in action. Open up the 07-audio.html example in your browser, and you'll see three cubes with pictures of animals. The following screenshot shows this example:

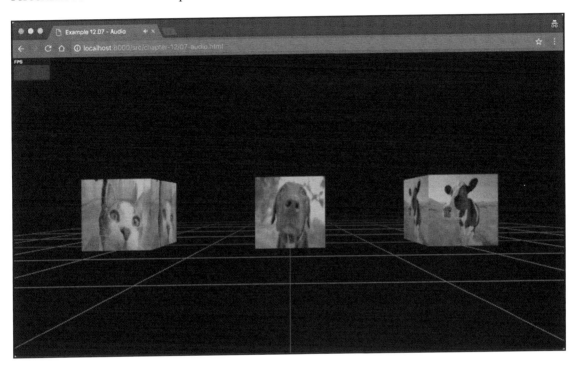

This example uses the first-person controls we saw in Chapter 9, *Animations and Moving the Camera*, so you can use the arrow keys in combination with the mouse to move around the scene. What you'll see is that the closer you move to a specific cube, the louder that specific animal will sound. If you position the camera between the dog and the cow, you'll hear the cow from the right-hand side and the dog from the left-hand side.

In this example, we used a specific helper, THREE.GridHelper, from Three.js to create the grid beneath the cubes:

```
var helper = new THREE.GridHelper( 500, 10 );
scene.add( helper );
```

To create a grid, you need to specify the size of the grid (500 in this case) and the size of the individual grid elements (we used 10 here). If you want, you can also set the colors of the horizontal lines by specifying the colorCenterLine and colorGrid property

Accomplishing this only takes a small amount of code. The first thing we need to do is define THREE.AudioListener and add it to THREE.PerspectiveCamera, as follows (in this example, we do this three times, once for each sound):

```
var listener1 = new THREE.AudioListener();
camera.add(listener1);
var listener2 = new THREE.AudioListener();
camera.add(listener2);
var listener3 = new THREE.AudioListener();
camera.add(listener3);
```

Next, we need to create THREE.Mesh and add a THREE.PositionalAudio object to that mesh, as follows:

```
var cube = new THREE.BoxGeometry(40, 40, 40);
var material_1 = new THREE.MeshBasicMaterial({
  color: 0xffffff,
  map: textureLoader.load("../assets/textures/animals/cow.png")
});

var mesh1 = new THREE.Mesh(cube, material_1);
mesh1.position.set(0, 20, 100);

var posSound1 = new THREE.PositionalAudio( listener1 );
var audioLoader = new THREE.AudioLoader();
audioLoader.load('../../assets/audio/cow.ogg', function(buffer) {
 posSound1.setBuffer( buffer );
 posSound1.setRefDistance( 30 );
 posSound1.play();
 posSound1.setRolloffFactor(10);
 posSound1.setLoop(true);
});;
```

As you can see from this code snippet, we first create a standard THREE.Mesh instance. Next, we create a THREE.PositionalAudio object, which we connect to the THREE.AudioListener object we created earlier. Finally, we add the audio and configure some properties which define how the sound is played, and how it behaves:

- setRefDistance: This determines the distance from the object from where the sound will be reduced in volume.
- setLoop: By default, a sound is played once. By setting this property to true, the sound is looped.
- setRolloffFactor: This determines how quickly the volume decreases as you move away from the sound source.

We've added first-person controls to this example, so you can walk around the scene. When you do this, you'll notice that the volume of the sound and the direction you hear it from depends on where you are in the scene. For instance, if you move the cow to the front like this, you'll mostly just hear the cow:

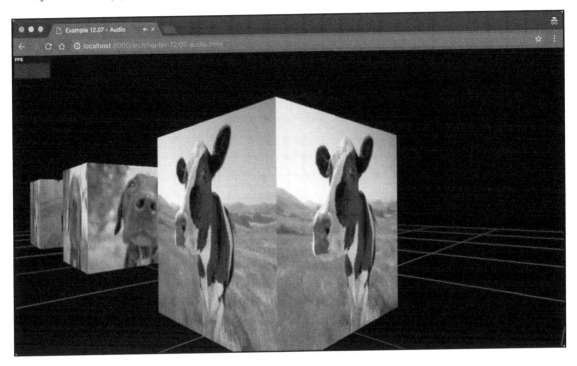

The cow, with the dog and the cat will be much fainter from the left speaker. Internally, Three.js uses the **Web Audio API** (`http://webaudio.github.io/web-audio-api/`) to play the sound and determine the correct volume. Not all browsers support this specification. The best support currently is from Chrome and Firefox.

Summary

In this last chapter, we explored how you can extend the basic 3D functionality from Three.js by adding physics. For this, we used the Physijs library, which allows you to add gravity, collisions, constraints, and much more. We also showed how you can add positional sound to your scene using the THREE.PositionalAudio and THREE.AudioListener objects. With those subjects, we've reached the end of this book on Three.js. In these chapters, we covered a lot of different subjects and explored pretty much everything Three.js has to offer. In the first couple of chapters, we explained the core concepts and ideas behind Three.js; after that, we looked at the available lights and how materials affect how an object is rendered. After the basics, we explored the various geometries Three.js has to offer and how you can combine geometries to create new ones.

In the second part of the book, we looked at a few more advanced subjects. You learned how to create particle systems, how to load models from external sources, and how to create animations. Finally, in these last couple of chapters, we looked at the advanced textures you can use in skinning and the postprocessing effects that can be applied after the scene is rendered. We end the book with this chapter on physics, which, besides explaining how you can add physics to your Three.js scene, also shows the active community of projects surrounding Three.js that you can use to add even more functionality to an already great library.

I hope you've enjoyed reading this book and playing around with the examples as much as I have enjoyed writing it!

Other Books You May Enjoy

If you enjoyed this book, you may be interested in these other books by Packt:

Learning D3.js 5 Mapping - Second Edition

Thomas Newton

ISBN: 9781787280175

- Work with SVG geometric shapes
- Learn to manage map data and plot it with D3.js
- Add interactivity and points of interest to your maps
- Compress and manipulate geoJSON files with the use of topoJSON
- Learn how to write testable D3.js visualizations
- Build a globe with D3.js and Canvas and add interactivity to it.
- Create a hexbin map with D3.js

JavaScript and JSON Essentials - Second Edition
Bruno Joseph D'mello

ISBN: 9781788624701

- Use JSON to store metadata for dependency managers, package managers, configuration managers, and metadata stores
- Handle asynchronous behavior in applications using callbacks, promises, generators, and async-await functions
- Use JSON for Angular 5, Node.js, Gulp.js, and Hapi.js
- Implement JSON as BSON in MongoDB
- Make use of JSON in developing automation scripts
- Implement JSON for realtime using socket.io and distributed systems using Kafka

Leave a review - let other readers know what you think

Please share your thoughts on this book with others by leaving a review on the site that you bought it from. If you purchased the book from Amazon, please leave us an honest review on this book's Amazon page. This is vital so that other potential readers can see and use your unbiased opinion to make purchasing decisions, we can understand what our customers think about our products, and our authors can see your feedback on the title that they have worked with Packt to create. It will only take a few minutes of your time, but is valuable to other potential customers, our authors, and Packt. Thank you!

Index

2

2D geometries
  about 163
  THREE.CircleGeometry 166, 167, 168
  THREE.PlaneGeometry 164, 166
  THREE.RingGeometry 169, 170

3

3D file formats
  importing from 285
  MTL 285, 286, 287, 288
  OBJ 285, 286, 287, 288
3D geometries
  about 177
  THREE.BoxGeometry 177, 178
  THREE.ConeGeometry 184
  THREE.CylinderGeometry 181
  THREE.PolyhedronGeometry 190, 192
  THREE.SphereGeometry 178
  THREE.TorusGeometry 186
  THREE.TorusKnotGeometry 188, 189
3D object
  axes 21
  camera 21
  cube 21
  plane 21
  rendering 21, 23, 24, 25
  sphere 21
  viewing 21, 23, 24, 25
3D text
  creating 215
  custom fonts, adding 218
  rendering 215, 216
3MF
  reference 270

A

advanced materials
  about 139
  shaders, creating with THREE.ShaderMaterial
    147, 148, 154
  THREE.MeshLambertMaterial 140, 141
  THREE.MeshPhongMaterial 142, 144
  THREE.MeshPhysicalMaterial 146
  THREE.MeshStandardMaterial 144
advanced properties, materials
  alphatest 122
  depthFunc 122
  depthTest 122
  depthWrite 122
  polygonOffset 122
  polygonOffsetFactor 122
  polygonOffsetUnits 122
  precision 122
alpha map 387, 388
ambient occlusion map
  subtle shadows, adding with 380, 381, 382, 383
ambient occlusion
  using 438, 439
AMF
  reference 270
ammo.js
  about 461
  reference 463
animations
  ball, bouncing 33, 34
  creating 308, 310
  creating, with external models 344
  cube, animating 32
  implementing 307
  loading, from COLLADA model 350, 352
  loading, from Quake model 353, 354

objects, selecting 310, 311, 312
requestAnimationFrame 30
scene, expanding 29
skeletal animation 328
  with bones 340, 342, 343
  with mixer and morph targets 329, 330, 332, 334, 336, 337
  with morph targets 327, 329
  with skinning 340, 342, 343
  with Tween.js 313, 315, 316, 317
Assimp
  reference 270
Autodesk
  reference 270
AWD
  reference 270

B

Babylon
  reference 270
ball-and-socket-joint-like constraint
  creating, with ConeTwistConstraint 488
ball
  bouncing 33, 34
basic lights
  about 81
  THREE.AmbientLight 81, 83, 84, 85
  THREE.DirectionalLight 103, 104, 105
  THREE.PointLight 97, 99, 100, 102, 103
  THREE.SpotLight 89, 90, 91, 92, 95, 96, 97
basic properties, materials
  colorWrite 120
  dithering 120
  flatShading 120
  fog 121
  id 119
  lights 120
  name 119
  needsUpdate 120
  opacity 119
  overdraw 119
  premultipliedAlpha 120
  shadowSide 120
  side 120
  transparent 119

uuid 119
  vertexColors 120
  visible 120
billboarding 254
binary operations
  intersect function 227
  subtract function 222, 223, 224, 225
  union function 229
  used, for combining meshes 220, 221
Biovision (BVH) format 345
Blender
  model, exporting from 282, 283
  model, loading from 282, 283
  reference 278
  Three.js exporter, installing in 280, 281
  working with 279
blending properties, materials
  blendDst 121
  blendDstAlpha 121
  blendEquation 121
  blending 121
  blendSrc 121
  blendSrcAlpha 121
blur shaders
  working with 448, 449, 451, 452
Bokeh effect
  adding 434, 436, 437
bones
  animating, with Blender 346, 347, 348, 350
  for animation 340, 341, 343
bump map
  about 375
  canvas, using as 411
  used, for creating wrinkles 375, 376
BVHLoader
  skeleton, visualizing 360, 362

C

camera, controls
  DeviceOrientationControls 318
  EditorControls 318
  FirstPersonControls 317, 323, 324
  FlyControls 317, 321, 322, 323
  OculusControls 318
  OrbitControl 325, 326

OrbitControls 317
OrthographicTrackballControls 318
PointerLockControls 318
TrackballControls 319, 320
TrackDallControls 317
TransformControls 318
VRControls 318
camera
  orthographic camera, versus perspective camera
    69, 70, 71, 73
  output, resizing on browser resize 38
  types 68
  using 317
  viewing, at specific points 74, 75
canvas
  rendering to 408
  using, as bump map 411
  using, as texture 409
Chrome
  filesystem, executing 17, 18, 19
CoffeeScript
  reference 222
COLLAborative Design Activity (COLLADA) 270
COLLADA model
  animation, loading 350, 352
  loading 290, 291
constraints
  ball-and-socket-joint-like constraint, creating with
    ConeTwistConstraint 488
  ConeTwistConstraint 478
  detailed control, creating with DOFConstraint
    490, 492, 493, 494
  DOFConstraint 479
  hinge constraints, using 482, 483, 484
  HingeConstraint 478
  object movement, limiting 478
  PointConstraint 478
  PointConstraint, using 479, 480, 481
  SliderConstraint 478
  SliderConstraint, using 486, 488
Constructive Solid Geometry (CSG) 220
CTM 270
cube
  animating 32
custom effects

creating, with blur shaders 448, 449, 451, 452
creating, with shaders 442, 444, 446, 447
THREE.ShaderPass, using 439, 441, 442
custom fonts
  adding 219
custom postprocessing shaders
  creating 452
  custom bit shader, creating 456, 457, 458
  custom grayscale shader, creating 452, 454,
    455, 456

D

dat.GUI
  reference 35
  using 35, 36, 37
displacement map
  used, for altering position of vertices 379, 380
Document Object Model (DOM) 36
DOFConstraint
  detailed control, creating 490, 493, 494
Draco
  reference 271

E

easing 313
emissive map 389, 390
environment map
  used, for creating fake reflections 393, 394, 395,
    396, 397, 398, 399, 400
external models
  BVH model 345
  COLLADA model 344
  DirectX models 345
  FBX model 344
  fbxLoader, using 356, 358
  glTF models 344
  gltfLoader, using 355
  legacy DirectX models, loading through xLoader
    359, 360
  MD2 model 344
  reusing, from SEA3D project 362, 363
  SEA model 345
  skeleton, visualizing with BVHLoader 360, 362
  used, for animations 344

F

fake reflections
  creating, environment map used 393, 394, 395, 396, 397, 398, 399, 400
fake shadows
  creating, lightmap used 383, 384
fbxLoader
  using 356, 358
Field Of View (FOV) 72
file formats
  3MF 270
  AMF 270
  Assimp 270
  AWD 270
  Babylon 270
  COLLAborative Design Activity (COLLADA) 270
  CTM 270
  Draco 271
  GCODE 271
  JSON 270
  MTL 270
  NRRD 271
  OBJ 270
  Packed Raw WebGL Model (PRWM) 271
  PlayCanvas 271
  PLY 270
  Protein Data Bank (PDB) 270
  STereoLithography (STL) 270
  SVG 271
  TDS 270
  Virtual Reality Modeling Language (VRML) 270
  Visualization Toolkit (VTK) 270
Filmbox (FBX) format 356
Firefox
  filesystem, executing 17, 18, 19
FirstPersonControls
  using 323, 324
FlyControls
  using 321, 322, 323
fog
  adding, to scene 50, 51
Frames Per Second (fps) 267

G

GCode
  reference 271
geometries
  2D geometries 163
  3D geometries 177
  about 53, 163
  creating, by extruding 204
  extruding, from SVG 208, 209, 210, 211
  functions 54, 55, 57, 58, 59, 60
  loading, from external resources 270
  properties 54, 55, 57, 58, 59, 60
  THREE.ExtrudeGeometry 204, 205
  THREE.TubeGeometry 206, 207, 208
Git
  repository, cloning 13
GitHub
  reference 13
GL Transmission (glTF) format 344
GLSL
  reference 150
gltfLoader
  reference 355
  using 355

H

head-up display (HUD) 254
hinge constraints, parameter
  axis 483
  mesh_a 483
  mesh_b 483
  position 483
hinge constraints
  using 482, 483, 484
HTML skeleton
  creating 19, 20, 21
HTML5 canvas
  particles, styling 239
  using, with THREE.CanvasRenderer 239, 241
  using, with WebGLRenderer 242, 243, 244, 245

I

IEWebGL plugin
  reference 9

intersect function 227

J

JSON 270

K

Keyhole Markup language Zipped (KMZ) models 350
Khronos Texture (KTX) 371

L

legacy DirectX models
  loading, through xLoader 359, 360
lens flare 110, 112, 113, 114
lens flare, argument
  blending 112
  color 112
  distance 112
  opacity 112
  size 112
  texture 112
lighting
  reference 79
lightmap
  used, for creating fake shadows 383, 384
lights
  about 80
  adding 26, 27
  basic lights 81
  reference 100
  special lights 106
  THREE.AmbientLight 80
  THREE.AreaLight 80
  THREE.DirectionalLight 80
  THREE.HemisphereLight 80
  THREE.LensFlare 80
  THREE.PointLight 80
  THREE.SpotLight 80
Literally library
  reference 409
loaders
  THREE.DDSLoader 369
  THREE.EXRLoader 373
  THREE.KTXLoader 371
  THREE.PVRLoader 370

  THREE.RGBELoader 374
  THREE.TGALoader 370

M

materials
  adding 26, 27
  advanced materials 139
  advanced properties 119
  basic properties 118
  blending properties 118
  LineBasicMaterial 118
  LineDashMaterial 118
  MeshBasicMaterial 117
  MeshDepthMaterial 117
  MeshLambertMaterial 117
  MeshNormalMaterial 117
  MeshPhongMaterial 117
  MeshPhysicalMaterial 117
  MeshStandardMaterial 117
  MeshToonMaterial 118
  ShaderMaterial 118
  ShadowMaterial 118
  textures, using in 365
mesh
  about 53
  attributes 61, 64, 66
  combining, with binary operations 220, 221
  functions 61, 64, 66
  materials, combining 130, 132
  multiple meshes, merging into single mesh 267, 268, 269
  position 61
  rotation property 61
  scale property 61
  starting 123
  THREE.MeshBasicMaterial 124, 127
  THREE.MeshDepthMaterial 128, 129
  THREE.MeshNormalMaterial 133, 135, 136
  translateX(amount) property 61
  translateY(amount) property 61
  translateZ(amount) property 61
  visible property 61
  with multiple materials 137, 138, 139
metalness map 385, 386
MIP map 367

mixamo tooling
  reference 344
model
  exporting, from Blender 282, 283
  loading, from Blender 282, 283
  loading, from other supported formats 292, 293
Mongoose
  reference 16
morph targets
  about 327
  using 329
MTL 270, 285, 286, 287, 288

N

normal map
  used, for creating detailed bumps 377, 378
  used, for creating wrinkles 377
Notepad++
  about 11
  reference 11
Npm-based web server
  testing, on Node.js 16
NRRD
  reference 271

O

OBJ 270, 285, 286, 287, 288
object movement
  limiting, with constraints 478
objects
  grouping 264, 265, 266
OBJExporter.js 270
OpenGL Shading Language (GLSL)
  about 453
  reference 453
OrbitControl
  using 325, 326
orthographic camera
  bottom 74
  far 74
  left 73
  near 74
  right 73
  top 73
  versus perspective camera 69, 70, 71, 73

  zoom 74
overrideMaterial property
  using 51, 53

P

Packed Raw WebGL Model (PRWM)
  reference 271
particle system
  creating, from PLY model 303
particles
  styling, with HTML5 canvas 239
  styling, with textures 245, 246, 247, 249, 250,
    251, 253
PDB 298
Perlin noise
  reference 411
perspective camera
  aspect 72
  far 72
  fov 72
  near 72
  versus orthographic camera 69, 70, 71, 73
  zoom 72
Physi.js
  material properties 469, 470, 471
  supported shapes 472, 474, 475, 476, 477,
    478
physics
  scene, creating 462, 463, 464, 465, 467, 468
Physijs, meshes
  Physijs.BoxMesh 472
  Physijs.CapsuleMesh 473
  Physijs.ConcaveMesh 473
  Physijs.ConeMesh 473
  Physijs.ConvexMesh 473
  Physijs.CylinderMesh 473
  Physijs.HeightfieldMesh 473
  Physijs.PlaneMesh 472
  Physijs.SphereMesh 472
PlayCanvas
  reference 271
PLY model
  particle system, creating 303
PointConstraint
  movement between two points, limiting 479,

480, 481

points 232, 235

portable version Mongoose

  testing, for for macOS and/or Windows 17

  testing, for macOS and/or Windows 16

postprocessing passes

  about 420

  additional passes 428

  advanced EffectComposer flows, using masks
    429, 430, 432, 433

  ambient occlusion, using 438, 439

  bloom effect, adding with THREE.BloomPass
    424

  Bokeh effect, adding 434, 436, 437

  output of multiple renderers, displaying on
    screen 427

  overview 420

  reference 421

  scene output, as set of dots 426

  starting 422, 423

  THREE.AdaptiveToneMappingPass 420

  THREE.BloomPass 420

  THREE.BokehPass 420

  THREE.ClearPass 420

  THREE.CubeTexturePass 420

  THREE.DotScreenPass 420

  THREE.FilmPass 420

  THREE.GlitchPass 420

  THREE.HalfTonePass 420

  THREE.MaskPass 420

  THREE.OutlinePass 420

  THREE.RenderPass 420

  THREE.SAOPass 421

  THREE.SavePass 421

  THREE.ShaderPass 421

  THREE.SMAAPass 421

  THREE.SSAOPass 421

  THREE.TAARenderPass 421

  THREE.TexturePass 421

  THREE.UnrealBloomPass 421

  TV-like effect, creating with THREE.FilmPass
    423, 424

postprocessing

  render loop, updating 418

  THREE.EffectComposer, configuring 418

  THREE.EffectComposer, creating 417

  Three.js, setting up 416, 417

Power VR 370

Protein Data Bank (PDB) 270

Python-based web servers

  testing, on most Unix/macOS systems 15

Q

Quake model

  animation, loading 353, 354

R

render loop

  updating 418

repository

  cloning, with Git 13

requestAnimationFrame 30

RGBE 374

roughness map 385, 386

S

scene, components

  camera 42

  lights 42

  objects 42

  renderer 42

scene

  creating 42

  creating, with physics 462, 463, 464, 465, 467,
    468

  expanding, with animations 29

  fog, adding 50, 51

  functionality 42, 43, 44, 46, 48, 49

  loading 274, 275

  overrideMaterial property, using 51, 52

  saving 274, 275

SEA3D project

  models, reusing 362, 363

shaders

  creating, with THREE.ShaderMaterial 147, 148,
    154

Shadertoy

  reference 452

shadows

  adding 26, 27

skeletal animation
  about 328
  multiple THREE.AnimationClip objects, using 337, 338, 339
skinning
  for animation 340, 341, 343
SliderConstraint, parameter
  angular_higher 488
  angular_lower 488
  linear_lower 488
  linear_upper 488
SliderConstraint
  movement to single axis, limiting 486, 488
sound sources
  adding, to scene 494, 495, 496, 497
source code
  archive, downloading 14
  archive, extracting 14
  examples, testing 15
  obtaining 13
  repository, cloning with repository 4, 13
special lights
  about 106
  lens flare 110, 112, 113, 114
  THREE.AreaLight 108, 109
  THREE.HemisphereLight 106, 107
specular map 391, 392
sprite maps
  about 254
  working with 255, 256, 258
STereoLithography (STL) 270
Sublime Text Editor
  about 11
  reference 11
subtle shadows
  adding, with ambient occlusion map 380, 381, 383
SVG 271
  geometry, extruding 208, 209, 210, 211

T

Targa 370
TDS 270
texels 367
textures, usage

custom UV mapping 401, 402, 403, 404, 405
repeat wrapping 406, 407, 408
textures
  applying, to mesh 366, 367, 369
  canvas, using as 409
  loading 366, 367, 369
  particles, styling 245, 246, 247, 249
  using, in materials 365
  video output, using as 413, 414
THREE.AmbientLight
  about 81, 83, 84, 85
  THREE.Color object, using 85, 88
THREE.AnimationAction object 329
THREE.AnimationClip object
  about 329
  creating 332
THREE.AnimationMixer object
  about 329
  creating 333
THREE.AreaLight
  about 108, 109
  color property 107
  groundColor property 107
  intensity property 107
THREE.BloomPass, property
  kernelSize 425
  Resolution 425
  sigma 425
  strength 425
THREE.BoxGeometry 177, 178
THREE.BoxGeometry, property
  depth 178
  depthSegments 178
  height 178
  heightSegments 178
  Width 178
  widthSegments 178
THREE.CanvasRenderer, attributes
  blending 240
  color 239
  opacity 239
  program 239
  rotation 240
  transparent 240
THREE.CanvasRenderer

HTML5 canvas, using 239, 241
THREE.CircleGeometry 166, 167, 168
THREE.CircleGeometry, property
  radius 168
  segments 168
  thetaLength 168
  thetaStart 168
THREE.Color object
  add(color) 87
  addColors(color1, color2) 87
  addScalar(s) 87
  clone() 87
  convertGammaToLinear() 87
  convertLinearToGamma() 87
  copy(color) 86
  copyGammaToLinear(color) 86
  copyLinearToGamma(color) 86
  equals(color) 87
  fromArray(array) 87
  getHex() 87
  getHexString() 87
  getHSL(optionalTarget) 87
  getStyle() 87
  lerp(color, alpha) 87
  multiply(color) 87
  multiplyScalar(s) 87
  offsetHSL(h, s, l) 87
  set(value) 86
  setHex(value) 86
  setHSL(h,s,l) 86
  setRGB(r,g,b) 86
  setStyle(style) 86
  toArray 87
  using 85, 88
THREE.ConeGeometry 184
THREE.ConeGeometry, property
  height 185
  heightSegments 185
  openEnded 185
  radialSegments 185
  radius 185
  thetaLength 185
  thetaStart 185
THREE.ConvexGeometry 200, 201, 202
THREE.CylinderGeometry 181

THREE.CylinderGeometry, property
  height 182
  heightSegments 182
  openEnded 182
  radialSegments 182
  radiusBottom 182
  radiusTop 182
  thetaLength 182
  thetaStart 182
THREE.DirectionalLight 103, 104, 105
THREE.DotScreenPass, property
  angle 426
  center 426
  scale 426
THREE.EffectComposer
  configuring, for postprocessing 418
  creating 417
THREE.ExtrudeGeometry
  about 204, 205
  amount property 205
  bevelEnabled property 205
  bevelSegments property 205
  bevelSize property 205
  bevelThickness property 205
  curveSegments property 206
  extrudePath property 206
  shapes property 205
  steps property 206
  uvGenerator property 206
THREE.FilmPass, parameters
  grayscale 424
  noiseIntensity 424
  scanLinesCount 424
  scanlinesIntensity 424
Three.js exporter
  installing, in Blender 280, 281
Three.js JSON format
  using 271
Three.js online editor
  reference 318
Three.js, versions
  three.js 21
  three.min.js 21
Three.js
  geometries 163

reference 11
requisites 11, 12
setting up, for postprocessing 416, 417
THREE.LatheGeometry
  about 202, 203
  phiLength 204
  phiStart 203
  points 203
  segments 203
THREE.Mesh
  loading 271, 272, 274
  saving 271, 272, 274
THREE.MeshBasicMaterial
  about 124
  color 124
  wireframe 124
  wireframeLinecap 124
  wireframeLinejoin 124
  wireframeLineWidth 124
THREE.MeshDepthMaterial
  about 128, 129
  wireframe 128
  wireframeLineWidth 128
THREE.MeshLambertMaterial
  about 140
  color 140
THREE.MeshNormalMaterial
  about 133, 135, 136
  wireframe 135
  wireframeLinewidth 135
THREE.MeshPhongMaterial
  about 142
  color 142
  emissive 142
  shininess 142
  specular 142
THREE.MeshPhysicalMaterial
  about 146
  clearCoat 146
  clearCoatRoughness 146
  reflectivity 146
THREE.MeshStandardMaterial
  about 144
  metalness 145
  roughness 145

THREE.ParametricGeometry
  about 211, 212, 214
  function property 213
  slices property 213
  stacks property 213
THREE.PlaneGeometry 164
THREE.PlaneGeometry, property
  height 166
  heightSegments 166
  width 166
  widthSegments 166
THREE.PointLight
  about 97, 99, 100, 102, 103
  color property 99
  decay property 99
  distance property 99
  intensity property 99
  position property 99
  power property 99
  visible property 99
THREE.Points
  about 236, 237, 239
  creating, from advanced geometry 259, 260, 261
THREE.PointsMaterial 236, 237, 239
THREE.PointsMaterial, properties
  blending 238
  color 238
  fog 238
  map 238
  opacity 238
  size 238
  sizeAnnutation 238
  transparent 238
  vertexColors 238
THREE.PolyhedronGeometry, property
  detail 192
  indices 192
  radius 192
  vertices 192
THREE.PolyhedronGeometry
  about 190, 192
  THREE.DodecahedronGeometry 196
  THREE.IcosahedronGeometry 193
  THREE.OctahedronGeometry 195

THREE.TetrahedronGeometry 194
THREE.RingGeometry, property
 innerRadius 170
 outerRadius 170
 phiSegments 170
 thetaLength 170
 thetaSegments 170
 thetaStart 170
THREE.RingGeometry
 about 169, 170
 THREE.ShapeGeometry 171, 174, 175, 177
THREE.Scene object
 add(object) 53
 children 53
 fog 53
 getObjectByName(name, recursive) 53
 overrideMaterial 53
 remove(object) 53
 traverse(function) 53
THREE.ShaderMaterial
 attributes 149
 defines 149
 fog 148
 fragmentShader 149
 lights 149
 linewidth 148
 shaders, creating 147, 148, 149, 153
 Shading 148
 uniforms 149
 vertexColors 148
 vertextShader 149
 wireframe 148
 Wireframelinewidth 148
THREE.ShaderPass
 using, for custom effects 439, 441, 442
THREE.ShapeGeometry
 about 171, 174, 175, 177
 options property 174
 shapes property 174
THREE.SphereGeometry 178
THREE.SphereGeometry, property
 heightSegments 179
 phiLength 180
 phiStart 180
 radius 179

thetaLength 180
thetaStart 180
widthSegments 179
THREE.SpotLight 89, 90, 91, 92, 96, 97
THREE.SpotLight, property
 angle 90
 castShadow 90
 color 90
 decay 90
 distance 90
 intensity 90
 penumbra 90
 position 90
 power 90
 shadow.bias 91
 shadow.camera.far 91
 shadow.camera.fov 91
 shadow.camera.near 91
 shadow.mapSize.height 91
 shadow.mapSize.width 91
 shadow.radius 91
 target 90
 visible 90
THREE.SpriteMaterial, properties
 blending 257
 color 256
 fog 257
 map 256
 opacity 257
 sizeAnnutation 257
THREE.TextGeometry, property
 bevelEnabled 217
 bevelSegments 217
 bevelSize 217
 bevelThickness 217
 curveSegments 217
 extrudePath 217
 font 217
 height 217
 size 217
 steps 217
 uvGenerator 217
THREE.TorusGeometry 186
THREE.TorusGeometry, property
 arc 187

radialSegments 186
radius 186
tube 186
tubularSegments 187
THREE.TorusKnotGeometry 188, 189
THREE.TorusKnotGeometry, property
  heightScale 190
  p 190
  q 190
  radialSegments 190
  radius 190
  tube 190
  tubularSegments 190
THREE.TubeGeometry
  about 206, 207, 208
  closed property 208
  path property 208
  radius property 208
  radiusSegments property 208
  segments property 208
ThreeBSP
  intersect function 220
  reference 220
  subtract function 220
  union function 220
TrackballControls
  using 319, 320
Tween.js
  reference 313
  used, for animations 313, 315, 316, 317
tweening 313

TypeFace.js
  about 218
  reference 219

U

union function 229
UV mapping 369, 401, 402, 403
UV mappings 404, 405

V

vertexShader program
  reference 154
video output
  using, as texture 413, 414
Virtual Reality Modeling Language (VRML) 270
Visual Studio Code
  about 11
  reference 11
Visualization Toolkit (VTK) 270

W

Web Audio API
  about 497
  reference 497
web workers
  reference 463
WebGLRenderer
  HTML5 canvas, using 242, 243, 244, 245
WebStorm
  about 11
  reference 11

31446011R00291

Made in the USA
Lexington, KY
20 February 2019